RAISED ON RADIO

Power Ballads,

Cocaine & Payola

RAISED ON RADIO

The AOR Glory Years
1976–1986

PAUL REES

CONSTABLE

First published in the United States of America in 2026 by Da Capo Press,
an imprint of Hachette Book Group

First published in Great Britain in 2026 by Constable

1 3 5 7 9 10 8 6 4 2

Copyright © Paul Rees, 2026

The moral right of the author has been asserted.

All rights reserved.
No part of this publication may be reproduced, stored in a retrieval system, or transmitted, in any form, or by any means, without the prior permission in writing of the publisher, nor be otherwise circulated in any form of binding or cover other than that in which it is published and without a similar condition including this condition being imposed on the subsequent purchaser.

A CIP catalogue record for this book is
available from the British Library.

ISBN: 978-1-4087-2111-7

Printed and bound in Great Britain by Clays Ltd, Elcograf S.p.A.

Papers used by Constable are from well-managed forests
and other responsible sources.

Constable
An imprint of
Little, Brown Book Group
Carmelite House
50 Victoria Embankment
London EC4Y 0DZ

The authorised representative
in the EEA is
Hachette Ireland
8 Castlecourt Centre, Dublin 15,
D15 XTP3, Ireland
(email: info@hbgi.ie)

An Hachette UK Company
www.hachette.co.uk

www.littlebrown.co.uk

This one's for Luke. For planting the seed and keeping the flame burning.

CONTENTS

	Cast of Characters	xi
	Prologue	1

Part One: New Frontiers

One:	When, why, and how it all began, and for the greater part on a February evening in 1964.	9
Two:	Journey, REO Speedwagon, Styx, and Kansas lift off.	17
Three:	Enter the Wilson sisters.	27
Four:	From a basement in Boston.	38
Five:	The makings of Toto.	43
Six:	Because every player needs a stage…	48
Seven:	Vindication of the "mad scientist."	54
Eight:	Three Brits and three Americans.	63
Nine:	The advent of Sammy Hagar and the Babys; further adventures of REO and Styx; Kansas and Blue Öyster Cult strike gold…	68
Ten:	The second band on Atlantic Records to go platinum.	75
Eleven:	Trouble with the Wilshires.	81
Twelve:	The price of making it.	86
Thirteen:	Styx pulls back the curtain.	93

Part Two: Take It on the Run

Fourteen:	In which Toto find their voice.	101
Fifteen:	The man with the golden throat.	106
Sixteen:	Boston and Foreigner follow up.	113
Seventeen:	Styx surge; REO stall; the Babys bust up.	118
Eighteen:	Affairs of the Heart.	123
Nineteen:	Toto birth "Hold the Line"; Cheap Trick take Japan.	128
Twenty:	Rainbow makes "Since You Been Gone."	134
Twenty-One:	Portrait of a young woman in a men's urinal and the damage done.	139

Twenty-Two:	Michael Bolton and Blackjack: the AOR supergroup that never was…	144
Twenty-Three:	Journey evolves; Survivor starts; Toto crash-lands.	150
Twenty-Four:	Kiss do disco with Desmond Child.	155
Twenty-Five:	The birthday present that went to Number One.	159
Twenty-Six:	There's something about Patricia.	162
Twenty-Seven:	Journey finds its missing link.	166
Twenty-Eight:	The trouble with Boston, Heart, Kansas, Pat Benatar, Cheap Trick…	171
Twenty-Nine:	Billy Squier and the "Big Beat."	176
Thirty:	Canada calling.	180
Thirty-One:	"Keep On Loving You" and the perks of being a radio programmer.	187

Part Three: Jukebox Heroes

Thirty-Two:	Clocking in at the hit factory.	195
Thirty-Three:	New adventurers in AOR…	200
Thirty-Four:	Foreigner Makes 4.	206
Thirty-Five:	Strangers waitin', up and down the boulevard…	213
Thirty-Six:	The revolution will be televised.	220
Thirty-Seven:	Quarterflash and their one-hit wonder.	227
Thirty-Eight:	Toto: house band on the biggest album of all time.	231
Thirty-Nine:	Chicago, Asia, and the fine art of reinvention.	240
Forty:	It's the thrill of the fight…	246
Forty-One:	Assorted ups and downs in '82: sex addiction and alopecia included.	250
Forty-Two:	Def Leppard and Mutt Lange catch fire.	257
Forty-Three:	Excess—almost—all areas.	264
Forty-Four:	A tale of two Canadians.	268
Forty-Five:	Journey's highway run into the midnight sun.	272
Forty-Six:	Dennis DeYoung's Waterloo.	278
Forty-Seven:	Night Ranger breaks big. Kansas and Rainbow break up.	281
Forty-Eight:	"Love Is a Battlefield" and the art of the hit.	288
Forty-Nine:	The woes of Boston and Heart.	291
Fifty:	Yes and Genesis join Asia's AOR Trail. Going tricky.	296

Part Four: No Brakes

Fifty-One:	It came from New Jersey...	303
Fifty-Two:	Mutt Lange with the Cars and David Foster with Chicago: the great dictators.	307
Fifty-Three:	Steve Perry goes solo.	313
Fifty-Four:	A video kills Billy Squier's star.	317
Fifty-Five:	Chasing the mighty dollar.	323
Fifty-Six:	Toto, Survivor, and the tale of two new voices.	328
Fifty-Seven:	Don Henley and Cyndi Lauper make "Boys of Summer" and "Time After Time."	334
Fifty-Eight:	Styx comes undone.	339
Fifty-Nine:	REO throw away the oars, forever.	342
Sixty:	Bryan Adams and *Reckless*.	345
Sixty-One:	Foreigner sends in the choir.	350

Part Five: Don't Stop Believin'

Sixty-Two:	Heart's reinvention and resurrection.	359
Sixty-Three:	Starship plays the mamba.	366
Sixty-Four:	John Parr: man in motion.	371
Sixty-Five:	Cautionary tales.	374
Sixty-Six:	Van Hagar.	379
Sixty-Seven:	Journey comes back together, breaks apart.	384
Sixty-Eight:	Highway to the danger zone...	391
Sixty-Nine:	Europe calling.	396
Seventy:	A prayer for Bon Jovi.	403
Seventy-One:	The big short.	409
Seventy-Two:	Aerosmith makes *Permanent Vacation* and the Year of Rock.	416
Seventy-Three:	In the still of the night...	422
Seventy-Four:	Def Leppard pour some sugar on.	429
Seventy-Five:	End Days.	435
Seventy-Six:	Aftermath.	442
Seventy-Seven:	Resurrection.	449

Acknowledgments	*457*
Notes	*459*
Index	*493*

CAST OF CHARACTERS

Lee Abrams: *Radio executive*
Bryan Adams: *Singer-songwriter*
Paul Ahern: *Manager, Boston*
Don Airey: *Keyboard player, Rainbow*
Rick Allen: *Drummer, Def Leppard*
Dick Asher: *Record company executive*
Irving Azoff: *Manager, REO Speedwagon, the Eagles*
Mike Baird: *Session drummer*
Russ Ballard: *Singer-songwriter*
Tony Banks: *Keyboard player, Genesis*
Pat Benatar: *Solo artist*
Cliff Bernstein: *Co-manager, Def Leppard*
Dave Bickler: *Frontman, Survivor*
Ritchie Blackmore: *Guitarist, Rainbow, Deep Purple*
Jack Blades: *Bassist, Night Ranger*
Michael Bolton: *Solo singer; frontman, Blackjack*
Jon Bon Jovi: *Frontman, Bon Jovi*
Graham Bonnet: *Singer, Rainbow*
Tony Brock: *Drummer, the Babys*
David Bryan: *Keyboard player, Bon Jovi*
Chuck Burgi: *Drummer, Rainbow, Balance*
Al Cafaro: *Record company executive*
Jonathan Cain: *Keyboard player/songwriter, Journey, the Babys*
Bun E. Carlos: *Drummer, Cheap Trick*
Denny Carmassi: *Drummer, Heart, Montrose*
Peter Cetera: *Frontman/songwriter, Chicago*
Bill Champlin: *Singer/keyboard player, Chicago*
Mike Chapman: *Songwriter/producer, Pat Benatar, Warrior, Blondie*
David Chase: *TV writer, producer, director, creator of* The Sopranos
Desmond Child: *Songwriter*
Tony Clarkin: *Late guitarist/songwriter, Magnum*
Phil Collen: *Guitarist, Def Leppard*

Cast of Characters

Phil Collins: *Singer/drummer, Genesis*
David Coverdale: *Frontman, Whitesnake, Deep Purple*
John Crawford: *Guitarist/songwriter, Berlin*
Kevin Cronin: *Frontman/songwriter, REO Speedwagon*
Bob Daisley: *Bassist, Rainbow, Uriah Heep*
Paul Dean: *Guitarist, Loverboy*
Brad Delp: *Late frontman, Boston*
Dennis DeYoung: *Singer/songwriter/keyboard player, Styx*
Thomas Dolby: *Solo artist; session keyboard player*
Neal Doughty: *Keyboard player, REO Speedwagon*
Geoff Downes: *Keyboard player, Asia, Yes*
Dennis Dries: *Frontman, White Sister*
Elliot Easton: *Guitarist, the Cars*
Phil Ehart: *Drummer, Kansas*
John Elefante: *Singer, Kansas*
Joe Elliott: *Frontman, Def Leppard*
Paul Elliott: *Music journalist*
Mike Fisher: *Manager, Heart*
Roger Fisher: *Guitarist, Heart*
Steve Fossen: *Bassist, Heart*
David Foster: *Record producer, songwriter, arranger*
Fergie Frederiksen: *Singer, Toto*
Les Garland: *Co-founder, MTV*
Neil Giraldo: *Guitarist/producer, Pat Benatar*
Jeff Glixman: *Record producer*
Roger Glover: *Bassist/producer, Rainbow, Deep Purple*
Randy Goodrum: *Songwriter, keyboard player*
Barry Goudreau: *Guitarist, Boston, Orion the Hunter*
Lou Gramm: *Frontman, Foreigner*
Alan Gratzer: *Drummer, REO Speedwagon*
Al Greenwood: *Keyboard player, Foreigner*
Myron Grombacher: *Drummer, Pat Benatar*
Sammy Hagar: *Solo artist; frontman, Van Halen, Montrose*
Bruce Hall: *Bassist, REO Speedwagon*
Jimmy Haslip: *Bassist, Blackjack*
Don Henley: *Solo artist; singer-songwriter/drummer, the Eagles*
Herbie Herbert: *Manager, Journey*
Trevor Horn: *Record producer*

Steve Howe: *Guitarist, Asia, Yes*
Rob Hyman: *Songwriter/singer, the Hooters*
Jimi Jamison: *Singer, Survivor*
Mick Jones: *Guitarist/songwriter/producer, Foreigner*
John Kalodner: *Record company executive*
Tony Kaye: *Keyboard player, Yes*
Kelly Keagy: *Drummer, Night Ranger*
Holly Knight: *Songwriter*
Danny Kortchmar: *Session guitarist, producer*
Bruce Kulick: *Guitarist, Kiss, Blackjack*
Robert Lamm: *Keyboard player, Chicago*
Laurie Larson: *Radio DJ*
Cyndi Lauper: *Solo artist*
Kerry Livgren: *Guitarist/songwriter, Kansas*
Kenny Loggins: *Singer-songwriter, solo artist*
Lee Loughnane: *Trumpet player, Chicago*
Steve Lukather: *Guitarist, Toto, multiple sessions*
Eric Martin: *Solo artist*
Jim Masdea: *Drummer, Boston*
Doc McGhee: *Manager, Bon Jovi, Kiss*
Andrew McNeice: *Journalist; CEO of MelodicRock.com*
Peter Mensch: *Co-manager, Def Leppard*
Eddie Money: *Solo artist*
Giorgio Moroder: *Record producer, songwriter*
Neil Murray: *Bassist, Whitesnake*
Ron Nevison: *Record producer*
Rick Nielsen: *Guitarist/songwriter, Cheap Trick*
Terri Nunn: *Singer, Berlin*
Ric Ocasek: *Late singer-songwriter/producer, the Cars*
Derek Oliver: *Music journalist*
Keith Olsen: *Record producer*
Steve Overland: *Frontman/songwriter, FM*
Hugh Padgham: *Record producer*
Richard Page: *Frontman/songwriter, Mr. Mister*
David Paich: *Keyboard player/songwriter, Toto, multiple sessions*
Carl Palmer: *Drummer, Asia, Emerson, Lake & Palmer*
Chuck Panozzo: *Bassist, Styx*
John Parr: *Singer-songwriter, solo artist*

Alan Pasqua: *Session keyboard player*
Joe Perry: *Guitarist, Aerosmith*
Steve Perry: *Frontman/songwriter, Journey*
Jim Peterik: *Guitarist/songwriter, Survivor*
Tom Petersson: *Bassist, Cheap Trick*
Ricky Phillips: *Bassist, the Babys*
Tim Pierce: *Session guitarist*
Bob Pittman: *Co-founder/CEO, MTV*
Jeff Porcaro: *Drummer, Toto, multiple sessions*
Steve Porcaro: *Keyboard player, Toto, multiple sessions*
Martha Quinn: *VJ, MTV*
Trevor Rabin: *Guitarist/songwriter, Yes*
Mike Reno: *Frontman, Loverboy*
Gary Richrath: *Late guitarist, REO Speedwagon*
Donald Roeser: *Guitarist/singer, Blue Öyster Cult*
Gregg Rolie: *Keyboard player, Journey*
Marv Ross: *Guitarist, Quarterflash*
Rindy Ross: *Singer, Quarterflash*
David Lee Roth: *Frontman, Van Halen*
Richie Sambora: *Guitarist, Bon Jovi*
Boz Scaggs: *Solo artist*
Tom Scholz: *Guitarist/songwriter/producer, Boston*
Neal Schon: *Guitarist/songwriter, Journey*
John Sebastian: *Radio executive*
Tommy Shaw: *Guitarist/songwriter, Styx*
Fran Sheehan: *Bassist, Boston*
Mike Shipley: *Record engineer*
Gene Simmons: *Bassist/frontman, Kiss*
Grace Slick: *Singer, Starship*
Henry Small: *Singer, Prism*
Patty Smyth: *Singer, Warrior*
David Spero: *Radio executive, artist manager*
Rick Springfield: *Solo artist, TV actor*
Billy Squier: *Solo artist*
Paul Stanley: *Guitarist/frontman, Kiss*
Jim Steinman: *Songwriter, record producer*
Frankie Sullivan: *Guitarist/songwriter, Survivor*
John Sykes: *Late guitarist, Whitesnake*

Bernie Taupin: *Songwriter*
Joey Tempest: *Frontman, Europe*
Mickey Thomas: *Singer, Starship*
Mike Tramp: *Frontman, White Lion*
Joe Lynn Turner: *Singer, Rainbow*
Steven Tyler: *Frontman, Aerosmith*
Jim Vallance: *Songwriter*
Ross Valory: *Bassist, Journey*
Eddie Van Halen: *Late guitarist, Van Halen*
John Waite: *Frontman, the Babys; solo artist*
Steve Walsh: *Singer, Kansas*
Diane Warren: *Songwriter*
Fee Waybill: *Frontman, the Tubes*
John Wetton: *Late singer/bassist, Asia, King Crimson*
Richard Williams: *Guitarist, Kansas*
Pete Willis: *Guitarist, Def Leppard*
Ann Wilson: *Singer/songwriter, Heart*
Nancy Wilson: *Guitarist/songwriter, Heart*
James "JY" Young: *Guitarist/songwriter, Styx*
Robin Zander: *Frontman, Cheap Trick*

RAISED ON RADIO

PROLOGUE

Steve Lukather: "For forty years now critics have hated and eviscerated us. We truly are the redheaded stepchild of rock 'n' roll."

Dennis DeYoung: "I'm a song guy. You give me a good song, and a singer, and I'll follow you."

"WE JUST WROTE THIS SONG ABOUT TWO WEEKS AGO," JOURNEY singer Steve Perry tells a baying crowd at the Oakland Coliseum. Behind him at a blood-red baby grand piano, Jonathan Cain, the band's newest recruit, begins a chiming keyboard pattern. It's joined by Neal Schon's crunching guitar riff, and then bassist Ross Valory and drummer Steve Smith weigh in with a hulking, Led Zeppelin–like groove. The song they intro is titled "Separate Ways (Worlds Apart)." It'll be another four months before Journey gets around to recording it, but it already sounds like a hit. A driving, euphoric FM radio anthem.

This much has been standard for the band ever since the release of *Escape*, their seventh album and the first to feature Cain, back in July 1981. A US Number One, *Escape* is well on its way to shifting more than ten million copies. The tour to support it opened in Osaka, Japan, on

July 27, 1981. Tonight, Saturday, June 26, 1982, is the 131st and penultimate show of the band's long run before a sellout 57,500-person hometown crowd. The final date, six days from now, will be played to 83,214 folks packed into the Rose Bowl football stadium, a six-hour drive down the West Coast from here in Pasadena, California.

It's a mild evening, a gentle breeze blowing into the stadium bleachers from off the San Francisco Bay. The lights of the city, where Journey started up nine years previously, form a twinkling backdrop against the ink-black night sky. There is as well a tangible sense of occasion in the air. As "Separate Ways..." crescendos, Perry eases his high tenor voice to the upper limits of his three-octave range, seemingly effortlessly holding a single note at this extremity for six, seven, eight seconds, like a tightrope walker perfectly balanced over the edge of an abyss. No wonder when Freddie Mercury of Queen was once asked what it was like to be the greatest ever rock singer, he shot back, "I don't know, ask Steve Perry." Perry's vocal gymnastics climax the song, the Oakland audience roaring him on.

The five *Escape* songs in Journey's set tonight draw an even more tumultuous response, in particular its two keening ballads, "Open Arms" and "Who's Crying Now," but most of all the last song they play from off the album. Introduced by Cain's tumbling piano line, "Don't Stop Believin'" is met with rapture. The audience as one takes up its refrain as if it speaks to them, and for them, about all the seductive power and glory of this music: "Streetlights, people, livin' just to find emotion, hidin' somewhere in the night."

Frozen there at this moment, Perry in a black tuxedo and tails, Schon like an off-duty astronaut in his white jumpsuit, Cain with his eyes squeezed shut, lost to the music, Journey is at its zenith as America's preeminent rock band. So too is this the high point for the whole genre of music they have come to embody—AOR. Aside from *Escape*, two other multiplatinum AOR albums, Foreigner's *4* and *Hi Infidelity* by REO Speedwagon, had topped the American charts in 1981. Toto, one of Journey's opening acts in Oakland, is on the way to four million sales of their *IV* album, released that April, and propelled by a brace of blockbuster singles, "Rosanna" and then "Africa." There is no bigger, no more evocative music reigning over the American airwaves just then than AOR.

For all that, there is a simple truth: No genre of music more than AOR has been so widely misunderstood, so consistently scorned. There was disco, the other derided movement in music overlapping it in the mid- to late 1970s. But disco's reevaluation came about so much sooner and more generally. No, AOR is out on its own in the unloved stakes. In the words of Toto's venerable guitarist, it is the redheaded stepchild. This in spite of it being one of the most enduring forces in American popular culture.

Even the brand name AOR is misleading, if not downright inaccurate. An abbreviation of "album-oriented rock," it was initially coined to encapsulate a radio format pioneered by consultants such as Lee Abrams in the late '60s and early '70s, one that was based upon playing album tracks by rock artists rather than the Top 40 pop hits of the day. Ironically, it has ever since distorted a crucial point—that so much of the music made during the halcyon period spanned by this book, between 1976 and 1987, was in thrall to the power of the song, to the sheer, boundless sense of joy encapsulated by the three-minute pop single. "More Than a Feeling," "Hold the Line," "Keep On Loving You," "Don't Stop Believin'," "Summer of '69," "I Want to Know What Love Is," "Livin' on a Prayer"—each one is a perfectly realized moment of magic.

AOR was further damned by the other term applied to it at the time—"corporate rock." The implication being that this was music made by committee and rolled off a production line to a fixed blueprint. Something mechanical, sterile, and wholesale. Altogether too easy to mass-produce. In reality, AOR's figureheads were masters of their craft. Their prowess was learned and honed through years of toil at the coalface of dingy rehearsal rooms and in subterranean recording studios. Galaxies removed from basic routine, their music was instead intricately made and recorded. The greatest of their records shine still as exquisite examples of minimalist art: verse–bridge–indelible chorus.

In this regard, these are classically produced pop songs in just the same way as those by the Beatles, or the Beach Boys, or any from out of Motown's wondrous hit factory. In short, they were songs made for the radio, and more specifically, the FM radio format dominating America's airwaves throughout the '70s and beyond. Broadcasting out across its heartlands in pristine stereo, FM was the daily diet of millions of folks crisscrossing its highways and byways in their cars. By the 1980s and the Reagan era, AOR was as much the reigning soundtrack of Middle America as country music is today.

For a kid growing up in the suburban England of Maggie Thatcher and Radio One on tinny medium wave, the stars of AOR were barely present, hardly heard. The biggest of the American bands—Journey, Foreigner, Boston, REO Speedwagon, Toto—scantly featured at best in such specialist magazines as *Kerrang!* or *Sounds*. Or else one might catch an occasional song of theirs on Radio One's late-night (which is to say, marginalized) *Friday Night Rock Show*, introduced by its laconic host DJ Tommy Vance as if from a deep slumber.

To that kid, AOR was music to be discovered by happenstance. Unlike punk, new wave, or two-tone, AOR was never ordained as cool, credible, or even acceptable by the self-styled critical cognoscenti of the day. None of the aforementioned bands ever once graced the cover of *Rolling Stone* magazine. On the contrary, when it wasn't being ignored for the greater part, AOR was dismissed as an aberration, like an unpleasant stench stirred up but bound soon enough to vanish into thin air.

Except AOR didn't disappear. Rather, it clung on, exiled for years to the cultural wilderness, and then, slowly but surely, seeped back into the mainstream. It ingrained itself into the fabric of American music.

Raised on Radio is nothing so much as a long overdue celebration of AOR and its leading lights, a first complete telling of its and their story. And, like all good stories, it has a well-defined beginning, middle, and end.

At the outset there was Tom Scholz. A bookish sort, native of Boston, Scholz for seven years from 1969 spilled the sounds in his head onto tape in the basement studio he'd built with his savings from working as a research scientist at Polaroid. Laboring alone in the main, Scholz was a true maverick obsessive. When at last his homemade recordings went out into the world under the banner band name of Boston, the cover of their self-titled debut album of 1976 was adorned with a guitar-shaped spaceship. Fittingly, since this was music that seemed to have been beamed in from another world. The Eagles' astral harmonies colliding with Jimmy Page's hard-rocking guitar. A lead singer, Brad Delp, whose voice soared to the stratosphere. Unerringly melodic songs heaving with hooks. These were its constituent parts, and they birthed AOR. For in Boston's wake followed Foreigner, Heart, Kansas, Styx, REO Speedwagon, Toto, Pat Benatar, and Journey.

From there came the long middle of AOR's heyday, the time of its greatest songs and, yes, also a litany of supernova albums, from *Escape*, *4*, and *Hi Infidelity* up to *Slippery When Wet* by Bon Jovi and Def Leppard's *Hysteria*. During what was the last genuine boom period of the music business, these were among its tentpole blockbusters.

As well, AOR's ranks swelled with a deep pool of stellar talent. Mad professor genius Scholz. Toto's crack collective of musicians, aside from their own band, so in demand they were essentially the backing group on the biggest-selling album of all time, Michael Jackson's *Thriller*, and thousands more besides. Steve Perry's golden voice. All were reined together by a rarefied group of supreme record producers, names such as Keith Olsen, Roy Thomas Baker, David Foster, Ron Nevison, Robert John "Mutt" Lange, the powers behind AOR's throne. Each as driven and domineering as the other.

In tandem, they created, shaped, and influenced the prevailing sound of popular music through the '80s. Clean, polished, finely nuanced, bittersweet pop melodies married to plangent guitar riffs. Power ballads and driving-with-the-top-down rockers. AOR begot such global smash hits as Don Henley's "Boys of Summer" and Cyndi Lauper's "Time After Time" every bit as much as it did "Africa" or "Don't Stop Believin'."

Ludicrous, too, is the notion that it was somehow safe and sterile. "Africa" surged over a drum loop almost before such a term had entered the popular lexicon. "Don't Stop Believin'" stretched out like elastic before finally pinging into its chorus. Mutt Lange pieced together the records he made as if they were porcelain mosaics. This was music forged from daring and vaulting ambition.

Until it wasn't. Inevitably, AOR grew to be so big, so top-heavy, it eventually tumbled. Toppled back to earth from becoming a parody of itself. As the hits increasingly got to be written by song doctors, the sound became one that might as well have been taken from off the peg. From there it was an ignominious drift to the margins and then to what seemed sure to be obscurity.

That, though, hasn't proved to be the end of AOR's story. Rather, with the noughties came classic rock radio, high-concept TV, iTunes, and Spotify. A popular culture informed by soundtracks, streaming, and playlists. Ever more easy access portals into music history, the charge points that resurrected AOR to life. "Don't Stop Believin'" playing out the climactic episode of *The Sopranos*. More than a 130 different versions of "Africa" populating YouTube and TikTok. The path Mutt Lange's signature multi-harmony production has beaten from Def Leppard to Shania Twain and on to informing the sound of the preeminent superstar of today, Taylor Swift. Billions of Spotify streams, and a surfeit of glorious songs that have undeniably entered the canon of popular standards.

Across its full span, this is a story of questing and endurance and ultimate triumph against the odds. A hero's tale, in other words. Or, as the song says:

Workin' hard to get my fill.
Everybody wants a thrill.
Payin' anything to roll the dice,
Just one more time...
Don't stop believin',
Hold on to that feelin'.

PART ONE
NEW FRONTIERS

CHAPTER ONE

WHEN, WHY, AND HOW IT ALL BEGAN, AND FOR THE GREATER PART ON A FEBRUARY EVENING IN 1964.

"Perhaps you should work at this music thing, son."

Steve Perry: "My creative influences, my writing influences, my good times and bad times—all centered around the fact I had a radio in my car...Radio taught me about writing songs, taught Jon [Cain] to write songs and Neal [Schon] to play guitar. We were raised on radio."[1]

Billy Squier: "I was very much a child of FM radio. It was a huge part of my life growing up in Boston. You know how today kids take online college courses? For me, listening to WBCN in Boston was like an online college of musical knowledge. I'm borrowing that phrase from Peter Wolf of the J. Geils Band. Peter used to do a late-night blues show on WBCN on the weekends. I called Wolf 'Professor,' and you could liken the disc jockeys to the faculty. They were teaching us.

Without them and the stuff I gleaned from them I probably wouldn't even be here."

Ann Wilson: "I remember being in the car with my dad, on the way to the hospital to see newborn Nancy. 'Sixteen Tons' by Jimmy Dean came on the radio. I'll never forget hearing that. I was three and a half."

Steve Perry: "[Hearing Sam Cooke's 'Chain Gang' on the radio] changed my life. My mom had an old Thunderbird with a six-by-nine-inch speaker on the dashboard. What an inspirational moment that was. And it led to my love affair with Aretha Franklin and Gladys Knight."[2]

Mick Jones: "My grand moment of enlightenment came one evening watching *Sunday Night at the Palladium* on TV with Mum and Dad. Buddy Holly was a featured guest on the show that night. No sooner had Holly walked onstage and started his set than I burst into tears. Mum was frantic, but I couldn't begin to articulate how I was feeling right then. I was just completely blown away by this gaudy-looking guy with horn-rimmed glasses and a Fender Strat. That was the moment I first knew what I wanted to do with my life."

Jim Peterik: "I was four years old. I had two older sisters who were bringing home 45s. They'd stack them up on the RCA Victor spindle record player. Elvis Presley was probably my first hero. I saw him on *The Ed Sullivan Show*, and he was amazing. For Halloween when I was five, I had a little ukulele, and my mother put 'Elvis' on it in masking tape."

Tom Scholz: "I actually grew up listening to classical music, Beethoven and Tchaikovsky and Rachmaninov. I didn't become interested in pop music until I heard the Kinks."[3]

Steve Lukather: "I can tell you the exact date I decided what I was going to do with my life. It was the evening of February 9, 1964. I was six years old, and I saw the Beatles on *The Ed Sullivan Show*. That for me was like the part in *The Wizard of Oz* when everything turns from black and white into color."

Jim Vallance: "Anyone I've talked to, or read about, they all were watching Ed Sullivan that night, and they all were blown away. Tom Petty, Don Henley, everyone."

Dennis DeYoung: "My good friend Dave had bought *Meet the Beatles*, and he had a pair of Beatle boots. There was so much hype in the United States. 'The Beatles are coming! The Beatles are coming!' I was skeptical on the whole thing. I heard 'I Want to Hold Your Hand' on the radio, and didn't like it. I still don't. I think it's okay. We had a Sunday night dance at Harlan High School. That's where all the chicks were, all the Catholic schoolgirls from the area would go there on Sunday nights. That was more important than the Beatles. The dance was 7 p.m. till 10 p.m. You'd get there at 7:45 p.m. or 8 p.m., not too late to miss anything, and Ed Sullivan came on at 7 p.m. I wanted to get in the car, go get gas, and get to the dance. But my buddy Dave said, 'We've got to watch the Beatles.' I lived in a two-flat. We were on the top floor, and my grandparents were on the lowest. I sat there and watched the Beatles in our front room. [Sings:] 'Close your eyes and I'll kiss you...' My jaw hit the floor. It was an epiphany. And I, like millions of others, went, 'That's a good job.'"

Bryan Adams: "My parents had a Chevy Corvair. I've memories of being five, six years old and how my brother and me used to laugh and make fun messing about to the Beatles' 'She Loves You,' repeating the 'yeah-yeah-yeah' parts to our parents ad nauseam."

Nancy Wilson: "The first time I heard 'Fool on the Hill,' we were in a car. The local radio station was going to play the *Magical Mystery Tour* album in its entirety. It was appointment listening. I was at a choir competition and Ann came to pick me up in the red Chevrolet Impala we bombed around in. We called it the Astro Plane. My choir won the contest and then it was, 'Okay, they're gonna play *Magical Mystery Tour* right now!' The timing worked out. We sat in the car in the school parking lot with rain pelting down on the roof and allowed our brains to be melted. The genius of Paul McCartney alone in that song."

Billy Squier: "To have been a teenager in the 1960s, it was absolutely the greatest gift I could've been given. It was an era of possibilities. Anything was possible, and that's the way we lived."

Joe Elliott: "Marc Bolan was the marker for me. Everybody I'd seen before that was other people's music. This was my guy. 'Hot Love,' 'Jeepster,' 'Telegram Sam,' 'Metal Guru'—all the singles. I was a singles-based listener, because I couldn't afford LPs. I'd save my dinner money up through the week, 12 pence a day, and on a Saturday, I could get a single for 60 pence. It would be T. Rex, or Slade, or Sweet. Pop-rock songs. Big guitars and drums."

Joey Tempest: "I remember David Bowie's 'Space Oddity' grabbing me because of the production. I thought it was wild."

Joe Elliott: "I know we can't talk about him, but the Gary Glitter singles were phenomenally brilliant. The first time I heard Glitter was at a kids' disco at the Top Rank club in Sheffield. I was kissing this girl under the stairs. The drums came on for 'Rock 'n' Roll (Part 2).' I said, 'I'll be right back!' I legged it straight up to the record shop with the 60 pence I had left and bought the single. The girl is probably still under the stairs, a skeleton waiting."

Ann Wilson: "Oh, they were all men back then. John Lennon, Paul McCartney, Robert Plant, Rod Stewart, Elton John, Harry Belafonte. There were a few female singers I really loved, like Judy Garland who was just an over-the-top, blow-you-away singer. But there wasn't a female rock 'n' roll icon yet."

Nancy Wilson: "Lennon and McCartney were both incredible guitar players, acoustic and electric. Elton John's piano playing was a big influence on my guitar playing. Eric Clapton. Jimi Hendrix. Jimmy Page, Stephen Stills, and Neil Young. Pete Townshend. Those were my muses. Rock 'n' roll was my aim, and there were no great women rock 'n' roll guitar players at the time. Even onstage today, I channel Jimmy Page more than I do somebody like Bonnie Raitt or Shawn Colvin."

Steve Perry: "My dad was a singer, and I watched him from an early age. At four I recall looking up at him onstage and thinking: 'I can do that.'"[4]

Lou Gramm: "Mom and Dad were both musicians. My dad played trumpet in high school. After high school he formed a big band, and my mom auditioned as the singer and got the job. They played for four or five years around the Rochester, New York, area. Then they got married."[5]

Rick Nielsen: "My parents were opera singers, so I toured with them all over the country. Now I look back and see that it was in a way very shady. Anybody who dedicates their lives to being a musician has made certain mental and physical and monetary concessions, and because of it they end up being a little funny in the head. I don't mean my parents were crazy, it's just that the life is conducive to that."[6]

Gary Richrath: "I grew up in Peoria, Illinois, which isn't too interesting. The first music things I heard were the Everly Brothers and a lot of country guitar. My uncle was a country guitarist, and he gave me a guitar and said, 'Learn how to play this. It'll keep you from starving.'"[7]

Steve Lukather: "The only other passion I had as a small kid was Tonka trucks. They were made out of real steel back then and I used to collect them. I loved to see the garbage men come up our street, because of the huge truck they'd be riding in. At seven years old, I thought that was the coolest thing in the world. I told both of my parents, 'If I can't be a musician, I want to be a garbage man.' They said, 'Well, perhaps you should work at this music thing, son.'"

Eric Martin: "My dad was in the army. We lived in Italy, Germany, and all over the United States at the posts where he would be stationed. I made friends with other guys who played music. I was too skinny for sports. But if I played music, I thought maybe I'd get a little respect, and girls would like me."

Rick Springfield: "When I was sixteen, I was in a bad mental state and tried to hang myself. I was so depressed. I didn't want to go to school because I was failing, and I wasn't really popular... I always found joy in writing and staying home and playing the guitar or reading, so that was my solace."[8]

Bryan Adams: "My father subscribed to this thing called the Columbia Record Club. Once a month, they would send you a catalog and if my father bought an opera record from it, you'd be allowed to choose three other records for free. I'd say to my father, 'Can I have this one, and that one?' If I was lucky enough, he'd get them for me. I always chose the records with the hairiest bastards on the front cover. That's how I found a lot of music—from image. It was all visual. It was how I discovered Creedence Clearwater Revival and Janis Joplin. One of the best records to pore over was *Machine Head* by Deep Purple. The inner sleeve had all these photographs of them recording the album. You could see their guitars and amps, which was amazing to me. I started trying to write songs when I was fifteen."

Tommy Shaw: "I wrote my first song around age five. It was called 'India Was the Town That I Was Born In.' I didn't know much about geography at the time."[9]

Dennis DeYoung: "The first song I ever wrote was called 'So Long Now.' It sounded like a Beatles song. What else would it be? The lyrics went: 'Fussing and fighting in thunder and lightning... Love was there, but now the cupboard was bare.' I smell a Pulitzer!"

Desmond Child: "As soon as I was old enough, I was climbing up on the piano bench and banging away, creating my own melodies. I wrote my first song when I was fifteen. I was in eighth grade. My cousin had a girlfriend, or a girl that he was interested in, Laura Stern. My cousin and I are almost the same age, and we're more like brothers, very competitive. There was something about Laura. She had the same look as Laura Nyro with the long brown hair. Her family were all musicians. I managed to get an invite to her birthday party at the Stern house. Being poor, I didn't have a gift to bring, so I decided to write her a song. It was called 'Birthday Blues.' It went [sings], 'Birthday blues, brand-new shoes. The wanting toos, all the yous you'd like to be.' I played it to her at the piano, with her sat up next to me, and when she looked at me, it was like I'd won her over. Not that I wanted her so much, because I was really gay. But being so competitive with my cousin, I thought, 'Well, what if I stole his girlfriend?' I wanted to be somebody who could write songs that would grab people's hearts. That's where the journey began."

Bruce Hall: "My first band was called Purple Haze, and we played at St. Pat's, a church in Urbana, Illinois. They had teen dances. It was every Friday night, and they were big. I mean, kids from all over came."[10]

John Elefante: "My brother and I started our first band when I was ten years old. We were called the DJs, Dino and John. I was the drummer. Then we formed a band with my cousins who're also Elefantes. There were four cousins. We had this one gig at a teen center. There were a lot of kids there. Some of the other singers in the band sang songs, and then we started to run out of material. My mother was there, and she told me, 'John, go up there and sing that one you sing at home all the time.' I went out and sang the Jackson 5's 'I'll Be There.' We left out the drums. I used to sing it pretty close to the original. And that was it. Everybody else in the band said, 'Hey, you're our new singer.'"

Jim Peterik: "My band the Ides of March had a Number Two hit in 1970 with a song called 'Vehicle.' That was a tremendous landmark in my career. It was mind-blowing. Suddenly, we were on the road all over America and Canada. The summer of 1970, we were playing with Led Zeppelin, Janis Joplin, the Grateful Dead, Jimi Hendrix, and

Brownsville Station. We were in Calgary, Canada, opening for Led Zeppelin. They invited us to a big party after the show. We showed up, and we were kids from Berwyn, Illinois. I mean, we had never seen an orgy before. We learned really quick how the big world of rock 'n' roll works. It was too crazy. There were too many drugs. I went to use the john and there was Bonzo in the bathtub with a groupie. Crazy shit. It just wasn't our scene. We weren't comfortable with that kind of thing, so we excused ourselves from the party and went across the street to a Dunkin' Donuts."

John Kalodner: "All I knew was that I wanted to make records, be famous, and fuck girls."[11]

CHAPTER TWO

JOURNEY, REO SPEEDWAGON, STYX, AND KANSAS LIFT OFF.

"There was no good reason to believe we could be anything but what we were, which wasn't much."

Dennis DeYoung: "It was 1961 when we met, on an August day. I heard John Panozzo and his brother Chuck practicing. They were twelve years old, and I was fourteen. I played accordion. We formed a band the very next day. We called ourselves the Tradewinds, and we were playing music to make our parents happy. We did music from the 1930s, '40s, and '50s. Dance band music, basically. We played weddings and anniversaries, mostly in the beginning to relatives, or friends of relatives who would hire us. We were nice boys. Good kids. I didn't have any thoughts about becoming a professional musician. Ours was a working-class neighborhood. My dad was a printer. He used to show me his hands. 'See these hands?' he'd say to me. And they were permanently stained blue from the ink. He'd tell me, 'Don't end up like me, digging a ditch for a living. Go to college. Be smart. Make something of yourself.' I went to the University of Illinois as a journalism major. Got a degree and became a schoolteacher. Got married and had a kid before I had a record deal. So, I was a little older. That has always, I think, informed my view of how I see myself as a professional musician. Not a rock star, but a dude who makes his living at the greatest job in the world, which is being a rock musician."

James "JY" Young: "Styx were all from the south side [of Chicago], considered the working-class side of town. Dennis was the oldest guy in the band, and he's obviously a very talented guy. The Panozzo brothers lived down the street from him, so it was kind of natural for them to at least try to work together. I drove a cab part-time in Chicago to make ends meet. It took about a year to get that recording contract and then we were devoted to the whole thing from there."[1]

Chuck Panozzo: "We signed our contract with Wooden Nickel Records in 1970. I was teaching high school at the time, as was Dennis. I taught art. Dennis was a music appreciation teacher."[2]

Dennis DeYoung: "Everything was stacked against us, like it's stacked against everybody who starts out. In our case, we had so many false steps to get to what you would call success. There were many times when I really believed that it wouldn't happen, even though I'd convinced myself. I was the driving force, always, in the organization. I believed long before I should have. There was no good reason to believe that we could be anything but what we were, which wasn't much, but somehow you see good in yourself."

James "JY" Young: "The record company was trying to get us to wear upside-down crosses just to make us outrageous. But there were very strong Catholic upbringings for both Dennis and the Panozzo brothers. For me, I just looked at it as a joke. I didn't know about the devil."[3]

Chuck Panozzo: "We were going absolutely nowhere career-wise. I went without pay for incredibly long periods of time."[4]

Dennis DeYoung: "I don't know how to write a song, I really don't.

Songwriting's a skill that's not really tied to musicianship, or any number of things. It's magic. Talk to any songwriter and they'll tell you this: 'I'm there and suddenly there's a song. I don't know how that happened, because there's no good reason for it.' Yet, there it is. So I had to unlock this in me. In 1972, I sat down and wrote 'Lady.' I didn't know what it was, swear to God. Because I had never written a hit record in my life. The way 'Lady' all of a sudden explodes into this loud band? That was the template I discovered completely by accident. 'Lady' is that way because 'JY' has always got to be the hard rocker, right? And I'm the melody guy. So when I played the melody and he walked in the room, and he recorded what we call the uninvited power chords, it made it into *a thing*. I gave it to the producer when we were doing our first record and he said, 'Well, let's save that for the second album.' The second album in 1973, 'Lady' appears, and it's released as the first single. It's one of the most catastrophic failures in all of Western mankind. I mean, it bombed. That second album was essentially me introducing myself as the songwriter. There were seven songs on the album, and I had five of them. And the record was a stiff. And I thought, 'Well, they hate me. They truly hate me.'"

Neal Doughty: "Alan Gratzer lived right across the hall from me in my dorm at the University of Illinois. We were just about the only hippies on the engineering campus. A minority of two against the world. I walked into an engineering class one day and saw 'REO Speedwagon' written on the board in giant letters. It was a milestone in the history of transportation: a high-speed, heavy-duty truck. It was the only name we ever considered."[5]

Irving Azoff: "I was at school at the University of Illinois, and a couple of my fraternity brothers were in bands. I [was] sort of putting my way through college booking bands. Some of these people were at the University of Illinois in Champaign, and some of these people were really talented. So a natural outgrowth of this, rather than just be a booking agent, was to manage these guys and try to escape the Midwest.

I managed REO Speedwagon, who were local guys. I also managed another artist I really believed in. His name was Dan Fogelberg."[6]

Gary Richrath: "Dan Fogelberg was in a band in Peoria. At that point, they were our rival. Dan's band did all Who material, and he used to fling the microphone cords. [My band] were the Yardbirds. There was actually a lot of music there then, but after about a year, a year and a half, it just tapered off, and everything moved to Champaign. Which is where REO got together and where Dan moved. Danny started getting into this acoustic thing, and I started getting into REO. That was during 1970, 1971, and everybody came to the University of Illinois to get out of the draft. I was sixteen then."[7]

Alan Gratzer: "Dan used to live about two houses down from me. It was real funny. Here we were, this hard rock band, and Fogelberg would come out before us with an acoustic guitar and play all the songs off his first album. No one knew who he was, but he was good enough so that people didn't boo him offstage."[8]

Gary Richrath: "I was the biggest guitar player in Peoria. And when I moved to Champaign, I joined the biggest band in Champaign. And then that band became the biggest band in the Midwest. So we've always been big—we just didn't let anyone know about it."[9]

Kevin Cronin: "I was a guitar teacher. For one summer I sold women's shoes, which was an education. And when I got a call from Gary Richrath about joining REO, I was driving a yellow cab in Chicago. I thought the name sucked, to tell the truth. But I went with it."[10]

Gary Richrath: "We were [Irving Azoff's] failure. He wanted me to be like Peter Frampton, but Frampton wasn't that impressive a guitarist—someone to aspire to like Beck or Page, Townshend or Clapton."[11]

Kevin Cronin: "Every song we play, Gary's all over it for me. We either wrote it together, produced it together, rehearsed it together, arranged it together, fought over parts that we played."¹²

Irving Azoff: "Essentially, I landed in California. My grandmother was here, and my aunt was here. And it was the lesser of two evils to New York. We'd secured a record deal [for REO] on what was then Epic Records."¹³

Gary Richrath: "We were just a bar band with a huge local following, and one day some producer came out, signed us to a label, and said, 'Go make an album.' Back in the bars, it's not like they have a spotlight on you, so I played high and fast because I wanted people to notice me… The rest of the guys played fast, too. It was keep up or get out."¹⁴

Herbie Herbert: "I put [Journey] together, absolutely, man by man. Personally, I handpicked each person. It was my band, and I had total authority, and total autonomy, and total control, and nobody minded one fucking bit."¹⁵

Eric Martin: "Herbie used to tell me stories all the time about how he started out. It was him and another guy named John Villanueva who basically were the roadies for Santana. They were at Woodstock. Herbie was a big guy. He went out to the scaffolding and did the sound for Santana at Woodstock. Herbie went on and managed a band called Frumious Bandersnatch, which Ross Valory was in, and he knew Gregg Rolie and Neal Schon from Santana. Neal Schon was this new young gun. He was, like, fifteen years old and the story was that Eric Clapton wanted him to join him for the Delaney and Bonnie years. Herbie wanted to take all these guys and make a great rock 'n' roll band."

Neal Schon: "Those years with Carlos were crazy. We lost many brain cells a long time ago. Probably when I was nineteen, I really peaked on my craziness."¹⁶

Herbie Herbert: "When the band played without Carlos, Neal played all the solos so well nobody noticed the difference. Then the percussionists walked out and in effect you had Journey right there."[17]

Ross Valory: "When I left the Steve Miller Band, Herbie had left the Santana organization, as had Neal Schon and Gregg Rolie. Herbie got the bright idea, let's put Neal and Gregg, Ross and George Tickner, and Prairie Prince of the Tubes together and create what had been loosely the Golden Gate Rhythm Section. Many artists had been coming to the Bay Area to record. Herbie's idea was to create a Wrecking Crew, so to speak, that could back anybody up. But it quickly evolved into what was a very experimental band on its own."[18]

Gregg Rolie: "Journey at first was really a players' band. There was a lot of solo work… We toured eight months out of the year and then we'd go in and record, and then do it again."[19]

Eric Martin: "When I first met Herbie, I went into his office and there was this huge painting of Journey hung up on his wall. There's Neal Schon with a necklace of bones around his neck. They looked so organic, earthy, jazzy back in 1974, 1975. Herbie scared me, even though he looked like a gigantic hippie. He wore overalls with pot plants on them. He weighed a couple of hundred pounds. He used to sit on the couch at Bill Graham's office and just watch Bill. He idolized Bill. Bill was a great man, but he was a screamer. He was a really aggressive guy, and Herbie had a little of that. He was a mellow guy, too. He smoked a lot of pot. He had this huge desk, with all of these Indian carvings in it, and a gigantic calendar on this desk. He was a planner, a general. Then he had his roach clip and his big, fat joints that looked like submarine sandwiches. There would be all this wafting of smoke in his office. What you saw was what you got. He'd have two milkshakes, two hamburgers. And Journey was Herbie's baby, man."

Phil Ehart: "Four of us had gone to high school together, but from the very beginning, three things made Kansas unique: the songs written by Kerry [Livgren], the vocals of Steve Walsh, and Robby Steinhardt's violin."[20]

Steve Walsh: "Don Kirshner signed us on a demo that I wrote all the songs for. He wanted us because we'd got a violin, and he thought he was gonna hawk us as some kind of hillbilly hoedown group. The songs I had submitted, oh God, they were awful... So, we go in to record our first album [in 1974], and we have already hired Kerry, who has just introduced us to his whole repertoire of musical compositions, which were at least 180 degrees away from mine. Man, when we delivered that album, Kirshner didn't know what the hell to think."[21]

Phil Ehart: "We spent years in bars doing nothing but playing all these greasy, sleazy, old dives all over Kansas."[22]

Jeff Glixman: "Kansas was a very good band, but they were a little too arty-farty for my taste. I became really enthused when they started putting the songs together for their second album."[23]

John Elefante: "I was always appreciative of a very musical band with a great singer, like Kansas. They could play songs with hooks, and then break out and make a ten-minute thing out of it. They would blow your mind musically."

Steve Walsh: "We opened for Queen, Mott the Hoople... Hell, we did everybody. Freddie Mercury was an asshole. He was a prima donna. A diva, if you will. That's about having an ego bigger than you are talented, bigger than you deserve."[24]

Kevin Cronin: "The first six years of our career were rather rocky. I left the band for a couple of years to pursue a solo career, which was short-lived."[25]

Alan Gratzer: "Whenever we would be reviewed, we'd almost immediately be lumped into this 'Midwestern' genre. 'Midwestern rockers, no substance, no this, no that.' When we'd play a live show, and it was a great show, sold out, people storming the stage, four encores, we'd read the next day that we didn't do so well. We just had to take it with a grain of salt."[26]

Gary Richrath: "Irving thought that the only way for us to make it was to play all the time, and he was right. It ended up, though, that we had to make our records in three weeks, and naturally, they suffered from being done so fast. But if we stayed off the road for a month, we were broke."[27]

Kevin Cronin: "This guy who was kind of a mover and shaker in LA, he hung out with us. And the Eagles. He said he'd discovered this new drug, and it wasn't addictive, and it made you creative, the sessions go better in the studio. 'It's called cocaine.' We were like, 'Yeah! It's not addictive and it makes you really creative...Let's go!' It became a part of our culture for a number of years. You got to the studio and by midnight everyone's tired. Well, take a toot and suddenly it's four o'clock in the morning and you're still playing."[28]

Dennis DeYoung: "I'd been preaching to the guys in Styx for two and a half years that the record company were idiots. We were with a local record company. I think it was a front for a Chinese laundry. We were stuck in Chicago playing. We couldn't get on a tour. I mean, they were real idiots. Because when we played 'Lady' every night, the crowd would go mental. Of course there's other songs they like, but that's the one. You didn't have to be a rocket scientist to see that."

James "JY" Young: "'Lady' wasn't a hit the first time it came out, but we had a radio station in Chicago that believed in it. WLS, which went 50,000 watts clear channel out from Chicago all the way to Daytona Beach and the East Coast."[29]

Dennis DeYoung: "We were playing night after night in Chicago. What we didn't know was, the kids would hear 'Lady' being played live and they were going home and requesting it to the biggest radio station in Chicago and the Midwest, WLS. Two and a half years later, we were up to our last chance. It was our last album on our deal, and we were finished, we didn't have any success. We stopped by WLS to drop off an album. It was like seeing the pope. You couldn't go into WLS if you were nobody. Everybody who was played on WLS was already somebody. It was a closed-door policy. But they let us in the building and told us, 'Jim Smith, the program director, wants to speak with you.' JY and I go in, and we give Jim Smith the new album. We're in a big conference room, nice chairs. Nice guy. He goes, 'I'm not going to play anything from the new record, but tonight at eight o'clock I'm going to play "Lady." And I'm going to play it once a night until it's a hit. Because I think it's a hit, and I thought so two and a half years ago.' Jim had ascended the totem pole at the station in that two and a half years. He did what he said, and because he did that, I'm talking to you now. If he doesn't do that, you don't even know who Styx is, you would never know."

James "JY" Young: "Getting that first hit record is the next essential step in the process. 'Lady' was Number One in every city across North America. That's really when we broke out on a national level."[30]

Dennis DeYoung: "The minute I saw that, I said, 'Okay, follow me, boys. I know the way to go.' After the success of 'Lady,' I knew instinctively that what I was doing was correct for who we were. Because I never wrote a song in Styx that I didn't write knowing the characters that were going to record it. I knew we had this pretty unique power harmony we could do. Some say aggravating. Ah, fuck 'em. It was unique in its own way. And then in 1975 we did *Equinox*, which is a pretty darn good record. It had eight songs. Seven of them I was involved in the writing and singing. It was my vision for the band. And it did good, but again, instead of being platinum or gold like it should have been… I went through a really tough period emotionally, trying to deal with that."

James "JY" Young: "Tommy [Shaw] came along in late '75 when John Curulewski decided he was fed up with Dennis."[31]

Dennis DeYoung: "John didn't want to do it anymore. It was a personal thing inside of his family. I've never talked about it, and I never will."

Tommy Shaw: "They flew me up from Alabama and I auditioned, sang the high note on 'Lady' and was hired."[32]

Dennis DeYoung: "Our road manager said he knew this kid. Tommy comes up to my house. He's living with his parents and playing acoustic guitar in a bowling alley in Alabama. He comes in and I say, 'How old is that person?' He's five-seven, he had long blond hair, and he looked like he was seventeen. We had a tour coming up. We had to play 'Lady.' Nobody gives a shit about anything else. John was the highest voice in Styx. He had a remarkably high falsetto voice. He sounded like a black chick. We needed somebody who could sing that highest part. I went to the piano, and I said to Tommy, 'Sing this.' He sang it perfect. He sat back down and pulled out a reel-to-reel, and he played me a tape that had 'Crystal Ball' on it. Not the 'Crystal Ball' you know, but the demo Tommy brought in. It sounded like America, or Crosby, Stills & Nash. I heard his acoustic playing and his sense of melody, and his harmony. I knew I needed a writing partner. I wanted a songwriter who could sing. I had JY and Dennis, and I needed one more. Because you had John, Paul, and George. See what I mean? Everything was about the Beatles."

CHAPTER THREE

ENTER THE WILSON SISTERS.

"Boys will be boys, men will be slimeballs."

Ann Wilson: "My father was in the Marine Corps. He was John Wilson. My mother was a stay-at-home mom, which people could do in those days. She took care of us kids and ran the household and the finances. She was Lois Dustin Wilson. They were liberal. Mom just wanted for us to be happy, basically. She said it again and again. 'I'm not going to tell you what to be or do necessarily but be blissful and do what you really love.' And we did."

Nancy Wilson: "We had what was basically a music university growing up in our living room. Dad was the leader of the Marine Corps marching band. He had a conductor's baton. He would put on marches and conduct to the classical music in the air in the living room. We'd do interpretive dance scenes from *West Side Story*, jumping off the back of the couch. It was a complete musical family—aunts and uncles, grandparents, cousins. We'd have family get-togethers whenever it was possible, large groups of us, and do the harmony singing, the Irish ballads and the off-color English pub ballads, like 'Great Titanic.' Songs our grandparents would drink their beer and sing along to."

Ann Wilson: "It was a pretty normal upbringing, but there were hard things about it. I was always the new kid in school because we were a military family and having to move every eighteen months or so. The Marine Corps would tell you where you were going to be stationed next and off you would go. I was never a popular kid. I wasn't like a cute blonde girl. I was really sort of an outcast. More apt to be in the folk music society than a cheerleader."

Nancy Wilson: "Dad retired from the Marine Corps because of Vietnam. He didn't believe there was any nobility to that war. That's when we settled as a family in Seattle. We lived in our tight-knit little bubble of music and comedy. That had been our language and our safe zone as a traveling family. Our parents were very encouraging. It was the neighbors, the Joneses, that said, 'Don't let Nancy play guitar, it'll ruin her fingernails.' Well, they were right, but I didn't really care about fingernails. I got proficient on guitar instead of worrying about my fingernails."

Ann Wilson: "It wasn't until I was in high school that I realized I could sing and carry a tune."

Nancy Wilson: "Ann had the voice of doom, and I was really consumed by being her accompanist on guitar, piano, ukulele, anything with strings on it, basically. I had babysitting jobs. I gave guitar lessons to local kids. I tried to get a job as a mechanic at a gas station, because I was interested in cars. They said it was a man's job and I couldn't do it. Ann had one other job in her life besides music. In high school she got a job at McDonald's. She put on the outfit. Her second day on the job, she complained to the management that it was a dangerous place to work because the floors were so slick with grease from the fryers. She was immediately fired. Her one, true, actual job lasted two days."

***

Ann Wilson: "Being in front of an audience, for me it was just having the privilege of singing the songs. I was very zealous."

Nancy Wilson: "I was in all of Ann's bands before Heart. They were plentiful. Dad lent us his reel-to-reel Sony tape machine, and he and Mom helped us make payments on cheap guitars. Lucky for us they were so supportive. They knew we were good at it, and we were getting proficient really fast."

Steve Fossen: "Roger Fisher and I teamed up starting our senior year in high school. He came over to my parents' house. We were sitting in the basement, and he said, 'Hey, let's start a band.' We shook hands on it and said, 'We're not stopping until we make it big.'"

Mike Fisher: "Roger and I had been in a series of bands. Roger played guitar and I kind of managed. I wouldn't even say managed, because I didn't have the slightest idea what management was. Our first band was called the Deserters, which is ironic."

Steve Fossen: "Roger and I put together a four-piece called Army. Mike Fisher was involved before he went to Canada to avoid the draft."

Mike Fisher: "This was 1967. The Vietnam War was raging, and I was eligible to be drafted. I received a notice to report for induction and basically didn't. I was so sick the day I was supposed to go I couldn't even get out of bed. I don't know, maybe it was psychological. The government created a case against me, the United States versus Mike Fisher. I packed a garbage bag full of clothes and goodies and left. Roger and our bass player, Steve, drove me in my car to Bellingham, which was close to the Canadian border, and I stayed with a friend."

Roger Fisher: "Steve and I drove back home, and 5 a.m. the next morning, the FBI were at the door asking for Mike Fisher."

Mike Fisher: "I decided that I was definitely going to leave the US. I figured the justice system wasn't working properly if this can happen. I went up to Canada. It was easy. No one was waiting for me at the border, and Canada was very sympathetic to draft dodgers."

Steve Fossen: "Then it was Roger and me for the next three or four years. We changed our band's name to White Heart, then shortened it to Heart. We thought it was a great name. The word 'heart' means so much to so many different people. Roger and I were super-motivated and ambitious. We annoyed the heck out of everyone else in the band with our enthusiasm, enough so that they all quit. We found ourselves homeless. All we had was our Chevy van full of equipment. We were sleeping in people's backyards."

Ann Wilson: "After high school, I went to art college, the Cornish College of the Arts in Seattle. I found out really quickly I wasn't meant to be a fine artist. I answered a newspaper ad for a singer and went and auditioned for these guys, Steve Fossen and Roger Fisher. We drank coffee all afternoon and jammed, and they hired me."

Roger Fisher: "The vibe with Ann was so amazing. It was just like fireworks going off. There was no doubt there was magic there. We played solidly for the next nine months. We only took Thanksgiving and Christmas off, because Steve and I wanted to get out of debt."

Steve Fossen: "Ann was pretty much a folk singer at the time. We got her to sing some Janis Joplin, and more things like that."

Mike Fisher: "Roger's band was playing in Bellingham, and I decided to risk going down to see them. I had a fake ID and a cute little Triumph sports car at the time. I was going to college up in Vancouver and working construction. I went down and that's when I met Ann."

Ann Wilson: "We were playing at this club in Bellingham called the Iron Bull. We were working out this Janis Joplin song, 'Move Over.' I was smoking a cigarette and drinking a beer, a real sort of hard-ass chick in those days. Michael walked in. He looked at me, I looked at him, and it was one of those things where your gazes grab each other and won't let go."

Mike Fisher: "Man, sparks flew. We were just instantly in love at first sight. We started corresponding after that night, and I came down again to hang out with them in Portland. Anyway, Ann decided she'd rather be with me than be in the band, so one day she just showed up at my doorstep with her suitcase."

Ann Wilson: "Oh, when I went to Vancouver I was following my heart."

Mike Fisher: "I was renting this amazing property in West Vancouver. It was kind of an upper-class neighborhood. A mini-château house on a two-acre estate, with a smaller round house next to it, overlooking a babbling brook that flowed down from the mountainside."

Ann Wilson: "Michael had the smaller cottage that was kind of in the back of the woods. This little round house. That was where we lived for a good six months before the band followed me and wrecked our solitude."

Mike Fisher: "One night I had this incredible, lucid dream. This vision of a band playing. I could hear the music. It was a combination of the aggression that Rog has and the incredible soulfulness of Ann when she sang. I couldn't think of any other band like that, one with the power of Led Zeppelin and the amazing connection I'd seen Laura Nyro have with her audience. I thought what if we could marry those two together somehow? I couldn't sleep for the next two nights. I stayed up and worked on equipment ideas and designs and business plans. I suggested to Ann we call Rog and see if he'd be up for this. Rog was over-the-top fired up. Steve wanted in, too. So they came up to Vancouver."

Steve Fossen: "At the time, the economy in Seattle was pretty bust. There was a big billboard that went up that said, 'The last person out, turn off the lights.'"

***

Mike Fisher: "We moved into the big house on the property. Ann and I, Steve and his wife and their child, and for a while, Rog and his wife. The house had a huge basement with a stone fireplace. A great rehearsal room."

Ann Wilson: "I wasn't pleased about it. Not at first. It wasn't my idea. I wanted the romance of just being with him in this little house to go on forever. When the rest of the guys in the band and their wives started to trickle in, and wanted to throw down their sleeping bags, I was kind of like, 'Get a hotel!'"

Mike Fisher: "I sat the three of them down on the couch and laid out the five-year plan."

Steve Fossen: "We hired a couple of Canadian musicians and within six months we were one of the top bands in Vancouver. That's when Ann got turned on to Led Zeppelin and Robert Plant. From then on, her singing got way more aggressive."

Mike Fisher: "Nancy came up to visit Ann. She and Ann sat down on the couch, brought out their acoustic guitars, and started singing together. Man, it was incredible. Because they had been singing together their whole lives. We wanted Nancy in the band right away, but she was going to school."

Nancy Wilson: "I was at Pacific University in Oregon, studying literature and creative writing. The campus was in the tiny town of Forest Grove. I'd walk down the block from the campus and go play acoustic sets at a local bar, the Pepper Grinder. I got $20 one time for playing 'Stairway to Heaven' by myself. I'd try to slip in a few original things, too. I was working on music of my own. 'Soul of the Sea' was one of the songs I was writing at the time that ended up on the first Heart album."

Mike Fisher: "Nancy kept coming up to visit Ann, and we would always have her sit in with us on songs. She had such an angelic persona. So soft and gentle in her manner."

Roger Fisher: "I was uncontrollably out of my wits about her. Completely smitten."

Nancy Wilson: "Finally, I dropped out of college. Quit and went to Vancouver to be in Ann's band. It was an auspicious beginning. A lot happened really quickly."

Ann Wilson: "Nancy joined us in early '74. It made Heart vastly more interesting for me. Nancy's a great harmony singer, and a great acoustic guitar player. She added to the band what I felt was missing."

Steve Fossen: "Shortly after Nancy joined, we came to the attention of Mike Flicker and Mushroom Records in Vancouver. We did a demo, which they liked, and they agreed to finance our debut album."

Mike Fisher: "Mike Flicker was this hotshot producer who'd moved up to Vancouver from LA. He came and saw the band, but didn't think they cut it. He thought he might be able to do something with Ann, but he didn't want to mess with any of the other guys. I just said, 'It's going to be the band or nothing.'"

Ann Wilson: "We made *Dreamboat Annie* in the summer of 1975. It was going from zero to ten. It was the first time I'd been in a recording studio doing my own original stuff. I knew absolutely nothing about singing on a big studio mic. Mike Flicker was my mentor. He taught me everything I know in those early recording sessions."

Nancy Wilson: "To me at the time, it seemed like Abbey Road. But Can-Base was just a hole-in-the-wall recording spot in Vancouver. We met Howard Leese there. He was a co-producer with Mike Flicker. Howard was a cool guy. He played guitar and keyboards, and he wound up being in the band. We were so hell-bent on making something cool happen, and so doggedly determined to be good. We were up early. We were on time. I think we actually pulled it off."

Roger Fisher: "I was always pursuing Nancy, but she was very aware that I was fairly adept at getting together with girls. That wasn't a popular topic with Ann and Nancy, they really looked down on it. I saw Nancy out to the car one day and we kissed, and that was that. *Man.* We just started hanging out all the time. A friend had given me a jar of psychedelic mushrooms in honey. We ate those mushrooms all the time."

Mike Fisher: "The two brothers and sisters together, it was a recipe that could only go right, at least for a while. We were so tight. It was a wonderful, powerful energy that we had."

Nancy Wilson: "Bad idea! In my mind, it was more a professional arrangement than a real relationship. It was easier to have somebody to bunk with in a hotel than have to pay for the extra room. There was an easier communication through line between the two brothers and the two sisters. Those guys had started the band, and I was new to it, and Roger had a crush on me. I kind of went along with it for a while there, but for me it was never like the ultimate relationship I was looking for. It made things more practical on different levels. But still, a bad idea."

Roger Fisher: "Ann and Mike and Nance and I moved into an A-frame house in a place called Point Roberts. That was at a time when Nancy and I were creating together. The marriage of our inspiration and talent together just produced really beautiful stuff. Ann and Nance were working on this song idea one day. They said, 'Hey Rog, we were thinking there could be this other guitar part over what we're playing here. Can you think of anything?' I listened, and in my head, I heard, 'Dah, da-da-da-da, dah!' Then I just sat and played them the riff for 'Crazy on You.' We had a democracy that every idea would be tried. It just so happened most of mine were pretty good."

***

Steve Fossen: "It was 'Magic Man' that was the song that changed everyone's lives. It was the first song of mine I heard on the radio."

Nancy Wilson: "Mike Fisher was Ann's 'Magic Man.'"

Ann Wilson: "I thought my voice sounded high and shrill, and kind of nervous. But you know, there were a couple of tweaks Mike Flicker gave me. Like, 'Don't say, "*Ow!*" say, "*Ohh*." Little things that just helped it to sound better."

Roger Fisher: "When *Dreamboat Annie* came out in September '75, it was being distributed around Canada and nothing was happening. We were playing a residency at this nightclub called Lucifer's in Calgary. Oh my God, we hated it. It was a popular place with older people who spent money buying a lot of alcohol. We attracted a hippie audience, and they didn't drink that much. Plus, we kicked ass and were too loud. They kept telling us to turn down."

Mike Fisher: "But they paid really well. Ultimately, we decided it wasn't the right place for us and we needed to quit. Ann and I went upstairs to meet the manager, and as soon as we sat down, he said, 'Well, guys, I'm going to have to let you go.' Literally, the same day the phone rang, and it was Shelly Siegel, the head of the record company, asking us if we could get out of our residency because we had an opportunity to go open for Rod Stewart in Montreal."

Nancy Wilson: "We took the train across the country to get our big break opening for Rod Stewart. It's kind of a romantic rock story."

Steve Fossen: "After that, we opened up for every band you could think of. We toured Europe with Nazareth. My father was always pretty skeptical about the whole music thing. He would keep saying to me, 'Hey, when are you going to get a real job?' A critic from the *Seattle Times* flew over to Paris to interview us. They ran a picture of the band with the Eiffel Tower in the background in the paper. Dad never mentioned getting a real job again."

Roger Fisher: "Around that time I really started to understand this wasn't my band so much. It was Ann and Nancy's band. It was a hard pill to swallow. I'd realized their songwriting was really good, above anything I'd ever done, but it was difficult to accept I was kind of just a musician in their band."

Ann Wilson: "No, I have to take issue with the idea that it's mine and Nancy's band. I think of Heart as belonging to all. Now, if other people were going to go round the democratic process, they would just go straight to Nancy and I and say, 'Girls, what do you want?' And that made the men in the band furious. We always treated them as equals, but nobody else did."

Mike Fisher: "To me, the Ann and Nancy thing was more of a marketing thing, initially anyway. It was the way to sell the band."

Ann Wilson: "Mushroom Records certainly decided to capitalize. I think it was because they couldn't think of anything better. Two sisters, wow! Think of all the possibilities for titillation. They took out a full-page ad in *Rolling Stone*. A picture of Nancy and me, looking at each other lasciviously, our bare shoulders together, and with the caption, 'It was only our first time.' I mean, that was not even run past us. Objectification at its finest, and that's how they were going to portray us."

Nancy Wilson: "Chauvinism was so rampant at the time. If you were a pretty girl, you had to endure it. I think we just took it with a ton of salt, like over the shoulder. Like, boys will be boys, men will be slimeballs."

Ann Wilson: "All of that made us really angry. Nancy and I weren't raised with any of that kind of stuff. Our mother was probably an early-generation feminist. She was just so dignified, so respectful, and she passed that on to us. When we saw ourselves being treated in such a sleazy, cheesy way, we totally rebelled. Also, Mushroom Records wasn't paying us. They were trying to treat us in the old-fashioned way when it came to that as well. Ride them hard, use them up, don't give them anything, and then do away with them."

Mike Fisher: "Shelly Siegel had an incredible coke habit and that megalomania ego thing going on. This little band Heart was only popular because of him in his mind. Meanwhile, our album is taking off like crazy but as an opening act we're not making any money. We were making more from doing nightclubs. We opened for Rush, ZZ Top, all these different bands doing big shows. The record company wasn't giving us any tour support. Mike Flicker got in some arguments with Shelly about it, and Shelly fired him. But see, when I negotiated the record deal with Mushroom, I had put in a 'key man' clause in the contract because Mike was the reason we wanted to be there. When they fired Mike, they violated our contract, and we didn't need to be with them anymore."

Ann Wilson: "Thank goodness Mike Flicker was also being mistreated and he decided to leave the company. Mike was our 'key man' in our contract. We exercised that option, and we left, too."

CHAPTER FOUR

FROM A BASEMENT IN BOSTON.

"I felt, kind of naively, that someday it was going to happen."

Fran Sheehan: "By the time I got to high school I was playing in bands around Boston. Barry [Goudreau] and I knew each other, and Sibby [Hashian] and I knew each other."[1]

Barry Goudreau: "Sib served in Vietnam. He was an officer in the army."[2]

Fran Sheehan: "I remember all of us playing a Hell's Angels bar one night. There was a rail around the band, so the Angels could gulp a handful of whites and just hang on. They'd scream at us. They'd throw bottles off the ceiling. We're talking about dues."[3]

Tom Scholz: "I started playing piano... and the organ when I was at MIT in Boston, just for the fun of it. I played in local school bands."[4]

Barry Goudreau: "I was in my last year at high school and Tom had just graduated MIT. My band needed a keyboard player, and we placed an ad in the local paper. Scholz answered the ad. He was just starting to play guitar, too, the first month we were together. One month he was learning how to play the guitar. The next month he was unbelievable. It wasn't long before it turned out to be his group—and we were doing his material."[5]

Tom Scholz: "I realized there was absolutely no future in trying to play in bands in bars if I really wanted to do this…from an artistic sense. So I stopped it altogether. I found that the only way that I could really get the ideas on tape that I was hearing in my own mind was if I did the parts…I started around 1969. That's when I wrote my first song, which was 'Foreplay.' It was an instrumental piece."[6]

Jim Masdea: "Tom asked to come to my home in Jamaica Plain, where I grew up, bringing his keyboard, his guitar, and everything, and we would start writing original material. He came from the end of 1969. Everything was set up in my basement."[7]

Tom Scholz: "The most important thing was to find a singer I really believed in and to stick to him like glue."[8]

Fran Sheehan: "Barry hooked Brad up with Tom and himself."[9]

Brad Delp: "In the summer of '69 I was playing in a cover band with Fran Sheehan. We didn't have many gigs. We were mostly rehearsing. The drummer from that band mentioned that there was a group playing at a nearby club that was looking for a singer. I went to see them at a little club on Revere Beach. It was a three-piece band then because their singer had just left. The guitarist was Barry Goudreau. Tom Scholz was playing Hammond organ and kicking bass with the bass pedals of his Hammond. Jim Masdea was playing drums. Barry was the only one singing at the time. Two songs that I remember them playing were 'Green Onions' by Booker T. and the M.G.'s and 'Casey Jones' by the

Grateful Dead. I spoke with them after their set and they said they had recorded some original songs at a local studio and wanted a singer to go back in with them and record some more. I auditioned for them about a week later and got the gig, partly because I could sing 'Rocky Mountain Way.' Tom was a big James Gang fan. And partly because I don't think they had anyone else come down to audition."[10]

Barry Goudreau: "Brad was actually my brother-in-law."[11]

Tom Scholz: "I met Brad, soft spoken and unassuming, when he auditioned in a recording studio outside of Boston one night to sing several songs I had written. Having endured countless sessions with other singers, most with undeserved egos, I had only the faintest glimmer of hope that he might be good enough to squeak by as a suitable vocalist. He didn't warm up. He just listened to the pre-recorded instrument track once. Then he started to sing. I don't know if it took two seconds or three, but before he finished singing the first line, I knew that some guardian angel had just delivered to me one of the best vocalists ever to step up to a microphone. Then he kept going and I realized he wasn't just one of the best, he was amazing. High notes I hadn't heard followed by harmonies, and he overdubbed exact duplicate layered tracks, all with ease, all with emotion, and yet all technically precise."[12]

Brad Delp: "I always knew singing in a band is what I wanted to do. But I wasn't doing anything personally to promote it. I felt, kind of naively, that someday it was going to happen."[13]

Tom Scholz: "Jim Masdea and especially Brad contributed greatly, but there was no band, and I actually always worked individually with Brad, or Jim."[14]

Fran Sheehan: "Those guys started playing together a little bit. And they started doing some tapes. I think they were called Mother's Milk then. Sib did a stint with them. Whenever I was off the road from playing, they would bring me some of the tapes and I'd sit in and sing backup."[15]

Tom Scholz: "I was working [as a senior product designer] at Polaroid and the money I made went into recording demos. Then after I'd blown enough money doing that…I decided I would put my own little demo studio together. I cobbled something together from a few tape machines, bought as junk."[16]

Brad Delp: "Tom had an old reel-to-reel tape recorder. We got hold of another one and Tom figured out how he could bounce the tracks back and forth. I don't recall even having a mixer. We went from one tape to another. Ultimately, Tom had been saving up some money to put a down payment on a house. He was married at the time. He took that money, which was all they had, and bought an eight-track recorder."[17]

Tom Scholz: "Gradually, I put a better studio together over the years. This was where I did most of the work and developed 'Peace of Mind,' 'Rock & Roll Band,' and 'More Than a Feeling.' That whole process took until 1975."[18]

Barry Goudreau: "Tom had a very focused way of doing things. That was very powerful, actually."[19]

Tom Scholz: "All of these demos were done the same way. Jim Masdea played drums, and I would overdub all the instruments. Brad Delp would overdub all the singing parts. I made so many tapes and sent them out, and I'd just get all these rejection slips back. Being married and looking at thirty coming up, it was time to throw in the towel…So I was gonna finish this last demo, sell the equipment, and stop pissing away all the money doing stupid recordings."[20]

CHAPTER FIVE

THE MAKINGS OF TOTO.

"They instinctively put that wibble-wobble in there."

David Paich: "Jeff [Porcaro] went to a different high school than I did. Jeff went to Grant High, a public school in Hollywood. I went to an all-boys prep school, Chaminade. My dad, Marty, was the musical director for a TV show called *The Glenn Campbell Goodtime Hour*. My dad happened to hire Jeff's dad, Joe Porcaro, for the orchestra on the show. I got to sit in every once in a while, and play a cue or a walk-off, and Joe noticed. He says, 'My son's got a band. I should hook you two up.' Man, Jeff was incredible. He was fourteen at the time, and he played better than most adult drummers. We just bonded and started our brotherhood friendship right there."

Steve Lukather: "Jeff Porcaro and David Paich's band in high school was called Rural Still Life. They were three years older than Jeff's youngest brother, Steve Porcaro, and me. I spent more time at the Porcaro household than I did my own. Their father, Joe, was a highly respected jazz drummer who'd recorded with Sinatra. David's dad, Marty, was this genius cat—a pianist, conductor, and arranger who'd produced Sinatra, Sammy Davis Jr., and the great country sessions for Ray Charles."

David Paich: "Still Life was the best band I've ever been in. There was Jeff, me, a bass player, guitar player, horn section, and sometimes background singers. Joe Cocker's *Mad Dogs and Englishmen* record was our blueprint for our band. We would go to high schools and have this choir and the keyboards. Jeff eventually brought in another drummer, Kelly Shanahan, because we were really into the Buddy Miles Express, too, and Buddy used two drummers live. It was rocking."

Steve Lukather: "Jeff had this distinct aura about him. He would walk into the room with his glasses and a vest on and the whole place would light up. He was a rock star *before* he was a rock star. When he was eighteen, nineteen, Jeff was playing in Steely Dan. That was a massive influence on us at Grant High, Steely Dan."

Danny Kortchmar: "Starting from the mid-'60s, all hell was breaking loose in Los Angeles. All the great musicians were there. Everybody knew each other. Another thing was the sessions were live. In other words, musicians got together in the studio and played live, which happens very infrequently now. That's one of the reasons the records sounded like they did, and why they were popular, I think. They had humanity in them."

Jeff Porcaro: "Sessions are work. It was a job. You have to pay for your mortgage on your house and your car, and you have to eat. I've done kiddie cartoons in the morning and TV commercials for Toyota, and I've also played with Steely Dan. It's alright, it's harmless."[1]

David Paich: "The very first session I did playing live was for Seals & Crofts at Santa Monica Civic. I was sixteen, and they were opening for the Carpenters. I passed my baptism test right there. Then my dad got to arrange something for Sonny & Cher. Jeff had already joined Sonny & Cher. He'd left high school early. He was telling them all about me, so

I got the job. All my best friends were playing in the band. David Hungate, on bass, I met him there. Sonny really liked the way I played. I was the musical conductor, so I would conduct stuff or play keyboards, too. That was better than any ride you could possibly imagine. First of all, we were traveling on Hugh Hefner's Playboy jet. It had Playboy Bunny stewardesses on it, okay? Now, I'd just gotten out of my all-boys high school. My eyes were as big as saucers. It was fantastic."

Danny Kortchmar: "How good were those guys? They were among the most brilliant musicians in Los Angeles. They were kind of the younger cats, behind us in the Section, but they were amazingly good. Great drummers know the difference between a dotted eighth note and a straight eighth note. Real rock 'n' roll is right in between those two and that's where the swing comes from. You don't get the rock without the roll. Jeff and all the great drummers didn't even think about it. They instinctively put that wibble-wobble in there."

Steve Lukather: "Jeff got to play on, and Paich co-wrote, one of the most successful and influential records to explode out of LA in the 1970s, Boz Scaggs's *Silk Degrees*. It was a game changer of a record."

Boz Scaggs: "I tend to gravitate toward a strong musician-arranger. The likes of David Paich. I could give him my ideas of a song roughly, and he could round it out and give me an arrangement that I could then spring off of and write lyrics and create melodies. Between the two of us we came up with a number of songs."[2]

David Paich: "It was the first time Boz had ever co-wrote with anybody. He basically gave me total musical freedom. I had Jeff Porcaro and David Hungate doing the tracks. I'd sit down at the piano and play each song for those two guys, live. It was rocking from the beginning. The first song we did was 'Slow Down.' We got it on the second take. I went and saw a Rod Stewart concert, and I was very impressed with Kenney Jones, the way he played. I came back and we did 'Jump Street.' I told Jeff not to play the bass drums, just the hi-hat and snare like Kenney Jones was doing. 'Jump Street' is my version of the Faces. It was an inspiring album, because we got to use strings and a little bit of horns. 'Lido Shuffle,' Boz heard a Paul McCartney song that inspired him. It was like a magic carpet ride, a piece of cake to make, as they say."

Boz Scaggs: "That was probably the most successful collaboration that I've ever had."[3]

Danny Kortchmar: "There was competition. Positive competition that your record had to sound as good as a Steely Dan record, or an Eagles record. Everybody was shooting very high, sonically in terms of the sound, and in terms of the songs on every level."

David Paich: "The sound of *Silk Degrees* came from several guys on the West Coast right then. Mainly, it was because the players out there had real clean sounds. Jeff Porcaro's drum kit sounded amazing. David Hungate was one of the best bass players around. He had a nice, clean sound. We were at a brand-new studio, Davlen Sound, which had the first Trident board in LA. It had a Bösendorfer piano. It was perfect for us. Tom Perry did a great job engineering. We took the band on the road, which was really fun. It was a blast."

Mike Baird: "Boz Scaggs's *Silk Degrees* was an epic record, and David Paich was *really* the one producing. He was writing the songs. You're thinking, 'Well, Boz is going to be using the same guys on the next album.' Because *Silk Degrees* was a big hit, right?"

David Paich: "I thought I'd had enough creative input on *Silk Degrees* to deserve a co-production credit. Everybody told me that I'd literally produced the album. I ran this by my dad. My dad said, 'Ask him for co-production, and if you can't get that then it's time to start your own band.' I asked Boz for co-production and he wouldn't give it to me. Boz did his next album, *Down Two Then Left*, with Jeff, Hungate, Lukather, and Ray Parker Jr. Every musician in town wanted to do that album, after they saw me, Jeff, and Hungate do *Silk Degrees*. They started thinking, 'If they can do it, we can do it.' Well, magic just doesn't fly out that way."

Mike Baird: "That next album went right into the frigging toilet. Boz made the decision that he could do it all by himself, and there are tons of artists that have one hit album, and they don't go any further, because they don't realize what it took for them to get there."

Bill Champlin: "Right on the heels of *Silk Degrees*, Paich is sitting there going, 'Wow, I got double scale, but this thing is raking in cash right and left and I'm not getting as much as I wish I did.'"

David Paich: "Neil Diamond asked me to join his band. He was opening the Aladdin in Las Vegas. Neil was huge at the time. I turned him down. I said something to the effect of, 'I'm going to need my own solo spot in your show.' Neil said, 'Well, I'll have to catch you later.'"

Steve Lukather: "David and Jeff were getting free time to work weekends on their own demos at Davlen Sound, where *Silk Degrees* had been made."

David Paich: "When *Silk Degrees* started selling like hotcakes out the door, CBS had begun courting us, suggesting we put a band together. Now, we didn't tell them that we were already going to do it. We were like, 'Hey, that's a great idea! We'll think about it.' Then we made our demos. The president of the West Coast for CBS signed us. That was the start of Toto."

CHAPTER SIX

BECAUSE EVERY PLAYER NEEDS A STAGE...

"To be driving and to hear a song played on FM radio in America, it was like having your clothes blown off."

Derek Oliver: "You have to keep in mind, radio was the reason that sound took off in America."

Lee Abrams: "I remember the exact day I first listened to radio. It was December 11, 1962. My parents had gotten a radio for Christmas, and they didn't want it, so they gave it to me. I just started turning the dial and found a real loud station, and I was addicted from that day on. The music, the magic between the songs, the production values, the theater of the mind of it. In the mid-'60s I was managing bands around Chicago, and every band played the same songs, 'Midnight Hour' and 'Louie Louie.' We wondered, 'Is this what people really want to hear?' So we started doing questionnaires outside of the dances my bands would perform at every weekend and found that in America the mainstream Top 40 audience was starting to fragment. There was becoming a group of people, mainly guys aged between about fifteen and twenty, who were rejecting the mainstream Top 40 and really focusing on an iteration of bands that didn't have a name as such but included the Yardbirds and the Animals, and of course the Beatles and the Stones. This audience grew, and by 1966 and 1967, if you were in the know you knew who Jimi Hendrix was and you'd heard about Cream."

Billy Squier: "I was still in high school in 1967, so seventeen. The culture was changing quickly and there was too much out there that wasn't going to be attended to by traditional Top 40 AM radio. Top 40 radio in America was kind of like the network news. You get the hits, repeated, and it's a very short span of information you're getting. It was the mainstream. Within a very short time, it seemed as if these FM stations were popping up in all the media centers—San Francisco, Los Angeles, Cleveland, New York. There was this movement that was coming into its own."

Lee Abrams: "We wanted to create a format that was as commercial as possible. We called it album-oriented rock, AOR. On Top 40 radio, you knew every song. On this new format, we wanted everybody to know the artist. So it had tremendous familiarity, but also a progressive identity and some depth to it. I was still very young at the time, just eighteen, but I was working as a program director at an FM station in Detroit, WIRS. It was very successful. I got a call from the afternoon guy at the AM station, who told me he'd got a friend in Raleigh, North Carolina, who owned a big signal radio station, AM and FM. The AM was very successful, but he didn't know what to do with the FM. He asked me if I'd talk to him. The owner of this station flew to Detroit where I was. We had dinner, and by dessert, we'd signed a deal for me to consult his radio station and turn it into an AOR station. We did that and the ratings were number one in ninety days. I knew I had something really strong here, so I started a consulting company. Off of Raleigh, we were able to sign up other stations in Pittsburgh, Buffalo, Kansas City, and Columbus, Ohio. Those stations all went to number one. From that point on, we were just getting one station after the other."

***

Bob Pittman: "In 1973, 1974, FM became standard equipment in the car. That was really the changing point, I think."

Lee Abrams: "FM was all about fidelity. It was just as clear as a bell. To a lesser degree, it was also stereo. A lot of the big records that were to come out at that time were very stereo-centric. There were those two things, and then of course when it became present in cars, that was it. First by car converters. For $50 you could go get an FM converter for your AM radio. Then as standard equipment. Driving in your car and listening to FM radio, the sound was unbelievable. You just couldn't stop that train once it started."

David Spero: "In your car, you'd have FM in stereo. For the first time, you were hearing these records the way that they were made. You really hear that separation in your car—the vocals in one channel, the music in the other. We were delivering the sound that the artists wanted you to hear."

Chuck Burgi: "I couldn't wait to get into my folks' car and turn the radio on. We were fifteen miles from the center of Manhattan, I could see the Empire State Building from the roof of our house, and all the local radio stations had these amazing compressors. So when you turned on a car stereo, everything sounded bigger. It didn't even have to be a special system. It would still sound amazing."

John Parr: "To be driving and to hear a song played on FM radio in America, it was like having your clothes blown off."

Hugh Padgham: "When I first went to LA was also when I first heard FM radio properly in a car, and it absolutely freaked me out. I mean, it was literally like the curtains opening. My God, I got to know very quickly which cars had the best stereo in them. Even though Lexus were quite staid-looking cars, they had really good sound systems. Whenever I went to America after that, I would always ask to have a Lexus as my rental car."

Les Garland: "Then audience research became fashionable."

Laurie Larson: "John Sebastian and his partner Steve Casey were pioneers in music research for radio. They did call-out research and auditorium research and figured out what people really wanted to listen to. Call-out was where you call people up and play them clips of five, ten songs down the phone. Auditorium testing, you'd pay folks $50 a pop to come out and hear your whole playlist. It would end up costing the stations, like, $30,000, but it was worth it."

John Sebastian: "The research methods that I introduced in the '70s, it's the same things that I'm doing programming a radio station even today. I was really able to relate to real people. How they listen to radio, and what they care about. I was able to really zero in on the fact that they wanted less talk, less disc jockey patter, if you will, less repetition."

Laurie Larson: "John and Steve were egotistical, of course. But John really cared about getting to the truth. Steve had horrid taste in music. He was like this weird computer nerd."

Bob Pittman: "I had a great interest in social methods. I was a sociology major in college. I thought it could really help us to understand what songs to play, what people really like and not what I think they like. I was one of the people that really brought call-out research into radio."

Les Garland: "I've always lived by the belief that a hit, is a hit, is a hit. It gets down to the definition of a hit, but a smash, huge hit is a hit, is a hit, right? And radio was essential in breaking an artist and hit songs."

Al Cafaro: "For a song to be a hit on radio, it had to be new. It had to be fresh sounding. It had to have something very distinctive about it, whether it be extraordinary melodies or playing, or just very colorful lyrics. It wasn't hard to determine what people would be interested in listening to."

Lee Abrams: "There was a certain sound that developed, a very American, Midwestern sound. Generally, it was high-pitched, but not always. Strong vocals, real strong melodies, great guitar playing, and real drumming. This sound was 180 degrees from what was also emerging at that time, which was disco. It was an interesting thing. We studied why people, rock listeners, didn't like disco. Rock was about listening. Disco was about dancing. Rock was dressing down. Disco was dressing up. Rock was for the regular guy and girl. Disco was perceived to be fashionable and elite."

Les Garland: "We'd do artist studies with our audience. Take a little tape recorder and go interview people at random at the local mall. Ask them questions about what they did and who they listened to. Play them excerpts of songs in the Top 10, and 90 percent of the time, the person you would be interviewing would be able to tell you the name of the song and the artist. I don't know that hits today are anything like so ubiquitous in that way. Whether it's Spotify, Apple, Sirius, SoundCloud, all those sources of music have fragmented what used to happen on the radio."

John Sebastian: "A great radio song gives you goose bumps. What's true of a lot of hit songs is, almost from the beginning, even before the vocal comes in, you feel there's a magic about them. There's something memorable. It's really hard to pinpoint, but it's something that you hear almost immediately."

Steve Overland: "As a songwriter, you learn how to craft a radio song. You've got to hit people with the chorus. You've got to get to it quickly. You've got to grab attention, otherwise people will move on."

Les Garland: "All the producers and artists that I came to know, one thing I noticed was that nothing made an act happier than to hear their song on the radio for the first time. It was a big deal for the artists themselves. They all talked about it, and they all wanted their songs to sound great on the radio. That became a part of the decision-making in the way they would record and mix. They would consciously mix records for radio."

Dennis Dries: "The famous Record Plant studio in Hollywood used to have a little shed in the parking lot that housed an FM radio broadcast receiver. You could go into the shed and put your tape in, dial in the radio in your car in the parking lot, and hear what your song sounded like compressed through a radio player. That's how much it mattered."

Lee Abrams: "There were big rock records starting to happen at radio. When *Frampton Comes Alive!* dropped at the beginning of 1976, we didn't have to do any research. As soon as we played it, the phones lit up."

Laurie Larson: "When I first heard Steve Walsh of Kansas's voice on the radio? The way it made me feel. Like I wanted to drive twenty miles over the speed limit with the windows down. The way you'd sit in the parking lot listening to the last notes of a song before you'd go into work. That's your magic. You feel like you've grown wings. You soar like an eagle. There's no higher high, really there isn't. Man, I miss that era."

CHAPTER SEVEN

VINDICATION OF THE "MAD SCIENTIST."

"Everybody wanted to cash in on what we had stumbled onto."

Tom Scholz: "I had two more songs to finish. I finished those up...and within a matter of a few weeks Epic came in with a good offer to make an album."[1]

Derek Oliver: "The signing was great news following the six years of heartache that had preceded it, but it didn't come without a price. The managers, Paul Ahern and Charlie McKenzie, insisted that they change the drummer, so Jim Masdea was cut loose, much to Scholz's chagrin, and Sib Hashian was hired to take his place."[2]

Jim Masdea: "Tom never wanted to have anyone else compete with him...I have an amazing feel, and it inspired him so that it allowed him to not have to try to stay in time. He was free to play on top of my percussive foundation. If you take the foundation out from under your house, what do you have? You have a pile of shit. Yes, Tom did all the production. He finished everything. But the foundation decides what the finished house looks like... Over five years, he was riding my back... [He] pushed me out in the spring of 1975. Then at the end of '75, at Christmas, the deal was signed."³

Brad Delp: "[Jim] actually told me he was losing interest in playing drums. I know Tom felt very bad when the whole thing happened."⁴

Tom Scholz: "I got so used to that isolation. It was the only way I could work. John Boylan, the producer Epic chose [for the *Boston* album], offered me a deal. I would make the record in my basement and wouldn't tell anybody, and he would take Brad and Barry Goudreau, and a couple of guys he knew out to LA. They would record some songs out there, and Epic would think all the recording was done in LA."⁵

Brad Delp: "I don't remember the exact address, but it was on School Street. It was the house that Tom was renting at the time. Three-quarters of that album was done on that equipment in Tom's basement."⁶

Tom Scholz: "'Let Me Take You Home Tonight' was the only song that ended up being included that was recorded in LA. Meanwhile, I would make a master with all the instruments on it back in my basement. I had to record all the songs exactly the same as they were on the demo... The only thing that had changed was Sib Hashian played a lot of the drums instead of Jim Masdea."⁷

Jim Masdea: "I worked for seven years. Sib was in there for a couple of months before the album came out. I'm the guy that put the work in, not Sib. He was never in my basement. He never worked on writing the music. He simply is the first cover drummer. He covered my intellectual property. I think Tom felt guilty, so when they set up the studio at his house to do the drum recording, he had me come over and do 'Rock & Roll Band.' I'm actually on most of the songs, fixing stuff, but [Tom] never admitted that."[8]

Tom Scholz: "Working with Brad was always a lot of fun. We had almost a Vulcan mind link. When we were working, we spoke in shorthand terms."[9]

Brad Delp: "Everyone was happy with it but me. I can still listen to the first record and hear when I was flat on this note or that note."[10]

Tom Scholz: "It was my music, and of course I was writing about images that were in my mind. In the case of 'More Than a Feeling,' it was sort of a bittersweet ballad…There actually is a Marianne. She wasn't my girlfriend. I think I was maybe eight or nine and I had a much older cousin who I thought was the most beautiful girl I'd ever seen. Her name was Marianne. I was secretly in love with my cousin."[11]

Brad Delp: "I had a test pressing of ['More Than a Feeling']. I had some friends that I went to school with over at the house to listen to it before the record came out. I can see how the A&R guys passed on the demo, because I really didn't hear it myself fitting in with what was on the radio."[12]

Tom Scholz: "My initial feeling was it would be the best single shot. Then I listened to it, decided it wasn't a single at all, and got very depressed about it."[13]

Jim Masdea: "Tom had me fix stuff on 'More Than a Feeling,' [and] on 'Hitch a Ride,' the cymbal work, Sib couldn't get the cymbal work."[14]

Tom Scholz: "In the back of my mind I had a guitar sound that I was always striving for. There's no way to put that into words, of course, but I knew it when I heard it. I would just keep experimenting with the equipment until I managed to stumble onto the sound…What ended up going on the record was sort of a very pure form of what I could do, and what I wanted to do."[15]

Derek Oliver: "Tom Scholz is an interesting guy. He's super-intelligent, but also quite belligerent. There's very little room for arguing with him. What he says is how it is so far as he's concerned, but he's a tremendous talent. To have had that vision at that point, and then carrying it out."

Tom Scholz: "The 'mad scientist in the basement.' That was something that Epic really cultivated in the early days. The fact is I do work in a basement, so that part is accurate. A scientist? I do have a couple of degrees. Whether that makes me a scientist or not I'm not so sure. Mad? I suppose some people would think so. So I suppose it's not altogether undeserved. I'm not even sure that I don't like it, to tell you the truth."[16]

Brad Delp: "There is only one person who can make a Boston album and that is Tom."[17]

Tom Scholz: "We took the instrumental tracks out to LA and Brad overdubbed the vocals. Then John Boylan and I mixed it. Then I went back to work at Polaroid, because I wasn't expecting anything to happen with this music."[18]

Barry Goudreau: "We had hoped that we would sell 200,000 records. Because if you sold 200,000 records, the record label would let you make another record."[19]

Tom Scholz: "Sony's creative department sent me their three selections for the album cover, which were a head of Boston lettuce, a slice of Boston cream pie, and a pot of Boston baked beans. I don't know where they got confused between selling records and produce, but I was definitely not down with the idea of putting out any of those things. I mean, did they even listen to the music? My only input was telling a manager, who was going to relay on my wishes, 'How about a guitar that's a spaceship?' That's the only thing. Every time I look at that logo to this day, I go, 'Wow, I'm so lucky that this guy came up with this brainstorm.' Roger Huyssen is the artist who did it, and his creation of that particular Boston guitar was totally his and it just blew me away and still does to this day. [For the cover], he came up with the idea of the Earth exploding and everybody escaping. And I thought, 'You know, that's exactly what this is. This is an escape. That's what the music is, it's exactly what I think of it.'"[20]

Paul Ahern: "With 'More Than a Feeling,' I knew we'd get twenty-four-hour-a-day airplay. And airplay was the key to it all. It starts off sweet and then gets heavy, which does not disqualify it from housewife airplay time."[21]

Tom Scholz: "A lot of credit must go to our managers, Paul and Charlie, who went round to just about every American radio station to make sure that the DJs had a copy of the record."[22]

Lee Abrams: "After *Frampton Comes Alive!*, the *Boston* album was next to happen in August 1976. It also had a tremendous impact at FM radio. This was really well-produced music for the American market particularly. It wasn't particularly experimental, but it had great melodies, great playing, great production, and that music became a big part of our music programming."

Al Cafaro: "Of course, *Boston* just took right off. Because it sounded different. It was a phenomenon."

Tom Scholz: "We were a totally experimental band. We played in a basement."[23]

John Kalodner: "First of all, *Boston* was a bolt out of the blue and it blew my mind. I later met Tom Scholz, which was one of the biggest disappointments in my life, but that's a whole other story. But anyway, it was a spectacular record. The sound of it, the songs, the vocals, it had everything."

Jim Vallance: "Bruce Fairbairn and I studied that first Boston album. It was really our template, our school. We had so much admiration for the craftsmanship. It was so radio friendly. We wanted to sell records and be on the radio, so we gravitated more toward it than any of the punk bands of the time."

Joe Elliott: "Talk to any of the punk guys, and they were all secret rock fans, they just dare not say it. Jonesy of the Pistols will tell you he loved that first Boston album. In Def Leppard, we all wanted our records to sound like the first Boston album."

Joey Tempest: "I went with my parents to Florida in 1976. I heard 'More Than a Feeling' on the radio in the car. I was sitting in the back seat, asking my mum to turn the radio up. It sounded *so* good. That experience stays with me forever."

Paul Elliott: "I loved 'More Than a Feeling.' Even as a kid of ten growing up in England, I loved that song. I don't think any song has ever been sung better than Brad Delp singing 'More Than a Feeling.' That guy touched the world with that one performance. It's a magical thing. The way it lifts up on, 'I see my Marianne walking away…' It's a masterpiece. Who doesn't feel good when they hear that song?"

Billy Squier: "I mean, 'More Than a Feeling' was a completely unique sound. The whole of the first Boston record, Tom Scholz's guitar sound is tremendous. Any time you hear 'More Than a Feeling' on the radio, it kicks your ass. It's a great riff, and Tom got it right."

David Spero: "I was just moving into management at that point. I was up at Epic playing them some Michael Stanley tunes that would become his next record. Steve Popovic, who was the A&R guy for us and vice president of the label, he was going, 'I've got to play you this record.' He played us the *Boston* record. I mean, we were sitting there like, 'Hey, this is *our* career we're here to talk about!' But that was a new sound. That was an exciting sound. Everything on *Boston* you could relate to, same as with Fleetwood Mac and *Rumours* and the Eagles with *Hotel California*. Those were songs that hit people hard."

Paul Elliott: "That record is ground zero for AOR, of course it is. It's the incredible level of melodic sophistication on *Boston* and pure great songwriting. That doesn't come out of the blue. It's a synthesis of all the music Tom Scholz was into. It's halfway between Led Zeppelin and the Eagles, isn't it?"

Barry Goudreau: "We sold a million copies, I think, in the first month. Things were happening so fast we didn't have time to think about it."[24]

Tom Scholz: "Once it got past 200,000 copies the figures didn't mean much anymore. By then we'd covered all our costs. The only challenge I ever had was subsistence. The rest is something of a bonus."[25]

Brad Delp: "We went out on an eight-week tour when the first album came out. The shows were all in clubs."[26]

Roger Fisher: "I think Boston's very first gig was opening for us."

Mike Fisher: "Providence, Rhode Island, I think it was. We were supposed to be the second on the bill to Jeff Beck. They were very competitive. It was their hometown, and they were very much like, 'This is our town, and you should be opening for us.' They were so hardcore about it, we just said, 'Fine, go ahead.' A lot of bands poo-pooed Heart because we had girls in our band, but boy, when they had to follow us, it wasn't easy for them."

Barry Goudreau: "The first arena show we played was at the Civic Center here in Providence, Rhode Island. We were opening up for Jeff Beck. We had just finished the club dates in the Midwest. We're halfway through our set and I look over to my left, and there's Jeff Beck and Joe Perry both standing with their arms crossed watching."[27]

Jim Peterik: "I opened for Boston on their second show in 1976. Brad Delp was still a scared rabbit. I was a seasoned pro by that time because I'd been on the road since I was fifteen. Brad was standing there shaking before going on. I said to him, 'Brad, it's no big deal—get out there.' I literally pushed him out onstage, and you know what? He suddenly became Sammy Davis Jr. and performed his ass off."

Brad Delp: "We did the best that we could. We shunned using any vocal tapes. Everything was live… We opened for Black Sabbath for a week or so, and then we played with Foghat and some other bands."[28]

Donald Roeser: "Boston opened for us in Boston. I was only mildly jealous of other artists that were more successful than us, but you had to like that record. There was no way you weren't going to like it. It was staggeringly good. I guess our audience liked it. They didn't go berserk in the moment, but immediately after that the record went off like a rocket. They were all over the radio for more than a year, because there were so many hits on it."

Tom Scholz: "There were tons of bands that happened afterward that had harmony guitars, harmony singing, and involved arrangements. Everybody wanted to cash in on what we had stumbled onto."[29]

Dennis DeYoung: "Allow me thirty seconds of sour grapes. Start your watch. The problem with Styx was, we made our first album in 1972, but we didn't get our real big success until 1977. All the bands like Boston, we were perceived as following them, but we had made seven albums in that style by then. I thought Boston had good songs, good band, liked the record. They just went from zero to 100 mph, and here we are going at five miles an hour."

***

Billy Squier: "When *Boston* came out, I had a band called Piper. Boston sold 17 million records, and Piper sold 170,000 records. So I wasn't feeling too good."

Barry Goudreau: "We weren't due our first royalty payment until the middle of 1977. As a gesture from the record company, they gave us a non-recoupable advance at the end of '76, which was $25,000. To me, it was more money than I had ever made in my whole life two or three times over. Naturally, I went out and bought a new car. A Porsche 911. I thought if the whole thing ended tomorrow, at least I would have a nice car out of it."[30]

Tom Scholz: "A year or two before I got the album deal, my department manager [at Polaroid] came around and said, 'Tom, listen, I've got to lay off a few people. We're cutting back a little... and if you're gonna be leaving here to become some kind of rock 'n' roll musician...' I said, 'Ed, that's a million-to-one shot. I just do that for a hobby.' As I'm leaving Polaroid a year and a half, two years later, I'm in the elevator waiting for the doors to close. He comes screaming into the hallway, stops the elevator doors, and says, 'A million to one?'"[31]

CHAPTER EIGHT

THREE BRITS AND THREE AMERICANS.

*"I realized just how much of
a control freak I am."*

Mick Jones: "I was high and dry in New York after Spooky Tooth broke up. I was twenty-six, twenty-seven and considering going back to England and starting over a whole new career. Going to medical school or becoming a dentist. Leslie West was searching for a second guitarist. At that time, I'd been introduced to Bud Prager, who happened to be managing Leslie. I did an audition for Leslie, and he really liked the way that I played. It was a little weird for me, because obviously Leslie was the focal guitarist, and I was more or less hired as a rhythm player. He was very warm and welcoming, and I thought it was worth giving it a shot. But it got a bit down and dirty. Leslie had a heroin problem, which I'd never encountered before. We made the one album as the Leslie West Band and toured, and they were good shows. The problem was that Leslie would get offstage and, more often than not, he would take the guitar that the opening act had lent him, go back to New York, and pawn it in one of the guitar shops on 48th

Street, then make it back in time for the next show. This was a continuing cycle to pay for his habit."

Lou Gramm: "[My band Black Sheep] went through several personnel changes. We would play songs like 'All Right Now' by Free and 'Feeling All Right' by Joe Cocker...I wound up going on welfare for a while. I scrubbed rich men's latrines."[1]

Mick Jones: "I ended up back in New York and without anybody really to help me with my career. I had, though, developed a relationship with Bud. He liked my playing and my English style, my appearance. Leslie went into rehab and all the time we thought he was doing great and getting clean, but in fact he did a deal with one of the other inmates and they swapped each other's urine every day. It got to the point where I challenged Bud to get Leslie cleaned up, and if not, I told him I was going to leave the band. One of the last things that happened in the band, we were doing a show out of state and toward the end of our set Leslie walked offstage and basically disappeared. He had left again for 48th Street. Anyway, I laid into Bud, and he laid back into me. I ended up telling him that if I was to form a band myself, he'd have to become the manager. He took up the challenge. He had to borrow $100,000 from his wife's trust fund to become my manager. She didn't know much about it at the time.

"Quite quickly, I wrote four songs, one of which was 'Feels Like the First Time.' I'd already found a keyboard player, Al Greenwood. Ian McDonald, another Englishman in New York, had played guitar, keyboards, and flute with King Crimson. Dennis Elliott came in soon after Ian. He was Ian Hunter's drummer. Bassist Ed Gagliardi was the last of the musicians to come into the fold. I had a name for the band, too, Trigger. But no singer. We auditioned at least forty singers. I'd met Lou when I was on tour with Spooky Tooth. The local record promotion guy up in Rochester was a Spooky Tooth fan and in his spare time managing Lou's band Black Sheep. He brought Lou and one of the other members of the band to our show."

Lou Gramm: "The summer of Black Sheep's demise, I attended a Spooky Tooth concert at Rochester Auditorium Theater...We met the band after the show [and] I gave Mick copies of our two albums."[2]

Mick Jones: "Lou and I chatted, nothing specific. After six months, we still hadn't got a vocalist. I was finishing off the demo of 'Feels Like the First Time' and I'd got this pile of albums to listen to stacked up in the studio on the mixing desk. I wanted to take my mind off what I was doing. The promotion guy had given me the Black Sheep album, so I put it on the turntable. Within ten seconds, I heard *the* voice, the one I had pictured for the band. I tracked Lou down to a building site in Rochester. When I called him, he was actually in the middle of carrying a pile of bricks on a hod up a ladder. He came down to take the call."

Lou Gramm: "Mick Jones somehow called my father's number and asked for me. My dad called me in my apartment."[3]

Mick Jones: "I persuaded Lou to come down to New York for a few days. The first day he joined us, we ran through a couple of songs with him. For me it was like being hit by a bolt of lightning. Lou had a feel for soul music and then again, this indefinable magic. He hadn't, though, ever worked with anybody who could help him shape his voice—with the phrasing, the key, and on melodies—which I would be able to do."

Lou Gramm: "The first song that Mick and I wrote together was 'Long, Long Way from Home.' They're very autobiographical lyrics. I really left the small town for the 'apple in decay.' When I went to New York for my audition, there was a garbage strike, and no garbage had been picked up for three weeks. The whole city stunk to high heaven."[4]

Mick Jones: "With Lou on board, we completed our demo tape and sent it to Jerry Moss at A&M, one of the great record men of the era. I found out later that Jerry had gone on holiday the morning our tape arrived. The tape also went out to Atlantic and got returned to us."

Lou Gramm: "Bud had the penthouse suite on top of a twenty-story building in Manhattan. He had all the offices around the outside, and so the inside was just an empty space. That's where we rehearsed. About seven record companies came and saw us play, and they all passed on us."[5]

Mick Jones: "Then John Kalodner arrived on the scene. He was the new kid on the block at Atlantic."

John Kalodner: "Atlantic was a unique company, because they had a lot of great rock bands. Obviously, Led Zeppelin, but also Yes, Genesis, Emerson, Lake & Palmer. And then again, they had a great history of soul music."

Mick Jones: "Kalodner wanted to hear our tape, and from that point on caused pandemonium at Atlantic, pestering everyone on the label to listen to our demo. He became a right royal pain in the arse on our behalf, but he got us heard. The tape finally made its way up to Atlantic's president, Jerry Greenberg. John brought Jerry down to our studio."

John Kalodner: "I went with Jerry Greenberg, and we saw them rehearse in Bud Prager's loft. I just said to Jerry that they were going to be a gigantic band. I was so sure of it. That's how strongly I felt about it. I never thought I might be wrong. I consider myself the best A&R person of the modern era, but you're wrong sometimes. You're right most of the time, but you're always wrong sometimes. But I wanted to sign Foreigner so badly for the three things that later on I would always look for in a group. A great lead singer, great songs, and star power, which was Mick Jones and Lou Gramm together. Those were the three things."

Mick Jones: "Within a few days, we signed to Atlantic."

John Kalodner: "I signed them over the head of A&R at Atlantic. He wanted to fire me. So Jerry Greenberg put me out to the Atlantic offices in California, which was where I wanted to be anyway."

***

Lou Gramm: "John Kalodner says to us, 'I think your songs are great... The problem is the demos and the songs you played live for us and everybody else averaged about six and a half to eight minutes. You could never get that played on the radio. Let's get three or four of the songs and trim down to 3:15, 3:30.' That's just what FM and hit radio wanted. Once we played the edited versions of the songs for Jerry Greenberg, he had a contract with him that day. We did business that day, and within two weeks we were in the studio recording."[6]

Mick Jones: "It was also John who, not unwisely, suggested we ditch Trigger as our band name. I instead came up with Foreigner to reflect the makeup of the group, three Brits and three Americans. Since we had three rookies in the band, I felt I had to lead the way in all other respects and very much took the reins. During that period, I first realized just how much of a control freak I am."

CHAPTER NINE

THE ADVENT OF SAMMY HAGAR AND THE BABYS; FURTHER ADVENTURES OF REO AND STYX; KANSAS AND BLUE ÖYSTER CULT STRIKE GOLD...

"All of a sudden, bam! The world opens up."

John Waite: "I pride myself on being down-to-earth. I'm a pretty working-class guy. I come from great people. We're not affected by artifice. I come from a background where people mean what they say."[1]

Sammy Hagar: "Once I discovered rock 'n' roll and pussy, I barely made it through high school."[2]

John Waite: "I was very hip to Black music and country."[3]

Sammy Hagar: "I learned how to play that style of guitar from Ronnie

Montrose. I still play like Ronnie. He had that profound an influence on me."[4]

Denny Carmassi: "When we were making the *Montrose* record in 1973, it was all new to me. It was only the second time I'd been in a recording studio. Ted Templeman and Don Landee were producing, and it was fresh and exciting. It still sounds pretty good today. 'Rock Candy,' 'Bad Motor Scooter'... I'd no idea what we'd done with that record at the time. We were opening for Boston three or four years later, and Sammy said, in his own inimitable way, 'You know, Carmassi, those guys love that first Montrose record.' They were big Montrose fans. I never even realized we'd been that big."

John Waite: "[London-based producer] Adrian Millar was trying to put together a band that was going to take over the world. I liked the way he talked, but I couldn't see it in a practical sense. It just seemed impossible. But I said I had a couple of songs, and I said I could sing... That's the first time I said it without blinking. It just came out of nowhere. We went into the studio and cut these two demos of me singing on the mic, in the studio, two-inch tape. It crystallized everything. I saw myself immediately. When I was in the position of being that person, I wasn't going to compromise for anybody."[5]

Denny Carmassi: "We learned a lot from Ronnie's work ethic. I can only speak for myself, but Ronnie set the bar for me. Being prepared, showing up on time, and still having a good time with the music. Ronnie Montrose showed me how to fold my T-shirts in a suitcase. It was four guys and a road manager in a station wagon with luggage in the back, flying around, commercial flights. When Montrose opened up for the Who at Madison Square Garden, that was a high point in my life."

John Waite: "Adrian was always trying to pull his tough-guy shit on me... One time, after a meltdown, he stormed out and came back in and said, 'You're nothing but a bunch of fucking babies!' And then he walked out and walked back in and said, 'That's it!' When spelling it out—I have dyslexia—I couldn't differentiate between putting a 'y' on something or 'ies.'"[6]

Denny Carmassi: "Sammy was a pretty good bandleader. I'm sure he was learning at that level as he went along."

John Kalodner: "Hagar had a strong work ethic. He did not have drug or alcohol problems. He wanted to be a star."

Sammy Hagar: "I got home from the Montrose tour with nothing in my pocket, no money in the bank...I had nothing going on, nothing coming up. I didn't think I could make my next month's rent. But almost immediately a publishing royalty check from the first Montrose album, for $5,100, showed up in the mail...So I went out and bought a $5,000 Porsche."[7]

John Waite: "We weren't getting signed. People were interested but they weren't getting it. I said to Adrian, 'Why don't you film it on videotape?' Which was very hard to come by. It was rare. It was just coming into being. We could just go in and make a video. I said, 'Somebody's going to go for this—absolutely! Come on, let's film it!' And he did. Adrian hired a studio, and we put our best clothes on, and we took it around the record companies. We had a deal inside a month. Everybody was on the verge of video, but the Babys just got there first."[8]

Sammy Hagar: "My first album, *Nine on a Ten Scale*, came out in May 1976. I went out on tour almost immediately with Joe Cocker, Ted Nugent, lots of others. I opened for everybody. [Capitol Records] pulled the plug on that record at 27,000 copies."[9]

John Waite: "Bob Ezrin was in town, and he was doing some of the other bands that were on Chrysalis. We became part of a deal, because he'd had lots of success with Alice Cooper. Bob came on like he understood, and he swore to me he got it. He was like, 'Just come to Toronto. I've got this studio. It's going to be the best, man.' I was a kid, so I kind of believed the hype. We packed our bags and went to Toronto... and it didn't work out. Almost immediately, there was echo on everything, which we hated... When we came back on the plane, nobody spoke. We were destroyed. He was really a cunt. Right there was the end. Because we were never able to pay back the price of that [first] album."[10]

Dennis DeYoung: "I had such a huge part in the *Crystal Ball* album. It's the truth. What can I tell you? We'd brought Tommy Shaw in, and the dynamic was easy. The song 'Crystal Ball,' I said to Tommy, 'You've got to have a hook. You have a continual verse. It's beautiful, it's perfect, but now you've got to sing "crystal ball" somewhere.' He went away and rewrote the song with a chorus, and we recorded it. When we'd finished the album, I went back and listened to all the music, and I said, 'Well, the title of the record is *Crystal Ball*.' Why? It's the best song. What's the first single off *Crystal Ball*? It's 'Mademoiselle.' Who's singing it? Tommy. Now, obviously I could have said, 'Nobody sings this shit but me.' I was the *capo di tutti i capi*, right? But no. It was like, 'Well, Paul sings that one, John sings that one.' That's how it worked. We wrote 'Mademoiselle' together, but it sprung from his musical idea. So Tommy went from the bowling alley in Alabama to getting the first single and the title of the album."

Gary Richrath: "Everybody hates [the *REO* album of 1976], but I like it. That was the last time we used a producer [John Stronach]. The guy hated us. He didn't like us, or anything about us. It was Kevin's return to the band, and it had some good songs on it, but I didn't play the way I wanted to on the album. That's the least-selling album we have. It made us feel terrible. I was running around saying that it sounded just like I wanted us to. And then, you know, it sold five or six copies. We were trying to be too much like the Eagles. We went overboard with the California sound, or whatever, and stopped being a rock 'n' roll band."[11]

Kevin Cronin: "I write nice songs. [Gary's] influences could be more along the lines of Jeff Beck, Eric Clapton, Jimi Hendrix. Whereas my type of influences are the Beatles, Stephen Stills, and Elton John."[12]

Gary Richrath: "I really wanted Kevin back because I had wanted us to be both acoustic and electric. I got that from 'Stairway to Heaven' and other Led Zeppelin songs where they start quiet and then, all of a sudden, bam! The world opens up."[13]

Dennis DeYoung: "I was going through some really dark times doing *Crystal Ball. Really* dark times. It was self-doubt. Believing that you'll never measure up, the curse of great expectations. It swallowed me up whole. Most of 1976 was not good for me."[14]

Donald Roeser: "The path to success was fairly clear. You got radio play, you sold records, and you toured and sold tickets."

Kerry Livgren: "There was a lot of pressure to write hit singles. That's what the record company wants. That's what they always wanted, and we kind of steadfastly refused to do that...We needed some kind of quantum leap to get on the charts. Tremendous pressure. By the time our fourth album came out, it was like, 'Hey guys, if you don't do it this time...' They didn't say, 'We're gonna drop you' but it was implied. That would have been the end of it."[15]

Donald Roeser: "In 1976, I was living in a house in Melville, New York, which is on Long Island. I'd just gotten the first four-track reel-to-reel TEAC recorder, which enabled non-professionals to overdub for the first time. The first song I wrote on that machine was '(Don't Fear) the Reaper.' It was the song that bumped us up into arenas. Columbia Records had stuck with us, but *Agents of Fortune* was our fifth LP, and by that time they sort of expected us to be mainstream and to sell some tonnage, as they called it back in the day. We did some of that thing of going into radio stations to promote the record, but for whatever reason, '...Reaper' sort of rose out of its own worth as a recording. We didn't have to do a lot of promotion on it. Although, of course, the major labels back then knew how to take a song and sell a lot of records once the value of the property was established. They'd move bulks of those records into the stores once they realized that they had a hit on their hands."

Richard Williams: "We were in rehearsals to record [*Leftoverture*]. The album is basically done and we're getting ready to go record."[16]

Phil Ehart: "We were packing up our stuff when Kerry walked in with his last-minute addition."[17]

Richard Williams: "Kerry was just on a writing streak. You didn't want to turn the tap off… He comes in and goes, 'I've got one more song.'"[18]

Kerry Livgren: "I said: 'Guys, maybe you should listen to this.' Eyebrows were raised."[19]

Richard Williams: "He starts playing 'Carry On Wayward Son.' We worked it up a little bit. We went on into the studio… We were actually hearing it as the tape was rolling. The album version was probably the first time we ever played it correctly."[20]

Jeff Glixman: "I didn't even use the twenty-four tracks I had available to me on that song… I cranked it up and let it rip. Phil was with me. I ran a pass to tape, and we then listened to it back and Phil goes, 'What do you think?' I said, 'If it wasn't us, I would think it was fucking awesome.'"[21]

Kerry Livgren: It's an autobiographical song. I've always been on a spiritual sojourn, looking for truth and meaning. It was a song of self-encouragement."[22]

Jeff Glixman: "It took me years to catch up with some of the philosophical issues [Kerry] was dealing with at a very young age. He worked his way through various religions on his way to Christianity."[23]

***

Kerry Livgren: "And, of course, it changed everything for Kansas."[24]

Richard Williams: "That was *the* song that made our career."[25]

Jeff Glixman: "I called Don Kirshner and I said, 'Don, we've got a hit.'"[26]

Kerry Livgren: "Oh, it was night and day. All of a sudden, we were playing in Madison Square Garden. It changed dramatically for us."[27]

Phil Ehart: "We didn't realize it at the time—I mean, who would?—how timeless [*Leftoverture*] would be. I've been around musicians that I respect very much, and they've flat-out told me, 'I think Kansas has made one of the best rock albums ever made.'"[28]

Tony Clarkin: "I always admired American bands, but especially Kansas. With British bands, we had hefty singers with heavy backing, but we never got the sophisticated sound and harmony vocals of the American bands."

Kerry Livgren: "All the factors combined came together in that time and that place on *Leftoverture*. That was by far the most fun."[29]

CHAPTER TEN

THE SECOND BAND ON ATLANTIC RECORDS TO GO PLATINUM.

"They were very heady times."

Mick Jones: "I wanted us to work with Roy Thomas Baker on our first album. Roy, though, was booked up on Ian Hunter's *Overnight Angels*. But he did recommend Gary Lyons to me, who had engineered the Queen stuff for him. Gary, in turn, wanted to bring along a co-producer, John Sinclair, who also happened to be Trevor Horn's brother-in-law. I rolled the dice and gave it a go."

John Kalodner: "I hand-picked the producers for the first Foreigner record, which was John Sinclair and Gary Lyons. Although Mick Jones really had a sense of what the band should sound like, too."

Mick Jones: "It was the first project Gary and John had produced in their own right. We recorded the album at Atlantic Studios in New York. One of the first songs I wrote on the piano there was 'Cold as Ice.' It was the same piano Aretha Franklin had used on a bunch of her hits. Fucking hell, I thought I'd better play it right, so I really applied myself.

There was some soul in that piano for sure. The song itself was a little bit Queen-influenced. Not stolen but inspired by."

Lou Gramm: "When we heard 'Cold as Ice' back in the studio, we knew it needed something that wasn't in there yet. Something that would be an attention grabber. Mick came up with that a capella part, 'Cold... cold...cold...as ice.' I thought it was awesome, but something else was slightly off about it. This was in February. It was brutally cold. We were in Manhattan recording. It got to the point where there was a flat note, or somebody's timing was off. We just stopped what we were doing. We got our coats on, and we walked around the block. This was in Columbus Circle, so the New York blocks took about forty-five minutes to walk around. By the time we got back we were freezing cold. We took our coats off and got in front of the mics, and we nailed it first time."[1]

Mick Jones: "Billy Joel used to cover 'Cold as Ice,' but in the wrong key. I had to teach him how to do it right."

Lou Gramm: "Mick had quite the temper...He was a charmer and could be fun to be around, but he also tended to be a taskmaster and could rub people the wrong way."[2]

Mick Jones: "When we were finished recording, Gary and John took the album off to London to do the mix. Without a green card, I still couldn't leave the country. Ian McDonald had a green card, so he was able to go with them."

John Kalodner: "I was kind of overseeing things from the West Coast, hearing the tapes as they were coming in every day. When they started trying to mix the record, it was a mess."

Mick Jones: "Ian would call me with updates, and obviously he would be with Gary and John in the studio. I was saying to him, 'How's it going?' And he'd say, 'Um...Um...I can't say right now.' I soon gathered there was something wrong. They sent me a couple of the mixes and they were interesting, but so far away from the image I had of what we were doing."

John Kalodner: "I had to fly back to New York and meet with Bud Prager, the manager, and Mick Jones. Between us, we picked an Atlantic Studio engineer, Jimmy Douglas. He was the number one guy at the studio. We fired the producers and had him mix the record."

Mick Jones: "Ian and I and Jimmy Douglas got the tapes back from London and had to remix the album in a very short amount of time. Racking up costs, which would become the norm for us. We were already by then running a month over our deadline. That would eventually be nothing for us, but we managed to get it to the point where I thought it was representative of the idea I'd had from the beginning of how the band should sound."

John Kalodner: "It turned out amazing. It was just a question of getting the right combination Mick wanted. The big vocals, and the power of the band."

Mick Jones: "When we'd finally finished the mastering, I went home and played the album. I was lying on the floor in the apartment, just looking up at the ceiling. I think I'd had a little smoke. I put it on pretty loud and it was one of the most glorious moments of my life. I felt it was good enough to definitely earn us the beginnings of getting a name, you know. I knew that it was going to do something and if it didn't then everybody was fucking stupid."

Lou Gramm: "We were rehearsing to go on tour. Dennis Elliott and I lived in Westchester. We didn't live in Manhattan. We would ride with each other into the city. He had an old Buick Riviera that was in beautiful shape. We had just started going down the West Side Highway. We were listening to WNEW and Scott Muni says, 'Here's a new band. Three Brits, three Americans. Wait till you hear this music…' And he started 'Feels Like the First Time.' We went crazy. Jumping up and down in the car. Dennis had to pull over to the side of the road and stop. It was an awesome moment."[3]

Les Garland: "I knew who Foreigner were. I knew about Mick Jones and his past with Spooky Tooth. Lou Gramm was an amazing singer. Bud Prager, the manager, was a legendary guy. You could put your faith in anything Bud touched. So it had all that good stuff going with it. Good label, good songs, good manager, good musicians, and certainly, good timing."

Mick Jones: "This was 1977. Disco was the big thing in America, punk was dawning, so it seemed even more unlikely that a band like Foreigner would be able to break through. I don't think anybody in their right mind could have projected what that record was going to become. I certainly never envisaged it, because the only other new rock band to have had anything like that kind of success was Boston."

Dennis DeYoung: "You had Boston, and then Foreigner came along. Those were good bands. They made good music."

Derek Oliver: "In the UK it was all pure pop music, which was just awful. The best-selling singles in the UK that year were Wings's 'Mull of Kintyre' and David Soul's 'Don't Give Up on Us.' Or else you had the beginnings of punk. I couldn't buy into that because the playing was so bad, and the songwriting was so rudimentary it didn't even infiltrate where my head was at. If you got exposed to Foreigner, you were immediately transported into another world."

Steve Smith: "I heard the first Foreigner record, but that wasn't my music. I was twenty-two, twenty-three years old. That was the music of a younger generation."

Eric Martin: "Lou Gramm, man. He killed me back in the day."

***

The second band on Atlantic Records to go platinum.

Lou Gramm: "Success came right away in the States."[4]

Mick Jones: "Almost nobody else up to that point, including the Stones and Zeppelin, had sold a million records straight off. The *Foreigner* album passed that mark within weeks. We raced to two, three, and then five million sales. The only two bands up there with us that year were Fleetwood Mac with *Rumours* and the Eagles with *Hotel California*. I can only put that down to how strong the songs were since we didn't have a particular image or gimmick. They were very heady times."

Dennis DeYoung: "The fact of the matter is, Foreigner, like all of those bands in the '70s, were immediately dismissed by people in the rock press. Because they had the audacity to write memorable songs that people liked."

Billy Squier: "Mick Jones lived a block around the corner from me in New York. There were things about Foreigner's music I was hearing that I was digging. What I didn't dig was that these guys were marching on without me."

Lou Gramm: "Bud booked us a tour with the Doobie Brothers."[5]

Mick Jones: "The little run we did with the Doobie Brothers was great. That opened us up to a big audience. By the end of that first tour, we were headlining arenas in the States ourselves. That's a testing experience, the kind of thing that separates the men from the boys. Quite often, we found that AC/DC would be our opening act. They were also signed to Atlantic, and there was a faction at the company that was desperate to break them in America. They were an especially tough act to follow, as were Cheap Trick, who also opened up for us back then."

Lou Gramm: "There was a lot of pressure onstage because we weren't really a band at that point. It was disjointed and it showed...Mick is driving, let's put it that way."[6]

***

Mick Jones: "I enjoyed the whole experience, completely and massively, though it was hard to grasp how big the whole thing was. We did one of Bill Graham's famous Day on the Green shows at Oakland Coliseum in May 1977. The Eagles were headlining, we were opening, and Heart and the Steve Miller Band were also on the bill. There was something like 80,000 people there that day."

Steve Fossen: "It was a great time to be in a rock band that was in the public consciousness. You had all these bands kicking off out there. Boston, Aerosmith, Foreigner, and Van Halen was just getting going. All of us were taking what the British Invasion bands had done and re-Americanizing it for an American audience."

Mick Jones: "Bill invited me up onto the stage just before the stadium gates were opened. It was a daytime festival, so this was around 8:30 a.m. All of a sudden, people began to run out from the black holes in the stands, like scurrying mice. It's mind-blowing to see that number of bodies gathered together in one place."

Lou Gramm: "My first royalty check...was close to six figures."[7]

Mick Jones: "I don't think at the outset that personally things changed for us too much. I mean to say, a couple of the guys went out and bought stuff—put down payments on cars. But nobody was of that spendthrift nature, really. Everybody was settled and I know they were thrilled. There was a certain amount of pride involved, too, that we had done it. It was also important to me that we would be able to sustain and build upon what the first album had done for us. I didn't waste any time in getting down to writing new songs with Lou. We played both 'Hot Blooded' and 'Double Vision' for the first time at the California Jam in March 1978, in front of 200,000 people. With a crowd that big you can see the curvature—it tapers off at the corners and forms an arc. That's a wild thing to look upon from the stage. I was the most experienced guy in the band, but nothing quite prepares you for that kind of success."

CHAPTER ELEVEN

TROUBLE WITH THE WILSHIRES.

"When you have all that money
you get sidetracked."

Nancy Wilson: "When your own music that you wrote becomes familiar to people, that's the gold ring. All of the little living rooms and church groups and campfires and hole-in-the-walls that you played before, it's like suddenly people know your songs. Not the covers you used to do, but songs *you did*."

Ann Wilson: "That first big success is exciting. *Very* exciting. It just seems like the good news keeps on coming. Pretty soon you've got money pouring in, too, and back then, everybody's buying sports cars and fur coats. And houses and gifts for their parents."

Steve Fossen: "Roger and Nancy and Ann and Mike had their little clique. They were off doing their thing. Well, Howard, Mike [Derosier, drums], and me had our clique, too, and we experienced all this stuff that not too many people get to experience. You buy yourself a nice car. I got a Saab two-door Turbo. My dad's Scandinavian and they were supposedly very safe cars. It was pretty neat. I had a lot of fun. You get a nice house. Maybe you overspend a little bit. Then there was the kind of keeping up with each other thing. The couples had two incomes, so they could get houses on the lake."

Ann Wilson: "Michael and I bought a house and a Jaguar XK-E. Those were our two big 'beautiful people' expenses."

Steve Fossen: "The thing is when you have all that money you get sidetracked. That was kind of weird because we were so focused before that."

Mike Fisher: "Our second album, *Magazine*, was going to be our masterpiece. We had such high hopes for it. The basic tracks had been partially done with scratch vocals before we left Mushroom Records."

Ann Wilson: "There's actually two versions of that record. We were fighting with the record label at the time."[1]

Mike Fisher: "That was a nightmare to go through. We'd got a really good offer from CBS for a new label that they had set up, Portrait. Then when we actually signed with Portrait, we got into a legal situation with Mushroom. They had the tapes for the new album we'd started to work on. Mushroom decided to finish it with other players and put it out. We had to go to court to injunct them. We won the case, and they were ordered to recall all the records they'd shipped and so we could complete our parts for it."

Ann Wilson: "Then we [could] put out our version."[2]

Mike Fisher: "Mushroom gave us two weeks to put our performances on there, before they were able to release the album again. That was not enough time to finish the record the way we wanted. Straight afterwards, we had to go into the studio again for Portrait, and in another rush put down our actual second album. *Little Queen* was a record that was made under extreme duress in marathon recording sessions."

***

Roger Fisher: "Being on the road for so long touring the first album, especially me and Mike Derosier, we just felt so stifled because it was difficult to find time to practice. We would go down to soundcheck and just jam. One of those times on the first tour, Mike came running up to the stage shouting, 'What is *that*?'"

Mike Fisher: "Those were some of my favorite times when Rog and Mike would jam at soundcheck. I got this eight-track and set it up so I could record each instrument, right off the preamps on the mixing console. They were the very first ideas for some of those songs and then the band could progress with them from there. 'Barracuda' was originally recorded right off the desk on a simple cassette tape."

Roger Fisher: "It was just something we were messing around with, but Mike said we should develop it. And I kept coming up with more guitar parts that fit."

Ann Wilson: "It was a song written out of being insulted. And I guess I realized, 'Yeah, well, this is kind of a slimy business.'"[3]

Mike Fisher: "We were in Detroit and doing a thing for the guys who put the records on the racks in stores. This one guy came up to Ann in the lobby and said, 'How's your lover, Ann?' Wink-wink, nod-nod, and he meant Nancy. Ann just froze solid. She was so offended. The next day we played at the university in Ann Arbor, opening for Bob Seger, and that's where I heard Rog and Mike doing that soundcheck. The day after that we were in Cleveland. I came back to the hotel room and Ann had written the lyrics. I read Ann's lyrics and just thought, 'Wow.' I gave her the cassette I'd recorded of Rog and Mike, and then the band fit the parts together really well."

Roger Fisher: "We recorded the *Little Queen* album at Kaye-Smith in Seattle, and we were really under the gun to get it done. We were taking seemingly too long on 'Barracuda,' but it was just getting better and better as we fine-tuned it. That song was like a big train with an energy and momentum of its own, and it didn't want to be just good enough, it wanted to be great. We all knew it was really special, so we just kept going at it."

Mike Fisher: "Rog and I were there all night long just recording the lead guitar parts to 'Barracuda.' We recorded so many tracks of guitar, it drove the engineer mad with all the splices he had to do. Of course, Rog's lead guitar part ended up being epic, and Ann's vocal performance was thrilling."

Ann Wilson: "People always ask who the porpoise is in the lyrics. Nancy is the porpoise. We used to call each other that. I think it was an extension of the walrus, because we were big Beatles fans."[4]

Nancy Wilson: "Ann and I have always been the left and right hand of the same musical being. We couldn't be more different as people. She's like our dad and I'm more like our mom. She's way more of a soldier, a warrior. But both of us have always been like the eye of the hurricane with Heart."

Mike Fisher: "*Little Queen* came out on Portrait in May 1977. Just one month after Mushroom released our version of *Magazine*."

Steve Fossen: "Of course, Ann and Nancy wanted all of the attention to be on themselves. At the same time, they were being pushed into it by the record company, I know that. But it was troubling to me. I just thought of the band as being musicians. It just so happened it was two females being supported by an army of men. I didn't really ever go, 'Oh, she's a woman, and she's a woman, so it's women's music.' I guess I should have."

Ann Wilson: "The other guys jokingly used to call Mike and I and Nancy and Roger the 'Wilshires.' Did I ever think it was bound to go wrong? Oh yes, constantly. But it worked for a good while. It worked out fine because we were all more like siblings together. It was family.

But the typical things started to eat away at the perfection of all that. Whenever you're in a relationship with someone, the green-eyed monster is always right around the corner. You're watching to make sure he's not looking at anybody else. Being so jumpy about all that. And people just find fidelity extremely difficult. That ultimately was the undoing of the Wilshire tribe."

CHAPTER TWELVE

THE PRICE OF MAKING IT.

"Self-destructive son of a bitch."

Brad Delp: "They kept adding dates to the tour... The venues started getting bigger as the eight-week tour lasted ten months."[1]

Fran Sheehan: "I would be twitching in bed, going over the songs in my head, staring at the ceiling. Then the sun would come up and I would still be lying there thinking, 'Oh no, I gotta play in front of 20,000 kids tonight.'"[2]

Barry Goudreau: "Boston toured right through the fall of 1977. We played every major, secondary, and tertiary city in the country twice."[3]

Brad Delp: "We actually headlined our own show at Madison Square Garden at the end of the tour."[4]

Fran Sheehan: "Just imagine how nervous we were before Madison Square Garden. And it sold out. I could barely breathe, but once we set foot onstage, it was wild. It was like the whole stage was ready to just take off."[5]

Brad Delp: "We went to the Grammys the first year. Ella Fitzgerald was sitting behind me... I could never figure out why I was there. I could see what Tom was doing there."[6]

Barry Goudreau: "We were just running as fast as we could, trying to keep up. Then, of course, the day we got home the record label was in touch saying, 'Well, when's the next record coming out?'"[7]

Kevin Cronin: "[By 1977 with REO], we'd had six albums, but no one had ever captured the energy of our band in the studio. All those early records just sounded kind of dull, and they didn't rock."[8]

Gary Richrath: "We got fed up with everybody asking us, 'Why don't you do a live album?' I heard that for seven years, from everyone."[9]

Neal Doughty: "We recorded [*Live: You Get What You Pay For*] over four nights in different towns, traveling with a big recording truck."[10]

Kevin Cronin: "We got a good deal on a plane, because under the guise of flying around a rock 'n' roll band they were running guns around the country and the whole baggage compartment would be full of pot. We'd be wondering why our guitars wouldn't fit anywhere."[11]

Neal Doughty: "That became our first gold record. Epic flew us to London to present it to us at their annual World Convention. They made a big deal of this 'new' American band."[12]

Kevin Cronin: "Certainly in REO Speedwagon's case, nothing great that we ever did was ever planned. It was all just happy accidents."[13]

Gary Richrath: "Kevin and I knew the songs were there, but we also knew by then exactly what was wrong with them. I guess you could say we were starting to have a bit between our ears besides vacant space."[14]

Jeff Glixman: "[For Kansas] there was also, now, the expectation of success, whereas before there was the dream of success. There were many complications as we were preparing for the next record. Let's just say that *Point of Know Return* was the most difficult record I've made in my entire career."[15]

Kerry Livgren: "When you're in your early twenties and suddenly become famous, women literally chase after you, and it's almost impossible not to give in to temptation. What began to change us was success. It was very satisfying, but it also left an inner void. When your dreams come true, where do you go from there?"[16]

Jeff Glixman: "The laughs were gone. The tension going on at the time contributed to the overall feel of the album. It's not an angry album, but there's a frustration to that album that gave it a certain power. Steve Walsh was angry the entire album. He quit in the middle. I said, 'Steve, you can't quit in the middle of the album. Let's get it all done and it will sort itself out.' He quit after the album, too, so I guess it didn't sort itself out… Then he got back with them, immediately."[17]

Kerry Livgren: "Again, ['Dust in the Wind'] was a last-minute song. And it was not even really a song. It was this acoustic guitar figure that I developed to practice with, and my wife kept walking by my music room saying, 'Kerry, you gotta do something with that, I'm telling you.' One day I came up with the melody and the lyrics. The last day, I walked in and played that song for the guys."[18]

Richard Williams: "He was reading a book about Native American Indians. It kind of inspired him to write the lyric. Between the lyric and the haunting melody, and everything about it, it was timeless when we did it and it's remained timeless."[19]

***

Jeff Glixman: "We all knew it was going to be a huge hit."[20]

Richard Williams: "The writers started receiving these huge checks. All of us were working our butts off, so it was hard to accept. Some guys were buying cars, boats, and houses, and I was still living in my mom's basement."[21]

Eddie Money: "I had a psychiatrist tell me that I represented the American male alter ego. I'm into blue-collar rock. My father was a cop. My grandfather was a cop…I quit the police department when my father was Patrolman of the Year. I had some friends of mine that were fooling around with words. They said to me, 'You know, if you take the laugh out of Mahoney—the "h" and the "a"—you could be Eddie Money.' I said, 'I don't have any money.' I thought it sounded pretty cool. I kept it."[22]

Alan Pasqua: "The Doors' producer, Bruce Botnick, called me when I first moved to LA. He was my only contact there, and he was working at CBS and Epic Records at the time. He said they'd signed this new artist, Eddie Money, and he was going to make his first record. They needed a piano/keyboard player and Bruce asked me to come over, said Eddie wanted to meet me. I walked in and the first thing out of Eddie's mouth was, 'Hey, Al, I don't want to hear any jazz shit.' Perfect, I knew exactly what I should not do. When I think back on the crew that was assembled for that *Eddie Money* record, Gary Mallaber [drums] and Lonnie Turner [bass], they were from Steve Miller's band. These guys were insane musicians. I got thrown in with them, and you sink or you swim. Eddie was from the East Coast like me, so we had this kindred, full-of-shit spirit. He always played the tough guy, but he wasn't really."

Eddie Money: "I was going with a girl at the time [I wrote 'Two Tickets to Paradise']. She was in college, and I was in college, and her mother wanted her to meet somebody that was actually making a living. She had been dating the mayor's son, and I didn't have any money to take her to Bermuda or Hawaii or anything like that. So I wanted to take her on a Greyhound bus ride to the California redwoods. It would only cost maybe $62 for the both of us. But she dumped me, and it never happened. I think she went to Bermuda with the mayor's son."[23]

Alan Pasqua: "Eddie's hits, 'Baby Hold On to Me,' 'Two Tickets to Paradise,' he played those piano parts for me in Bruce's office. He said, 'This is the song, man.' I'm a quick study, so when he played it, I figured out what he was doing and just played it back for him. I didn't try to elaborate. This was meat and potatoes. It was, 'Take your creativity and stick it.' I got it. But then on 'Baby Hold On to Me,' Eddie sings the bridge, 'Rich man, poor man…' and I play this fill. It just happened. There was a gap in the vocal, and it seemed like that was a moment for me to shine and play something that led him into the next line. That stuff wasn't written on paper. But see, if you have a good song, the world is an oyster. Eddie had a great voice, and we wrote some *great* songs."

Eddie Money: "The first record sold, like, two million copies. I played Madison Square Garden. I was sweating a lot. I was backstage looking at my wardrobe case. My father was across the room, and he said, 'Look at you. Look at how tired you are. If you'd have stayed on the job, you would have been retired. You would have been out on three-quarters.' That cop mentality."[24]

Alan Pasqua: "The first tour with Eddie was horrible. We were doubling up on rooms. We toured in a station wagon. We took a lot of flights, stayed in really shitty hotels. Eddie was fine. I guess there was some similarity to the way he and I looked back then. On a few occasions, there were photos in the newspaper of me walking through the airport with a caption like, 'Eddie Money playing tonight in Cleveland.' And it would make him crazy. He would tell me he was going to fucking kill me."

Eddie Money: "I just wasn't used to having too much money to buy exotic drugs. I'd barely enough money to buy a can of Chef Boyardee ravioli. Then, all of a sudden, bang, I'm famous. Wango—got a new Mercedes-Benz, brand-new house with a thirty-six-foot swimming pool, ducks in the backyard. Big fucking deal. I had to go out and get high and blow it all. Self-destructive son of a bitch."[25]

John Waite: "[The Babys] landed in LA and the limo took us to the Hyatt House, the mythical rock 'n' roll hotel. It was a far cry from Lancaster, I can tell you. Oh man, there were the prettiest women everywhere. We were in the Rainbow bar every night. It was absolutely insane."[26]

Ron Nevison: "[The Babys] were a great band that just didn't have the right single. Their label, Chrysalis, brought me in [for the *Broken Heart* album, 1977]."[27]

John Waite: "How much did I enjoy working with Ron Nevison? Not much."[28]

Ron Nevison: "I found them the songs 'Isn't It Time?' and 'Every Time I Think of You.' John [Waite] hated those songs, but he was always a royal pain in the ass anyway."[29]

John Waite: "That's bullshit. That's simply not true. Because he was on the next album. If I fall out with you, you've done something serious... ['Isn't It Time?'] finished the album. We were proud of it. It went to Number 14 on *Billboard*."[30]

Rick Nielsen: "We came out with our first album [*Cheap Trick*, February 1977] in an era that was a rebellion against radio at the time. Disco had mostly saturated the airwaves from 1973. Right here in Chicago, there was a big bonfire in the park where they burned all the disco records."[31]

Bun E. Carlos: "In 1975, I got a rehearsal tape with ten songs on it. Ten real killer songs that Rick had written in the previous months. Every song but one ended up on our first three LPs."[32]

Robin Zander: "'Dream Police,' 'I Want You to Want Me,' and 'Surrender' were all written around the same time. They were all presented for our first record and not one of them made it. 'What else you got? Anything better than that?'"[33]

Rick Nielsen: "Critics liked us more than anyone, but that can be the kiss of death. You have to go beyond the initial hype everyone gets. If I was a record buyer and I had a choice between buying, say, the first Cheap Trick album when it came out, or the new Led Zeppelin album (*The Song Remains the Same*) that was released around the same time, I would have bought the Led Zeppelin."[34]

Bun E. Carlos: "Everybody back home said to me, 'You're playing with Rick Nielsen? He's such a jerk.' There were the crazy nights Cheap Trick would play the clubs. The late sets would get pretty rowdy. There was the Carnival Game. I would start off a little shuffle, and Rick would take the mic: 'Ladies and gentlemen, welcome to the Cheap Trick carnival. Tonight, we're asking for volunteers—do I have a young lady in the audience? Well, step right up and you'll win a prize if I fail to guess your weight within five pounds. Just step right up. Now, in order to guess your weight, you'll have to sit...on...my...face!'"[35]

CHAPTER THIRTEEN

STYX PULLS BACK THE CURTAIN.

"There's a lot of different things going on—from messages to tight pants."

Dennis DeYoung: "When I sat down and wrote *The Grand Illusion*, whatever I was going through during *Crystal Ball*, I had cleared. I began to say, 'How does this whole thing work?' By which I meant, we're trying to sell albums and concert tickets. And we're really just a small part in this huge thing called capitalism. What's our role in that? And I said, 'Well, our role is to create an illusion for people's possible edification, but mostly for entertainment.' That's what we do. It's an illusion."

Tommy Shaw: "We've always been different personalities—the zany one, the teen idol, the heavy metal monster. I think there's a lot to like about the band because there's a lot of different things going on—from messages to tight pants."[1]

Dennis DeYoung: "I wrote these lyrics about the band coming onstage. 'Welcome to the Grand Illusion. Come on in and see what's happening. Pay the price, get your tickets for the show. The stage is set, the band starts playing. Suddenly your heart is pounding, wishing secretly you were a star.' Out of all those fans out there, so many of them are looking at that stage, wondering what that's like. 'That could be me.' That's the appeal of it. But then I said, 'Don't be fooled by the radio, the TV, or the magazines. They show you photographs of how your life should be. But they're just someone else's fantasy.'"

Tommy Shaw: "Around the time of *The Grand Illusion* we couldn't get work. We didn't have a track record as headliners, and we couldn't get anyone else to let us play with them onstage because we were kicking their asses so bad."[2]

Dennis DeYoung: "We hadn't gotten real big success yet, and I was wondering would we ever. Those lyrics come from the idea that this is an illusion that we're creating. I'm telling you it's an illusion. I sat down with the band and said, 'We're creating an illusion, guys. How do we fit into this? What's your take on it?'"

James "JY" Young: "We had three highly motivated writers that all had a different mindset, a different skew on what they wanted to do."[3]

Dennis DeYoung: "JY wrote 'Miss America.' Tommy wrote 'Fooling Yourself.' JY, Tommy, and I wrote 'Superstars.' See what I was saying about Styx being *a band*?"

James "JY" Young: "On that record, we were more in sync, personally and professionally as individuals, than we ever were before or after."[4]

Dennis DeYoung: "I never felt it was my band. Never. I felt it was *our* band, but that I was the leader. That's all. What does leadership do? I once said something on a *Behind the Music* thing that was misinterpreted by morons. I said I was the president of Styx. I meant that in terms of the United States. We have Congress, the Senate, and the Supreme Court. In other words, the president doesn't rule by fiat. What leadership to me is, you set a goal, you keep the troops together, and you be the cheerleader toward meeting that goal. You cannot rule any group of adults like a dictator. Unless you've got some hold over them. What have you got? Pictures of them with goats? Cocaine coming out of their asses? No, you do it two ways. Through success. I was the only one in the band that'd had real success as a writer. And I was a motivator. But all of those records? Those are the result of five mooks in a room."

James "JY" Young: "['Come Sail Away'] is what Led Zeppelin perfected with a power ballad. 'Stairway to Heaven.' Start slow and finish big. That was the big turning point. It shot us off into outer space. We were at our creative peak."[5]

Dennis DeYoung: "When I first played 'Come Sail Away'—the part of the song that goes, 'A gathering of angels appeared above my head,' and then goes into, 'Come sail away.' I could feel, 'I have got something here.' It's just electricity. It just goes right through you. You start to get goose bumps and start to shake just a little..."[6] Our manager, Derek Sutton, and our promotion man, Jim Cahill, wanted 'Superstars' to be the first single. I said, 'That is the weakest song on the album.' 'Superstars' was sitting between 'Fooling Yourself' and 'Come Sail Away.' Like a cute girl between Salma Hayek and Elizabeth Taylor...It's not a bad place to be. It's that old story that if you want to look attractive, then surround yourself with ugly people."[7]

Al Cafaro: "Styx was one of the funniest bands. Very few radio programmers were Styx fans, as I recall. But they all knew they had to play Styx. They knew Styx was going to deliver a record, it would go on the radio, and the phones would light up, and it was going to sell. It would always happen with Styx. It was almost like a moan. 'Oh, *another* Styx record I gotta play.'"

Dennis DeYoung: "In one year I went from, I was making good money in the band from *Equinox* and *Crystal Ball*. A lot more than my dad made for a living, immediately. And then *The Grand Illusion*. '*How much* did I get?' It was an unheard-of experience from a working-class, blue-collar part of Chicago."

James "JY" Young: "Five young men had finally gained success. We achieved our goal and finally the money and all the trappings came rolling in for us."[8]

Tommy Shaw: "Much of *The Grand Illusion* album was to do with the disillusionment of finding out that the things we had dreamed about weren't quite what they were cut out to be."[9]

Dennis DeYoung: "I was stunned by how my family and my friends suddenly viewed me. There's a change that happens. You realize that your friends can feel threatened by your success. Something you never saw coming. Because you didn't aspire to leave them behind. They're your friends. It's just that their fears are pure human emotion. Even in my family, the amount of money I suddenly had, you could feel a change in how they viewed me as well. And it scared me, I didn't like it. I used to have dreams of bringing home all this money in giant refuse bags. These bags were all around me. Because at some point I viewed the money as garbage."

James "JY" Young: "Going from having very little to having lots is a transition that affects you personally, professionally, and emotionally in ways that you didn't expect."[10]

Dennis DeYoung: "Your whole life you've been looking to fill this hole within you. I've always said, ambitious people are forever trying to please someone who cannot be pleased. That's what drives people. Is that your mom or dad? I don't care, tell your shrink. For me, it was my mother I wanted to please. Once you get there, you think all holes will be filled. All will be glorious and wonderful because you've done it. Then you find you're the same mook as the day before. You thought your family would be happier for you. But they have their own fears of being left behind. Not being needed. That suddenly I would be a different person. But I didn't feel like a different person. And I was really consumed with one thing. How did we deal with this? Because prior to it, all we were doing was competing with Queen and Aerosmith. We just wanted to kick their asses. That's all we cared about. Suddenly, you're competing with yourself, and that was the trickiest thing to do. Can we keep this thing going?"

PART TWO

TAKE IT ON THE RUN

CHAPTER FOURTEEN

IN WHICH TOTO FIND THEIR VOICE.

"Bobby was a party boy.
And straight-up crazy."

Danny Kortchmar: "I was really jealous when David Paich and Jeff Porcaro put a band together. I felt like, 'Jesus, we should have done that!'"

Steve Lukather: "A big rave was going on around town over who the guitar player would be. That chair was still open, and more than anything in the world, I wanted to be the guy to fill it. My cause was helped by the fact I was so close with Steve Porcaro. Sure enough, Jeff called to invite me down to Davlen Sound to play on a track Paich had just written. It was obvious they wanted to check me out up close, and I wanted to impress them so badly, I was shaking with nerves by the time I got there."

Tim Pierce: "The studio musician, that's a person who has to come up with multiple ideas and concepts instantly and never falter. Lukather had that skill when he was nineteen. He was already fully formed. He could do anything in any style. He was phenomenal."

Steve Lukather: "Davlen was such a great studio. The room was big and loud. It had a beautiful Bösendorfer piano. There were a whole bunch of other guys who thought they were in line for the gig, so the vibe on the scene was very much, 'Who the hell is this punk-ass kid jumping the queue?' Neither was Paich or Jeff about to make things easy for me. In fact, for several months the two of them delighted in fucking with me. They kept having me come on down to Davlen, but never let on whether or not I was actually in the band."

David Paich: "I didn't know Lukather at the time. I think there were one or two other people auditioning for the guitar slot, too."

Steve Lukather: "One time, I turned up with the girl I was seeing. Her name was Christy. She was beautiful, blonde, six years older than me, and a divorcee. My mom was appalled. Paich and Jeff had me wait outside in the corridor with Christy and my guitar, just to fuck with me some more. Finally, Paich came out of the studio. He looked at me, looked at Christy. Then he swept her up and stuck his tongue right down her throat. What's more, she went for it."

David Paich: "Oh, man. Lukather is not going to let that one go. I told you I went to an all-boys' school. What happened was, Luke was out in the hallway learning the songs. Meanwhile, his girlfriend came into the booth and kind of snuggled up next to me as I was standing there. I simply took advantage of the moment."

Steve Lukather: "My face was on the floor. But as far as I was concerned, I wanted the gig so bad he could have her. My weekend visits to Davlen carried on going. The way things would go down, Paich and Jeff would cut tracks live to tape. Paich would also add Moog bass and, man, he was so good at it. Then I would overdub onto the tracks. Together, Paich and Jeff were intimidating, but also like this magnetic force. Here they were, two of the hottest young cats in LA, and they were tearing it up right in front of me. On any given day, I would watch magic go down between them with a shit-eating grin on my face. I was so happy just to be there in that room, I could have burst into flames."

Steve Porcaro: "We were all about the groove and the pocket, and cool chord changes and a good melody."[1]

Steve Lukather: "We knuckled down to make the first Toto album in October of 1977. Punk rock was at the peak of its influence in the US. We had been with Boz Scaggs in London and seen all these guys with blue mohawks and leather jackets walking down the street. We were like, 'What the fuck's this all about? These guys can't play. And they *spit* on each other.' Our heroes were Steely Dan. As far as Paich and Jeff were concerned, musicianship was a prerequisite of their band. They had wanted guys who could not only play, but also sing and write music. Paich would reference Fleetwood Mac and the Eagles, the kind of bands in which every member contributed. In Steve Porcaro, they had a genius keyboard player. David Hungate was the most seasoned cat of us all. He was nine years older than Steve and me, but hilarious and a first-take guy. Paich had also decided that we had to have a lead singer. He got fixated on a high tenor voice like Lou Gramm's."

David Paich: "You bet I was very aware of our competition. Boston had not long released their record, and they had a real high vocalist. Foreigner had a great vocalist. I said, 'We're going to have to raise the bar here. We're going to have to go outside of the group and find somebody.' Meanwhile, I was singing some of the demos, and I have a low range. I can't climb up into the stratosphere above the music. We looked around at a few singers. Mickey Thomas, who was with the Elvin Bishop Group, was one. Jeff and I had played on Mickey's solo record with Steve Cropper and 'Duck' Dunn. We were like one half of Booker T. and the M.G.'s on that record. Then I asked Kenny Loggins, and then Leo Sayer. Michael McDonald had just come to town, and we dug him immensely. I actually called Michael to offer him the job and he told me, 'Damn, I just signed on with the Doobie Brothers four days ago.' Otherwise, Mike McDonald would have been our lead singer."

Bill Champlin: "I used to do a ton of vocal session dates with Michael McDonald. Him and Bobby Kimball."

Steve Lukather: "The other guy Paich and Jeff were hot on was Bobby Kimball. Bobby was in a band with a friend of theirs, Joe Schermie. Joe had been the bassist in Three Dog Night. They went along to see Bobby rehearse with Joe. Bobby wasn't a schooled musician, but he had a powerful sound to his voice. He was a big personality, too."

David Paich: "Bobby was in a group called SS Fools. It was like the backing band for Three Dog Night. He could sing really high, but he had more of a Southern blues feel, and he could break windows with his volume. Everybody would be in awe of him when he opened his mouth."

Bobby Kimball: "[My influences were] Black music. That's what shaped the way I sing. I played with some great cats from Louisiana. It was a music mecca for bands where I grew up. There were so many 5,000-seater clubs, and they were full every weekend. The drinking age in Louisiana was eighteen. Can you imagine how many eighteen-year-olds were coming across the border to hear some great live music and get a buzz on?"[2]

David Paich: "Bobby had a pretty untrained voice as far as the recording process goes. I was working with a diamond in the rough here. He could sing, but I had to get rid of his vibrato and make him sound like Lou Gramm."

Bobby Kimball: "We got together and recorded one of my songs that I had written two days before. We got it in two takes. The second take of 'You Are the Flower' was on our first album, and it's still one of my favorite songs. I couldn't believe how fast they locked into the groove and made it sound like magic."[3]

***

Steve Lukather: "I was the rock 'n' roll guy. But we also had that R&B thing going on. Even when we played straight notes, we didn't play them like rock guys would play them. Ours would have a little more swing. Subconsciously. That's what you can't program into a computer. You can't name it, you can't put your finger on it or touch it, but it's there. It happens to be a gift from God."

Steve Porcaro: "[What we didn't have was] a poet in the band, which we sure could have used. There was no Bono. We tried to bring him in with Bobby. He was an amazing singer... but we didn't really know Bobby all that well."[4]

David Paich: "We soon discovered Bobby was *very* different to the rest of us."

Steve Lukather: "Like Hungate, Bobby was older than the rest of us. Ten years older. He was the outsider. He'd been working on the road for pretty much his whole life. Bobby was a sweet cat, but also a party boy. And straight-up crazy. Bobby ran with a rough crowd. There were some very interesting goings-on at his house. One time I was there with my girlfriend and a bunch of people came out of Bobby's bedroom, all of them butterball naked. They wanted the two of us to get involved in their whole scene. I was like, 'Ah, no, we're going to leave now.' You never knew what might happen when you were at Bobby's place. There were no goats at least."

CHAPTER FIFTEEN

THE MAN WITH THE GOLDEN THROAT.

"That guitar and my voice went together like salt and pepper."

Ross Valory: "[The first three Journey albums all] went gold. For each of those albums to sell 500,000 copies is no sharp stick in the eye."[1]

Herbie Herbert: "By the third album the inmates were allowed to run the asylum. Meaning that Journey got to produce *Next* [in 1977]. There was a real cult following. [But] Boston, Foreigner, Styx...all these bands had their hits way before Journey had theirs. They were standing on the platform watching the taillights of the caboose go wailing away in the distance."[2]

Neal Schon: "The label said, 'We think you need a frontman.' They wanted to get us on the radio. And sell some records. And so they gave us an ultimatum—'Get a frontman, or we're gonna drop you from the label.'"[3]

Robert Fleischman: "We started in Texas for some practice shows and played with REO Speedwagon and Judas Priest. The band would do three or four songs, and then they would introduce me. The front row was always diehard Journey fans, and they would flip me off and say, 'Fuck you!' Every time I got up on the stage, that's what I was up against."[4]

Herbie Herbert: "Neal loved Robert Fleischman."[5]

Neal Schon: "'Wheel in the Sky' is an early song I wrote with Robert Fleischman."[6]

Robert Fleischman: "Neal and the band had the music already. I came up with the melody. One day, I was given a poem by Ross Valory's wife, Diane. So to make everyone happy, I plucked out the line, 'Wheel in the sky,' and then I wrote the rest."[7]

Neal Schon: "The lyrical content came from a poem that Ross Valory's ex-wife wrote and handed me on a napkin. We were traveling as a band, like nine guys in a station wagon in those days, and at one point, everybody had to take a restaurant break. I pulled out the acoustic guitar, sat on the hood of the car, and I banged out that song."[8]

Robert Fleischman: "They were very nice to me except when we were on the road. Management—that was another story. [Herbie] thought I was cocky. But name me one lead singer who's not a little cocky. Later on, we opened up shows for Emerson, Lake & Palmer."[9]

Gregg Rolie: "We were opening for ELP and [Robert] kind of made an ultimatum in Fresno. That he wanted us to play the new songs, but we were just trying to get the band across. He said he wouldn't go on and that was a mistake on his part. Herbie made the decision right there to fire him. Nothing was really written in stone until that happened."[10]

Herbie Herbert: "[Fleischman] was just a poodle in heat to deal with as a manager. He was like, 'Oh everybody, would you clear the dressing room? That person is smoking over there.' That kind of, you know, oh man, please. If this is before he's got his first paycheck what's gonna happen?"[11]

Robert Fleischman: "Like any relationship you want out of, it's always a personality difference that's the excuse."[12]

Eric Martin: "Steve Perry lived in this funky little town off of Highway 5, or 101 going from San Francisco to LA. It was one little strip, a real nothing of a farm town."

Steve Perry: "Three years old, I started singing around the house. My mother said I used to hit a high C that would go through her head."[13]

Tim Pierce: "Steve Perry's voice is God-given. But basically, he's channeling Otis Redding. He would admit that, and he was in the right place at the right time with that gift and that voice."

Steve Perry: "I was in a band called Alien Project. We were about to get signed to Columbia Records. The weekend before the bass player got killed in a car wreck on the 101. About a week later, I got a call from a gentleman who was running Columbia Records named Don Ellis. He said, 'Forgive me for being so quick about this, but we have a band named Journey on the label. Are you interested in meeting them?'"[14]

Herbie Herbert: "Somewhere along the line I got a Steve Perry tape. I listened to him for about sixty seconds on the tape and tried to chase him down."[15]

Ross Valory: "I was in the position to actually hear the demo album that he'd done with the band he had been working with prior to Journey, the Alien Project. I was simply amazed by it. What a voice."[16]

Herbie Herbert: "He'd already left the music business. I talked to his mom, and he was working on a turkey farm in Visalia, pounding nails with his stepfather Marv on the weekends... When I tried to talk him into coming up and spending a week with me at my house he couldn't afford to. I told him I'd pay him the money he was gonna lose, pay his expenses, he can sleep on my couch."[17]

Steve Perry: "There was a club called the Star Wood at the corner of Santa Monica and Fairfax [in LA]. I remember going there and watching Journey perform... Neal Schon with his white Stratocaster and his Twin Reverb Fender kicked back at an angle... he killed me. I wasn't that excited about the rest of the players to be perfectly honest with you."[18]

Herbie Herbert: "It was not an easy negotiation by any stretch. He was afraid of Aynsley Dunbar not having a groove, being too white of a British drummer with very minimal exposure to soul or R&B."[19]

Steve Perry: "[Herbie] said in essence, if not the actual words, 'This is your new singer, deal with it.' I don't think I would've been in the band if Herbie had not just said, 'Look, guys, get used to it, keep going, and shut the fuck up and write the music.' Had it not been for Herbie my life would be profoundly different right now. He gave me my chance."[20]

***

Gregg Rolie: "Neal and I were looking for someone with more of an edge, but Herbie brought us Steve Perry. We thought that he was a bit of a crooner."[21]

Neal Schon: "Herbie goes, 'This is your new singer.' And we're all looking at each other going, 'Really? Okay.' Because it was a radical change. It was like A to Z. There was no proving to us that he could sing."[22]

Steve Perry: "Herbie wanted me to fly out and meet Neal. I think it was in Denver, Colorado. They were opening for Emerson, Lake &

Palmer... Neal and I wrote our first song together that night in the hotel room, after the show—'Patiently.'"[23]

Neal Schon: "I have great memories of when Steve and I first met."[24]

Herbie Herbert: "When I put Steve Perry in the band, Neal Schon was not even on speaking terms with me, because that guy hated [Perry] so much. He flat out didn't want him. I just knew I was right."[25]

Steve Perry: "[Neal and I] lived together when I first joined the band. He gave me the back bedroom at his place. But we were also working together. And a lot of time spent together can chew on a friendship."[26]

Neal Schon: "We were like brothers. We spent a lot of nights out way too late doing things we shouldn't be doing."[27]

Steve Perry: "Of course there were differences between us all. It's called *a band*!"[28]

Neal Schon: "The second song I ever wrote with Steve Perry was 'Lights.' It had a different feel when Steve first showed it to me. It was more old-school blues, but when I put that rolling rhythm around it took on a whole different perspective. It's become a freakin' anthem."[29]

Steve Perry: "All of a sudden, as one of my girlfriends said, that guitar and my voice went together like salt and pepper."[30]

Gregg Rolie: "We started writing songs for singing first... It was all about the vocals."[31]

Steve Perry: "They put me in a little apartment on Bay Street [in San Francisco]. I went to [their practice space] every day and wrote songs with the band. Then Roy Thomas Baker comes in. We had enormous respect for him, because he'd produced Queen and Free. He was so much fun. The studio [His Master's Wheels] had an old Neve console and a large tracking room, and the next thing you know, he's really giving us a different sound."[32]

Herbie Herbert: "They're releasing [the *Infinity* album] in February '78 when the Number One record was *Saturday Night Fever*, the Number One record is *Grease*, and everything else is Donna Summer and 'Disco Inferno.' There's just no prayer, no chance, no way, Jose. I put together this package that was so cheap with Journey, Montrose, and Van Halen—five grand for all three bands. And I made it work."[33]

Steve Perry: "It was eight weeks of 3,000-seater proscenium-stage gigs. Van Halen opening, Ronnie Montrose second, and then Journey. This went from the beginning of March to the end of April. [Van Halen] was so on fire and Eddie Van Halen was the driving, demonstrative force of that group... Every fucking night I'd stand on the side of the stage and watch their set. I would bring Neal with me and say, 'Check this out.' Neal was blown away by Eddie."[34]

Steve Smith: "I did the tour playing with Ronnie Montrose and his band. It was Journey's first headline tour of the US. They really knocked me out. They were great live, fantastic. Everyone in the group was a powerful musician. From my jazz orientation, the way I saw them was, for a rock band, these guys were really good players. Including Steve Perry. He was an incredible singer and instrumentalist, his voice being the instrument."

Steve Perry: "That album is still selling. That's unheard of from a group without a hit single. You want to know how we sold those copies? The road. We toured nonstop for seven months... and people who saw us bought that album."[35]

Herbie Herbert: "How in the fuck did we sell three million records under the radar on an album that never made it into the Top 50 on the *Billboard* album chart? With single tracks that had never been on the Top 50, or any chart? We hooked up with companies that were the pioneers of 'foreground' music. These guys had every retail outlet, every shopping mall, every restaurant. We got airplay as foreground music, which makes gross impressions just like radio."[36]

Steve Perry: "Neal and I went to a pizza place, and I went over to the jukebox and saw 'Wheel in the Sky' in the machine—an ecstatic feeling. I didn't tell Neal. I just put two quarters in, pushed the button, and sat down, and the song started. Neal looked at me and started laughing. It was a monumental moment."[37]

CHAPTER SIXTEEN

BOSTON AND FOREIGNER FOLLOW UP.

"We had a lot of really good songs on our album. They had one good song on theirs."

Mick Jones: "I didn't have much of a break between the two albums. There were a few songs that didn't end up on our first record that were on *Double Vision*. I wanted to keep the momentum going. It was a lot of work within a short period of time, and it led to me feeling a little burnt out. But it was a case of striking while the iron was hot."

Barry Goudreau: "As the band members, we had hopes going into the second record...that the rest of us would get a little more leeway and we'd have more input into it. But it didn't really turn out that way. Tom continued working the way he had, and in fact he was taking less ideas from the rest of us than he did before."[1]

Tom Scholz: "When I'm recording, I pretty much work alone. I'm not that well versed in psychological matters. [But] I've always approached everything I do with the thought that if I'm gonna do it, I'm gonna do it the best I can. Other than the people in my life, the art is absolutely the most important thing."[2]

Mick Jones: "A young Mutt Lange lobbied to produce our second record. He was only just starting to make a name for himself having worked with Graham Parker and Boomtown Rats. Once we met, it seemed to me as though he was going through something in his life and wasn't in the best shape. So we went instead with Keith Olsen, who had produced Fleetwood Mac's first album with Stevie Nicks and Lindsey Buckingham."

Lou Gramm: "Keith [Olsen] had just come off *Rumours* by Fleetwood Mac, which was a monumental album. He was on his game with us."[3]

Mick Jones: "It was an interesting record to make. We started off in the Atlantic Studios once again. I figured we needed a very strong opener for the album, and 'Hot Blooded' was written in the studio. We were just jamming around. Dennis and I were kind of messing about on a certain rhythm, and it got more and more intense. All of a sudden, I could smell burning. I looked around and my amp was on fire. Right then, I thought we've got to get 'hot' in the title of the song."

Lou Gramm: "I think 'Hot Blooded' is fairly self-explanatory. It's a hunting song. The lyrics are about as suggestive as they can be without crossing the line."[4]

Mick Jones: "Five of my seven kids have a Foreigner tattoo somewhere on their bodies. One of them has the first album cover done. Another has 'Hot Blooded.' I got a call one night from Ted Nugent. He said to me, 'Mick, there's cats around that would chew your old boots off to play a solo like that.' Ted was crazy, but a great guitar player and that was cool."

Lou Gramm: "We were singing the verses of the [title song] and recording, but I didn't have a title yet. I couldn't think of anything that made sense. In my vocal booth, I had a little five-inch TV up there. Without the sound on, I was still watching the Rangers against Montreal in the Stanley Cup playoffs. We took a break, and I turned the volume up just as one of the Montreal Canadiens skated in front of John Davidson, the Rangers' goalie, and high-sticked him, knocked him out cold. The coaches and trainers went over and helped him, held on to him and skated him off back into the dressing room. Every now and then, they gave updates on John Davidson. They said, 'He's starting to feel a little better, but he's experiencing double vision.' I heard that and I thought for about two seconds, and I go, 'That's it!'"[5]

Tom Scholz: "Fun is when you're writing a song and you're trying a rough shot at a demo and... it works. That's when it's fun. After that, it's work."[6]

Barry Goudreau: "My involvement was about the same. I played guitar on 'Don't Look Back' and the song that Brad wrote ['Used to Bad News']."[7]

Brad Delp: "Tom, to this day, will tell you that he would never do it again. He thinks that the second record suffered because there was record company pressure."[8]

Tom Scholz: "That was the last time I let anything like that affect anything that I did. The individual acting as my manager was out of my life from that point on."[9]

Mick Jones: "I agonized over every note and detail. I was very hard to please. Those were magical times when the album was perceived as a true work of art."

Lou Gramm: "I wasn't green behind the ears anymore, but I was soaking up everything that was going on. I would sit there for all of the late-night sessions. When we packed up and called it a night at a quarter to five in the morning, and I would hear the conversations between Keith and his engineer and between Mick and Ian and Keith... I would be there and putting my two cents in. Pretty soon they would start asking me for my two cents."[10]

Steve Lukather: "Paich wrote the string charts for Foreigner's second record."

David Paich: "I requisitioned my father, because we only had about two weeks to do it. They were getting ready to leave for Japan. I think David Foster had been doing some of their arrangements, too. I worked with Keith Olsen. Keith was hot on me. He said to Mick Jones, 'You've got to use this guy here.' When they played the stuff back to me, it was mixed like a record already. The songs were very good. It was a good experience. I liked working with them."

Keith Olsen: "Everybody was saying that Foreigner sounded just like Boston. And everybody was worried that *Don't Look Back* would be released and wipe out Foreigner... Our album came out. Their album came out. Theirs sold 500,000 and started slowing down. Ours sold seven or eight million. Gee. We had a lot of really good songs on our album. They had one good song on theirs."[11]

Mick Jones: "It ended up selling even more than the first record. The last I heard it was up to ten million copies."

Al Cafaro: "You could tell that there was a style of music going on. You would hear that kind of a band and go, 'Yep, put it on the conveyor belt.' I don't want to take anything away from their individuality and uniqueness, because that would be unfair. In and of their own right, they were all exquisitely, finely crafted pieces of music. They were powerful. They sounded great loud, and when you were driving in your car. Women loved those bands."

***

Mick Jones: "We went straight from the studio into the tour. I'd been impressed by the use of shadow and light and shade from that Orson Welles movie, *Touch of Evil*. I had this idea of having our own thing going on like that, so I had these huge louvre windows put on either side of the stage with lights working behind them. They could be open or shut to create different sheets of light. The whole thing ratcheted up our costs to hundreds of thousands of dollars."

Tom Scholz: "When I got off the road after the tour, I wasn't sure that I ever wanted to go on tour again. I was going to hang it up and just record. I was more than drained. I was demoralized. I wasn't sure I wanted to be in the music business. I didn't like what I had seen. Brad and I had made a lot of money for a lot of people, and I didn't like what they were doing. I began to feel guilty about enabling people to do things I didn't approve of."[12]

Mick Jones: "We did a show with the Rolling Stones at JFK Stadium in Philadelphia. There were 90,000 there. Peter Tosh opened the show. We went on right before the Stones and to a roaring success. For me at least, it was like reaching the summit of a long climb. I suppose we began to feel indestructible. It was great, though, because there was also a feeling of power."

CHAPTER SEVENTEEN

STYX SURGE; REO STALL; THE BABYS BUST UP.

"He came up with a broken bottle, out of nowhere."

Dennis DeYoung: "I said to the guys, 'How has this accumulation of money to all of us changed us over the course of the last twelve months?' And that's what *Pieces of Eight* was about. It's the antidote to *The Grand Illusion*. We analyzed what had happened and how did we feel about it."

Tommy Shaw: "I think it was the best album of that lineup, because we were still working together so much and the sounds that everyone came up with really contributed, and it never got that far left into the ballad-ish things."[1]

Dennis DeYoung: "It's *The Grand Illusion Part Two*, I always thought. So it's a concept album, but I don't even know what the hell that means. *The Dark Side of the Moon* is a concept album, but I have no idea what it's about. The songs all kind of flow together and it's very nice. I think in some way that picking the topics that I did was a way of saying, 'Can we all get together on the same page?' Try to get a cohesiveness to what we're doing as a band. And it worked."

Kevin Cronin: "We were at a party in Champaign. There were all kinds of nefarious activities going on. And when I woke up the next day, somehow that phrase—*You Can Tune a Piano, But You Can't Tuna Fish*—was in my mind. Everybody thought I was crazy."[2]

Bruce Hall: "We knew that we needed to make it where we were a bit more radio friendly. Because the band was…kind of like a jam band. More like the Allman Brothers or something like that. Not the kind of stuff that is going to get you on the radio."[3]

Kevin Cronin: "That album didn't do as well as we'd hoped. We had some songs we really felt were strong—'Roll with the Changes' and 'Time for Me to Fly.' But there was a schism at Epic Records. They dropped the ball, and the album just got kind of left in the lurch."[4]

James "JY" Young: "*Pieces of Eight* has the two best rock songs that Styx ever did in 'Renegade' and 'Blue Collar Man.'"[5]

Tommy Shaw: "I wrote 'Renegade' on piano. I was sitting in my room in Niles, Michigan, and I had an upright piano in there. I just started playing these triad chords. With my piano skills that was just about as far as I could get. Then I started playing it on guitar. I wrote all the words down when I was playing it on piano there. It became a rock song when I took it to the band."[6]

Dennis DeYoung: "When it came time to pick the single, everybody pretty much went, 'Yep, that's the one.' Nobody ever said, 'It's got to be Dennis's *Pieces of Eight* song.' It was obvious it was 'Renegade.' So, Tommy, run fast with that and I'll be right behind you with all the guys loving it and all the girls screaming. What's wrong with this?"

Tommy Shaw: "['Blue Collar Man'], it was the end of a tour and a bunch of us went deep-sea fishing in Maui. Before we got to our boat, somebody gave us a little Maui Wowie, so by the time we got to the dock, we were all high as kites. We got on the boat, and for forty-five minutes we sat there not saying anything. I kept listening to the waves breaking. It was this lurching sound that became a soundscape that stuck in my head. I thought it might make a good intro for a song."[7]

Dennis DeYoung: "You like 'Blue Collar Man'? How does it start? *'Da-da-da, DA DA!'* Tommy didn't write that. I wrote that."

James "JY" Young: "Tommy...had a friend that was laid off and had to go stand in the unemployment line and felt the shame of having lost his job. Tommy really tied into that with the lyrics."[8]

Tommy Shaw: "I grew up in a blue-collar family. That's what inspired the song lyrically...It still speaks to people. I get letters from fans who tell me, 'I went through this when I got laid off.'"[9]

James "JY" Young: "It's said that great works of art come from creative tension, conflict, or troubled times. The fact that Dennis, Tommy, and I were headed in different directions worked well, leading to songs of an incredibly high standard. There was a magic about that collective of people at that point in our lives."[10]

Dennis DeYoung: "We never got into a fistfight. We didn't argue, I'm telling you. No punch-ups. No screaming matches."

John Waite: "We were making our third Babys album [*Head First*, 1978]. We'd gone down to San Diego to play a show. And it sold out. We got, like, two songs before the end and Mike [Corby, guitar/keyboards] smashes his guitar and starts screaming, 'Fuck off! Fuck you!' at the audience. And he walked offstage. We had no idea what happened... Then we got on the bus to come home, and Mike was getting really drunk. He came and sat up in the front seat and started to tell me what he felt about me. That I'm fucking useless. And I lost it. We get into a complete fistfight on this bus. We got dragged apart. We get off the bus, and it started up again. We were rolling around, really hardcore, and he came up with a broken bottle, out of nowhere. It was Michelob. I hate Michelob beer. A broken bottle! Wow! Where did that come from? Tony jumped on him. Ron Stone jumped on him."[11]

Tony Brock: "If Michael hadn't left, we wouldn't have had a record deal anymore."[12]

John Waite: "The record company got wind of what had happened, and the situation was out of my hands. That's the truth. I'd swear to it on a whole stack of Bibles."[13]

Ron Nevison: "John Waite...I had a difficult time with. I wanted to strangle him. I just didn't want to go to jail."[14]

John Waite: "Jon Cain came to the auditions and could play keyboards and some guitar, so he was just the all-rounder we were looking for."[15]

Jonathan Cain: "Before I joined the Babys I worked for Manpower stacking beer cases and sweeping stores in a stereo shop. Coming home so tired that I wouldn't even have the strength to touch the piano. It was either push a broom or sing Top 40 songs. I'll push a broom any day."[16]

John Waite: "Jonathan Cain and Ricky Phillips came in and brought a brand-new energy to the Babys. And we really needed it. Because up to that point, it was kind of lonesome. I suddenly found I could become fearless, and we became a seriously good live band."[17]

Ricky Phillips: "We were very serious about the music. The first thing John Waite ever said to me was: 'If you have an idea for a song I don't care what time of day or night it is, call me. I'll put on the coffee pot.'"[18]

John Waite: "I watched a video of the Babys performing 'Money' on the *Chuck Barris Show*, and it's just off the hook! You can tell by the way I was dressed and the way I kind of acted that it was my moment in that time."[19]

Ricky Phillips: "It was wine, women, and song, or sex, drugs, and rock 'n' roll. Whatever you want to call it."[20]

Tommy Shaw: "I was young, somewhat single, ready to take it all in, and I did."[21]

Dennis DeYoung: "Right around '77, I started getting a grip and getting some therapy about who I am. I'm okay, I'm not perfect, but I'll be this guy, and you can think what you want. I've been the sober man in a room full of drunks. I didn't have to be some hedonistic fucking moron. And I bragged about being married from the very beginning. What did I care? My wife, who I've known forever, has protected me and loved me. Have I mentioned that she is also a sharpshooter? I wasn't aware of that when I married her."

CHAPTER EIGHTEEN

AFFAIRS OF THE HEART.

"I'm with this incredible, beautiful, talented woman and I'm out being unfaithful to her."

Steve Fossen: "During the course of recording the *Dog and Butterfly* album, we discovered we had a bunch of aggressive songs and a bunch of mellower songs. We decided to put the aggressive songs on one side of the LP and the mellow songs on the other. Mike Flicker was still our producer, and he had a great set of ears, so he could make the best out of everything."

Ann Wilson: "I think Nancy's at her best when she's playing acoustic guitar. That's always my vote. I don't think you could call her a virtuoso in the Segovia sense, but she's an original. She can make a guitar move and come up with parts that are so cool, and so her. That's when she's at her most real. She's not thinking about herself."

Nancy Wilson: "The greatest God-given gift from above is my love affair with the guitar. It's my language. It speaks to me, and I speak with it."

***

Roger Fisher: "A song like 'Mistral Wind,' it's just so powerful and otherworldly."

Nancy Wilson: "It's a really perfect example of everything Heart's good at in seven minutes. It's acoustic. It's poetic. And then it's huge rock. It's a journey through the lyrics. It takes you through Ulysses's journey, basically. I love that one. It's not three chords, let's put it that way."

Steve Fossen: "A lot of people consider that song to be Heart's masterpiece. It was kind of the culmination of all we'd done and the things we'd dreamt about. It was a very special song to us."

Roger Fisher: "Me and Ann were really buddies, and we had great times for a while there. Nobody else in the band more than she and I, I think, had the sense of profoundness of 'Mistral Wind.'"

Ann Wilson: "For some strange, unknown reason, it seems to be a prerequisite for singers, and to a lesser degree, a lot of people in groups and artists, they're the ones who see the world in a different way. They don't have the same aspirations as other people. They definitely don't want to marry young and retire. They want to live a life."

Roger Fisher: "Oh, it got to be tense making that album. Ann and Nance were raised by these two beautiful people, John and Lou Wilson. John was the officer in the Marines, but Lou was the real officer. The way she raised her girls, it was like, if you have a chance to take power, gain rank, you take it. They had that built into their constitution. As Ann realized that she had more and more power, she wanted it just to be her and Nance's band. That was what was going on."

Mike Fisher: "In our entourage of employees, some people felt like the combination of the brothers and sisters wasn't a good thing. We were too powerful, and they tried to undo that actively. There were these forces acting against us during the recording of *Dog and Butterfly*."

***

Roger Fisher: "And boy-oh-boy that was tough."

Steve Fossen: "With Roger and Mike being boyfriends of the stars, they were, can I say annoying? They got annoyingly full of themselves. They just rubbed people the wrong way by thinking they could tell everyone what to do and what to play. It was difficult."

Roger Fisher: "I kind of helped them with their decision-making by doing really stupid stuff. I'm with this incredible, beautiful, talented woman and I'm out there being unfaithful to her. It was a little bit excusable in the sense we were all doing stuff like that at that time, but it was convenient to help get me out of the band."

Steve Fossen: "Roger was not faithful to Nancy. When you're not faithful to somebody, it's easy for the other person that's being hurt to say, 'That's it, you've stepped over the line.'"

Roger Fisher: "I was actually set up one night. I was set up to have sex with these two women. The next day, Ann and Nance found out all about it because it was a setup. That was the big excuse for them to say, 'Okay, you're out.'"

Steve Fossen: "When Roger and Nancy broke up, Rog really had a tough time dealing with it."

Mike Fisher: "Roger actually continued in the band without being with Nancy. They were in the band together for, like, a year. It was a really awful period. For me, it was really heartbreaking to see my beautiful dream coming apart."

Roger Fisher: "It was excruciating. I was just absolutely heartbroken and then Nancy started going out with Mike Derosier. I had to be around that, and it was so painful. It was just torment."

Mike Fisher: "I just didn't feel like I was getting the support from Ann that I should have gotten. I felt kind of betrayed by her. That's kind of how we became unwound together. She didn't really see it happening. I was enduring this heartbreak for a long time."

Steve Fossen: "Then we came to find out that Mike was straying on Ann at the same time. When he told her she just said, 'Okay, that's it, we're done.'"

Mike Fisher: "Ann and I had bought a couple of places together. One was on the Oregon coast, down at Cannon Beach. The other was a chalet at a skiing resort up in the mountains. The last time I was with Ann was at the Cannon Beach house."

Steve Fossen: "Playing the live shows, Roger was kind of on his own island. Then, when we started up the initial sessions for the next record, he was not focused. We would be rehearsing a song one day, come back the next to record it, and he'd have either forgotten his part or made up a new one that didn't gel with what we'd already come up with. It was hard to make any kind of progress with having to start over every day."

Roger Fisher: "I'd never have not wanted to have learned those painful lessons. There are things I wish I had done differently, but no regrets."

Steve Fossen: "We had a meeting. We had this corporate agreement, and we could vote people out. That's what we did. Ken Kinnear, our manager at the time, he dealt with it for us. He told Rog and Mike what happened and why."

Roger Fisher: "Mike and I were in eastern Washington watching a band that we loved play. We had a great time partying with those guys. The next morning we were at a restaurant and somehow, we got a call on the pay phone in the front of house. I don't know how that happened. Our manager told me, 'Well, Rog, the band got together last night, and they voted you guys out.'"

***

Steve Fossen: "I don't know how they took it."

Roger Fisher: "I said to Ken Kinnear, 'Oh my God, thank you so much.' It was a huge relief. It really was."

Mike Fisher: "The fact was that there were all these people behind the scenes that were pushing this, and Ann and Nancy couldn't see that they were being manipulated. I didn't want to be part of that at all, so it was a relief to me, too."

Steve Fossen: "Next thing we knew, Mike and Roger weren't around. When that happens, you figure you've got to move on. We weren't going to stop and feel sorry for ourselves."

Mike Fisher: "The dream of what our band could become never really got all the way there. It could have done. It came close but didn't quite make it."

Steve Fossen: "At the beginning, it was musicians playing and pulling together. It wasn't men versus women. Heart had that chemistry. I don't think they've ever had that chemistry again in their band."

Ann Wilson: "We didn't have the stamina that, say, Fleetwood Mac had. At that point, we just needed a breather. Everything had got so big and huge. Money, fame, interviews. And all of a sudden, the emotional toll just kind of ate us."

CHAPTER NINETEEN

TOTO BIRTH "HOLD THE LINE"; CHEAP TRICK TAKE JAPAN.

"We kept telling everybody, 'Double platinum, baby.'"

Steve Lukather: "We were listening to everything that came out in real time. Everything that was on the radio. And that was rock with melody. We were following in the footsteps of Boston and Foreigner. Those bands were having the hits. Our take on that would be to add a little more of an R&B and jazz influence. That's what we snuck into our pop music."

David Paich: "We were very aware of the recording process, but also of how things sounded on the radio. That's another reason we did the band, we loved hearing ourselves on the radio. We'd all been on radio before the Toto band, but we wanted to hear *our own* music. That was a big deal. DJs could play your record and get you noticed just in LA."

Steve Lukather: "To make the *Toto* album, we based ourselves out at Studio 55 in Hollywood. That was the producer Richard Perry's place. Perry was another legendary cat from that time. He'd made records with

Barbra Streisand, Fats Domino, Carly Simon. It was a beautiful big room with polished wood floors and a great custom-made console. I got to learn on the job. I was enthralled with every part of the process. Man, we loved big productions. Starting with *Sgt. Pepper's*... and all the way up to *The Dark Side of the Moon*.

"On breaks, we'd all go to this joint called Mikado, which at the time was one of the only Japanese restaurants in LA. It was also one of the few places where I could drink underage, because the staff never ID carded me. There was one night Jeff ordered a frozen Mai Tai, which was always the signal he was going to tie one on. In short order, he'd sunk ten of them. He was about to pour the last of the bottles over his head when, I shit you not, who walks into the place but Marlon Brando. This was Brando in his big, beefy phase. He stopped in his tracks. He looked at all of us intently, but especially at Jeff, who by this point had hot sake dripping down his face. Brando didn't say a word. Just shook his head and moved on. Man, we pissed ourselves laughing at that."

David Paich: "What you hear on that record is the culmination of years of study... playing with people like Steely Dan and all of the others. You learn how to be more proficient at the craft. People criticize us for being too proficient. I wouldn't criticize a doctor for being too proficient at doing open heart surgery."[1]

Steve Lukather: "At the same time as we were cutting our record, Paich was also off doing a disco record with Cheryl Lynn. Often as not he would be late along to our sessions. The rest of us would sit around and jam. That's what we did. We sat in a room and played together. That's what's so funny about all the shit we took for being slick, soulless studio musicians. Dude, we sat in a room and played a take until we all sounded good together. Usually, it was the first one, but no more than three takes, ever."

David Paich: "'Hold the Line' came very quickly. I was inspired by Sly and the Family Stone. They had that song 'Hot Fun in the

Summertime.' We used to play it with our high school band, and I liked that beat. I also liked the way Fats Domino played triplets on 'Blueberry Hill.'"

Steve Lukather: "Paich invited Jeff, Steve, and me up to his place in Westwood. He played this riff for us he'd got on his little spinet piano. He told us he'd copped the vibe from Sly Stone."

David Paich: "I'd just got my first apartment. When I got the opening riff, I must have played it for three days straight on my upright piano. I mean, people were banging on the doors. 'Stop playing that piano!' The rest of the song fell into place as soon as I got with the band. When we went down to the studio, I started playing the riff and Luke joined in, Hungate and Jeff, too. I gave Bobby a couple of lyrics and told him to take it from there. The next time we played it, Bobby was singing, and our band was playing. Everybody just looked at each other, dumbfounded."

Steve Lukather: "When it came time for me to cut my solo, there were a bunch of other cats in the control room that day. Buddies of Paich's and Jeff's. Jim Keltner among them. What's on the record is what I played right then. It's a one-take solo, apart from the multitracked harmony section at the end. Paich wanted to have that because he'd heard it on the first Boston album. By the end of the take, the guys were jumping up and down in the control room."

David Paich: "Bobby sang the shit out of that song, too, but it was in his own style."

Steve Lukather: "A problem with Bobby did become apparent. There were issues with getting him to sing the higher-key parts that Paich wanted. Bobby struggled with being able to sing those in tune."

David Paich: "When I did the backgrounds, I tried to stack them like Foreigner had done. That meant using the lead singer for all of the backgrounds. Then have the group go in and do two passes so it has the body of the band in there."

Steve Lukather: "Every one of Bobby's vocals on that record was painstakingly put together."

David Paich: "All of us were learning as we were working on the job. We thought we'd gotten lucky with Bobby, and that was the Toto sound for our first four albums."

Steve Lukather: "Not long after the album was released in October 1978, Tom Scott, the great LA Express sax player, sent us a Polaroid in the mail. It was a picture of a toilet, with a little 'Toto' logo written on it, and Tom's shit floating in the bowl. Tom had written across the photo: 'Nice name.'"

Rick Nielsen: "[Cheap Trick was] a live band. That's what we did. But we knew how to make records, too. Our band is rock 'n' roll. We were never just a studio band trying to make everything perfect. It was never supposed to be perfect. It was supposed to be cool."[2]

Robin Zander: "When we first got [to Japan], we were on the plane, we looked out the windows, and there were all these girls with signs, standing on top of the building, on the roof. There were at least a thousand of them up there. We were thinking to ourselves, 'Maybe the president's here, or something. What's going on?'"[3]

Tom Petersson: "That quirky, cartoon character thing [we had] going on. The Japanese got a kick out of it."[4]

Robin Zander: "We went to the radio stations. There'd be hordes of people, and they'd all be trying to tear you apart. Grabbing your clothes and ripping your sleeves off. I had an instance where a girl had a pair of scissors and went to cut my hair and stabbed me in the back of the neck. That was pretty scary."[5]

***

Rick Nielsen: "The record was being taped while we were performing. It wasn't really planned to be an album. We just recorded the shows we played in Osaka, Nagoya, Tokyo. And a number of months later, we were asked to mix it."[6]

Les Garland: "We used to have a term we used in radio. You'd get a song from a record company that was so great, maybe you'd never heard of the act, maybe it was a big act, but it was what we called an 'out of the box add.' That literally meant, when we took it out of the box, we played it."

Rick Nielsen: "Any city that had an FM station played 'Surrender'[7] ... We recorded and released 250 songs. And I think most people know about ten. 'Surrender' has got a kind of universal statement to it. I've never met anyone in the world who didn't think their parents were weird. And if you don't think your parents are weird, your friends do."[8]

Les Garland: "A friend called me from LA, played 'Hold the Line' to me over the phone. We put it on the radio that day. Those kinds of songs were just magical for the time and for radio. They towered above everything else that was going on out there."

David Paich: "What's made 'Hold the Line' endure? I read an Elton John book one time. He was talking about what made a great record, and he said, 'Give me good production. You can dance to it. And it has inspired performances.' That's about it. Great musicianship. Poignant lyrics, may I be so bold. A memorable chorus. And good production."

Steve Lukather: "I was sat at home one day and Paich called me up, very excited. He told me to turn on the radio. The local FM station, KMET, was playing 'Hold the Line.' I turned the radio on just as the DJ was saying, 'Los Angeles's own Toto there with a brand-new record.' I went running around the house with my first wife. It was the greatest rush in the world, man. That's an amazing feeling. And once you've had it, your life is never the same again. Now, did I think that it would last for fifty years? Fuck no."

David Paich: "We kept telling everybody, 'Double platinum, baby. Our first record's going double platinum.' All the management and record company people were kind of blinking and going, '*Of course*,' not really believing us. Then it went double platinum."

Rick Nielsen: "[*Cheap Trick at Budokan*] eventually became the largest-selling live album on import ever. People were paying four times the price. Something like $40 a copy. They couldn't import them fast enough."[9]

Steve Lukather: "Straightaway, we got our asses handed back to us by the rock critics. One guy wrote how he wished all of our parents had been sterilized, so we'd never have been born to make music."

Rick Nielsen: "Then after the [Japanese] tour was over, we'd fly back to Iowa and there's nobody there."[10]

Tim Pierce: "From our point of view as aspiring young musicians, Toto was among the biggest bands in the world from their first record. In LA, they were the pinnacle. These guys who could play on any record, and then do their own thing? They were *the* rock stars. What the critics said never mattered to any of us. We were working professionals doing a job. People on the outside could say whatever they wanted."

Eddie Money: "If I'd get a so-so review or a bad review, I'd be the stupidest guy in the world and call the [critic up] and go, 'I know where you live. I'm gonna blow your car up.' I was out of my mind. I was coming down off vodka, come on. I was probably running out of cigarettes. What are you gonna do?"[11]

David Paich: "We were floating on such a high carpet anyway. We thought we were bulletproof pretty much."

CHAPTER TWENTY

RAINBOW MAKES "SINCE YOU BEEN GONE."

---

*"Ritchie didn't like the way I appeared...
He locked my shirts in a trunk."*

Bob Daisley: "Ritchie [Blackmore] thought our version of the band wasn't successful because it wasn't flying up the charts. He was desperate to have a hit single and an album on a more commercial scale."

Roger Glover: "I'm a huge Ritchie fan. So when he asked me to produce Rainbow I thought, 'Why not? Why should I bear a grudge after Deep Purple?' It was a good opportunity for me. We started rehearsing in Connecticut. I soon became aware of the frosty relationship between Ritchie and Ronnie Dio. There was a huge gulf between the two of them over what they wanted. There was no material. Ritchie would start to play something, the band would jam along, and Ronnie would sit in a corner with a notebook, scribbling away. He hardly ever opened his voice. After ten days of this, things exploded, and Ronnie quit. By then, there was no one left in the band but Ritchie and Cozy Powell on drums."

Ritchie Blackmore: "We recorded [the *Down to Earth* album] in a castle because I like mucking around in castles. I don't know why, maybe it's reincarnation."[1]

Roger Glover: "Of course Ritchie wanted to go and record in a castle. We took over an eleventh-century château in France."

Ritchie Blackmore: "It was a place called Chateau Pelly de Cornfeld, just outside Geneva. We hired the mobile of Moulin Rouge—Jethro Tull owned it. It's like a lorry, so we took it to the castle and just passed the leads through the window and played in the old dining room. It was haunted as usual. It has to be haunted, otherwise I don't go there."[2]

Roger Glover: "I sort of helped Ritchie to reform the band. We brought in Don Airey on keyboards."

Don Airey: "I braced myself for all the old bollocks. Which is to say, the moods, and people being late, playing badly on purpose, and being rude to everyone."

Roger Glover: "I started to play bass and also to write songs, and we began work on the album without a singer."

Graham Bonnet: "They would play games of 'Name That Tune' in their downtime. Cozy had with him a tape of songs from the '60s. He played the others the first record I ever made, with my cousin, 'Only One Woman.' It was Ritchie who said, 'Where's *that* guy now?' Roger happened to also be working with one of my friends, Mickey Moody, who at the time was with Whitesnake. Roger said he could get in touch with me and arrange to bring me over for an audition. I didn't even know who Rainbow were. Anyway, I went over to the château. It was in a tiny village in the middle of nowhere. Not my scene at all. I had to learn a Deep Purple song for the audition, 'Mistreated.' I sang it in front of the four of them, off the microphone because I thought I'd screw up. They were sort of amazed at how loud my voice was for one thing and they offered me the job."

* * *

Ritchie Blackmore: "An incredible singer. He's got a three-octave range."[3]

Graham Bonnet: "I didn't think I fit with the band. I didn't look like them and I wasn't into their music. It was totally alien to me as a pop/R&B singer."

Roger Glover: "One day in the office, the manager Bruce Payne played me a recording of this Russ Ballard song, 'Since You Been Gone.' Bruce asked me if I thought it could be a hit and I said, 'Possibly. Why?'"

Russ Ballard: "I wrote most of my songs on a little upright piano that my mum bought me for my twenty-first birthday. 'Since You Been Gone' came very quickly, and it sounded to me like a hit when I did it. An all-girl band from South Africa, Clout, had covered it first. Then an American band, Head East, had a go. They did quite a light version. They'd also opened for Rainbow on tour."

Roger Glover: "When Bruce told me that Ritchie wanted to do it, I just said, 'Never.' Ritchie had done 'Stargazer.' This was a pop song."

Ritchie Blackmore: "The management said to me, 'What do you think of that?' And I said, 'It's a great idea. Let's do it.' Cozy went, 'No! I fucking hate this song! It's bullshit! I don't want anything to do with it.'"[4]

Roger Glover: "I told Cozy he'd no choice but to play on it. So with me playing a guide rhythm guitar, we managed to record just the drum track in one take. Cozy expressed his feelings about it by playing something overly simple. Strangely enough, that worked in the song's favor."

Graham Bonnet: "The château was dreadful for vocals. Too reverb-y. So Roger and I went over to Long Island to do my vocal tracks. Roger brought the finished album over to my house in Maida Vale and played it for me and my girlfriend. I was surprised at how good a job I'd done. And all of a sudden, the band became radio friendly. That's why we'd recorded 'Since You Been Gone' in the first place. Everybody knows that damn song now."

Russ Ballard: "I was in my back garden when I first heard Rainbow's version of my song. It was early summer, and someone had a radio on in another garden. Graham Bonnet's voice is very strong. There's something quite special about having a song you wrote be out there in the ether. They do take on a certain life of their own."

Ritchie Blackmore: "When it was, like, Number Two or Three on the charts, I heard from someone who went up to Cozy and said, 'Oh, I love "Since You Been Gone."' And Cozy said, 'Yeah, it's one of my favorite tracks.'"[5]

Graham Bonnet: "The tour we did was quite a long one. We went from coast to coast in America, and I probably enjoyed it too much. It was the usual stuff that you hear from every band. Loads of booze in the dressing room along with a lot of girls. Sometime in the morning each day it would be like, 'What happened last night?'"

Ritchie Blackmore: "Fucking hell, Graham...[He] was a nice enough guy, just completely...lost. One day I said to him, 'How are you feeling?' 'Oh, not too good. I feel kind of fuzzy.' Someone said, 'Have you eaten?' 'That's it—I'm fucking hungry!' He had literally forgotten to eat for ages! And all these singers used to say I was a mental case."[6]

Bob Daisley: "Ritchie could be contrary. You were flavor of the month one minute, and the next you were out. He didn't suffer fools gladly, or easily."

Graham Bonnet: "Ritchie didn't like the way I appeared. I just wasn't into the uniform—spandex pants and Cuban heel boots. I wore jackets and shirts. Things of mine would disappear. Ritchie would throw my sunglasses away. He locked my shirts in a trunk. That was something that did get a bit nasty."

***

Ritchie Blackmore: "We were a long-haired band, but Graham looked like a Las Vegas casino man. He had such a great voice, we thought, 'Oh, it doesn't matter. We'll rough him up a bit around the edges.' But he never took to that."[7]

Graham Bonnet: "My hair was also too short for Ritchie, and he wanted me to grow it. I rebelled when we were in Edinburgh."

Ritchie Blackmore: "We had a roadie guarding his dressing room to stop him getting out, because he was threatening to have his hair cut. It was very petty, but it had become an obsession with me. He got out a back window."[8]

Graham Bonnet: "I didn't see Ritchie or anyone else until I went onstage that night. Ritchie came on, clocked my haircut, and gasped. He walked straight back off and ended up playing the rest of the gig from behind his amps."

Ritchie Blackmore: "He was doing it just to annoy me. It's the principle. I took it as an insult. I don't think I spoke to him again after that."[9]

CHAPTER TWENTY-ONE

PORTRAIT OF A YOUNG WOMAN IN A MEN'S URINAL AND THE DAMAGE DONE.

"The great Bible Belt of America would turn against you."

John Kalodner: "Mick Jones and Lou Gramm knew from the first two gigantic albums that they needed more radio hits. At rock radio *and* pop radio."

Mick Jones: "Relations with Ed Gagliardi had become strained by the end of the *Double Vision* tour. With the direction the band was going, Ed just didn't quite fit. We were a mainstream rock band, and Ed was slanting more into a progressive rock sound in his playing. The other band members and I made the decision to let Ed go. That was a really tough thing to have to do, but I brought in Rick Wills to fill Ed's shoes. Rick was another Englishman, and he had great pedigree having played with Peter Frampton, David Gilmour, and Roxy Music."

***

Lou Gramm: "One of the negatives of back-to-back tours [was] it put us behind coming up with new songs for a third album."[1]

Mick Jones: "The *Head Games* album proved to be a not especially constructive period for the band. We moved our base of operations to LA, and once we were out on the West Coast, we started to live the life of rock stars. All of the acclaim we'd had went to our heads a little bit."

Lou Gramm: "Unfortunately, Mick and my bandmates didn't share my sense of urgency. I showed up promptly at 10 a.m. the first day of rehearsals. The rest of the group didn't show up until 3 p.m. because they had been partying the night before. This continued for several days."[2]

Mick Jones: "There was a lot of swanning around in Beverly Hills, partying, and general madness going on. Ian McDonald got mugged in his car at a traffic light. He was probably driving something ostentatious. That was a crazy period. The one bonus was that we did at last get to work with Roy Thomas Baker as our producer. Roy was a character, an eccentric. A very jovial fellow with a cynical sense of humor, but he knew his stuff. He was coming off having made a couple of great records with Journey and the Cars."

Elliot Easton: "Roy was this hilarious, *Monty Python* type of character. He was very much like, 'Hello, my loves.' He was known for his massive background vocals. At the time he worked with the Cars, he'd just had this huge hit with Queen and 'Bohemian Rhapsody.'"

Roy Thomas Baker: "The important things were always songs, performance, and musicianship. You can fart around in the studio, twiddle as many knobs as you want, but you've got to have those other things."[3]

Elliot Easton: "He used this unusual machine, a Stephens forty-track on two-inch tape. There were just a few of them in the world. Roy flew this thing around the world with him in three big camera trunks. When it broke, this one particular guy, John Stephens, would also have to fly out to wherever Roy was working to fix it."

Lou Gramm: "We thought we had the right producer in Roy Thomas Baker. But he seemed very distracted, like his mind was someplace else. We didn't feel he was completely with us in our work."[4]

Mick Jones: "We wanted to make a record with a slightly more abrasive sound to what we'd done to that point. I went over to England, just to change pace a little bit, and while I was over there, I wrote the music for 'Dirty White Boy.' Whenever I'd go back to England, it would readjust my listening. At that time, I would have had John Peel mostly on the radio. It was also the time of Johnny Cougar and 'My Sharona' by the Knack. That variety of songs and sound made an impression."

John Kalodner: "They had a star writer team in Lou Gramm and Mick Jones. They had a star singer. So I had to focus both of them on the songs. That was the trick, to get the focus on the songs. It was not difficult to get Mick Jones to listen to me. Or Lou for that matter."

Mick Jones: "The identity of the band usually comes from the singer. Well, it just does, it can't help but not. The singer is the focal point, and that voice has to get into people's psyche."

Lou Gramm: "*Head Games* was the first one that got away from us. The ideas were good, but we didn't follow up on them, and that was a symptom of our problem. It seemed like everybody had his guard up. Personally, I was disillusioned. I wanted to leave, get out of the band. There was this, like, complacency. It was really eating me up. It was ugly."[5]

Mick Jones: "Even with someone as accomplished as Roy, I found it hard to be produced by others. I was way too much of a perfectionist. I should have left things a little bit rawer in a few places. And I could certainly piss people off."

***

Lou Gramm: "We had to scramble to salvage the album and meet our deadline...I wasn't pleased with the result. It sounded unfinished."[6]

Mick Jones: "No, it wasn't a rushed album. But it's a record about which I've always had misgivings."

John Kalodner: "Then I had no fucking idea the *Head Games* album cover would get me into such trouble. That was really something."

Mick Jones: "Funnily enough, it was the idea of a woman in the Atlantic Records art department. Not that it absolves us of any responsibility. She was a friend of a friend, and out of curiosity, we gave her the record to see what she would come up with. That photograph of a young girl in a men's restroom was the result."

John Kalodner: "There was a great art director at Atlantic named Bob Defrin. He worked with Mick Jones and Bud Prager and me on this really interesting cover of this girl in a men's room where the urinals were. It wasn't really suggestive in terms of her being naked or whatever."

Mick Jones: "At the time I thought it was a humorous cover. A play on words, and it was a striking image."

John Kalodner: "I was completely unconscious to the fact it could offend people. When that was pointed out to me after the record had come out, I felt like, 'Oh yeah, that was probably a really stupid idea.'"

Lou Gramm: "In my local paper in Rochester, there was a huge picture on the front cover showing a big bonfire, and people throwing their Foreigner albums in it. They were saying our visual presentation of the cover was hideous, and suggestive, particularly to younger teens. A lot of big radio stations banned us. We had no airplay."[7]

Mick Jones: "Lou came to be of the opinion it was because of the cover artwork that our sales were harmed. Personally, I'm not sure that was the case, but it's true it caused us problems. The trouble was, if you stepped over a certain line, the great Bible Belt of America would turn against you."

Lou Gramm: "*Head Games* did less than half what *Double Vision* did. It didn't get good reviews. After a couple of singles, the record label called us in and told us, 'We're up against a brick wall. We can't spend good money to get no results.'"[8]

Mick Jones: By the time we finished touring *Head Games*, I felt exhausted and dissatisfied. There had been too much indulgence in every respect and not enough productivity. My reaction to that ultimately left us with four people in Foreigner."

CHAPTER TWENTY-TWO

MICHAEL BOLTON AND BLACKJACK: THE AOR SUPERGROUP THAT NEVER WAS...

"Everything ended up being a disaster."

Michael Bolton: "[Growing up] I had a big voice for a little guy. My hair was down to my waist. I had spectacles. Pretty wild. You didn't see many people like me about."[1]

Bruce Kulick: "Some of my first big live performances as a professional musician were with Andrea True. It was a big band with dancers and horns. Andrea was a porn star who wound up with a producer who could write hit songs. In 1976, she had a smash hit at radio with a disco song called 'More More More.' To this day, my wife remembers dancing and singing along to it in her bedroom. She'd no idea Andrea was a porn star, though."

Jimmy Haslip: "I toured with Tommy Bolin. I was just twenty-five when Tommy passed away at twenty-seven. I was a pallbearer at his funeral in Iowa."

Michael Bolton: "I was signed when I was sixteen to Epic Records. I knew nothing about the business, nothing about recording, except by that time I knew there were people in the industry who heard my voice and encouraged me to go for a career."[2]

Bruce Kulick: "My older brother Bob had great connections in New York. Bob had auditioned for Kiss in 1972, '73, when Ace Frehley got the gig. Through his networking, Bob heard there was this guy looking for two lead guitar players for a tour. Both of us went along and auditioned at a rehearsal studio in Manhattan. That's where we met Jim Steinman, and Bob and I wound up doing a year touring *Bat Out of Hell* with Meat Loaf. That was my first opportunity to go on the road with an actual rock band, but from the start, I knew it was going to be a weird experience. It was amazing at times, stressful at others. Once his dream came true, Meat Loaf got into drugs, cocaine, and he became erratic and difficult. His highs and lows were the hardest things to navigate. My brother and I didn't have problems meeting girls. Meat Loaf maybe did. Even though he was the star, he was three hundred pounds. At times he would be jealous of that and act out."

Jimmy Haslip: "When I got the call to work with those guys they didn't have a name for the band. It was a potential project, nothing more, and a lot to do with a lawyer named Steve Weiss. Steve called me and said he'd an interesting thing going on with a singer. They were on the verge of getting signed to a label, but they didn't have a band. He asked if I'd be interested in flying to New York to rehearse."

Bruce Kulick: "It was Michael Bolotin at the time, his actual name. Michael was working as a singer-songwriter out of New Haven. He'd worked up a batch of new songs. Johnny Winter actually played guitar on the two that got Polydor Records interested. But the label wanted

Michael in a band, not as a solo artist. So Blackjack was created. Steve Weiss was our attorney. Steve represented a little band called Led Zeppelin, and also Bad Company. I drove to New Haven to do a show with Michael. I thought potentially he was a rock star."

Jimmy Haslip: "I showed up at this rehearsal hall in New York. They also had a drummer come in, Sandy Gennaro, who'd been playing with the Pat Travers Band. Both Bruce and Bob Kulick were there as well. I thought Michael had a brilliant voice and everybody was a good musician, so there was no problem there. I remember Bob asking a lot of questions."

Bruce Kulick: "It was a weird dynamic. Another part of my strange growing up with my brother and his personality. It was clearly going to be Michael's band, but you know, we were all taken care of well enough that I didn't have an issue. Maybe Bob knew more about what could be on offer, but he started to make waves. Steve Weiss was like, 'This is a sweetheart deal. If you're going to sign it, sign it. If not, whatever.' All of a sudden, I was being asked, 'Would you be willing to do this without your brother?'"

Jimmy Haslip: "Bob seemed very knowledgeable about the business. Maybe they got nervous that he was going to screw up the deal. That's the impression I got. There's always something going on with a gig, especially when there's a lot of money involved and record company deals. Anyway, the management got rid of Bob. For my part, I was the new guy that just got off the airplane. It was a chance to do some touring and recording, and the music was cool."

Bruce Kulick: "I saw it as a great opportunity. Bob might have done some other important things already by then, but I was still struggling. So I did go ahead without him. We didn't necessarily need Bob, even though he'd co-written one or two of the songs. Of course, that caused some stress between my brother and me for a year or so."

***

Jimmy Haslip: "We got a deal with Polydor. They were ecstatic about the project. Michael and Bruce signed the contract. I don't recall Sandy or I being asked to sign anything. We just came along with the project. Polydor had really high aspirations. Right away, they arranged for us to record with Tom Dowd, the renowned producer, at Criteria Studios down in Miami."

Bruce Kulick: "It was incredible to be working with Tom Dowd. I was a big Eric Clapton fan, and Tom had done Clapton's *461 Ocean Boulevard* album at Criteria, and the Allman Brothers, too. Then again, all New Yorkers love to go to Florida. There I was at the Holiday Inn. 'Swimming pool! Wow!'"

Jimmy Haslip: "I was in Miami for nine, ten days in total. Basically, I felt more or less like a session player brought in to play what was on the table. Even still, there was a lot of give-and-take with Tom. It was great to be in a room with somebody like that, exchanging ideas."

Bruce Kulick: "I have to admit, I wasn't really one hundred percent down with how Tom Dowd wanted to present the band. But there was no way you could argue, because he's Tom Dowd. Plus, Polydor had practically bought Florida for him to make the record. They threw him a massive percentage. So we were up against that. Michael was more vocal about it than I was, but I knew that we didn't have much power. There were certain other things that freaked Michael out. I think Michael was nervous of Tom, but it wasn't my battle."

Jimmy Haslip: "We made a nice record. It seemed like success was in the air, but you can never tell what's going to happen. It's a roll of the dice always."

Bruce Kulick: "I'm not embarrassed about the *Blackjack* record, but I felt like we sounded more powerful in the rehearsal room. This was 1979, and Michael and I were very aware of other bands. Foreigner was one we both paid particular attention to. I mean, that was undeniable. The radio songs from that band and Lou Gramm's voice were just so great."

Jimmy Haslip: "There wasn't a lot of touring. Polydor got us an opening slot with Peter Frampton. We did a bunch of dates with him, and we got a good response from Frampton's audience."

Bruce Kulick: "The Frampton dates were a lot of fun."

Michael Bolton: "We used to throw stuff from the eighth floor of our hotel to see who could land it most directly in the middle of the pool. We had food fights in our rooms, sandwiches flying into the walls, that sort of thing."[3]

Jimmy Haslip: "Then they hooked us up with a couple of gigs at this chain of clubs, the Agora Ballrooms. One in Cleveland and another in Columbus, Ohio. We also did a video for one song, 'Without Your Love,' on the top of the Polygram building in the middle of Manhattan, with helicopters."

Bruce Kulick: "The video on top of the skyscraper? Pretty funny, too."

Jimmy Haslip: "The single got on the *Billboard* chart, but I think Polydor were expecting a little more."

Bruce Kulick: "The same week our album came out, Supertramp released *Breakfast in America*. That went on to become this gigantic record. We sold 150,000 copies of our album, but we were under a lot of pressure to succeed. If we didn't go gold, it was seen as a failure."

Jimmy Haslip: "Michael and Bruce got right back into writing songs for a follow-up record."

Bruce Kulick: "The top people at Polydor might have staked their reputations on Blackjack. I've a feeling that wasn't a good decision for them.

So you know what happens next. They tried to get rid of us, but Steve Weiss was one of the biggest entertainment lawyers on the planet for a reason. He told them, 'We have a two-album deal. We're recording.'"

Jimmy Haslip: "We did the *Worlds Apart* record toward the end of 1979, just to try to keep some momentum going. Eddie Offord was our producer. I was blown away by that, because Eddie had played with Yes and I was a huge Yes fan. We recorded up in Woodstock."

Bruce Kulick: "The studio was owned by Levon Helm from the Band. Interesting place. Not that far from the Aquarian era, if you know what I'm saying. I'm a huge Yes fan, too, and I knew what Eddie Offord was capable of, but unfortunately, he was going through a really bad time. He'd a cocaine habit he was struggling with, I believe. He was extremely erratic. We did the best we could, but Eddie had very little input. Jimmy took off. He was an incredible player, so there was other work waiting for him."

Jimmy Haslip: "After another ten days or so, I drove to Syracuse to join up with Dave Mason of Traffic's band for a tour. That was it for me with Blackjack. I had a whole other career as a session musician, but I really enjoyed playing with those guys."

Bruce Kulick: "A couple of the songs from the record were later on sampled and used by both Kanye West and Jay-Z. But at the time, it wouldn't have mattered if we'd made *Abbey Road*. Nobody was going to hear it. We might have been able to force the label to let us make the album, but they weren't about to give us any money to support it. You were lucky if you could even find a copy. The cover was dreadful, too. Polydor bailed on us. We'd had this team of people that really believed in us, but it wasn't to be for whatever reason. We just didn't hit the mark the way I'd loved for us to do. Everything ended up being a disaster."

CHAPTER TWENTY-THREE

JOURNEY EVOLVES; SURVIVOR STARTS; TOTO CRASH-LANDS.

"He drew out a big '79' on a mirror for me in blow. And the rest is history."

Steve Lukather: "The best and worst thing that can happen is for you to have a really successful first album. As soon as the record company went with 'Georgy Porgy' as the third single off *Toto*, we started to take a beating for being a pussy pop band. We lost all of our rock credibility."

David Paich: "All we had to that point was three-minute songs. So when it came time to make the second record, we saw it as a chance to expand our horizons."

Steve Lukather: "Never read your own press, good or bad. What we wanted above all else was to be taken seriously as a rock band."

David Paich: "We were being influenced by English groups in the main. Genesis and ELP, and Yes especially."

Jim Peterik: "After the Ides of March had disbanded, I caught pneumonia and ended up in the hospital. Through my haze of drugs, I started to chart the ultimate rock band from my hospital bed. I'd worked with Dave Bickler singing jingles in Chicago. We did the Schlitz Malt Liquor jingle together. I'd also written three songs for a band called Mariah. Frankie Sullivan was their guitarist. He impressed me right away with his smarts. The bassist Dennis Johnson and drummer Gary Smith had played together in another group, Chase. That band tragically went down in a plane crash, but those two gentlemen weren't on the flight. They became the rhythm section of Survivor."

John Kalodner: "I signed Survivor to Scotti Brothers, which was part of Atlantic Records at the time. I was aware of Jim Peterik from the Ides of March. Knew he was pretty talented. Frankie Sullivan I could see working out as songwriter. Peterik already was a pretty good songwriter. But I just had an instinct about the two of them together. If they could get in the groove with each other, I knew they'd be able to write *great* songs."

Jim Peterik: "Kalodner was an odd duck, but brilliant."

John Kalodner: "People paid attention when I came to see their band."

Jim Peterik: "He would stand in the room and make suggestions, whether you wanted them or not. A lot of times, he would simply say, 'You gotta start with the chorus—with the hook.' I will say he had very good commercial instincts. He knew what would get on radio."

John Kalodner: "That much is right. The melody was pretty much everything. If I could remember it, or relate to it within two to three listens, that meant most other people would be able to do the same. Radio did a lot of testing of songs in those days, and you had to get an immediate, visceral reaction."

Jim Peterik: "The producer we went with on the *Survivor* album was a guy named Barry Mraz. A perfectly good engineer, but pardon the term, also really kind of anal. Barry was one of those guys that did everything measure by measure. Kalodner came down to the studio one day to hear what we'd got. He sat there listening to everything we'd so carefully put down in silence. Then he looked over at me and announced, 'Mr. Mraz is a memory.' Kalodner hired Ron Nevison to make the record instead."

John Kalodner: "Along with the melody, it's all to do with the power of the production."

Jim Peterik: "Unfortunately, Kalodner also fired Ron Nevison. I ended up going up to Vancouver to finish the record with Bruce Fairbairn."

John Kalodner: "And it's about the vocals. Always, the vocals."

Jim Peterik: "I always intended to be the co-lead singer of the band with Dave Bickler. Whereas Frankie wanted the one singer in the Journey mold. He would make fun of my voice from the control room. Dave was a great singer, but I could sing, too. I just didn't want to buck the tide. I only sang one lead on the first record. I regret that I didn't push that harder."

Steve Smith: "I got a call from Herbie Herbert, asking if I was interested in coming to San Francisco and being the drummer in Journey. I really had no experience of playing with a singer at the level of Steve Perry, none at all. But it seemed interesting, and I felt like I could rise to the occasion. Once I got together with the band, we would rehearse five days a week, 11:30 a.m. to 5 p.m. The songs were written in rehearsal. We would create them in a collaborative way. Although when it gets down to the songwriting credits, there are established precedents. It's melody and lyrics that are copyrightable. For the most part, I didn't get a writing credit, but I participated like everyone else did in the development of all of those songs. We shared the publishing evenly. That was our way of having everyone get a piece of the creative process.

"The music was very close to finished from the rehearsal room. That meant we were able to make the *Evolution* record without having to spend a lot of time in the studio. In general, that was how Journey worked from the time I joined the band until 1985. The album started with a big rock ballad, 'Too Late.' I was a jazz drummer. I'd never played anything like that up to that point."

Jim Peterik: "The first album wasn't the sound I wanted for Survivor. It didn't have the power. Frankie and I decided to fire Dennis and Gary. We went to LA to audition for their replacements. Marc Droubay and Stephan Ellis auditioned on the same morning. Frankie had known Marc from way back in Chicago. Stephan I'd once seen play with a band in the middle of a skating rink. They became the second Survivor rhythm section."

Steve Lukather: "There was some fun stuff on the *Hydra* album, but it was a little heady."

David Paich: "Columbia Records, of course, thought we were going to give them *Toto 2*. Just like a new can of Coca-Cola, different packaging but with the same thing inside."

Steve Lukather: "We were under tremendous pressure to deliver the next 'Hold the Line.' On the contrary, we came up with a seven-minute title song about a serpent with many heads. We did have some funkier-sounding songs, too, like 'Mama' and '99,' but you'd never have guessed they were by the same band that had made 'Hold the Line.'"

David Paich: "It was fun to play those songs live at least."

Steve Lukather: "There was one night we had the Ramones of all bands open for us. What can I tell you, there were some strange fucking bills in those days. They were so bad people threw shit at them. After their set, they were so pissed with each other they got into a huge fistfight. We could hear the four 'brothers' beating the shit out of each other from our dressing room."

***

David Paich: "We only had the one small single off the record with '99.'"

Steve Lukather: "*Hydra* itself went gold, but we were coming off the back of a triple platinum record. It was perceived as a flop."

David Paich: "After that, we found out things weren't quite how we'd thought they were."

Steve Lukather: "For all our frustrations at the time, I did get to meet some very colorful people through my association with Mr. Bobby Kimball. One of them was a cowboy from Texas named Woody. He was kind of a drug dealer to the stars. Gary Busey and John Belushi were among his regular clients. I ended the year holed up in my new house in the Hollywood Hills on New Year's Eve, waiting for the Wood Man to show. When he did, he drew out a big '79' on a mirror for me in blow. And the rest is history."

CHAPTER TWENTY-FOUR

KISS DO DISCO WITH DESMOND CHILD.

"'What's my part?' 'Doo-do-do, do-doo-do-do.' 'No, come on!'"

Paul Stanley: "'I Was Made for Loving You' came out of a time when the band was a bit lost. We'd reached a point where we'd kind of forgotten why we were Kiss, and why we loved doing what we did. We were all, in some ways, drunk on success…There was every kind of vice that fame brings."[1]

Desmond Child: "Before my group Desmond Child and Rouge came out with our first record in 1979, we were doing a gig at a New York club called Trax. It was this underground place on West 72nd Street. Literally underground. It was the most happening club in Manhattan. We were getting ready to go on. There was no dressing room, there was just like a curtain we got ready behind, and the stage was right there. Paul Stanley poked his head around the curtain and said, 'Hey, guys, I'm Paul Stanley of Kiss.' I mean, we didn't know what he looked like. He didn't have his makeup on. He said, 'I just wanted to let you guys know that George Harrison of the Beatles is sitting at the front table.' I almost fainted. So we killed it. Before the encore number, of course, George was whisked off, so we didn't get to meet him. But through the whole thing he was smiling. I could see those big, white, fake teeth of his. Then Paul came backstage afterward and said, 'Hey, you guys were great.' I think he had eyes for Maria [Vidal]. Maria and I had been boyfriend and girlfriend, but we'd broken up by then for sure. I'd moved in with the guy across the street."

Paul Stanley: "I remember going to Studio 54. It was hedonism. Whatever your vice was, it was available. I would just go there, and people would dance all night."[2]

Desmond Child: "Paul said to me, 'You and I should write a song together.' I said we should write one for our album. Then I should write a song for his group. I knew nothing about Kiss. He looked at me and said, 'You *do not* know Gene Simmons.' But he went along with the deal. We shook on it. He wrote a song with me and our guitarist, David Landau, who was Bruce Springsteen's manager Jon Landau's brother, called 'The Fight.' Then Paul invited me to come to a lunch break at SIR where Kiss was rehearsing for their next tour. I got there dead on 1 p.m. The other guys in the band were passing me in the hallway, kind of bumping into me. Kind of like, 'Get out of my way.' Paul was waiting for me. There was a grand piano there with a big canvas cover. He helped me to pull the canvas cover back, and we sat next to each other, and I had the start, the first verse. 'Tonight, I will give it all to you…' I don't even know how to explain it, but it was Springsteen-like for sure, with maybe a little Meat Loaf in there. It was very Romeo and Juliet romanticism."

Paul Stanley: "All the songs at Studio 54 seemed to be about 'tonight'—and about having a good time in the present rather than thinking about the future. So I went home, set the drum machine to 126 beats per minute, and got to work."[3]

Desmond Child: "In the studio with Kiss, Paul went on to extrapolate and create the hook. 'I was made for loving you, baby.' Basically, mirroring the end of my verse. It's the same beat and feel as the Four Tops' 'Standing in the Shadows of Love.'"

Gene Simmons: "Paul walks in, 'Got a new song for you. It's called "I Was Made for Loving You."' 'Oh, that's great. What's the first line?' 'Tonight.' 'Oh, that's good. What's the second line?' 'I want to give it all to you.' 'Oh yeah, I know what "it" is! That's cool.' 'In the darkness there's something I want to do.' 'Oh, that rocks! What's my part?' 'Doo-do-do, do-doo-do-do.' 'No, come on!'"[4]

Paul Stanley: "Although we all looked at each other and said, 'This is a bit of a stretch,' we also all looked at each other and said, 'This song is undeniable. It's a no-brainer.'"[5]

Desmond Child: "I didn't even know they'd recorded it. I was in a cabin in upstate New York, and all of a sudden, I heard the song on the radio. It was a big hit. It was fantastic because it put me on the map."

Paul Stanley: "It became a double-edged sword, because it [was] such a massive hit, but it was also so contrary and contradictory to what we had done before. But look, at that point in our history, we had so many problems... We were becoming fat, wealthy musicians. We forgot what made us and why we loved what we did... and 'I Was Made for Loving You' was part of that."[6]

Gene Simmons: "I hate it to this day. Except, stadiums full of people, they jump up and down like biblical locusts to it, and so I sing along."[7]

Desmond Child: "We toured with Desmond Child and Rouge. It was the end of disco. We had two records come out in 1979. The record company did nothing with them. Disheartened, we went our separate ways. I regret that I didn't have my head together enough to deal with my sexual orientation in an honest way with Maria. I hurt her very deeply, and I was just reckless and selfish. I began this spiritual quest. I went to India and worked at an ashram. Then I came back and our voice teacher, all of us Broadway gypsies, this man named Bill Barber, he took over our lives. He was like a cult leader. We gave up our apartments. We moved to a commune in upstate New York. We weren't allowed to have couples. It was as if I were a eunuch, or something. The palace eunuch. The money I made from 'I Was Made for Loving You' was bankrolling the whole thing. I was being told the money wasn't mine, but that it belonged to our cause. I mean, I lost a lot of money. Eventually, I woke up and I left the cult."

CHAPTER TWENTY-FIVE

THE BIRTHDAY PRESENT THAT WENT TO NUMBER ONE.

"You better have some good drugs, because you can't figure shit out when it happens. It makes no sense."

Dennis DeYoung: "I met my wife when I was seventeen and she was fifteen. She was there through the whole thing. She was there when I had my dark days. In order for me to continue at the level I wanted to, I needed her. Her birthday was coming up. We'd just got off the road with *Pieces of Eight*. I said to myself I was going to write her a song, tell her how much I loved her. It was going to be a surprise. I made sure she was always out when I was doing the writing and the lyrics. This was not for the band. I was going to give it to her as a present, that's it. 'Babe' was written on the piano for my wife, and no one else.

"I call up John and Chuck. I say, 'Hey guys, come and do a demo with me over at Pumpkin.' That was the little local studio we would use. 'Okay, what's in it for us?' 'Pizza.' 'Fine.' I booked Pumpkin for two days. One day for the music. The next day for the lyrics. We went in and recorded it.

"Now, here's the thing. The ephemeral nature of life is such that if you try to analyze it, you're in trouble. You better have some good drugs, because you can't figure shit out when it happens. It makes no sense. I go over to the studio to do the demo, and I'm going to play it on a grand piano. I walk into the studio, there's no piano. I said to our producer, Gary Loizzo, 'What's wrong with you? I told you I was going to come over.' Over in the corner of the studio, there is a suitcase Rhodes. 'Bobby Whiteside' is stenciled on the side of it. Who's Bobby Whiteside? I don't know. He'd done a session, and he'd left his Rhodes there.

"We pull out the suitcase Rhodes. I'd never played a Rhodes. They're very different instruments to a piano. I'm noodling away on this thing, trying to get the lay of the land. I figured I'd start with something, so I said, 'Okay Gary, I'm ready to do the track. I'm going to do a little introduction.' That opening to 'Babe,' I was just noodling around with no idea it was being recorded. And it would not have sounded like it did if I'd played it on the piano.

"Here's another thing, JY and Tommy are on vacation when it's time for me to sing it. If Tommy and JY would have been there, they would also have put the 'Lady' power chords on it, but they weren't. It was all stupid, dumb luck, which as we all know is the best kind to have. I sang all the harmony parts. I did it, I mixed it. This was a little shit-nothing studio, but damn, did it sound good."

James "JY" Young: "Dennis wrote that song about his wife, Suzanne. It was the softest song we'd ever done to that point. I don't really like that soft a ballad personally."[1]

Dennis DeYoung: "We have the big birthday party, and I play the song for Suzanne. Did she like it? She told me she preferred Talking Heads. Let's get serious. She loved it. She didn't expect it. It could've been the worst song in the world. The more I played it for people, for friends, the more I got told it was a hit record. That's how it came to the band. But then, when we went in to record it for Styx, the demo I'd done had captured such magic, I was afraid to change it. I still don't like that vocal I did [for the *Cornerstone* album]."

***

James "JY" Young: "Dennis was much more of a mainstream writer. He sort of got dragged kicking and screaming into the rock thing by me, in a sense. I was clearly more of a rock 'n' roll guy."[2]

Dennis DeYoung: "Nobody had a bitch about 'Babe' when we recorded it. Our manager was the only one. [Huckster's voice:] 'Hey, you put this out and suddenly you'll have no rock credibility.' There are some people who would rather have a mediocre rock song than a pop song. That's fine, but ask your accountant what he prefers. Don't be an idiot. I don't like playing in front of fifty people. I've done that."

Al Cafaro: "When the radio programmers got given 'Babe' they had no choice. They *had* to play it. And it was a huge hit."

James "JY" Young: "It became our first Number One across the board nationally. I had some tough hockey players tell me that it was their and their wife's favorite song. So for me it was like, 'Well, it's not killing this rock image that we've built.'"[3]

Dennis DeYoung: "Is there jealousy? Is there envy? The competitive nature of putting people in a room together is that everybody, in some way, wants to feel that they are responsible for the success. Well, here's the problem. This one guy writes stuff that goes to here [just above his home studio's console]. The other guy writes stuff that goes to there [two feet above]. The second guy's accountant is very happy. It all plays in. People are human. With all the frailties that human beings have. How you handle that really defines how long your band stays together. I believe all boats rise with the tide. It wasn't a fucking beauty contest. It was the music. That's all that counts for me."

CHAPTER TWENTY-SIX

THERE'S SOMETHING ABOUT PATRICIA.

"I said, 'Absolutely not, I'm not playing with any girl.' Then I met her."

Pat Benatar: "I hate being vulnerable. When I was a kid [on Long Island], I loved to play little-girl games—until they started to take advantage of me because I was a girl. A kid named Joey lived across the street from me, and he'd push snow in my face before school. I could never do anything about it because I was a girl and real small. But after about a week, I got real pissed off. So I had two friends hold him on a slide. Then I punched his teeth out."[1]

Paul Elliott: "Pat Benatar was a ballsy operator."

Pat Benatar: "I wanted to be a schoolteacher. But it would have been a big mistake because I just don't have the patience at all. I was going through the training but then I got married and he unfortunately got drafted.[2]

"[Then] I was a bank teller for about two and a half years. I'd always been able to do whatever I wanted, and suddenly I had to face the reality of marriage and lots of bills. I sat in the teller's cage every day, looked at the money and thought, 'I know there's a way for me to have this without going to jail.' I wanted to steal it. I didn't want to sing, but I always knew that if I did it well enough, it could work. So I quit the job on impulse and became a singing waitress and played real sleazy bars.[3]

"I have the idea. I know what I want to do. I want to be Robert Plant. I don't want to be Linda Ronstadt. I love her. But I don't want to be singing, 'If you break my heart...' I want to be singing, 'Don't you break my heart, you're gonna die.' Or I want to be Lou Gramm. So I decided to start switching gender on a couple of cover songs. 'I'm telling you, get out of my face,' you know?

"I always loved science-fiction movies, especially the really crappy ones. There was this one Grade D movie called *Cat Women of the Moon*. I loved it because they wore these leotards and big eyeliner. I loved Sophia Loren and Audrey Hepburn and Brigitte Bardot. It was Halloween and we went to the Village. We went to Café Figaro, and they had a costume contest. And I won. I had on really exaggerated makeup and my hair was crazy, and I had this black leotard thing on... I just modified it and made it a little less like a costume.

"I finally get a showcase at a place called Tramps [in New York]. The first night it was my parents and my friends in the audience. That night somebody from the *Post* was there, and they wrote this incredible review. The next day all the record companies came down. The line was around the block.

"We signed [to Chrysalis], and we made a record, and it was crap. It was garbage. I needed, like, a big sound. I knew that. I didn't know what to do, but I figured that it was the guitar player. I want Robert Plant and Jimmy Page. I want Keith and Mick. I don't want to be a solo artist, I want a partner, so that we can play off each other.[4]

"Mike Chapman was brought in to produce four songs. I was talking to Mike, and I had done this ad nauseam speech to everybody about trying to get this Plant-Page thing going... And Mike was the only person who actually listened, and he said to me, 'I got your guy.' He was playing with Rick Derringer at the time, and Mike had done the Derringer record."[5]

***

Neil Giraldo: "I received a call, and they said, 'There's this person that's just got signed to a record deal and they're looking for a partner.' I said, 'Well, maybe I've heard of him. What's his name?' They go, 'It's not a "him," it's a "her."' And I go, 'Oh my God, it's a "her"? How's that going to work out?' I love women, but this is going to be difficult."[6]

Pat Benatar: "I'm in the room and they say, 'Neil Giraldo's here.' I have my back to the door. I'm not looking at him. I can hear him talking and I hear him say that he didn't bring a guitar. I'm thinking, 'Oh my God, what an ass.' I turn around ready to... and I see him and I'm like, '*Uh*.'"[7]

Neil Giraldo: "She turned around and I'm like, 'Wait, she's five-one.' I love short women. She's got dark hair. Then she started talking and she was super sweet. I'd never been with a normal girl in my life, and this person is so normal. So sweet."[8]

Pat Benatar: "It was like every cliché, every Disney movie thing you ever saw in your life. I couldn't even talk. He was a god. I was like, 'I don't care if he can play. He's in the band.'"[9]

Neil Giraldo: "The first thing I thought was, 'Where have you been all my life?' I told Patricia after our first day, 'Do you want to get married?' She goes, 'You're ridiculous. Get out of here.'"[10]

Pat Benatar: "I called up my girlfriend. I was living on, like, 81st Street and 1st Avenue, in this little apartment, and I was getting divorced, and everyone was really happy... He was a problem. And they didn't want everything to get screwed up. I go, 'I met the father of my children.' She slams the phone down, comes over to my apartment, and says, 'Are you an idiot?' But I knew."[11]

Neil Giraldo: "I put a band together. There was no band, nothing. I found a drummer and another guitar player and a bass player."[12]

Myron Grombacher: "At first, I said, 'Absolutely not, I'm not playing with any girl.' Then I met her and heard her voice, and I'd never played with anyone that could sing like that."[13]

Neil Giraldo: "We went to California, and twenty-eight days later the [*In the Heat of the Night*] record was done, and it was pretty simple."[14]

Pat Benatar: "When we did 'Heartbreaker,' I was like, 'Oh my God! Yes!' I knew we had it. Lyrically, it was exactly what I wanted to say. Musically, it was exactly what I wanted."[15]

Neil Giraldo: "She sounded great, but it wasn't what you hear today. What it was, was a very clean, clear, pristine voice. It wasn't the powerful voice that you know of... So I played way aggressive. The more aggressive I played, the more she had to compete to get heard."[16]

Pat Benatar: "'Heartbreaker' was released as the third single. All hell broke loose."[17]

Mike Chapman: "It's obvious. You hear the first few bars [of a] monster hit. Those are the kind of songs that I've always tried to write. Something that's instantly appealing. That people just crank up the radio and go, 'What's *that*?!'"[18]

Paul Elliott: "She was a class act, too. She handled herself brilliantly in that era. I don't think she ever sold herself cheaply in any way whatsoever."

Pat Benatar: "The first album cover doesn't look sexy to me. People look at it and go, 'What a *cover*.' I think, 'My teeth are too big, my eyes are too small.' But it created an image that everyone capitalized on... All of a sudden, you realize, 'Shit, people are looking at my crotch. This is embarrassing.'"[19]

CHAPTER TWENTY-SEVEN

JOURNEY FINDS ITS MISSING LINK.

"[I told them,] 'Number one: songwriting and composing. You guys are a bunch of zeros.'"

Steve Smith: "There's a tune on the *Departure* album called 'I'm Cryin'.' I can't even relate to how to describe that as a pop tune. It's a vehicle for all of the players involved. If you listen to that one song, you're going to hear so much from Neal Schon, from Gregg Rolie, from Ross Valory, from Steve Perry, and from me. It's quite loose. It's not a highly structured piece of music. It's a pretty unique kind of track that's all about the group performance. I did a lot of work with Ross to come up with drum and bass parts that really locked in together, but it's not just the rhythm section that made Journey different from the other groups. There were the non-typical arrangements, the blend of R&B influences with blues and rock, and the instrumental virtuosity of all the players in the band that made the group exceptional. We could play the songs and then stretch out on them. In a way like a jazz-rock fusion band."

Herbie Herbert: "I had to de-program them in a lot of ways. Originally, the band was very self-indulgent. A lot of long solo excursions were created specifically to set up Neal Schon for his guitar statements. But who was he talking to? [I told them,] 'Number one: songwriting and composing. You guys are a bunch of zeros.'"[1]

Steve Smith: "We really did need each other to make great music and take the fragments of ideas and turn them into complete songs. We were very good collaborators. I'll give you one example. On 'Walks Like a Lady,' Steve Perry has sole writing credit. But before Steve Perry came into the rehearsal room that day, Neal Schon and I were jamming on an idea inspired by 'Up from the Skies,' which is the first tune on Jimi Hendrix's *Axis: Bold as Love* album. Mitch Mitchell was playing brushes and Jimi's playing wah-wah guitar. Neal and I were jamming on that, and Steve Perry walks in and says, 'Keep playing that.' And he started singing, improvising over it, coming up with melodies and vocal phrases. Out of that eventually came 'Walks Like a Lady.'"

Steve Perry: "Some of the things vocally that I used to do. Why was I singing so high like that? What am I, crazy?"[2]

Dennis Dries: "Why Journey became so massive is because they had hooky songs. They had such great melodies. Pop melodies, but with heavier guitar and drums. Mix those together and it gave the rock 'n' roll of that era its magic."

Steve Smith: "We had an idea that we had something with 'Any Way You Want It,' but you never really know if a song's going to be a hit or not. That would be presumptuous. When we were writing the music, we were coming up with albums. We knew we needed to have hits, some songs that worked on the radio, but the big picture was to tell a story with ten songs."

Herbie Herbert: "Songs like 'Lovin', Touchin', Squeezin'' and 'Any Way You Want It' got so much airplay you got pounded by them, but they never really were hits. We did big promotions and access to Journey tickets and merchandise and meet and greets and things like that. And oh my God, the airplay we got from that was incredible. So every shoe store, shopping mall, and restaurant from Rusty Scuppers to Houston's, there they are. They come to a level of familiarity and recognition that means people really believe that those songs were hit songs."[3]

Dennis Dries: "I grew up at a time where you put the radio on in your car and you'd be singing along. That was part of the whole experience. Songs that got you humming right away. They were part of your life then."

Herbie Herbert: "I can remember sitting down one day and putting headphones on and watching a video of the last concert with Gregg Rolie back in 1980 in Tokyo at the Sun Plaza. And just being astonished at how good these guys could sing. They could pull off serious vocals."[4]

Gregg Rolie: "When I quit in 1980, I was just finished with the road and touring and being in a band."[5]

Neal Schon: "I had been watching Jonathan [Cain] with the Babys when they opened up for us and I saw that he clearly had something. He was the glue that held the Babys together."[6]

Gregg Rolie: "I pointed the band towards [Jonathan Cain]."[7]

Herbie Herbert: "Gregg Rolie picked Jon Cain."[8]

Jonathan Cain: "[The Babys] had been leveraged by the record company. And as talented as they were, they weren't really allowed to be the Bad Company type of band they wanted to be... They had hits but they got into debt. The manager ran the band into the ground. When I joined, believe it or not, they were almost $750,000 in debt in 1977, so that's pretty mind-boggling."[9]

John Waite: "Being in the Babys—being young and successful—was everything I thought it would be, and then some. But after the first couple of years the darkness descended. There were some volatile individuals in the band. We're talking almost asylum levels. We'd been 'the next big thing' twice before, and you can't keep doing that over and over again, can you?"[10]

Jonathan Cain: "We had the *On the Edge* album and after that [John Lennon was] shot. All the radio stations played nothing but Lennon music and our singles didn't matter anymore. That's when I got the call from Journey. John had already been planning on getting out of Chrysalis and going solo, so when I called him, he said, 'Go ahead and take it. It's a good thing.'"[11]

John Waite: "Jonathan Cain got offered the job with Journey, and that was the last straw. I just went, 'Fuck it, I'm leaving.' I had $6,000 for six years' work."[12]

Jonathan Cain: "John Waite was a great bandleader in the Babys. He ran the ship. But when I got to Journey, I saw this guy who was so musically involved. He could play the drums and the bass and sing like a bird... He knew where every little thing fit. He was, rhythmically, a genius... He had the innate instinct of an artist, like Sinatra. He was as good a vocalist as Sinatra. Sinatra could make anything feel like butter. Steve Perry could do that, too."[13]

Herbie Herbert: "The truth is Gregg Rolie said, 'Man, this guy, Steve Perry, he's out of control. He's gonna fix this whether it's broke or not. And I've been doing this forever. I've got more money than I'll ever need...' And he bailed."[14]

Gregg Rolie: "If Jonathan Cain had not been my replacement, and without his writing skills, I don't think they would have gone on to do half the things they did... But without Perry's voice and Neal's guitar it also wouldn't have happened."[15]

Steve Smith: "The members of Journey were all pretty alpha, all five.

You had two only children, Neal Schon and Steve Perry, and three oldest of their siblings. I'm the oldest of five, so is Ross. And Jon's the oldest of three."

John Kalodner: "It's really simple. Steve Perry's is the greatest voice in popular music, ever. And, yes, that is almost too much of a burden for one person."

CHAPTER TWENTY-EIGHT

THE TROUBLE WITH BOSTON, HEART, KANSAS, PAT BENATAR, CHEAP TRICK...

"You're bound to have this wall of animosity building up brick by brick."

Steve Fossen: "The first part of the *Bébé le Strange* album was when Roger was having all of his troubles. Once Rog and Mike Fisher were out of the picture, it went smoother."

Ann Wilson: "All the songs were written before the breakup... I've never been one to wallow really. I felt my pain and all that, but I've never been able to sit around and cry. Like, I'm trying to be as delicate as I can without saying that I stuck with it for the sex. But that's pretty much what it was."[1]

Nancy Wilson: "It's been said that five years is the life span of any new, hot rock band. They can do no wrong and every album is huge. Then five years go by, and people start to go, 'Ah, you know, it sounds like their other stuff.'"

***

Steve Walsh: "Hell, [Kansas] had been together five or six years at that time. Anybody who lives in the confines of a group for that long, while trying to exceed in a compelling medium, like songwriting was for us all, you're bound to have this wall of animosity building up brick by brick."[2]

Phil Ehart: "There was a lot of unhappiness and stress behind the scenes. Kerry and Dave were off in their own little corner, others took drugs. It definitely wasn't a fun band to be in at that time."[3]

Barry Goudreau: "Tom got us together for a meeting toward the end of 1979 and said, 'I'm not going to work all of next year. If you guys have other things that you are wanting to do, then now is the time to do it.' That is really what put the idea of me doing a solo record in my head in the first place. The album was written and recorded in six months. It was released in nine months… If I'd known it would be my first and only solo album, then I'd have taken more time with it."[4]

Brad Delp: "I still get a kick out of listening to that album [*Barry Goudreau*, 1980]. It was a real fun project for me… Barry allowed me to put a lot of myself into the lyrics and vocal parts."[5]

Barry Goudreau: "Brad being my brother-in-law and Sib my best friend, I brought them in to work on the recordings. After we had several songs together, we brought them to Tom in the hopes [he] would say, 'I like one of these songs. I'll consider it for a Boston record.' Obviously, having a song on a Boston record would be a really big deal. But he said, 'I'd like to produce the record.' We realized the record company was already pushing really hard for a new [Boston] record. There was no way they were going to let him record with me."[6]

Sammy Hagar: "Originally, Tom Scholz was going to produce my [*Danger Zone* album]. He came out and did pre-production, but his record company decided he should be working on another Boston record, not somebody else's record. They were going to sue him, so he left."[7]

***

Brad Delp: "Barry was in a bit of a difficult position to the extent that if the record sounded too much like Boston some people would be disappointed, and others would be disappointed if it didn't sound enough like Boston."[8]

Barry Goudreau: "The record label put out an advertising campaign that said, 'Six million people have heard the sound of this guitar, we'd like to introduce you to its owner.' Tom saw that as they were saying, 'Here's the guy behind Boston.' And he obviously was furious about it… Tom contacted the label and said, 'Listen, you've got to stop promotion on this, or you'll never see another Boston record.' And my record died a fairly swift death after that."[9]

Pat Benatar: "I was never so tense in my life [making the *Crimes of Passion* album]. I was freaking out so much I couldn't sing. I'd go home at night… and I'd be crying. I'd be, like, ripping my hair, taking Valium, and sitting in the hot tub going out of my mind. Neil would drive his car into the hills and sit there staring at Hollywood, because he didn't know what to do either."[10]

Rick Nielsen: "In 1980 things started to go wrong. The record company started to get real smart on us and, instead of fighting for us, our manager went along with it. I think we're a band's band, and we've made every mistake known to a band. But we have to take all the blame."[11]

Tom Petersson: "By that point we'd all gotten a bit burned out. We were averaging 290 shows a year and doing two albums a year. That was from 1977 to 1980. Things just kind of went out of control."[12]

Rick Nielsen: "We've been dumb artists. Anytime we think we're smart, all we have to do is look at ourselves. But at least we don't have to say we're quitters."[13]

Eddie Money: "I was drinking a lot of vodka. After work. You know, alcoholism runs in my family, and I was probably an alcoholic, and I was probably a cocaine addict, too. One night I was drinking a lot of vodka, and I thought I was snorting some cocaine. It turned out to be this fentanyl. It's the same thing that killed Prince. It's a very bad drug, it's like synthetic heroin. I fell asleep and went into a semi-catatonic state, and my nerves didn't twitch. So I killed the sciatic nerve in my left leg."[14]

Ron Nevison: "[Eddie Money is] a total asshole. I used to call [the *Playing for Keeps* album] 'Playing for Creeps.' I will tell you why...He sabotaged the album."[15]

Eddie Money: "I had doctors talking to me, telling me I was never gonna walk again...I walked from my bedroom to my music room with one of those walkers that the old ladies use. I'd come home from the hospital, crying my ass off, like a baby, like, 'What the fuck did I do to myself?'"[16]

Tom Scholz: "Concerned about egos, back in 1976 I naively suggested to Brad that we pay Barry Goudreau a share of the [*Boston*] record royalties equal to ours. Not just for the two cuts he played on, but for every song on the album. After performing with Boston for a scant three years, Barry left to pursue a career separate from mine."[17]

Barry Goudreau: "Actually, I was fired."[18]

Tom Scholz: "But he kept his share of royalties for all the songs he was not involved in recording and has continued to collect."[19]

Barry Goudreau: "Tom and I had a disagreement on what I was to receive when I left. We were equal partners in the band at that point. The band had sold tens of millions of dollars. I wasn't just going to walk away from it. There was supposed to be a settlement when I left, but weeks went by, and I didn't hear anything. Six months went by, and I couldn't get them even to return my calls. I wanted closure, so I went ahead and forced the issue to get things settled. In retrospect, I would not have done it. Being on the rocks with someone you were best friends with was very distasteful."[20]

Rick Nielsen: "The low point of the band was when Tom [Petersson] left. We didn't want him to go. We carried on, but it wasn't the same."[21]

Phil Ehart: "Kerry's religion was fine, but he wanted to make Kansas a sounding board for his beliefs. That sort of pontificating just didn't sit comfortably with us, especially Steve, who had to sing the songs with conviction."[22]

Steve Walsh: "It just started to really grind on me that I was having to mouth this inspiration in a way that I didn't feel comfortable with, at all. It was too specific. Way too specific."[23]

Jeff Glixman: "Steve did *Audio Visions* before he left for good. It got to the point where Steve and Kerry wouldn't be in the studio at the same time."[24]

Steve Walsh: "I had to walk away. Jeez, *Audio Visions* was a joke. We could barely stand in the same room the whole time. It was really bad. Shit, I just had to go. Cost me a hell of a lot of money, but I was young, and I thought, 'I'm bulletproof and I'm gonna live forever.'"[25]

Pat Benatar: "All the memories of [*Crimes of Passion*] are real shit. I only like a few songs on it, I don't like it as a whole record... Do you know what it's like to sing, 'You're a real tough cookie'? I mean, come on."[26]

Neil Giraldo: "Lindsey Buckingham once said that getting in a relationship inside a band is a big mistake. I never believed him. Now I believe him."[27]

CHAPTER TWENTY-NINE

BILLY SQUIER AND THE "BIG BEAT."

"I felt like, 'Okay, this is my time. People are listening to me.'"

Billy Squier: "I grew up on two-minute songs. I've always had a good pop and melodic consciousness. I was never trying to deny that, but I also wanted to be more of a hardcore rocker. I didn't want to be on the cover of teen magazines. I wanted to be on the cover of *Rolling Stone*. FM radio gave me the license to take what I liked from the past and throw it into something of my own in the present. It wasn't clinical. I had time to learn, and a lot of good teachers.

"I graduated in 1968 and went to New York, trying to get my career going. I was living pretty much on the street for a while. I had a band in 1972 called Kicks, which was a really good rock 'n' roll band. The drummer was Jerry Nolan, who went on to play with the New York Dolls. I left that band to come back to Boston to play in a band called the Sidewinders. A friend of mine named Bill Edmonds, who was working at EMI in London, had told me about them. They were making a bit of noise around Boston, and Bill told me they could really use my help, and I should be in this band. That would have been the beginning of 1973.

"One night we were playing a downtown gig at a notorious gay club called The Other Side. Quite a cool place. I met a woman at the bar name of Maxanne Sartori. Maxanne was the afternoon drive DJ on WBCN. I was totally smitten with her on-air personality. She was whip smart, clever, and funny, and she had great creative playlists. She was as good as it gets, and she had come down to check out me and my band. Maxanne was very into the local scene and trying to support local bands. She did the same thing with Aerosmith and the Cars, too. She was kind of the queen of the city. I talked to her that night, and the two of us ended up having a three-year relationship.

"My relationship with Maxanne really opened the doors of the music industry to me in a way I'd never even imagined. I was shown it wasn't just about the music, but how the game works. How you get your band on the radio. How you get to a record company. Through Maxanne, I met all of the promotion men from all of the major labels in the country. They'd come to town, take her out to dinner, and in which case I'd go to dinner with them. Maybe they'd liven things up with a little cocaine..."

Bruce Kulick: "Billy finally got a record deal out of a band called Piper."

Billy Squier: "The day I thought I'd finally become a singer I was singing a song on my second album with Piper [*Can't Wait*, 1977]. The song was called 'Little Miss Intent.' I came into the control room, listened back to it, and said, 'I sound like Paul Rodgers!' I mean, Paul Rodgers was the bar. There was something about his voice that really spoke to me.

"When Piper broke up and I didn't have a band, I had the freedom to write all kinds of songs. I heard lots of things on the radio, and I'd write different kinds of songs. I really liked Fleetwood Mac, so when *Rumours* came out, I started to write songs that sounded like them. Eventually, I realized you can't do that. If you do what's already happened, you're going to be late to the party. You've got to get on top of it. I became very conscious of trying to make the songs I was writing somehow identifiable. So that whenever you heard a Billy Squier song on the radio, you would know it was me."

Bruce Kulick: "Billy did some demos with my brother, Bob, and some great session players in New York. But when he wanted to make his album, Bob had a scheduling conflict. So Billy asked me if I would record with him. I loved working with Billy, and we did *The Tale of the Tape* up in Woodstock with Eddie Offord again. Eddie was a little more focused by then. I played rhythm guitar on every track and some leads, too. Billy's a good guitar player, but he'll always have a lead player with him. Whatever I played was the start of what he was going to do, if you know what I'm saying. Bobby Chouinard played the drums. He later died from cocaine. Bobby held the session hostage, I remember. He was like, '*I gotta have something!*' It's rock 'n' roll, right? But an incredible drummer. His pocket made that album, and I know that Billy loved him."

Billy Squier: "If you could have taken all of my songs, and laid them out on a table, from your left hand to your right in a 180-degree arc, that was the scope of my writing. Well, I took the 180-degree mark and cut 45 degrees off both sides. Basically, I jettisoned all the stuff that didn't meet the criteria I was looking for."

Bruce Kulick: "This guy had a notebook with him in the studio the whole time. He was meticulous with everything. He was looking for a sound that he called the 'Big Beat.'"

Billy Squier: "It was a very successful record in its own right. It wasn't a sales success, but it got a lot of radio airplay in America. There was one song, 'The Big Beat,' that was the most requested song on American radio for six weeks straight when it came out. *The Tale of the Tape* set me up. I felt like, 'Okay, this is my time. People are listening to me.'"

Bruce Kulick: "I didn't get to finish the album with Billy, because I had to go rehearse for a tour with Michael Bolton that never happened. So

I don't know in the end how much of that record was Billy's or Eddie's vision. But you can tell there's a big difference between *The Tale of the Tape* and the next one Billy made. He was to get even more polished and even more radio play."

Billy Squier: "I remember meeting Axl Rose after the first Guns N' Roses record came out. It was in New York at my local hangout, the China Club. Axl wanted to meet me, and he got someone at the club to call me up. Sure, I went down to see him. He told me, 'The first time I got laid, I was listening to "Calley Oh."' Second song, side one of *The Tale of the Tape*."

CHAPTER THIRTY

CANADA CALLING.

"I won't say I'm boring, but I'm not wildly exciting either."

Bryan Adams: "Mum was just a mum, and I mean that in the best way because she only cared about her boys. My father wasn't around a lot in the early days. He had left the military to join the UN as a peace-keeping observer for the India-Pakistan war. We traveled quite a bit in Europe after he left the UN and joined the diplomatic service, places like Austria and Portugal, and later to the Middle East and Israel. And of course, because both of my parents were British, we'd travel back to the UK to visit grandparents, aunts, and uncles, and have Christmases there. It was an interesting upbringing."

Jim Vallance: "My parents finally gave in and bought me a guitar when I was thirteen. I also got a drum kit from my grandparents and a little reel-to-reel tape recorder from Mom and Dad. From the age of fourteen, I started writing snippets of music. Not a whole song, but just so I'd have something to record. I reckon my first real song might have been when I was fifteen. Songwriting is a very slow evolution. You're always experimenting and thinking you can do better, trying something different and new."

Bryan Adams: "The first time I performed to an audience was with a band called Shock. We got a regular gig at a pub in Vancouver. The first night, because I was fifteen and too young to be in the place, I had to be escorted to the stage by a bouncer when we went on. At the end of the show, the bouncer took me backstage again. That went on for a day or two and then they went, 'Fuck it, you can just walk on yourself.'"

Jim Vallance: "There were lots of opportunities to make a living as a musician in Canada in the early 1970s. I'm talking a humble living, but in Vancouver and the vicinity there were twenty or thirty clubs with live music six nights a week. There were dozens of bands, and one particular booking agency called the Sam Feldman Agency that just kept them all going around the circuit. I was in three or four different bands. We worked Monday night to Saturday night every week, going from one club to the next. We'd go round all thirty of the clubs and then start again. There was good camaraderie. The musicians all knew each other."

Bryan Adams: "I used to audition for all kinds of things. I really wanted to be a guitarist, but every time I auditioned for work as a guitarist, I'd never get the gig. *Every single time*. Every time I auditioned as a vocalist, I got the job. They weren't like lead vocal gigs. It was sometimes singing harmony with a group or doing backups for other singers. I got to know the local scene and other musicians in Vancouver quite well."

Jim Vallance: "I'd done one year of music at the Vancouver university. It was classical music, there were no options back then for rock or pop studies. I met another fellow there, Tom Keenlyside, a saxophonist and flautist. Tom knew Bruce Fairbairn, so in the summer of 1973 when Bruce's band Sunshyne was looking for a drummer, Tom recommended me. I remember going to the first rehearsal, which was probably actually an audition, and that's where I met Bruce for the first time. It was kind of a jazz fusion band. Bruce was the trumpet player. We all had silly nicknames. Peter the piano player was 'Captain Boll Weevil.' Richard the bass player was 'Eddie Dexter.' I was the drummer, and I took the name 'Rodney Higgs.' Sunshyne morphed into Prism and the name stuck. It was silly, and pointless, and I regretted it, but I can't undo it now."

Bryan Adams: "I'd a friend who was a guitar player and I said to him, 'If we're going to make it, we have to do our own music.' His response to that was, 'Great, you do it.' So I must give him the credit for pushing me."

Jim Vallance: "I went traveling for a year, trekked around Europe and the Middle East. I returned to Vancouver expecting to get my job in Prism back, but they had got another drummer. I was shut out, and they were actively pursuing a record deal. But with no success at all. Bruce rang me up one day and asked if I had any songs. I gave them three or four songs I had on the shelf. They recorded them and got a record deal straightaway. So, I got invited back into the band and became the main songwriter. Prism went on to become a moderately successful Canadian band. By the time we finished the first album [*Prism*, 1977], we had a little bit of experience to go forward. We opened for Foreigner and Heart. Five guys in a rental car, sleeping in cheap motels and eating microwaved tacos at truck stops on the freeway. I hated it. It's not glamorous. I quit the band after the first tour and was once again unemployed."

Bryan Adams: "Maybe there are people out there that have always been brilliant songwriters, but I think it's a craft you learn by putting time in. And it's much like any other kind of craft. Like the first time you sit at a potter's wheel, the clay doesn't come together. Songwriting is the same. You have to work at it to get good at it."

Jim Vallance: "I was fairly busy as a session drummer. I played on a McDonald's commercial. Then, six months after I quit Prism, I ran into Bryan by chance in a music shop in Vancouver. I was in the store with a friend of mine, Ally Monroe. She was a piano player, and she knew Bryan.

She said hi to him and introduced me. I knew who Bryan was already, because he'd been in another Vancouver band called Sweeney Todd."

Bryan Adams: "Don't ask me about that band. I won't talk about them."

Jim Vallance: "Bryan and I had a quick chat. I told him I'd quit my band. He told me he'd quit his band. I can't remember if it was him or me, but one of us suggested we get together. A few days later, Bryan came over to my place. We had a cup of tea and wrote a song on that first day."

Henry Small: "Paul Dean and I had hooked up in Calgary in a band called Scrubbaloe Caine. A great live act. Our manager got us a deal with RCA, which we were very excited about, and we went down to LA to record. We had six days to do the whole thing, that's all. When we heard the result, we were not very pleased. The band continued for another six months before breaking up. Paul went on to Streetheart, and I moved down to Los Angeles."

Paul Dean: "Streetheart was a really great band. I used to think it was the Led Zeppelin of Canada."[1]

Mike Reno: "In my mind, Paul was in one of the greatest bands in Canada… He'd come home for Christmas in Calgary from Winnipeg, where Streetheart was from, and he got a phone call, and they'd canned him. He was in a bad state of mind."[2]

Henry Small: "Paul called me one day and said he was getting a new band together, which ended up being Loverboy, and would I be interested in being the singer. They were going to be getting $300 a week, paid for by their manager at the time, Lou Blair. I loved Paul's playing, but I had my mind set on making it in LA and so I declined Paul's offer."

Paul Dean: "Mike was working in construction during the day, carrying cement around. I thought he was an incredible singer."[3]

***

Henry Small: "What was funny about it, Mike Reno used to come and watch us in Scrubbaloe Caine. He was this fat kid that was kind of always hanging around. He'd be like, 'Hey, man, you're a great singer.' He was a really enthusiastic kind of guy. He took the job with Paul, obviously, and they did what they did."

Mike Reno: "I'm not flashy, or outrageous or flamboyant. I'm not especially witty. I'm not going to talk circles around you or flabbergast you with my wit. You won't die laughing at anything I say…I won't say I'm boring, but I'm not wildly exciting either."[4]

Bryan Adams: "With Jim and me, it was two guys sat in a room and bouncing ideas back and forth. Neither of us had anything else going on at the time. I had a load of shit ideas and Jim had a load of good ones. Jim was also a very proficient and talented musician. He played drums, bass, guitar, a bit of cello. There was momentum between us right away. First day we got together, we wrote a song. The next day, we wrote another. The third day one more, and suddenly we had all these songs. We'd go down into Jim's basement where he had a snare drum, bass drum, microphone, and a small TEAC four-track recorder. We'd just sit there and make demos. To the point we were spending twelve hours a day, sometimes more, trying to write songs."

Jim Vallance: "My first impression of Bryan was that he had a vibe. He was energetic, clearly smart, but I didn't grasp how talented he was until we actually sat down and got together. He could sing, play guitar, he could write, and he had endless energy and enthusiasm. So he was someone to really keep an eye on. It was one of those moments in time. I knew that he and I were going to do something together. I couldn't tell you what just then, but I knew we had potential as a songwriting team. We both write lyrics. We both write melodies. It was a little different song to song. There might be one song that I wrote a few more lyrics for than Bryan, and vice versa on the next song. But it was always very much a 50/50 split. There was never an argument about, 'I wrote one more word than you did,' or any of that. We wrote together and to this very day, the best idea wins."

Bryan Adams: "We worked quite differently, and I think that's probably why our partnership was successful. We'd make drum loops. Jim would play a beat, and he'd loop it on a piece of tape. He'd tie a pencil to the end of the TEAC deck and let the tape go round and round the pencil. When it came out the speakers, it was like we'd a drummer in the room with us. We would write songs to the grooves Jim put down. In between times, we'd be chasing Jim's roommate's cat around, trying to get it out of the basement because it would piss over everything."

Jim Vallance: "It was a rental house that I shared with another fellow, a musician named Wayne. There was just a corner in the basement, next to the furnace. It wasn't fancy. It was an unfinished basement, concrete floor, open ceiling beams, and I just carved out a little corner for my studio. I remember going down one morning after a big rainstorm the night before, and it was ankle deep in water. It was horrible, but that's where we started—a smelly, dusty corner of a basement."

Mike Reno: "Paul and I took our time finding the [other] members. They had to have the right attitude. We even talked about how we wanted to look, how we wanted to dress, how we wanted to present ourselves, what we wanted to talk about in interviews, how we wanted to lay it out."[5]

Paul Dean: "We were pretty ballsy back in those days, totally confident. Failure was not an option, and we were going to go for it."[6]

Mike Reno: "We were hanging out with our girlfriends. The girls were reading *Cosmopolitan* and *Vogue*, and I said, 'Look at how good these cover girls look on these magazines.' Paul shoots up and says, 'Let's call ourselves Cover Boy.' I thought about it and said, 'That's not half bad.' I got a call first thing the next morning and it was Paul. He said, 'We'll call ourselves Loverboy. If we don't get the shit kicked out of us in the first ten days, then maybe it'll catch on.'"[7]

Jim Vallance: "Bryan was signed to A&M Records in 1978. Without his knowledge, the record company remixed one of our demos, 'Let Me Take You Dancing,' and released it as his first single. Bryan rang me, and he was really upset with the fact that the track had been remixed to make his voice sound sped up. That was the first I'd heard about it, too, but I wasn't as upset as he was. To this day, just the mention of that song is enough to get Bryan all prickly."

Bryan Adams: "The first song I wrote that did anything was 'Wastin' Time' for Bachman Turner Overdrive in 1979. That was around the same time I also wrote 'Straight from the Heart.'"

Paul Dean: "It's amazing to think Bob Rock and Mike Fraser were the *engineers* [on the *Loverboy* album, 1980]. I mean, *what* a team."[8]

Jim Vallance: "There was kind of Canadian sound that developed. To his credit, I think Bruce Fairbairn invented that sound with his work with Loverboy."

Mike Reno: "The public jumped all over it... This was at a time when people would actually go out and *buy* a record."[9]

Jim Vallance: "Making Bryan's first album [*Bryan Adams*, 1980] was good fun. We were happy to have a record company supporting us, and proper studios. But we were still learning and not yet fully formed. The album sold a wee bit in Canada, but we were thinking way beyond Canada. It's so insular and xenophobic. As a Canadian, you just want to jump across the border."

CHAPTER THIRTY-ONE

"KEEP ON LOVING YOU" AND THE PERKS OF BEING A RADIO PROGRAMMER.

"They would get the ladies under the table and a new truck, and they didn't even have to play anyone's stinking record."

Andrew McNeice: "I run a little music shop in Hobart, Tasmania, and forty-four years on, I'm still selling copies of REO Speedwagon's *Hi Infidelity* album [1980]. It's like a greatest hits album, song after song. They just hit a hot spot."

Kevin Cronin: "The thing that was on my mind—and Gary's mind, too—was our personal relationships. It's an embarrassing thing to write. Some of the things I put in those songs are things I would be embarrassed to say even to one of my friends."[1]

Neal Doughty: "Several band members were going through some stormy relationships, but mine was falling apart completely. I ended up in the emergency room after a severe panic attack."[2]

Kevin Cronin: "Gary and I were in the eye of the hurricane... There was no one closer to it than Gary and me, and nobody was as close to him as I was. You write songs together. You produce records together. It's a pretty intimate situation."[3]

Bruce Hall: "With *Hi Infidelity*, it seemed like we were on to something."[4]

Kevin Cronin: "Epic Records was ready to drop us. They insisted we had to have a radio-friendly song on our next album. And everyone in the band and around us thought that if anyone could come up with that song, then it would be me."[5]

Gary Richrath: "We wanted songs that would be more acceptable to radio, which meant more structure and less flash."[6]

Kevin Cronin: "One night, I woke up at 4 a.m. with these three single piano chords stuck in my head. They were still there the next day, so I went down to SIR Studios where we were rehearsing, sat down at Neil's piano, and started to play. I must have played this part about a hundred times, and no one was taking any notice. Finally, Gary plugged in his Les Paul to a giant stack of Marshalls and started playing something. Now, I am convinced the only reason he did this was to try to drown me out."[7]

Gary Richrath: "When I listen to *Hi Infidelity*, if I was going to criticize my playing, it would be that I didn't play enough."[8]

Kevin Cronin: "But when I heard what he was doing I jumped up and said, 'That's exactly what this song needs!' And 'Keep On Loving You' took off from there."[9]

Bruce Hall: "We went into this little studio in downtown Los Angeles, Crystal it was called, just to make demos. We had this batch of songs. It was fun and it was easy. We got done with it... Because we just wanted to hear it in our cars. We wanted to see if it sounded all right. Next thing you know, we took the band into a professional studio, and we couldn't beat the demos. A lot of those songs are demos."[10]

Gary Richrath: "On 'Take It on the Run' I had two tracks for rhythm, two for the first harmony, two for the second harmony, and then one for the lead."[11]

Kevin Cronin: "Gary didn't think much of that song, but I heard something in it. Originally, it was called 'Don't Let Me Down.' I said, 'I think the Beatles already did a song called that!' But the chorus started with, 'Take it on the run…' I said, 'There's your title!' And of course, that song has one of the greatest opening lines in rock history: 'Heard it from a friend who heard it from a friend who heard it from another you been messin' around.' I wish I'd written that."[12]

Neal Doughty: "Usually by the time we were done making a record, I'd had enough for a while, and I wouldn't listen to it for maybe a month. *Hi Infidelity* was my favorite album from the day we finished it. I had that thing going in my car, on headphones in the tanning shed… It was just immediately my favorite record."[13]

Kevin Cronin: "When Epic heard our demo of ['Keep On Loving You'], they weren't even gonna put it out as a single. We persuaded them, and it got to Number One in America."[14]

Steve Overland: "Ed Sheeran could do a version of 'Keep On Loving You' and it would still be a great song. Great songs are great songs."

Kevin Cronin: "Most rock 'n' roll songs have said, 'Caught you cheating on me, baby, now get lost.' Or it's only okay for men to do it, but it's not okay for women… I still don't understand that double standard. 'Keep On Loving You' was my attempt to attack the double standard. Now that I think about it, it's almost a feminist kind of song."[15]

Neal Doughty: "Gary had always been the leader, but now the momentum was shifting toward Kevin. The record company even wanted it that way since his ballad finally got us a giant radio hit."[16]

Kevin Cronin: "REO has always been a rock 'n' roll band. But we learned we could play ballads and still have them be real powerful."[17]

David Spero: "That corporate rock thing was really starting to happen by then. It was Foreigner and Boston first of all, and then REO Speedwagon and Styx and Journey took off. These bands were doing anthems, and they were talking directly to *us*. That's when music connects—when they're really talking to us. Those bands found a way to do it."

Lee Abrams: "Those bands were the soundtrack of America at the time."

Kevin Cronin: "To see our album at Number One was mind-boggling. We ordered a bunch of Dom Perignon and just yelled like schoolboys. It was awesome! The days of touring in a Chevrolet station wagon were still fresh in our minds."[18]

Dick Asher: "It wouldn't have bothered me so much if the REO album had been a good album. But it just wasn't. The Clash had a super album, and it was not getting any [radio] support."[19]

Les Garland: "It was a pretty simple formula when you think about it. Get your song on the radio, get it played, and if it's a hit on radio, it will sell. Record companies, radio stations, record stores, that was the pipeline."

Steve Lukather: "Toto was on the same record label as REO Speedwagon. Columbia Records. Columbia gave us what was called 'independent promotion.' One of the great euphemisms of the music business."

Lee Abrams: "Independent promotion was very big in Top 40 radio. There were a lot of reports of corruption. Guys at radio stations that were making $300 a week were driving Porsches and taking lots of vacations. It cost money to make hit records. You'd have to pay off these people, or else give them 'incentives' to play your record."

Billy Squier: "The promo guys would come to town. It wasn't so much like, 'Here's $300, put the record on.' But if a guy comes, he's nice and he takes you out to dinner, gives you a little of this and that, and tickets to the show, you say, 'Yeah, okay, what's wrong with that?' I wouldn't exactly say it was criminal. Personally, I never heard of money changing hands. Like I said, you'd get taken to a nice restaurant. You'd get given illicit drugs. But everyone was a cocaine addict at that time. Everybody liked a little blow."

Steve Lukather: "Radio play was crucial to having a hit record and there were two ways to get it: someone at a station could actually like your record, or else you paid them to play it. That payment could be made in the form of money, drugs, chicks, boys, whatever the fuck someone was into. It was a crooked game, but everyone played. God knows how much was spent over the years on our behalf, but it always came out of our pockets in the end."

Laurie Larson: "Oh, I have so many stories. Even though we all had to sign anti-payola contracts, it was wink-wink, nudge-nudge. You didn't say anything about the trips to Hawaii. You didn't say anything about the program director and assistant director having new vehicles in the radio station parking lot. Then again, the program director would think a song sucked and didn't want it to affect their ratings. So they would say they had added it to the playlist. They would tell all the trade magazines that, but they wouldn't really do it. It was a win-win for those guys. They would get the ladies under the table and a new truck, and they didn't even have to play anyone's stinking record."

John Kalodner: "It was one of those things like drugs and alcohol. It could really affect decision-making and perception, because the independent promoters were so powerful and there was so much money involved, it could make you be not focused about the things you needed to be. You had to make the music be really great. If you got caught up with thinking about the next segment of radio, you were fucked."

Neal Doughty: "I did not like being that famous. They say it changes you, but it actually changes everything around you."[20]

Kevin Cronin: "I was convinced that the band's success and my emotional health were inextricably interwoven. If the band made it big, all my problems would be over. Well, guess again, Junior! Turns out the enormous popularity of *Hi Infidelity* only magnified my insecurities. Bummer, right? Hey, at least that 'Keep On Loving You' money helped take the sting out of my shrink bills."[21]

PART THREE
JUKEBOX HEROES

CHAPTER THIRTY-TWO

CLOCKING IN AT THE HIT FACTORY.

"Rock 'n' roll, what happened? It became this slicked-out thing."

Andrew McNeice: "The classic rock of the '70s was more British based, but the '80s belonged to America. And the music matched the times. People generally were happy. We didn't have social media fucking up everybody's lives. Everybody wanted to be part of the big booming American experiment. Journey, Styx, Foreigner, they were just ruling the airwaves, even here in Australia."

Joe Elliott: "My idea of America in totality came from TV. You know, you're living in Sheffield. You're in a factory. 'Hello America' on the first Def Leppard album [*On Through the Night*, 1980]? That was me in a basement factory that had no natural light, doing a job that could be done in two hours but I'm there for eight, and what had I been watching on telly last night? *Starsky and Hutch*, *Charlie's Angels*... There are all these palm trees and girls in bikinis. You're thinking, 'And I've got fifty years of *this*?' Fuck no.

"Mutt Lange came in for our second album, *High 'n' Dry*, and he pushed us in a whole different direction. He was a slave driver. Literally, within twenty minutes of meeting us he was like, 'No, stop. That's not good enough. Slow the song down and scrap those lyrics because they're shit.' I can remember him reaming our guitarist Pete Willis for just picking up an apple and taking a bite. 'Put that down and pay attention!' It was like going back to school. What he was saying was, we haven't got the time to fuck around. As hard as it was to get your head round, he wanted the best. He wanted to make history. We just had to get on the same page pretty quick and speed up our process."

Dennis DeYoung: "The *Paradise Theatre* album of 1981 was Styx's biggest success. Our first Number One. And that was my big idea. Shoot me."

Billy Squier: "Virtually no one gets to make a record like *Don't Say No*. I mean, you're talking about records that you wouldn't change a thing about. There aren't many. Even with the great bands. When I was getting ready to go in and make it, I was talking to Brian May about him producing the record. Ultimately, Queen went beyond schedule with *The Game*, and they had a tour booked, and Brian wasn't able to do it. But he said to me, 'Why don't you call up this guy in Munich that we used on *The Game*?' [Reinhold] Mack had made his bones engineering with Giorgio Moroder and Jeff Lynne with ELO, and when I heard *The Game*, it was the sound I'd always wanted to hear on my records. I was, like, '*This is the guy!*' The rest is history. We do *Don't Say No*. Huge record and off we go."

Paul Dean: "There are a million guitar players out there that could smoke me. But as a songwriter, I think I have a unique style. And if you don't have songs, you don't have anything really. That's where it all comes from."[1]

Mike Reno: "We don't do a lot of experimenting. We basically do songs about lost love and new love. We keep it simple. We're commercial. That's a dirty word to some people, but not to us. We're middle of the road, [and] we're not trying to hide it either."[2]

***

Paul Dean: "I was strolling through Kitsilano in Vancouver one spring day and the streets were mostly deserted. I thought, 'Where is everybody? The place is usually jumping. Oh, I get it. They're probably waiting for the weekend.' [The song] was originally called 'Waiting.' I got the music part started in Montreal a week later in my hotel room. I brought it to the band and Reno says, 'How about 'Working for the Weekend'?"[3]

Joe Elliott: "Mutt thought we had a potentially huge song for American radio in 'Bringin' On the Heartbreak.' That was his job—to take this band to the next level. And I couldn't sing it. Couldn't hit a barn door with a fucking banjo on that particular day. I made the mistake of walking into the next-door studio and watching David Coverdale do a vocal in one take. Different league. He came out of the booth, and he was like, 'Joseph, dear boy, whatever's the problem? Let's have a brandy.' To cut a long story short, the two of us drank a bottle of brandy. I walked back into our studio bouncing off the walls, and Mutt sent me home, sick as a dog. Next day, we'd nailed all the lead vocal parts of the song by late afternoon. Getting drunk with David got all of that anger at myself, and fear, out of my system."

Donald Roeser: "Once you had one hit, you were expected to have more. Everybody in the band wrote, so everybody in the band was trying to have a hit. I don't know if that was the best thing for us to do artistically, because you constrain yourself immediately when you're chasing what's popular. '...Reaper' wasn't written with that in mind, obviously. I don't know, did we do our best work when we didn't care about having hits? Probably. I just don't think we were cued to the mechanisms of hit radio. There wasn't anything about partying or romance in our songs. We sang about history, technology, and horror."

Steve Lukather: "You keep fighting those perceptions of you, and that was the *Turn Back* album in 1981. We blazed through it in three months, but it's a very strange record to listen to sonically. We were like, 'We want to be a hard rock band at all costs.' We tried too hard. Lost it. Pop radio didn't play us, and rock radio wouldn't play us anymore. So we were defeating ourselves."

Billy Squier: "I think 'The Stroke' is a very simple song with a tremendously seductive, innuendo-filled hook which is not about anything you think it is. I knew when we were doing it that it would be a smash. *Knew it.* Everybody was going to think it was about some sort of sexual situation that's taboo, but it isn't. So I was going to get all this controversy that was going to help it. Then there wasn't going to be anything else that sounded like it on the radio."

Joe Elliott: "Whenever I hear 'The Stroke,' I think of 'We Will Rock You.'"

Billy Squier: "My record company didn't know. Capitol didn't even want to put it on the record. They didn't like it at all. They wanted to put a ballad out as the first single. Thank God I had a good promotion man. His name was Ray Tusken in Los Angeles. He was a lot brighter than some of the other guys upstairs. The record companies did a promotional thing with radio called 'day parting.' What that was, they'd take songs that they wanted to test to the big target stations at weekends. They'd give them to the stations to play over the weekend and see what happened. They took 'The Stroke,' and it blew up. And that was that."

Donald Roeser: "I wrote 'Burnin' for You' for my solo record. Sandy Pearlman, our manager and mentor, convinced me to let the band record it for *Fire of Unknown Origin*. It was a bigger hit for Blue Öyster Cult than it would have been for me. And sort of by default, I became the hit guy. If you listen to the band's output after that, you can hear a conscious effort to get radio play."

Steve Lukather: "Then there was the showbiz side, which we never counted on. I was dressing like Kurt Cobain in 1975. It was old jeans and Pendletons, T-shirts and my hair was disheveled and completely ridiculous. I didn't give a fuck. The record company had me cut my hair and dolled me up like a fucking pouting businessman. I fucking hated it. Rock 'n' roll, what happened? It became this slicked-out thing."

Billy Squier: "Oh, I did everything to work my records. I loved them, and I wanted people to hear them. I didn't care if I had to get up early in the morning after a show and go do a radio interview to promote them. Those radio stations wanted me to come. I wasn't asking for an interview with them, they were begging me for one. So you were always in an environment where people were digging what you were doing. How can that be bad?"

Joe Elliott: "The two things Mutt really taught this band—dynamics, and don't get precious about anything. There were a lot of guitars thrown down and screaming ab-dabs in the studio. But as we went on, we started to hear performances from all of us that would make us look at each other and go, 'Is that really you?' Because Mutt would make you do everything again and again until he thought it was good. Then he'd tell you, 'There's a better one in you.'"

Paul Dean: "[Touring with] ZZ Top was tough. Their audience was hardcore biker blues fans... There was one gig in Cape Cod when all hell broke loose. I put on my [baseball] batter's helmet while the audience threw lighters, bottles, ice cubes, and coins—it all came raining down on us. That was a wake-up call."[4]

Steve Lukather: "Of course, the reviews for *Turn Back* were scathing. It got no higher than 30 on the chart, then petered out and died. We didn't even bother to go out on tour behind it. The top brass at Columbia were bummed out."

David Paich: "We were put under a lot of pressure. The record company let our managers know that they thought we were a one-hit wonder."

CHAPTER THIRTY-THREE

NEW ADVENTURERS IN AOR…

"Those hooks are the things you remember, man. In Germany, they call it the 'earworm.'"

Rick Springfield: "When I first came [to the US] from Australia, I lived in Hollywood. I would write to people I hardly knew in Australia just so I could sign 'Hollywood, California' on the return address."[1]

Mike Baird: "I'd been working with the producer Keith Olsen. He calls me up one day and says, 'Hey, can you come over to the house? I've got a project I want to discuss with you.' I went over to his pad, and he told me he was doing an artist named Rick Springfield. Keith goes, 'He's a soap opera guy, an actor, but he's had a music career prior to this.' Keith always used Sound City as a studio, and the guy that owned it, Joe Gottfried, had discovered Rick. Keith was wanting to have a lifetime lease on Sound City. Joe goes to Keith and says, 'Here's what I'll do. I'll lease the property to you for a lifetime, so long as you produce two hit songs for my artist Rick Springfield.'"

Rick Springfield: "I'd been listening to a lot of punk…I loved the whole thing of short songs and guitar, bass, and drums. Elvis Costello's *My Aim Is True* and the first Police album were very inspirational and the blueprints of *Working Class Dog* for me."[2]

Mike Baird: "It was meant to be Keith, me, Neil Giraldo, great guitar player, and John Pierce on bass. We show up for the date, and there's no bass player. The story goes, John didn't get the blow that he ordered, so he just never showed up. John will tell you that he never got the call, but who knows? It was a crazy time back then."

Steve Lukather: "The Tubes was an incredible, theatrical live act, but they didn't write hit songs and couldn't get on the radio. So in 1981 David Foster got the job of producing their new album, *The Completion Backward Principle*."

Bill Champlin: "David Foster's maybe one of the most creative human beings I've ever met. He also works the machine pretty well if you see where I'm going with that. When it gets down to just dealing with music, he's unbelievable. First of all he's a great piano player and an amazing arranger. So when you write with David you're writing with an arranger. Once the song is done, it's pretty much ready to go."

Fee Waybill: "Foster had never done a rock record before, [but] *The Completion Backward Principle* is pretty much my favorite album we ever made."[3]

Bill Champlin: "Oh yeah, I was all over that Tubes record. They were a Northern Californian band. Most of them lived in Pacifica, which is right close to San Francisco where I live. I had a ball hanging with them. They were really good and Fee's one of the best performers I've ever seen. Anybody who has nothing but a pair of Speedos on and is dry humping a television console onstage has got to be pretty rare. Totally fearless. But eventually their production was costing way more than they were making, so…"

***

Graham Bonnet: "We went to Sweet Silence Studios in Copenhagen to start up rehearsals for the next Rainbow album, *Difficult to Cure*. Russ Ballard had sent us another tune, 'I Surrender.' I did the backing vocal on that because we had nothing else to work on but for that one song. No other songs had been written. We were going to rehearsal every day, but Ritchie never came. Once in a while he would come in and ask how it was going. He might pick up his guitar and play a chord. It was very strange, and boring."

Roger Glover: "Usually, Ritchie's his own master and it's difficult to tell him what to do."

Graham Bonnet: "We were spending money we didn't have. I didn't know if we were making an album or not. Don Airey said to me that he was going to go home, and that he was leaving the band. So I said I was going to go, too. I went home to LA and stayed. I actually fired myself over the phone. They called and asked me to come back, but I didn't want to. Don, of course, never left. With hindsight, I should have stuck it out. My then-wife, and my mum and dad, they all said to me, '*What are you doing?*'"

Joe Lynn Turner: "My band Fandango was breaking up at the time. I got a phone call from Colin Hart, who was Rainbow's tour manager. He asked me if I fancied an audition. At first, I didn't believe it was Ritchie Blackmore he was talking about, it sounded too good to be true. But he put Ritchie on the phone. I jumped on a train to Syosset, Long Island. Colin picked me up and brought me to the studio. There were Ritchie and Roger Glover, sitting at the desk. I sang some tracks they had together. They asked me if I could write, and I said absolutely. Next thing I know, Ritchie grabs a couple of beers and says, 'You've got the job if you want it.' Did I want it? I needed it. They didn't even allow me to go home to my apartment in New York. They bought me T-shirts and jeans, and I started writing with Roger that very night in a hotel."

***

Henry Small: "Paul Dean called me and told me he'd recommended me to Prism's manager, Bruce Allen, because they were unhappy with their singer. I didn't have anything going on in Los Angeles at the time. I listened to the music. I liked some of it, some of it I didn't. But after Loverboy, I said, 'I'm not turning anything else down. I'm gonna do this, hell or high water.' So I went up to Vancouver and auditioned. At the time, they were in disarray. They really weren't getting along with each other. It wasn't a great gig, but they had a record contract with Capitol and the budget was $250,000 a year."

Rick Springfield: "Usually, it's a sense of inadequacy—or something negative—that drives a person to be creative...I do worry and I'm not always happy, but in my depression, I've written some good songs. It kind of lurks behind me, pushing me not to be an idiot."[4]

Mike Baird: "Rick's timing wasn't that great back then, and he was too loud in the 'phones. I didn't know if he was nervous, or what the deal was. Anyway, we cut this track, 'Jessie's Girl.' We did maybe two or three passes, and then we all went home."

Rick Springfield: "The riff came first. And although it's a pretty simple-sounding song, it wasn't easy to write...It's a bubbly and vivacious song, but it's dark. It's also covetous, which a lot of my music is."[5]

Steve Lukather: "Along with Fee, me and Foster wrote the signature song for that record, 'Talk to Ya Later.'"

Fee Waybill: "Foster said, 'We need a rock song. An uptempo, hard-driving rock song.' We didn't really have one. So Foster said, 'This guy I work with a lot is the number one session guy in LA and he's a great guitar player, and he's really quick.' We were working in a studio out in the Valley from four to midnight. Foster goes, 'Let's just you and I and this guy meet at 10 p.m. and see if we can come up with a song.' Steve Lukather is incredibly brilliant...I mean, instantly, within the first five minutes, he's got the riff and Foster goes, 'Okay, that's it, let's build on that...' By 4 p.m. when the band shows up for the regular session, the song's done. So that didn't go down all that well with them."[6]

Steve Lukather: "The vibe was pretty thick in that studio when I turned up to work on the album."

Bill Champlin: "In some ways the problem with David is, every time he's ever done a band, the band broke up when it was done. He's not really a band producer in that sense. He's better with one singer and dealing with that guy."

Rick Springfield: "I had to convince RCA to put [my dog Ron] on the cover [of the album]. I did this whole mock-up at home, used the shirt and tie that I'd worn for the album before, and they liked it. So I had to go out and buy a shirt 'cause Ron has like an eighteen-inch neck. I went to a Big and Tall Man's Store and asked for an eighteen-inch collar button-down. They wanted to know how long the sleeves should be. When I told them eighteen inches, the guy looked at me like I was some kind of asshole."[7]

Joe Lynn Turner: "We went from Long Island to Copenhagen. I was a little bit intimidated by Ritchie, but he's not a monster. He just really expects perfection. He expects everybody to do the best they can. If you measure up to that he's all yours. He was always experimenting. He changed musical styles like he did his socks, and just then, absolutely he wanted to be played on American radio. He saw everybody else going on the charts and said, 'Wait a minute. This is what I want.' You know, he loves ABBA. He does. He loves melody and composition."

Henry Small: "As we started rehearsing, a producer came up from Capitol, John Carter. He had a great track record. He goes, 'I'll take you,' which was me, 'and Lindsay Mitchell,' who was the main writer in the band to that point. Now, Lindsay at this point was so high he was smoking pot constantly. He was done with the band. He didn't admit that, but he was done. Anyway, John takes us down to Los Angeles, puts together a bunch of great studio musicians, and we did the *Small Change* album. Lindsay quit in the middle of making it, because he wasn't into it. He went back up to Canada, and suddenly *I* was Prism."

Joe Lynn Turner: "Ritchie and me were a good writing team. I'm a melody guy. I make melodies for days. Those hooks are the things you remember, man. In Germany, they call it the 'earworm.'"

Mike Baird: "Rick's a great guy, but here's the thing. A lot of the hits I've played on, I never thought they'd be a hit."

Rick Springfield: "When 'Jessie's Girl' was climbing the charts, there was a voice haunting me, telling me, 'They're going to find out you're a fake.'"[8]

Henry Small: "The album comes out, and it sells close to half a million copies. Capitol was quite enthused. We toured extensively, opening for everybody. And then the record company deducts all of their tour support from your royalties. You're working for the company store. So by the time you get home, you have no money. You learn about the music business, that's for sure."

Joe Lynn Turner: "When I got handed 'I Surrender,' it sounded somewhat different. I sang it my way. The way I phrased it, and I changed a few melody lines. Russ Ballard later on said a very nice thing about me. He said he never thought of the song as a hit until he heard my interpretation. Of course, he never gave me a writing credit."

Steve Lukather: "'Talk to Ya Later' became the Tubes' first radio hit. My credit on the record ended up being so small you'd have needed a jeweler's eye to find it."

CHAPTER THIRTY-FOUR

FOREIGNER MAKES 4.

"I fell on my knees and asked the Lord to get me out of this hell."

Mick Jones: "Cracks had begun to show. I felt we were losing focus generally, and divisions had opened up within the band. Both Ian McDonald and Al Greenwood felt they should have a greater input into the songwriting, which Lou and I had monopolized. I called a meeting that was attended by Lou, Dennis Elliott, Rick Wills, and me. The other three seemed to feel the same way as me, so the decision was made to fire Ian and Al."

Lou Gramm: "That was one of the worst moments of my life. They were good friends and very good players, and they didn't see it coming either."[1]

Mick Jones: "Just as it had been with Ed, it was a difficult and tortuous process. Of course I have regrets. You're in the studio and touring with these guys who also are your friends. It's like a second family. In hindsight, I'm not sure whether it was the right or wrong thing to have done. But it was certainly cold."

***

Al Greenwood: "Foreigner was one person doing everything. Basically, Mick Jones."[2]

Lou Gramm: "We had sixteen to eighteen songs. They needed work, but I thought they were strong."[3]

Mick Jones: "I totally went into the *4* record on a mission. I wanted to show more dimensions of the band and to create the complete album. Mutt Lange came over to New York to be interviewed for the job of being our producer, and he was so obviously on the ball. One of Mutt's great strengths is he'd come up in radio in South Africa. He'd started out singing jingles. Because of that background, he had a very acute pop sensibility, a flair for short, sharp choruses, and also an understanding of the discipline of being in a studio."

Lou Gramm: "Mutt didn't tactfully beat around the bush. He told us that if we released ten of the best out [of the songs we had], we'd be lucky if we had a Top 20 album. Then he left for two weeks while we frantically rewrote everything."[4]

Mick Jones: "Mutt was pushy, challenging, and absolutely relentless. The two of us are both quite strong-willed personalities and he didn't mind upsetting me, but we managed to harness that together. We pushed each other to be at our best. Believe me, it could very easily have gone completely the other way."

Lou Gramm: "Sometimes it was the case of seeking perfection at the cost of spontaneity. But that ultimately was up to Mick."[5]

Mick Jones: "Our first big bust-up was over drums. We were at the Record Plant in New York. The third or fourth day of the sessions, Mutt came in with these electronic drums he wanted us to use. I wanted real drums, but Mutt was insistent that Dennis's timing wasn't perfect. So I took Dennis out into the main room and together the two of us ran through one song, 'Break It Up,' the whole thing, top to bottom. Dennis was right on the money, absolutely flawless. I stomped back into the control room and said to Mutt, quite aggressively, 'Is *that* what you were looking for?'"

Thomas Dolby: "I was desperately trying to get a record deal, and in the meantime taking any gig I could to help pay the rent. I'd sent a demo tape with five or six songs on it to various record labels and publishers. One of those companies was Zomba, which Mutt Lange had formed with two compatriots of his from South Africa. Mutt was back in England on a break from recording *4*. He heard my tape, really liked the keyboard playing, and asked me to come over and work on the Foreigner record. I thought of Mutt as the AC/DC guy, and I'd never really been a guitar-rock fan. But he offered to pay me $500 a day, so I jumped at the chance. They were under the gun to finish the record. They'd already put keyboards on the whole album, but they weren't happy with them. When I got to New York, they were mostly recording Lou Gramm's vocals."

Lou Gramm: "Mutt worked us very hard. When I was singing the songs, he'd come into the studio and go, 'Can't you sing them a little more like this?' He would sing and I would go, 'Mutt, that sounds exactly like AC/DC. That's what *they* do, but we do something completely different.'"[6]

Mick Jones: "'Juke Box Hero' was made up of a couple of ideas. Lou came up with that initial line, 'Take one guitar…' We messed around with that, and then I put together the chorus part. I had the title as well. We morphed the two bits into one, and it just worked. I was pretty proud of the power we got in it."

Thomas Dolby: "Mutt was an incredible perfectionist, incredibly fastidious. He would make you do twenty-three takes of things even when you were way past the point of diminishing returns. He was staying in a suite in a hotel on Central Park South, and he let me have the pull-out couch in the living room. Often, he'd come back from the studio a couple of hours later than me. I would hear him in his bedroom, playing an acoustic guitar, singing Van Morrison songs. Two or three hours later, he'd get up and go back to the studio. In the studio, I worked more with Mick Jones than anyone else. He had the roadies set up some amps and a Fender Rhodes so that we could jam together. That, traditionally, is how musicians bond, but I don't jam. My fingers are always a couple of bars behind my brain. He must have thought I was a complete amateur."

Mick Jones: "With 'Waiting for a Girl Like You,' it was that feeling of just grabbing something out of the air and letting it flow. Then again, it was one of the most emotionally draining songs I've written."

Thomas Dolby: "I remember the night I did the intro to 'Waiting for a Girl Like You.' The brief they gave me was, 'See if you can replace the Fender Rhodes we have with a more interesting sound. And if you want to do some atmospherics before the song starts, then have a go.' I got my Micromoog, and one finger note at a time, I played these long sustained notes in the key of A minor with very slight variations. I'd hold the note and then just twiddle a knob here and there. I'd read how 10CC did something similar with the vocal tracks on 'I'm Not in Love,' pushing them up and down on the faders. It was 9 a.m. the next morning, early for rock musicians, when the band came in to listen to what I'd done. I put the tape on, let the intro go by, then a couple of lines into the rough vocal I stopped it. There was a hush. They all looked a bit perplexed, and then Rick Wills spoke up: 'It's a bit like massage music, innit?' I said, 'Um, I'd call it ambient rather than massage music.' To which he replied, 'Actually, I could kill for a massage right now. Can we get someone in?'"

Mick Jones: "The track we prepared for 'Urgent' had a bit of an urban vibe to it. It had the slap bass and the funk thing going on. I was living in a house in upstate New York at the time. I went home one afternoon, a beautiful day, and I sat in the living room with a little cassette player, going over and over the song. I wrote the lyric in a couple of hours, top to bottom. When you get that sort of flow going and it's fresh, you just have to ride it."

Lou Gramm: "We knew 'Urgent' needed something [else], but we didn't know it needed saxophone. I was looking through the *Village Voice* and saw that Junior Walker was playing at a club that was not that far away."[7]

Mick Jones: "We were on a break in the studio, and I was reading the *Village Voice*, just to check out who was in town. The instrumental track for 'Urgent' was playing very softly in the background and we'd left space for a solo. I'm flicking through the paper, I see Junior Walker's name, and I just put two and two together. The song felt like it had the feel of one of those classic Junior Walker things, like 'Roadrunner.'"

Lou Gramm: "We shut the lights off and turned the power off in the studio and went to see him."[8]

Mick Jones: "I went down to the club he was playing and sat through three sets. Eventually, his son, who was playing drums in his band, recognized me. Junior came out and his son said to him, 'Dad, this dude is serious, and he wants to talk to you.'"

Thomas Dolby: "I was around when they recorded Junior Walker. That was a very exciting session."

Mick Jones: "For all the stuff he'd done at Motown, Junior had never before overdubbed onto a track. That was the first hurdle, getting him comfortable. Then he goes over to the mic, pulls up a chair, and sits down like a jazz player. We did a few passes, and he was playing this sort of lounge-type of fill without any of his trademark high notes, or squeaks. He informed me this was his new style. I had to tell him, with all due respect, that his new style was not what we were looking for."

Lou Gramm: "We got him to play about five solos, took the best pieces, and we made it into one kicking solo."[9]

Mick Jones: "Mutt and I spent two nights completely dedicated to editing the solo and making it sound right. Junior did three or four takes. They were all great, but they weren't great all the way through, so we had to chop and change. The finished solo was made up of something ridiculous like twenty-four snippets of tape stuck together. Later, Junior came out and did the song with us at five arena shows and he played the identical solo, note for note. It was stunning."

Thomas Dolby: "Having been hired for two days, I ended up doing something like twenty-four days in the studio with them."

Mick Jones: "It took an agonizing amount of time to get that album done, almost a year all told."

Thomas Dolby: "It was not uncommon for Mutt to sit for twelve, thirteen, fourteen hours on the trot in the control room, working on just the drum sound. One day, just like any other day, we'd been sitting there like that, and Mutt suddenly pipes up, 'We need to go to the park!' So, we order a limo, and him and me and his engineer Mike Shipley drive off uptown. Mutt goes, 'Isn't there a giant toy store around here?' The limo driver says, 'FAO Schwarz?' 'Stop off there!' Mutt runs into the store, and he comes back out with every brand and size of Frisbee they had. We drive another few blocks to Central Park, where Mutt again runs off ahead of us. Next thing, we're all of us hurling these Frisbees around the park. After ten minutes at most, Mutt shouts out, *'What the fuck are we doing?!* We've got an album to make!' And back to the studio we go in the limo."

Mick Jones: "When I heard the finished record, I knew we'd made a big album. It did, however, come at a cost. I was there for every minute of the sessions, and I was in desperate need of a break. The effects of that have lasted right up to today. Even now, I've an almost pathological aversion to hanging out in recording studios."

Thomas Dolby: "I went home with a pile of cash in my pocket. That basically enabled me to pay for my own album."

Andrew McNeice: "It's not possible to think of a more influential band during that time frame than Foreigner. And in 1981, with *4*, they simply exploded that whole power ballad genre."

Mick Jones: "Rather than take any time off, we went back out on the road within two weeks of finishing the record. For eighteen months, we headlined stadiums and sold-out venues all over the world. It was tough to stay grounded in any possible sense. Jimmy Page and Robert Plant came to see our show in Munich. That was a huge surprise, I didn't even know they were there until they walked out onstage together. We did Little Richard's 'Lucille' with them. To me, it was a sign of validation. Like, 'Wow, we're being accepted on *this* level.' A huge feast followed that show at the Four Seasons restaurant in Munich. Let's just say we had lots of jolly good fun that night and leave it at that. The best word to describe the whole tour would be 'extravagant.'"

Lou Gramm: "Foreigner had reached a peak of success, and all the trappings of success were part of our lives…One particular day, I had a nightmarish night and just knew that I didn't want that stuff to be part of my life anymore. I fell on my knees and asked the Lord to get me out of this hell."[10]

Mick Jones: "There was a little too much imbibing the cocktails of the day, shall we say. All too often when happy hour would go on for much longer than sixty minutes. Very self-indulgent. Living the high life. No TVs flying out of hotel windows, just lots of money, and you can very easily lose focus when you're experiencing that type of success."

Lou Gramm: "We were emotionally, physically, and mentally spent."[11]

Mick Jones: "In the back of my mind there was also the constant question of where we could possibly go from that point."

CHAPTER THIRTY-FIVE

STRANGERS WAITIN', UP AND DOWN THE BOULEVARD...

"Steve Perry, Neal Schon, and Jonathan Cain. They were three of the most talented people I ever met."

John Kalodner: "It took Journey until 1981 to really become a powerhouse. Then they were the biggest American band."

Jonathan Cain: "Perry had that pop sensibility. I followed his lead, he followed mine—and Neal added the rock edge to it."[1]

Steve Smith: "I can't remember anything different about the way we made *Escape*, other than that we had Jon Cain in the band at that point. We had the same rehearsal space, at the warehouse we rented in Oakland, California. We would go there and spend five days a week writing and rehearsing, just the same as always."

Jonathan Cain: "We know what rock 'n' roll is and we know who our audience is, and it's a blue-collar band...We write songs for people who go to work every day."[2]

***

Steve Perry: "Everything I write comes back to high school. I know it sounds funny, but *everything*. It all comes from the emotions I grew into during my adolescence. Those moments are not to be tossed away. If something means something to you, go back and get it and make it part of your life. And anyone who doesn't understand how important that is, you tell them to fuck off."[3]

Steve Smith: "I don't feel like we were making music for our generation. We were making music for people in junior high school, high school, and people in their early college years."

John Kalodner: "I did a lot of work later on with Steve Perry, Neal Schon, and Jonathan Cain. They were three of the most talented people I ever met."

Steve Smith: "Jonathan's personality was injected into the band. He was a piano and synth player, versus Gregg Rolie, who was more of a Hammond B3 player. Plus, Jon could play rhythm guitar and that added another dimension to the music. The act of coming up with the music involved a lot of improvisation. Steve Perry, I think, is a gifted improviser. That band could play almost anything, and Steve would find a melody that would work over it."

Jonathan Cain: "[Perry] sang 'Mother, Father' in one take. I've never seen anything like him, and I probably won't ever again."[4]

Steve Smith: "We'd have our cassettes running and then we'd listen back and weed through the ideas. There was no set way of doing anything, but it was a process. There was time taken after the music was written to write the lyrics. Then we'd fine-tune the songs and rehearse them, so we were ready to perform them in the studio without a lot of takes."

Neal Schon: "I hated my 'Who's Crying Now' guitar work when I did it at first. I probably did, I don't know, fifteen takes. So, out of pure frustration, I played the simplest thing, just kind of like being a smart-ass. And I went, 'There you go. That what you want?' And they go, 'It's fucking perfect.'"[5]

Steve Smith: "I even worked out a lot of drum fills. For example, my fills for 'Open Arms' were all worked out."

Herbie Herbert: "Perry's in there trying to sing 'Open Arms' with [the producers] Kevin Elson, Mike Stone. And I'm going, 'He's singing his heart out, he's trying to nail this fucking thing.' Neal and Jon Cain were fucking just denigrating Steve and just talking stink. I mean, you know, it was, 'Is that Perry Como?' And they're just teasing him awfully. I took Neal and Jon into the back room and go, 'What the fuck are you doing, man? He's obviously written a fantastic song.' Jon Cain goes, 'He didn't write that, I wrote that.' And I was stunned. I just looked at him and my mouth dropped open. I go, 'Just making your behavior all the more unbelievable.' I mean, they were seriously giving him shit."[6]

Neal Schon: "I fought hard on 'Open Arms.' I was not getting it and didn't want to get it."[7]

Jonathan Cain: "On the last page of my notebook, I found three words scribbled: 'Don't stop believin''…The words my father had given me on a long-distance phone call one night."[8]

Steve Perry: "I came in one day and I've always liked quarter notes on the piano. I said to Jon Cain, 'We got to write something with quarters on the piano.' And so he started doing some changes. I picked up the bass…and I just start messing with that."[9]

***

Steve Smith: "That was another one where my whole drum part was worked out ahead of time. I approached it in rehearsal at first more like a jazz drummer, but then as a rock drummer I zeroed in on the best grooves and fills and they became fixed."

Jonathan Cain: "We broke all the rules with that song. The chorus only happens once, and it comes in right at the end. And Neal solos even before Steve sings."[10]

Steve Perry: "The song started to take on a life of its own... It literally became a Neal Schon, Steve Perry, and Jon Cain song because those are the three writers that contributed the most to the melodies that changed the hook lines, and the lyrics."[11]

Jonathan Cain: "I wrote it about the '70s... It represents all of what Journey is."[12]

Steve Perry: "We had just finished a show at Cobo Arena... one of my favorite places to play in Detroit. We had done a great show that night and the hotel we stayed at was right across the square from there. I was up on the top floor and wasn't tired... I [was] staring out the window, looking down, and the streetlights of Detroit at that time were kind of an orange color. The amber was washing down... It's like 3 a.m. and these people are still milling around. So I thought, 'Wow, "street people."' When it came time to write the lyrics, I told Jon Cain about this moment... And then we came up with 'hiding somewhere in the night.' It came from downtown Detroit. It really did."[13]

Steve Smith: "It seemed like a very good album to me, but I didn't know that *Escape* was particularly exceptional. And I didn't feel like it was going to be that much bigger than our previous albums."

Jonathan Cain: "I thought, 'They're either going to love this or hate it.' I had my fingers crossed going into it. Then, when our great hippie lawyer [Hal Kant], a really cool guy, heard [*Escape*], he said, 'Jon, you're never going to have to worry about where another dime comes from. This will be the font of life for you.' He was really sincere, and I guess he was right."[14]

Herbie Herbert: "We had this big party for *Escape* at Fantasy in Berkeley with all the press, media, and radio there to hear this new masterpiece. Perry's in there with Jon Cain, and somebody suggests, 'Wow, this is so great. Jon Cain sure did bring a lot as a songwriter.' And he did! But boy, Perry bristled so much at the notion that Jon Cain had contributed much of anything. He just proceeded to dismiss and diminish Jon Cain's contributions and involvement to the point where Jon Cain had to leave the room and was out in the parking lot. I mean, bawling like a fucking baby. So I went out to the parking lot and said, 'Now you see what happens when you run into an even bigger asshole than yourself. This is what it feels like… You have met your fucking match.'"[15]

Steve Smith: "We'd had albums that were platinum or double platinum. *Escape*, in its first year of release, sold five million copies."

Derek Oliver: "It was totally the sound of Middle America right then."

Paul Elliott: "They are fundamentally great songs, brilliantly performed. They're made to sound great on the radio. And if you've ever driven around America with the FM radio on, that's when that music makes complete sense."

Dennis Dries: "I heard 'Don't Stop Believin'' just yesterday. I was driving in my car, and it came on the radio. I reached down to change the station, but I stopped. I just couldn't turn it off. I ended up listening to the whole song and singing along to it. It's become part of our lives."

Donald Roeser: "We played the Fourth of July Festival with Journey. They were headlining to 100,000 people at the Rose Bowl in Pasadena. I remember meeting Angie Dickinson that day. That was a thrill."

***

Steve Perry: "The pace was fast, and we never stopped. It was the '80s. Everybody was pretty much having a good time, put it that way.

Partying comes with all sorts of toasty behaviors. And that's about all I'll say about that."[16]

Herbie Herbert: "Neal is doing cocaine, drinking, fucking the chicks, doing all the things that Steve couldn't do as a lead singer. And then going out onstage totally hammered and playing perfectly."[17]

Steve Smith: "In some ways it was a whirlwind. Things were moving at a fast tempo. Life had accelerated. It required a lot of me physically and emotionally to keep up with the demands of being in the band and performing onstage, and then trying to have a life as an individual with a wife and child.... But I had a perspective. I took the work seriously, but not the idea of being a rock star."

Steve Perry: "The hardest thing to explain to the rest of the band members [was] the neurotic fear that I'd be going through because I'm in one city tonight, and all I know is I've got to give it everything and I'm not going to skate it, I'm going to put it out there. And I would. And I wouldn't know how much I borrowed from tomorrow's show until the next day. So I'd wake up in the morning in fear. Do I have laryngitis? Is [my voice] gone? Is it there?"[18]

Herbie Herbert: "[Perry] would send Sigmund Freud to the hills, screaming and ripping out his hair. He's a tough nut to figure."[19]

Danny Kortchmar: "Steve's a great cat. Of course, his voice is just as good as you expect it to be, but he's a lovely guy, too. I worked with him several times and thought the world of him."

Herbie Herbert: "If you were drowning in the ocean, and Steve Perry came along in his luxury liner, he would offer you a life raft in such a way that you would decline it. I'm not just talking about you. I'm talking about anybody. The terms and conditions would be such that you would have to pass."[20]

Steve Perry: "The beginning of the end was when Neal started his solo career. Neal did a solo album with Jan Hammer [*Untold Passion*, released in November 1981]...I said to Herbie, 'I think this is a bad idea.' That it would fracture the band on some level."[21]

CHAPTER THIRTY-SIX

THE REVOLUTION WILL BE TELEVISED.

"People say to me, 'When did music change?' Easy. The summer of 1981."

Bob Pittman: "The president of NBC was a guy named Herb Schlosser, and Herb had decided I was his protégé. He said to me, 'You take the slot after *Saturday Night Live* and do anything you want to do.' What do I do? I do video radio. Music news with video clips. A show called *Album Tracks*. At that time, everybody was playing around with these videos, trying to figure out what to do with them. They were produced primarily to be shown on TV shows in Europe, like *The Old Grey Whistle Test*, *Top of the Pops*, and *Rockpalast* in Germany. After that, I jumped over to a new company being formed by Warner Bros. and American Express, Warner-AmEx, to program The Movie Channel."

Les Garland: "I was a year and a half into my contract with Atlantic Records out in Los Angeles. In January of 1981, Bob Pittman phoned me. He was second-in-command at this new company, and his question to me was, 'What percentage of the artists at Atlantic Records get to make music videos?' I guessed 25 percent of the acts. Let's say you had signed a new American act and wanted to break them in Europe. It was less expensive to send a video than to send the act to tour in Europe."

Bob Pittman: "I programmed The Movie Channel sort of like a radio station. It was a twenty-four-hour paid TV service with subscription fees. Low-tech, on-demand programming. We decided that we were ready to do another network, and I put forward a plan to do a music video radio station. The board of directors at Warner-AmEx thought it was a crazy idea, but my boss, Jack Schneider, God bless him, got us a meeting with Steve Ross, who was CEO of Warners, and Jim Robinson, who was the CEO of American Express. Doug Morris at Atlantic Records was an old friend of mine, and I got him into the meeting, too, so he would vouch for me."

Les Garland: "A month later, Pittman phones again. He goes, 'Confidentially, we're thinking of starting a music video channel on cable.' I thought it was a killer idea. Then he says, 'But hey, Gar, we're looking to raise $40 million, and I need support from the Warners side. Would you be willing to talk to Doug Morris?' I phoned Doug. I go, 'First of all, Pittman's brilliant. Second, this is a brilliant idea.' Doug went into the meeting and voted yes. I don't know for sure, but I've been told that Doug's was the deciding vote."

Bob Pittman: "It was actually Jim Robinson who really got the approval. He told me, 'The reason I did it was because I knew you'd had such success as a radio programmer, and we were betting on you.' That was the way it went down, and then of course we had to scramble to get this thing on the air. First off, we had to try to get the permission and license rights to actually play the music from all the record companies, which was a battle in itself. Then I wanted us to have VJs, because it was a video radio station. No one would bond with a jukebox. People bond with human beings."

Kevin Cronin: "I was the first person approached to be a VJ, and I turned it down. I thought, 'These guys are clueless.'"[1]

***

Bob Pittman: "I don't recall us ever having that kind of conversation about REO Speedwagon. On the last day of the auditions, my old assistant at NBC called me up and said, 'Hey, could you give an intern we have over here an audition?' I go, 'Look, I'll do you a favor. If she can get there before 5 p.m., we'll put her on tape.'"

Martha Quinn: "I got myself through New York University doing two things. I worked on the college radio station, and I did TV commercials for Clearasil, Country Town Lemonade, Aspirin, and Campbell's Soup. I graduated in July 1981, but I was still working at my college dorm and also interning at WNBC Radio. I go up to WNBC one day, and the guy I was interning for, Buzz Brindle, tells me about MTV. Buzz says, 'Martha, that's what you should do.' He picked up the phone and dialed Bob Pittman. I dashed over to this TV studio in Hell's Kitchen wearing sneakers and a T-shirt that my friend from Nashville had given me that had an iron-on patch, 'Country Music Is in My Blood.' I didn't have an ounce of makeup on."

Bob Pittman: "The next morning the guys called me up and said, 'Hey, we need to show you something. This woman you sent over, she's great.'"

Martha Quinn: "Could you even imagine. I'm twenty-three years old. I'm out of college for two weeks. The executive producer of MTV at the time, Julian Goldberg, calls me into his office at Hell's Kitchen, sits me down, and says to me, 'So, how would you like to go on TV, talk about rock 'n' roll, and fly around the country interviewing rock stars?'"

Bob Pittman: "The biggest problem we had in the beginning was that most artists didn't have videos. It was mostly English artists. They called it the second British Invasion. But who'd heard of Flock of Seagulls, Madness, and the Police? These were not big acts. REO Speedwagon, Styx, Journey—that was the big American acts. I think we had 250 videos to start this channel, and that was it. The bet we made was that if it succeeded, they would start to make more videos in the industry. Then the launch night, August 1, 1981, was a disaster. The first hour we were on air, the VJs would say, 'This is...' and the wrong song would play."

Martha Quinn: "I'd only been there for a couple of weeks. All of the crew and VJs, they rented a school bus for us. I guess it was the only thing they could find, but we were driven out to this bar in New Jersey called the Loft. It was down in the basement. They had a couple of TVs put up around the place."

Bob Pittman: "We didn't have much money. The reason we used the moon landing stuff for our graphics was because it was high quality and free. The original idea at the top of the hour was to have Neil Armstrong say, 'One step for man, one giant leap for mankind.' That and...'MTV!' We sent Neil Armstrong a letter saying, 'We're going to use your voice. If we don't hear from you by this date, we deem that to be permission.' A week before we launched, we got a letter telling us we couldn't use it. Fuck it, we had to go without the voiceover. Years later I met Neil Armstrong, told him the story, and he said, 'Nobody ever asked me.'"

Les Garland: "They were only in Des Moines, Iowa, and Tulsa. They had a total of maybe 200,000 homes."

Bob Pittman: "We were not on in Manhattan. We went out somewhere in New Jersey. Buggles was the first video played, of course."

Pet Benatar: "We were the second video played on the inaugural day. A performance video of the Rascals song we'd covered."[2]

Bob Pittman: "Pat Benatar's 'You Better Run' was *supposed* to have been the second video, but something else might have gone out. The launch was such an absolute catastrophe, the first hour showreel we put out was not the first hour of MTV. It was a reconstructed version of what we wanted it to be."

***

Pat Benatar: "It seemed like they played us round the clock, every hour...In one week our world changed."[3]

Les Garland: "In October of 1981, Pittman asked me if I'd be interested in coming into MTV as the highest-ranking officer and to oversee programming. Off I went to New York. I had my yellow pad out on the red-eye, and I'm scribbling out a bunch of notes to myself. I'm thinking about what MTV is. The next morning at 9 a.m., there was a memo out to multiple vice presidents. 'In the event you are ever asked by anyone, anywhere, what is MTV, here's your answer: MTV—Music Television—is the world's first twenty-four-hour music video channel in stereo on cable television.' It was the old Marshall McLuhan rule, 'If we say it, and they print it enough, people will eventually get it.' People have told me I invented what they now call a mission statement."

Martha Quinn: "You could work in a deli that Les Garland comes into, and he orders his sandwich and walks out, and you will know that he's a character. That's not something that you have to figure out over time."

John Parr: "I'd hang out with the boss of MTV, Les Garland, and he was crazy, a lunatic. We'd go out drinking and he'd stop traffic in Times Square just for fun. He'd actually walk out into the middle of the street."

Les Garland: "In the early days, a high amount of my time was dedicated to creating believers. We had to go out and prove to the record labels that music videos were very similar to records, or songs on the radio, and that if it's a hit, it's a hit, it's a hit, and it will translate to music sales. MTV was born out of AOR radio. I mean, the first words uttered on MTV were, 'Ladies and gentlemen, rock 'n' roll.' That was the original idea."

Bob Pittman: "Those kinds of bands had music that was very popular. And at the end of the day, we were music television, and a hit song would drive anybody. I don't care how cool you looked. If you didn't have a hit song, you weren't going to have a hit video."

***

Kevin Cronin: "We had the Number One record when MTV started out, so that just fueled the phenomenon even further."[4]

Mike Reno: "Loverboy sent them two or three videos for the first week they opened, because they didn't have enough to play twenty-four hours a day...So, they played us, like, ten times a day, and it made us hugely famous."[5]

Les Garland: "In truth, MTV really didn't take off all that quickly. It was very difficult for us to get distribution at cable. The cable operators didn't get it, or really believe in it. It took well over a year, going on two, before we busted into the Top 10 major markets."

Eddie Money: "[My manager] Bill Graham was a very smart man. He said to me, 'I think this MTV is going to be really big.' So we made videos. The first video I made was for 'Shaking.' It really helped my career I gotta tell you."[6]

Cliff Bernstein: "Polygram [Records] didn't have any videos to give MTV. All they had were these live videos that we shot of Def Leppard...And all of a sudden, the record started selling—apparently with nothing going on. It was because [MTV] was playing 'Bringin' On the Heartbreak.'"[7]

Martha Quinn: "I didn't actually quit my job at the NYU dorm right away. At first, it still seemed very odd because we were putting our blood, sweat, and tears into this project that nobody saw. Because we weren't in Manhattan. None of our friends saw it. *We* didn't see it. It was this weird kind of twilight zone. You had to say to people, 'No, I swear I have a job.'"

Billy Squier: "People say to me, 'When did music change?' Easy. The summer of 1981. MTV. To me, this was a good idea that went totally off the rails."

***

Steve Lukather: "Then all of a sudden, MTV comes along. Wait a second. What is this? Is this good or bad? It was like the first time we saw the drum machine work. We were kind of skeptical at first, but they told us, 'This is going to be great promotion. It's going to be a free channel, no commercials on it, nobody makes any money. It'll be in the eyeballs of everybody across America.' They sold everybody into giving up the rights to everything, because nobody was going to make any money. Bullshit like that."

Bob Pittman: "Now, over time, what's interesting is that those artists that didn't look good, the ones that looked sort of nerdy and goofy and awkward, they fell out of favor. It took a while, but it hurt their brand because they didn't look as cool as they sounded."

Billy Squier: "I knew Bob Pittman, really smart guy, really liked him, but what MTV did, not intentionally, was destroy the sanctity of the listener and the radio. You put on the radio and hear a song. You don't see an image, but you hear the lyrics. You might even make up your own lyrics because you can't hear what they're singing. But you can make that song your own. It's like Axl Rose getting laid to 'Calley Oh.' That's his song. And you can't do that with a video. MTV completely shattered that bond."

CHAPTER THIRTY-SEVEN

QUARTERFLASH AND THEIR ONE-HIT WONDER.

"For six months, I was a deer in headlights."

Marv Ross: "Rindy and I met in high school [in Portland]. We played our first gig as seniors as an acoustic duet, doing Dylan and Joni Mitchell kind of stuff."[1]

Rindy Ross: "I played saxophone briefly in the fifth grade and put it down because I was the only girl saxophone player in my fifth-grade class, and I was quite intimidated."[2]

Marv Ross: "We went through college and played just whenever we could, little college gigs. We got our teaching degrees. Rindy taught fifth grade, and I ended up teaching junior high English."[3]

Rindy Ross: "[Marv and I] were married by then... We put together a covers band in central Oregon that was called Jones Road, because we lived on Jones Road. We played bars on weekends."[4]

Marv Ross: "We had quite a bit of success playing in the central Oregon area, and we just decided, 'Let's take a shot at this.'"[5]

Rindy Ross: "Marv was getting itchy... He said, 'I really want to try to do music full-time.' He was ready to just go for it. I ended up taking a year's leave of absence because I wasn't."[6]

Marv Ross: "We moved back to Portland and started a band called Seafood Mama. We played everything from country-rock to a little bit of new wave, to swing music."[7]

Rindy Ross: "There were five of us. We had bass and drums and guitar, and me picking up the saxophone. I still had my father's saxophone and decided to see what I remembered about playing. I was playing by ear various solos and stuff that I had heard, especially with Marv's original tunes. We were playing at least three nights a week and sometimes more than that. We played for about three years, finally working our way into downtown Portland [when] we had enough of a following to play at more coveted clubs."[8]

Marv Ross: "In that band we recorded 'Harden My Heart.'"[9]

Rindy Ross: "Marv had this song. He took the title from a poem that a friend of ours had written. [It] was one of those things that happened really quick. We recorded it in our basement with this reel-to-reel that we had financed from getting a little loan from Marv's dad."[10]

Marv Ross: "I was playing this melody that ended up being the sax solo that started the song. I actually wrote that on guitar."[11]

Rindy Ross: "Marv said, 'Well, I want you playing saxophone on something at the beginning,' and he kind of came up with a couple of notes and had me just fool around with it."[12]

Marv Ross: "That's the one thing that sort of caught my eye and ear.

That 'harden my heart' phrase. I called the friend who wrote poetry and said, 'I'm gonna use this thing. I'll pay you some money for it.'"[13]

Rindy Ross: "It was a 45 that we put out locally and distributed ourselves."[14]

Marv Ross: "The Seafood Mama version sold 10,000 copies in Portland and Seattle. We thought it sounded like a hit song, but you never know."[15]

Rindy Ross: "An A&R person from the Geffen label came up to see us. Geffen was a new label. They had signed some big heavyweights, including John Lennon, Elton John, and Donna Summer."[16]

Marv Ross: "They gave me an advance. I'd never seen money like that... They gave us a budget for the record, which was $100,000. We could afford to get an apartment in LA and go down there and start working at the legendary Record Plant with John Boylan, who produced Boston and Linda Ronstadt."[17]

Rindy Ross: "John Boylan said that he really liked the band, but he wasn't sure that we worked well as far as the instrumentation. He decided that the deal would just be for Marv and me, which was really difficult. We'd been a band."[18]

Marv Ross: "It was just the two of us with studio musicians. The album took almost a year to record and during that time we found the other four musicians playing together in a Northwest band called Pilot. We got the name Quarterflash from a book about early Australian slang phrases. In the early 1900s, Australians would refer to newcomers to the country as being 'one quarter flash and three parts stupid.'"[19]

Rindy Ross: "We began to really focus in on a new band... and having it be definitely kind of an AOR rock niche instead of a bar band all over the map."[20]

Marv Ross: "My guitar solo was changed [on the re-recorded version of 'Harden My Heart'], but that was the only thing really. Of course, it was recorded at the Record Plant instead of our basement in Portland, so the sounds of everything were better. We did not anticipate it being *such* a big hit."[21]

Rindy Ross: "I couldn't believe any of it was happening, honestly. For six months, I was a deer in headlights."[22]

Marv Ross: "Geffen threw us out on tour with Loverboy right away, before the record even got going. All of a sudden, instead of playing bars, we were playing in colleges and ice rinks. So, we jumped to that 8,000 to 10,000 people kind of thing."[23]

Rindy Ross: "We were thirty when we were signed. Not twenty-one. And I think just having that little bit of extra life experience, we were not too dazzled. Like, not too full of ourselves."[24]

Marv Ross: "[We went on and made two more albums], and it had run its course. We were assigned to John Kalodner... We'd go have a meeting with him, and he clearly was not interested in anything we were doing. Luckily, we'd made a lot of money. [That] gave us financial freedom to take some time off and figure out what we wanted to do with the rest of our lives."[25]

Rindy Ross: "We decided not to sign to another record label. We came home to Portland. It felt like our writing, and our creativity, was not our own. And we had no control over it after that experience."[26]

Marv Ross: "[But] I feel so lucky to have had a hit song that everyone knows."[27]

CHAPTER THIRTY-EIGHT

TOTO: HOUSE BAND ON THE BIGGEST ALBUM OF ALL TIME.

"If this is a hit, I will run naked down Hollywood Boulevard."

David Paich: "We pretty much figured the next album was going to be our last one with Columbia. The record company's thinking was, 'We'll see how this one performs and then decide if we pick up their option.'"

Steve Lukather: "Columbia was, like, 'If you guys don't have a hit this next time, you're toast.' That was a wake-up call. We decided to stop fighting what we are, and just *be*. First day of the sessions, Paich came in with 'Rosanna.'"

David Paich: "It's as close as I ever got to consciously putting my head to writing a hit. You can't do that all the time, but at that moment, I'd been working with all kinds of different people, so I was able to put the amalgam formed into one song."

Steve Lukather: "When Paich brought it to us, it had a Bo Diddley groove. It ended up being what it became within a period of ten minutes.

We started jamming, got the feel of the verse, and then it was, 'Roll the tape!' The take you hear on the album was take two."

David Paich: "That song really shows off Toto at its best. It had everything in it from the brass to the individual solos, to the harmonies, to Luke and Bobby sharing the lead vocals. We put so many hooks into 'Rosanna,' that's how we knew it was going to be a hit."

Paul Elliott: "There's something playful about 'Rosanna.' Those guys grew up listening to Motown as well as rock music, and it was all in there."

Steve Lukather: "The live jam shit at the end? That was just us in our early twenties feeling our oats."

David Paich: "Rosanna Arquette was going out with Steve Porcaro at the time."

Steve Lukather: "The two of them were very much an item and Paich copped Rosanna's name for the song."

David Paich: "It wasn't about her. I just stole her name. Publicly, she didn't like being told the song was about her, but I found out from friends she kind of got a kick out of it."

Steve Lukather: "Man, Rosanna Arquette went through a long period of denial that the song was about her, and of hating it. Rosanna was not hard on the eyes at all, and she and Steve had a very passionate but tumultuous relationship. How can I describe her best? She's an interesting woman and a nice bunch of people. Anyway, the record company heard 'Rosanna,' lost their minds, and thank God, we had their blessings again."

David Paich: "We played 'Rosanna' for the president of Columbia. He said, 'Go ahead, finish the album.' I'd have to say it's the song that I'm most proud of, and it was our 'Sgt. Pepper…' for that album. It's a damn near perfect record."

Steve Lukather: "A little heat had been taken off of us. So let's go have some fun and the big production. We were checked into Sunset Sound with the great Al Schmitt engineering for us. Al had worked with Steely Dan and Neil Young. He was a no-nonsense New Yorker, a seasoned pro, and an all-around legend. We were in Studio Two. The Van Halen guys were in the front room making *Diver Down*. Prince was in Studio Three with his band. There was a basketball court in the middle of the complex and we'd all hang out there together between sessions. With the exception, of course, of Prince."

David Paich: "Lukather wrote the big ballad, 'I Won't Hold You Back.'"

Steve Lukather: "Paich was encouraging everybody else in the band, and me especially, to write. He was like, 'That ballad you were playing me? Come on, man, finish that.' I thought it was just too pop, but he insisted, 'No, we'll do a big Elton John production with the strings.'"

David Paich: "We got to use the London Symphony Orchestra on that one. Paul McCartney and Wings had just put out 'Live and Let Die.' When the orchestra came in halfway through that, I said, 'We've got to up our dimension here!' I got together with James Newton Howard and my dad and wrote a string chart for our song."

Steve Lukather: "It was a case of, 'We have the dough, so let's go to London!' If we were going to go out, we were going out with a bang."

David Paich: "That was an incredible experience. We were just beaming from ear to ear the whole time we were there."

Steve Lukather: "Marty Paich came with us to London. The two Paiches were a great combination, but Marty was a strict taskmaster. He drove his son really hard, but that's what made Paich such an outstanding musician. Like the rest of us, Marty would always call David 'Paich,' which we found hilarious. And when we were almost done with the record, Paich arrived with one last tune."

David Paich: "I'd started playing around at home with a new instrument I'd got from Yamaha, a CS-80. It had this brass flute sound on it, and no sooner had I played that than within a couple of minutes, I had that riff, 'Bom, bom, bom-bom-bom, bom-bom.' I brought that, and a verse and chorus, to the band."

Steve Lukather: "That song was literally built from the ground up. Paich had the melody and a chorus, but no other words. He played us the outline on piano. It was Jeff who leapt upon the idea of putting a percussion loop on it."

David Paich: "We said to Al, 'Do you know how to do a loop?' He just laughed. He took the tape, and we wrapped it around mic stands that we set out around the room. Thirty inches per second on two-inch tape is probably twelve feet long. We made a tape of Jeff and Roger Linn playing, and that's the intro. We kept this loop going while another machine was recording that and also all of our new overdubs. I put a guide track down with my keys. Hungate put on bass. Lukather came out with some brilliant guitar stuff. It was like the Beatles used to do it, one instrument at a time over the tape loop."

Bill Champlin: "With that West Coast thing, it was education-oriented music. There's a certain level of education and sophistication involved. I mean, as much as I love them, 'Africa' could not have been written by AC/DC."

Steve Lukather: "There was no such thing as 'world music' at the time. We were creating this shit from dust. When it came to the lyrics, Paich and Jeff ended up thumbing through all of these geography textbooks for inspiration. I said to Paich, 'Man, "I bless the rains down in Africa"?

What the fuck?' To their credit, they did manage to get the word 'Serengeti' into a rock song."

David Paich: "Finally, we got into the background vocals. In large part, they were the key to that record, I believe."

Billy Squier: "It's just one of the best songs ever written. David Paich is a brilliant songwriter, and it's got a brilliant production."

David Paich: "That was writing pure music from the heart, and us using all of our acquired knowledge of the process. We'd all of us raised our bar in general. That whole record was the band at our best, I think."

Steve Lukather: "Then right at the end of the tracking sessions, Hungate upped and quit. He picked a fight with Jeff, Paich, and me. That was ended by him shouting, 'I can't take this bullshit anymore,' throwing his Precision Bass across the room, and walking right out the back door. We were stunned. Because Hungate wasn't the kind of guy to show his emotions."

David Paich: "Hungate just didn't want to tour anymore. That's why he left. He was a homebody. We were lucky, because Mike Porcaro, Jeff and Steve's middle brother, happened to have been the bass player in Still Life in high school. We stuck him straight in, and he worked out perfectly."

Steve Lukather: "All around that same time, man, we were also playing on just about every other big record that was coming out of our hometown. My phone rang off the hook. Steve Porcaro, Jeff, and me did Don Henley's first solo album, *I Can't Stand Still*."

Danny Kortchmar: "The Eagles had broken up, and I guess Henley realized he couldn't just sit at home doing nothing. He asked me to produce it for him, and all the guys that played on it were my buddies.

Henley probably knew the Toto guys, but he'd likely never met them before, and he'd certainly not interacted with them on a musical level. So it was an eye-opener for him, and he loved it. How could you not? Jeff Porcaro, none better, ever. And Luke's an absolute virtuoso. He astonished Henley. The solo that Luke put down on 'Dirty Laundry' was absolutely brilliant, and yet he knocked it out real quick."

Steve Lukather: "Henley had cut a demo of 'Dirty Laundry' to a drum machine. Kooch said to me, 'Joe Walsh is taking the middle solo on this, do you want to do the one at the end of the track?' Walsh was a guy I stood in line to see when I was a kid, so I was thrilled beyond words. I nailed it in one take. The Eagles guys had a reputation for being very earnest in the studio. That gave me cause for concern, because I'm the exact opposite. Not to say I'm not a serious musician, but I am a silly man. Don, though, was happy to let us fly."

Danny Kortchmar: "That one turned into a lovefest between Don and the musicians."

Steve Lukather: "After that, we were basically the house band on *Thriller*."

David Paich: "I have two snapshots of *Thriller*. The first is of me sitting in a room with Michael Jackson, just the two of us, and him wanting me to put down a synth part on 'Billie Jean.'"

Steve Lukather: "It began for me with an 8 a.m. phone call. This was during a period of my life when every one of my acquaintances knew that a hang was always likely to be going on at my house, and I wouldn't be going to bed till seven in the morning. The phone was by my bedside. I snatched it up, and a high-pitched voice said, 'Hello?' I went, 'Fuck you,' and hung up. I figured it was friends fucking with me. The phone rang again. The same high-pitched voice said, 'This is Michael Jackson.' I said, 'Fuck you, Michael Jackson,' and hung up. Three hours later, Quincy Jones called."

***

David Paich: "The second snapshot is cutting 'The Girl Is Mine.' Walking into the studio and seeing George Martin, Geoff Emerick, Quincy Jones, Paul and Linda McCartney, and Michael in the same room. A pinch-me moment."

Steve Lukather: "The duet with Paul McCartney? I think I fucking pooped myself. Just a little nugget, a turtle head, at least. Man, it turned out to be a surreal scene. A camera crew arrived, and a very strange group of people showed up along with them. Dick Clark, the host of *American Bandstand*. George, Geoff, Paul, and Linda. Michael came in carrying in his arms Emmanuel Lewis, the little Black kid actor from that sitcom, *Webster*."

David Paich: "We started off jamming on the old Motown song, 'Signed, Sealed, Delivered.' Paul was doing a kind of blue-eyed soul thing. Michael tore into his part. He was spinning and dancing while he was singing. They were killing it. It was *unbelievable*."

Steve Lukather: "Steve Porcaro wrote 'Human Nature.' He had the original demo idea for it on a cassette. He used to play it for us in the studio and we'd go, 'No! Not stadium rock!' Steve got the last laugh on that one."

Paul Elliott: "Steve Porcaro told me once that his big brother was one of the best drummers in the world, but also a bit of an arsehole, and a slave driver with him. That had dented his confidence. And then he was the one that got the writing credit on the best-selling album of all time."

Steve Lukather: "It was basically a Toto song, written by Steve Porcaro, with an arrangement credited to me, that Michael just happened to have sung on. Michael didn't play anything per se, but he heard songs in his head. He'd make up demo tapes using his voice as all of the instruments. Whenever he got excited about something, he'd start to dance, doing that Michael Jackson thing. That's how you would know you were on to something good. Like with 'Beat It.' All Quincy had was Eddie Van Halen's solo, Michael's vocal, and one of Michael's tapes with him beating out a two-four rhythm on a box with his hands. There was nothing else on the track but for air. I came up with the basic riff and the bass part, and then Michael sang out for me the four-bar guitar part he wanted. I told him just that alone for four minutes would be monotonous, and I suggested that signature change-up—the 'duh-duh-duh-duh-*duuuh*' part. Soon as I played it for him, Michael started to move."

David Paich: "It was magical working with Michael and Quincy, I can't say that it wasn't."

Steve Lukather: "Don Henley just happened to be at Sunset Sound, hanging out, when we were going to play the master of our own new album from top to bottom for the first time. It was two-track reels, old school. Henley sat there on the couch, listening intently, and when it was done, he turned to us and said, 'That's a fucking good record.' And Don would tell it like it is, you know."

David Paich: "The first single was 'Rosanna.' It got to Number Two and became Record of the Year. We couldn't believe it when Columbia picked 'Africa' as a follow-up. We were, like, 'Are you guys kidding?'"

Steve Lukather: "I told Paich, 'If this is a hit, I will run naked down Hollywood Boulevard.' But with the *IV* album, we didn't have to arm-wrestle anybody to play our songs on the radio. 'Africa' came out, and the record went off like wildfire."

John Parr: "I'd had twenty years in the doldrums, trying to make it as a musician, working out of an eight-track studio in the Peak District in England. I was thirty-two. My wife and I were flat broke. She'd been paying the bills for four years. The first time I heard *Toto IV* I broke down. Sat and cried. My van had blown up. I was skint. My wife was keeping me. And here was this band, doing everything I dreamt of doing, but better."

Steve Lukather: "We turned down the cover of *Rolling Stone*. I don't know that anybody had ever done that before, but we knew that it was going to be a hatchet job. To us, it was like being asked to walk into a wood chipper headfirst. Also, we didn't want to have to suck Jann Wenner's dick. So, we became the first band in history to tell him, 'Fuck you.' Apparently, old Jann got his G-string in a bundle when the news was relayed to him. Probably the most punk rock thing anybody's ever done."

CHAPTER THIRTY-NINE

CHICAGO, ASIA, AND THE FINE ART OF REINVENTION.

"I can't honestly say we never thought about money...I had two children to send to school."

Bill Champlin: "I first got a call about Chicago right after Terry Kath passed away. They were being managed by the same people as I was being managed by, and they were snakebit at that point in the game. They'd just lost their battery. Terry was a monster, Jimi Hendrix's favorite guitar player, and I'm not the guy that can sit with a guitar round my neck and play it all night long even in the same zip code as Terry. I told them I wasn't the right guy. A couple of years later, I got another call. I had just written a song for them with their drummer, Danny Seraphine, called 'Sonny Think Twice.' I went in and met all the guys, and I actually played piano on the track. We put the song up a major third so Peter Cetera could sing it. David Foster was on Rhodes, and I was on grand. I got along with them really well and then Danny called me and said, 'Hey, man, we'd really love to have you in the band.' What they needed was my singing more than anything else."

***

Chicago, Asia, and the fine art of reinvention.

John Wetton: "I had become the protégé of John Kalodner from Atlantic Records. He had been grooming me for a band of my own for many years. When he moved to Geffen Records, the time was right."[1]

John Kalodner: "First of all with Asia, it was the power of John Wetton's voice. I'd seen him in Uriah Heep and a few other bands that he had played in. I loved Steve Howe's guitar work from Yes. I loved Geoff Downes, who was really talented, and Carl Palmer was from Emerson, Lake & Palmer. I knew these people were great."

Steve Howe: "The whole strength of radio in America was very exciting. Basically, our idea was to get something off the ground—to prove we could do it without the other guys in our old groups. A sort of personal satisfaction if you like. For so long it was the 'Yes guitarist' and the 'Yes-this,' and after a while you think, 'Can I get out of this shell?'"[2]

John Wetton: "It was [my manager] Brian Lane who suggested the name Asia. No one particularly liked it except me. I persisted and it became our name."[3]

Carl Palmer: "Emerson, Lake & Palmer could not have carried on as we were. We were not being played on the radio. So it was a case of repainting the armor."[4]

Steve Howe: "I can't honestly say we never thought about money because that would be silly. I had two children to send to school."[5]

Bill Champlin: "Chicago was in a slump. After Terry died, I think they lost a lot of their forward motion and direction. They were slobbering around in the mud, trying to figure out a way to get things going. Danny had a studio built in his house in Westlake. I went up there to listen to their stuff. I was like, 'Ah, none of this is even close to where Chicago needs to be at this point in the game.' Danny asked me what I thought David Foster would be like as a producer. I said, 'He'd be great, but you guys are probably going to end up having to throw away most of what you've been rehearsing. But the thing about David is, if you let him do his thing, he'll get you back on the charts.' Pretty much everything Foster did in those early days he really gave a shit."

David Foster: "I don't think I would have particularly liked the younger David Foster much. Because I was cocky and I was brash, maybe a little know-it-all. I'm thinking of particularly when I produced the group Chicago."[6]

Bill Champlin: "Some of the original members of the band ended up being unhappy with what David did to them."

Lee Loughnane: "First time we met him we had a bunch of songs that we wanted to play for him that we thought were going to be on our next album. He came in, he listened to all of the songs, and said, 'It's all mediocre.'"[7]

David Foster: "I had the job of telling Chicago that the songs they had written for *Chicago 16* were terrible and they had to start all over again. I went in there with eight cylinders going and all guns blazing. It was a dictatorship."[8]

Steve Lukather: "Anything that Foster was doing at that time, I would play on. I was part of his team, and he was good to me. That was when he was a human being, and before he slept with thousand-dollar bills around his cock. He'd got hired to resuscitate Chicago. Some of the band ended up hating how he changed their sound, but Foster was brilliant in his own way."

David Foster: "I was trying to imagine what a great Chicago record sounded like. Unfortunately for them, it didn't include a lot of horns."[9]

John Kalodner: "When I put the four of them together in Asia, they just came up with these incredible songs. It was simply their time."

***

John Wetton: "Prog still lived inside the four of us, but with Asia we sliced away the fat."[10]

Steve Howe: "Not to compare Asia to the Beatles, but if John and Geoff were Lennon and McCartney, I was George Harrison. I was fine with that. On the first record I was well accommodated."[11]

Carl Palmer: "Asia's music was pop music, but with an edge."[12]

Bill Champlin: "Cetera was in really good shape. He'd lost weight, he'd stopped drinking, he was screaming. Peter was as ready as anybody I've ever seen. And David and Peter really hit it off. They're both very talented people, and when you've got a voice like Cetera's to deal with, you're packing big ammo."

Peter Cetera: "[Foster's] intimidating, and when he came in the studio, we were all intimidated. I was intimidated. He made a little comment over the loudspeaker after a take. You know, 'That's not right. That bass part's not right.' So I put my bass down, I went inside of the booth, and I said, 'Don't ever talk to me like that again.' I think that was unique for him. We ended up writing a string of fantastic songs together. We needed someone to command the show, and he did. Some people liked it, and some people didn't."[13]

Steve Lukather: "Sure enough, in early '82 Foster called me in to help him out on *Chicago 16*. I felt a little uncomfortable going into that situation, because Chicago already had a fine guitar player of their own in Chris Pinnick. But Foster pretty much took over the band and told everybody where it was at. When we cut the basic tracks, I played along with Pinnick. Foster, though, didn't keep much of Doug's stuff and he had me come back in and overdub all the solos."

Bill Champlin: "Robert Lamm's piano playing is really cool, but it doesn't really go in the direction that Foster did. So we had to learn a lot of things that Foster played piano on. I mean, there were days when I might have thought, 'Hey, I need to sing a little more. I thought I got brought in here to sing.' But the way I looked at it was, 'Man, let's ride this train for as long as we can.'"

John Kalodner: "Then Mike Stone recorded this incredible album."

Geoff Downes: "Mike Stone was the perfect producer for Asia. The music was on our side of the glass, so to speak, but Mike made us sound ten times better than we dared to imagine."[14]

Bill Champlin: "We thought the record was done, and then Peter and David came up with 'Hard to Say I'm Sorry.' Or as Richard Marx called it, 'Sorry to Say I'm Hard.'"

John Wetton: "['Heat of the Moment'] was the last song to be recorded for the *Asia* album. No one else particularly 'got it'… The lyrics are an abject apology for my dreadful behavior towards a particular woman. The woman I would eventually marry, but divorce ten years later."[15]

Bill Champlin: "Our engineer, Humberto Gatica, did the mix of 'Hard to Say I'm Sorry.' Humberto's amazingly great, but he was a little too deep into reverb. There was too much echo going on. Importantly, Foster had Bill Schnee remix the song for the single release. Schnee's one of the greats of our time, and the record did so well that I think Humberto listened to it and went, 'Oh, less reverb—got it.'"

Geoff Downes: "John and I were in the States and ['Heat of the Moment'] came on the car radio. It was crazy. And very exciting."[16]

John Wetton: "It didn't fare too badly for something thrown into the pot as a bit of an experiment right at the end of the session."[17]

Geoff Downes: "For a short while Asia was the band of the moment. That's something nobody can take away from us."[18]

John Wetton: "We knew [the *Asia* album] was special, but we had no idea it would be quite so stratospheric. The singles, plus MTV, put ten times on our sales. We sounded terrific on the radio, courtesy of Mike Stone, so we had a lot going for us."[19]

David Foster: "I understand how [Chicago] was pissed off. Meanwhile, they went from 50,000 albums to seven million albums. They're still pissed off about it. [And] they're still working on the backs of those albums right now."[20]

CHAPTER FORTY

IT'S THE THRILL OF THE FIGHT…

> "[Stallone] says, 'Can you help me out?
> I want you and Frankie to write me an
> anthem that's gonna outlive you and me.'"

Jim Peterik: "I feel like I'm a chameleon in a way. I don't consciously do it, but I try to adapt to what's going on. Subliminally, I shape my songwriting style to what's happening."

Frankie Sullivan: "Sly Stallone and [Scotti Brothers co-founder] Tony Scott are incredibly good friends. When we'd go up to the Scotti Brothers offices, there'd be these big posters of Stallone on the walls… [*Rocky III*] had been done for a couple of months. Sly and Tony were having dinner at this Italian restaurant, eating pasta, and Sly goes, 'I don't like the music they're gonna put in the film.' Then he told Tony about this one spot in the movie where he wants the right song. Now, Tony Scott's sharp, and he told him, 'Well, I've got this band if you wanna give them a shot and have them submit some music for it.'"[1]

Jim Peterik: "I had a Samsung answering machine with a cassette in it. One night, I was listening back to my messages. I hear a couple from a friend and my sister. The third message is a familiar-sounding voice. It says, 'Hey, yo, Jim, that's a nice answering machine you got there. Give me a call—it's Sylvester Stallone.' I just went, 'Yeah, right.' God bless my wife, Karen. She asked me who it was. When I told her it was some joker pretending to be Stallone, she told me I'd better call him back just in case. I did and I said, 'This is Jim Peterik. Is this really Sylvester Stallone?' He goes, 'Hey, Jimbo! Call me Sly.' He told me he'd got this new movie, *Rocky III*, and for the soundtrack he wanted something with a pulse, as he put it. He says, 'Can you help me out? I want you and Frankie to write me an anthem that's gonna outlive you and me.' I made some kind of lame joke, like, 'Is the pope Catholic?'

"Stallone sent me a rough cut of the movie two days later. I had to rent a Betamax Pro machine to play it on. I'm watching *Rocky III* at the kitchen table in my house. I'd a guitar around my neck, and I just started playing that riff. I'm watching the punches being thrown and trying to coordinate the punches with the chords. You know, we knew we'd caught lightning in a bottle with that riff. Coming up with lyrics was another story. Frankie started the ball rolling. He said, 'How about, "Doing time, taking chances…"?' I liked that. Sometimes it just takes a starter nudge to get me moving. I go, 'How about this: "Rising up, back on the street. *Did* my time, took my chances…"?' I started jogging around the neighborhood, scribbling lyrics, and three days later we were in the Chicago Recording Company doing the demo."

Ron Nevison: "Jim came up with the more interesting melodic stuff and the ballads. Frankie came up with the riffs. Peterik was great."[2]

Jim Peterik: "Generally, Frankie was credited 50/50 unless I really felt there was something he was a part of, but not equally. Overall, he always wanted to add something, even on a song I thought was finished. He'd call me at 11 p.m. at night and say something like, 'Maybe we should write a third verse on that one.' I didn't think it needed it, but we'd stay on the phone and write a third verse together, and he became the co-writer. And he always contributed. He was a great guitar player, and he wrote great riffs. I am *the* songwriter, but Frankie always added something that gave the songs depth."

Jimi Jamison: "Bless Jim Peterik's heart, but he wrote every song. He wrote *all* the songs. Frank maybe came up with a line of the song, or a guitar riff here and there, but what songwriting Frank got, Jim pretty much gave it to him... Jim was Survivor, as far as I was concerned. And Frank hated that. He *hated* it."[3]

Jim Peterik: "The high note? 'And he's watching us all with the *eyeeeee...*' It's a B. I can only *imagine* that note, never mind try to sing it."

Frankie Sullivan: "Sly put us in the hot seat. I learned a lot in that school of hard knocks. For three weeks, I was put in a chair with an Oscar winner next to me, asking me to turn the drums up louder, because he liked the kick of the bass drum. The engineers were being very conservative with the levels, and he was like, 'Fuck that! I want to feel it.'"[4]

Jim Peterik: "We cut the track in a day and a half, mixed it, and boom!—sent it to Stallone. He goes, 'You really did it. You wrote one that's gonna outlive you and me.' But then he told us he was going to have to use the demo in the movie, he'd got no time to wait. So what you hear in the movie is our demo tape. It's great, but it's looser, and there's differences to the version we recorded for our *Eye of the Tiger* album. To redo it for the album, it took us a month and a half to re-create the spontaneity of the demo."

Dave Bickler: "By today's standards it was a pretty low-budget video, but it has a certain cool feel. We shot it in San Francisco."[5]

Frankie Sullivan: "That was the best music video you could ever ask for, the *Rocky III* movie. They used four minutes and fifty-eight seconds of our song, and in the beginning of the movie. Think about that. MTV was cool and all, but it wasn't Rocky."[6]

***

Jim Peterik: "The rest is history."

Paul Elliott: "Jim Peterik is a great character. I interviewed him once, and he told me how he'd been pulled over by a traffic cop for speeding. The cop says he's going to have to ticket him, and Jim says, 'Not that it will have any influence on you, but I am the guy who wrote "Eye of the Tiger." The cop goes, 'On your way.'"

Jim Peterik: "How many times have I had that riff sung back to me? Oh my God! That riff is in the water, man."

CHAPTER FORTY-ONE

ASSORTED UPS AND DOWNS IN '82: SEX ADDICTION AND ALOPECIA INCLUDED.

"Staying on top calls for keeping your fucking sleeves rolled up and your hard hat on."

Ann Wilson: "We took a year off. During that time, Nancy and I decided to write an album that was not like our previous records. That ended up being *Private Audition*."

Steve Fossen: "Why wasn't Mike Flicker involved with *Private Audition*? You got me there. I think Ann and Nancy wanted to stretch out a bit. The guy who was originally meant to step in and produce the album was Jimmy Iovine."

Ann Wilson: "[Jimmy Iovine] just didn't seem to like our music. It was real simple...And he was a coarse kind of guy in a way, and I got kind of sick of it."[1]

***

Steve Fossen: "Ann and Nancy would present these songs to Mike Derosier and me, and they wouldn't be in the vein of what people expected from Heart. Jimmy Iovine felt the same way about them as Mike and me. He said, 'Unless you guys go back and write some better songs, I don't want to produce this.'"

Nancy Wilson: "There's been some challenges, but with everything else around us. The politics and the drama that ensues around the peaceful center. It's like that movie *Twister*. You get caught up in the tornado and you see the cow fly by, and there goes the tractor. This is my favorite new analogy. That's what it feels like. You've got to hold on tight to something that's not going to get sucked into the stratosphere."

Steve Fossen: "We ended up using Iovine's engineer as our producer. We did *Private Audition* at the Capitol Records studio in LA, the famous room where the Stones had recorded. From the start, the whole vibe was not right. Ann and Nancy were kind of acting out their disappointment with what was going on. They were both fairly distracted by their breakups. Nancy and Mike Derosier were still in a relationship. Ann wasn't in a relationship. I don't know whether they were trying to exorcise the demons of what had happened, but they weren't as focused as they had been."

Nancy Wilson: "Ann and me are symbiotic siblings and somehow it works. I'm not ever sure how, to be quite honest. I know Ann sometimes better than she knows herself. So she's lucky to have me, and I'm lucky to have her. Ann's complex. She's a double Gemini. There's a lot of different Ann Wilsons, right? Catch the right one and that's the one you want to be with."

Ann Wilson: "My biggest fault, I think, is trusting people too much. I trust everybody to be real and to be honest, and I don't feel paranoid about people. I mean, you have to be careful with people. I think of myself as a strong person. Up to a point and then I'll go, 'Okay, no more.' I will just back away. I won't ever reach out and punch anybody. I'll just withdraw."

***

Steve Fossen: "Those *Private Audition* sessions were the low point of my time in the band. It was hurtful and disappointing. We were being told that Ann and Nancy thought the music was great, that this was going to be their big album. The proof is in the pudding, I guess."

Ann Wilson: "It didn't do as well as the albums before it. It was always a bit too 'off.' By that time, people expected Heart to sound a certain way, and it didn't have that. We suffered a real setback in terms of sales."

Steve Fossen: "Mike and I were asked to leave the band, and it was kind of a relief. We were pretty disillusioned with what was going on. They got some new musicians in, and really didn't do too well for a couple of years there."

Neal Doughty: "Kevin and Gary felt they had been rushed through the songwriting process [on *Good Trouble*]. Epic wanted the record out while the buzz was still going from *Hi Infidelity*. Kevin still says the songs weren't really finished."[2]

Pat Benatar: "The reason *Get Nervous* is different is because I didn't want to let myself get trapped in one particular category. People like to put you in little boxes and want you to stay a certain way, and that's dangerous."[3]

Billy Squier: "I'd like to hear a record that sounded like *Emotions in Motion* today. The songs were great, and the performances were great, but the sound was great, too. I have my own unique voice. I have my own unique way of writing. I don't mean like I was totally in a world of my own, but there were a lot of elements that went into that record that became identified with me. I mean, I used to hear people say that there was a Billy Squier sound."

Rick Springfield: "I had a huge house, money, a beautiful wife, kids, touring the world. And I realized it hadn't fixed me."[4]

Tim Pierce: "Rick was coming off 'Jessie's Girl,' and he was arguably the biggest star in America at that time. He had this Number One record, and a Number One TV show, but he traded his band. He kept his drummer, but otherwise he wanted new musicians. So I auditioned. That ended up being the start of a five-year working relationship."

Mike Baird: "Rick's just an incredibly talented guy. And he got more and more confident and just better and better. He knew exactly what he wanted. There are not that many artists that you work with that know what they really want."

John Elefante: "A friend of mine said to me, 'John, did you see Steve Walsh left Kansas? They're looking for a new singer, and you need to go for it, man.' One thing led to another. Sure enough, I started getting calls from Kerry Livgren and Phil Ehart. I didn't know they'd auditioned Sammy Hagar until years after. Now, Sammy's a fantastic singer, but he just wasn't right for that band."

Sammy Hagar: "David Geffen signed me. He only had John Lennon, Donna Summer, and Elton John at that time, and now he's signed Sammy Hagar. I liked that kind of company, so I stepped up. I put on some brand-new shoes, and said, 'I'm here, I'm ready to do this.' Then John Kalodner said, 'Here's a million dollars to make [the *Standing Hampton* album]. I'm not gonna let you out of your fucking house until you've given me twenty great songs.' We did twenty-eight."[5]

John Waite: "[After the Babys split], I moved to New York and Chrysalis said they'd make it up to me, pay my rent, and give me $200 a week. They found me a crash pad on 72nd Street. And I wrote and wrote, and I slept all day and went out at night."[6]

Tim Pierce: "I went to New York to work on John's first solo album, *Ignition*. It was kind of a dream come true for me. John's one of the greatest rock singers alive, and Neil Giraldo produced that album. If you look at the videos of Neil playing guitar with Patty in the '80s, there is no better example of an absolute rock star in the world."

***

Ritchie Blackmore: "Rainbow Americanized to a certain extent. The [*Straight Between the Eyes*] album was a lot glossier. [But] I don't get much enjoyment out of listening to rock 'n' roll. I often feel, what's the point? Mostly, I listen to organ recitals."[7]

Joe Lynn Turner: "I was a literature major in university, and I love to write. I write stories in my lyrics. That's basically what I do. 'Death Alley Driver' on *Straight Between the Eyes* was written about Highway 9. That was a truck route where all the drugs would be running north to south, from New Jersey all the way down to Florida. All the hookers and the no-tell motels on the side of the road. That's why I called it Death Alley. It's all about the cocaine."

Alan Pasqua: "I love Rick Springfield. I did his *Success Hasn't Spoiled Me Yet* album with him at Sound City. His wife, Barbie, was the receptionist at the time, and they started a relationship. They're still married today. And at the time, Rick was a poster symbol for all women."

Rick Springfield: "Sex addiction is...I wasn't addicted to sex. It was a habit I fell into as a young musician."[8]

John Elefante: "We put together twelve, thirteen songs, and then went to LA and started recording the *Vinyl Confessions* record. It didn't get any cooler than walking into a recording studio and seeing that big, beautiful console and a reel-to-reel tape machine. Everything about it was great. It was bigger than life. Because I didn't just join a band, I joined Kansas. It wasn't some mundane, three-chord group. This was sophisticated music. Kerry Livgren on his own is a modern-day Mozart, and I don't say that loosely."

Sammy Hagar: "Most artists, fame and fortune ruins them. As soon as they start making it, they lose it. It's a black hole. But fame and fortune make me hungrier. I want to stay on top. And staying on top calls for keeping your fucking sleeves rolled up and your hard hat on, getting in that tunnel, and going to fucking work."[9]

***

Pat Benatar: "The bigger you get, the less control you really have. So when something gets really screwed up, you have to pull out the big guns and say, 'Look, cut it out or I won't sing.' I wore tights onstage because they were comfortable. I didn't realize that when I put my leg up people went crazy. I was just putting my leg up…I used to think I could be real sexless onstage. It doesn't work. You're a female, and it comes out no matter what you do. Just having hips is enough."[10]

Alan Pasqua: "Rick, Sammy, Pat Benatar…The one thing that got all of them there is that they had this desire and hunger to create something and present it to the masses. That was the most important thing. Not 'I want to be famous,' but 'I love music, I have something to say, I want to say it, and I know I'm good.'"

Tim Pierce: "John Waite's difficult to work with, that's common knowledge. Why was he difficult? I don't think I want to go into that. I couldn't describe it, and it wouldn't be appropriate."

Andrew McNeice: "John's a very opinionated man. And as long as you agree with his opinions, you'll get on great with him."

Joe Lynn Turner: "My thing was, I had to wear a wig. I had an autoimmune disease as a child. And because of the injections I had to have, my hair fell out. None of it came back. So when I began rocking and rolling, I also started wearing hair. Just the other day, my wife had me cleaning out some closets and I came across some of my old wigs. I was going, 'Oh yeah, I remember this guy, and that guy.'"

Billy Squier: "In the middle of making the record with [Reinhold] Mack, who calls me up? Queen. 'Will you go on tour with us this year?' Sure. I felt pretty good just then. I'd finally got where I wanted to be. This was my life's journey."

John Waite: "I had a hit song called 'Change.' MTV had just started. They didn't have a lot of videos to play. But if you had a video you were suddenly in every home in America. I was getting played, like, eight times a day."[11]

John Elefante: "The first night of the tour was in Huntsville, Alabama. Guess who shows up? Steve Walsh with his new band, Streets. Right before I was ready to go on, somebody told me. That made it twice as hard, knowing that he was going to be sitting there looking at his successor. My brother overheard the guys in his band saying, 'This guy's a joke.' And then he heard Steve say to them, 'No, he's not, he's good.' When my brother told me, I felt really good about that. I didn't meet Steve that night. I've never met him. I've emailed him a bunch of times, but he's never answered me back."

CHAPTER FORTY-TWO

DEF LEPPARD AND MUTT LANGE CATCH FIRE.

"Bit too soft. Do it again…Too hard… Again. It needs to sound sexy."

Thomas Dolby: "When it comes to records produced in the '80s, we could just as well be talking about the golden age of Hollywood and Busby Berkeley musicals and a *Ben-Hur* cast of thousands."

Paul Elliott: "Joe Elliott wanted to be in the biggest band in the world, and that's unquestionably what Def Leppard set out to be with Mutt Lange. For all the talent in that band, they still needed a catalytic behind-the-scenes figure and they were open to being manipulated by someone who really knew what they were doing. That's naked ambition."

Joe Elliott: "At the beginning of the project, Mutt said, 'We can make *High 'n' Dry 2*, or something that no one's ever heard.' That made our ears prick up. And Mutt didn't know himself how he was going to do that, because he'd not done it before either."

Paul Elliott: "There's also the fact that Leppard made brilliant records in that period, and there's a lot of AOR influence in there. Say with Boston's production values and sense of melody."

Steve Perry: "I love Def Leppard. Mutt Lange took them to a pristine place of rock clarity and performance, to where it was something you could not ignore because it was so amazing."[1]

Thomas Dolby: "I didn't know anything about Def Leppard, but Mutt asked me to record a synth-drum intro for one of their new songs. He was talking about 'Rock of Ages.' It was mostly me and Mike Shipley at those sessions."

Joe Elliott: "We sat down and listened to cassettes of the Human League, Joy Division, and New Order. Heard all of this obvious drum machine stuff, and thought, 'Why can't a rock band integrate that into their sound?' It worked on pop music, and we were leaning more toward pop-rock anyway."

Mike Shipley: "On *Pyromania*, Mutt wanted to experiment and leave the drums to the very end. He would keep changing the arrangements, so therefore the drum parts would need to keep changing."[2]

Joe Elliott: "In the studio, we were playing the guitars and bass to a drum box. A tinny-sounding little thing, zero dynamics."

Mike Shipley: "The drums are all samples from a Fairlight... The bass drum, snare, and toms are all a machine."[3]

Thomas Dolby: "You're lucky if you can get a drum sound in a month with Mutt. The kick drum alone could easily take two weeks. It pays off, but it's not always very satisfying for the artist. Mutt once told me, 'Hey, if you do what we do, you're already married.' He also had me double every note played on guitar with a comparable synth note. The goal was to make the synth disappear altogether. So you thought to yourself,

'Well, if the goal is to make it disappear altogether, why am I doing this at all?' It was something of a mystery."

Joe Elliott: "And that wasn't really Pete Willis's cup of tea at all. Pete was into his riffs. But then, we had to part company with Pete for non-musical reasons."

Pete Willis: "I just really got out of my brains one night. Drank a bottle of brandy or something and was really ill. I probably shouldn't have gone to the studio the next morning."[4]

Joe Elliott: "We all drank, don't get me wrong, but when we drank, we just told dirtier jokes a little louder. Pete caused problems. He was disruptive and negative. The band had to come first."[5]

Phil Collen: "About a year prior, Joe had called me while they were on the *High 'n' Dry* tour and said, 'Can you learn these songs in two days? It's not going so great with Pete Willis.' So there was some stuff going on. And so when Joe phoned again when they were in the studio and said, 'Hey, do you wanna play some solos on the new record?' I said, 'Sure.'"[6]

Joe Elliott: "The band's direction changed drastically when Phil joined. I'd known him since 1979. We'd meet up when his band Girl were opening up for UFO. Him and Girl's singer, Phil Lewis, stayed over at my mum and dad's house. We went out in Sheffield and got pissed."

Phil Collen: "I came in and Mutt gave me a tape and said, 'Okay, this is a song called "Stagefright." Can you learn it and come back tomorrow with a solo?' I went in the studio the next day, picked up my Ibanez Destroyer, plugged it into my Marshall, and did a one-take solo. I didn't know that was an audition, but I guess it was."[7]

Joe Elliott: "All the time we were making the record, we would have cassettes sent over of what was being played on American radio. It was

Asia and Van Halen and Dio. What we were doing was nothing like how those bands sounded. We were building our sound up like LEGO."

Phil Collen: "It felt very different, because I'd never heard anything like it. But it also felt really right. It felt refreshing. 'Rock of Ages,' that song had Thomas Dolby on keyboards. And there's hardly any guitar in the verses. And the big deal with that was when the vocals and guitar come in on the chorus you get that 'super rock' sound."[8]

Thomas Dolby: "It starts with the songwriting with Mutt and goes into the arrangement. He'd go in the rehearsal studio with Def Leppard. He'd be very insistent on which cymbal the drummer hit going into which chorus. He wouldn't record anything until it was sorted out at the arrangement stage."

Joe Elliott: "We wrote all of the songs instrumentally with the lyrics in mind. They were all mathematically mapped out. Eight bars for the verse, four for the bridge, six to eight for a chorus. Then once the backing tracks were 80 percent finished, we'd take a song a day and pick the lyrics apart. We'd spend a couple of days on each song generally."

Phil Collen: "Mutt would put the main melody first and then all these harmonies around it. But he also never did gratuitous vocals. And there's an absolute way you can fuck a rock song up by singing too sweet and happy on the vocal. The approach has got to be that you're shouting the words. A lot of American bands, they sing better than we do but they also have a lot of gloss and polish on it."[9]

Bryan Adams: "The first thing with Mutt is, he's a really, *really* good songwriter. He understands voices really well, too. Anybody who's ever collaborated with Mutt, he'll have probably got the best vocals out of them that they've ever done. Ask Joe Elliott, ask Shania Twain. I'd say the same."

Joe Elliott: "Mutt would go to me, 'Bit too soft. Do it again... Too hard... Again. It needs to sound sexy.' *Fucking hell!* There was a lot of it that was done one line at a time, and occasionally you'd drop in a single word."

Thomas Dolby: "What was strange was Mutt's relationship to real life. He had a great resentment for almost anything *real*. Politics, sport, traffic…At the time he first recorded Bryan Adams, he was living and working in a sort of stately home in England. He had a studio in there with a big picture window. Amazing grounds, designed by Inigo Jones. In the view from his control room out through the window, between the speakers, there was a trout pond, and it wasn't quite symmetrical. Mutt is very, *very* into his stereo. Everything has to be perfect. It must have driven him nuts that this trout pond was not symmetrical. So he sent out for bulldozers. He stopped work on Bryan's record while they re-dug the trout lake."

Bryan Adams: "Whenever I've worked with Mutt, we'd spend hours working on something because it could always be better. That was the ambition. It was never, 'That's good, let's move on.' It was always, 'It's good, but I think you can do better.' It's like working with someone who can walk through the forest, hear birds chirping, and come up with a melody out of it. That's Mutt."

Thomas Dolby: "I'd certainly never worked with a master like Mutt. I thought he was over the top, and I wouldn't have traded places with him for the world. I think I'm a happier person than he is, but I'm glad I did those records with him."

Joe Elliott: "Mutt was pushing us to do a proper single. A band like Queen naturally had hit singles. Something exactly like what we grew up listening to. With big guitars the way 'Suffragette City' did. With the Sweet thing, the Queen thing, and the Boston thing. Played with aggression, but with melodies and harmonies. When we came up with 'Photograph' we were like, '*Hello!*'"

Cliff Bernstein: "We knew when we heard 'Photograph,' even though the record wasn't gonna come out for another five or six months, we knew we had a smash."[10]

Joe Elliott: "It's like, when you compare 'Photograph' to, say, 'Heat of the Moment' by Asia. They're six months apart, but they sound decades different."

Phil Collen: "With *Pyromania*, it was those guys finding their own thing. All of a sudden, they had their own sound. That became the pivotal Def Leppard sound, if you will."[11]

Joe Elliott: "Even then, we didn't know what we'd got till right at the very end. It was only when Rick and Mutt got together, and we had the combination of real, acoustic drums and electronic drums. It was like, 'Holy shit! This does not sound like the record we've been making for the past year.'"

Billy Squier: "Def Leppard are great guys, and I guess I was a small part of their success, since I brought them over to America and they blew up opening up for me on that tour."

Peter Mensch: "When Def Leppard went on tour with Billy Squier, they blew him offstage every night."[12]

Billy Squier: "They were still wet behind the ears, but they were really good."

Phil Collen: "We were Top 40. The equivalent now would be being played next to Beyoncé or Taylor Swift. It was that kind of thing. We were shifting crazy amounts of records."[13]

Joe Elliott: "Any day now, *Pyromania* will go past eleven million sales in America."

Phil Collen: "That's what Mutt wanted. He was like, 'It's so safe to just be a rock band'... Oh, it was Mutt's vision. We also wanted it, sure, because whenever you're in a band, you absolutely want to be the most popular and successful band ever. I never for one second just wanted to play for a bunch of seventeen-year-old boys. I wanted to play for everyone."[14]

CHAPTER FORTY-THREE

EXCESS—ALMOST—ALL AREAS.

"I had an alter ego, Reverend Joe. I would get tanked up and just start pontificating."

Steve Lukather: "All the cocaine, all the madness, all the shit that went with it. Yeah, it was all going on and everybody did it, or they're lying."

Jim Peterik: "I saw a lot of stuff. As for myself, I never got into it. I knew I had to go back to my hotel room after a show and write the next hit for the band. I wasn't into the party."

John Kalodner: "I did not drink or do drugs, ever. I was not involved. My focus was on having my artists be famous and on me being famous. I wasn't focused on partying."

Dennis DeYoung: "I never did drugs. No cocaine went up my nose and down the back of my throat. I didn't drink. I never smoked cigarettes. And when my children were naughty, I hired a very large Ukrainian woman to yell at them to save my voice."[1]

***

Steve Lukather: "The nought-point-nought-nought-nought-one percent that said they didn't do it, okay. The rest are fucking lying, I'm telling you."

Kevin Cronin: "Yeah, we partied our brains out! We were a rock band in the '70s and '80s. We were flying around in our own airplane, and we lived the life. We rocked."[2]

Steve Lukather: "Bobby Kimball's problems got even worse on the road. He would be great one night, awful the next. The fun with Bobby soon wore off. He made the grave mistake of starting to smoke the shit, and one hundred percent guaranteed, that will make you lose your fucking mind. The poor cat got strung out, and he became a liability. We were all casualties to a certain extent, but when you're the lead singer of the band...It would be the same as me taking a belt sander to my fingers so that I can't play. It was like, 'You've still got to bring it, man. You need a hamburger and a shower, because we hired that guy, not this guy.'"

Bruce Hall: "I don't remember the '80s. It was tough."[3]

Steve Lukather: "Bobby would go missing for days on end and not return our messages. When the cat did show up, his pipes were shot from staying up all night. Bobby was a sucker for drugs and women, and put those two things together for him and it would be a volatile combination."

Neal Doughty: "I had a few really bad marriages. I mean, it was all part of the party back then. Every woman I dated, I married. It took me four tries to find the right woman."[4]

Steve Lukather: "Out where Bobby lived in Toluca Lake, there was a Mexican restaurant he used to hang at, drinking and doing whatever else. Being the personality he is, this would be very obvious and out in the open. There were these two chicks in the place this one particular night and they dangled a carrot in front of Bobby's face. They told him they'd have a threesome with him if he got them four ounces of blow. That's 90 grams of cocaine! *Nine-zero!* But Bobby had a friend who would've been able to get his hands on that much shit at short notice. Like I said, Bobby ran with a scary crowd."

Desmond Child: "The artists were always very comfortable leaving me with their wives while they went off to their AA meetings. By the time they came back, I had redecorated their living room and moved pictures on the walls and fluffed up pillows. So the wives would always say, 'Oh, I love that Desmond—you should write with him again.' That was a saving grace."

Steve Lukather: "And of course, the two girls were undercover cops. The stupid fuck, Bobby was a big, loud, and proud Louisiana homeboy. When he made the deal, they busted him on the spot. It was on the TV news, so now we were all in the middle of a shitstorm. I got the phone call at six in the morning from my mom going, 'What the fuck are you guys doing?' It was a mess. A disaster. Jeff in particular was furious."

Joe Lynn Turner: "Sex, drugs, and rock 'n' roll. I certainly put in my time with all of that. A lot of women. There was plenty of alcohol, and everybody was giving you coke. I had an alter ego, Reverend Joe. I would get tanked up and just start pontificating about things that normal people don't even have a clue about. I read all of this incredible paranormal, metaphysical literature. I was into the occult. People still come up to me to this day and say, 'Man, *you were on fire!*' I've calmed down a lot since then. But you could get me going with the right combination of alcohol and spirit."

Steve Lukather: "Bobby, I'm sure, regrets his transgression to this day. At the time, he obviously felt terrible, and scared. Getting busted for possession with intent to sell was a heavy felony. If convicted, he was looking at serious jail time. Our managers had to go and bail him out of the tank and try to clean up his mess. We'd a tour booked. It wasn't the time to kick our lead singer out of the band, so we gave the brother another chance."

Dennis DeYoung: "There was the glamorizing of it, of course. 'Oh, look at all these rock 'n' rollers!' Yeah, they die young, they die stupid. You're in your sixties and you have health problems. Why? Because you were a fucking idiot. Pardon me for saying it, but I've been the sober man in a room full of drunks."

Steve Lukather: "Everything you've ever read about those times, it's true, multiplied by a hundred. We lived in an era where the fact of people doing drugs was part of everyday life. Everyone was partying, including the gardener. The first time someone offered me blow, they said, 'This shit isn't addictive—it's like having a cup of coffee.' It was easy to go along with the big lie, because there'd be blow at every session. It certainly brought out the worst in me. I made some of the most regrettable decisions of my life being high."

John Kalodner: "Being the only sober person in the room, you could really separate the good ideas from all of the cocaine and alcohol bullshit that came out of everyone else's mouths. What was important. And most of the things weren't important."

Steve Lukather: "The craziest situation I found myself in? I'd have to kill you right after I'd told you."

CHAPTER FORTY-FOUR

A TALE OF TWO CANADIANS.

"I remember calling my manager…and
saying, '…Selling a million records—
it's amazing. Where's the money?'
He told me there wasn't any."

Jim Vallance: "With the second album, *You Want It You Got It*, Bryan and I were writing better. We were surrounded by better people. The chart of our progress was on an upward curve. The second record did better in Canada than the first. A little bit better in the US, too, but Bryan was by no means a household name."

Bryan Adams: "In 1981 and '82, I was playing in America quite a bit, doing lots of shows."

Jim Vallance: "He was away for weeks at a time, but we would schedule writing time during his tour breaks. Literally, he would fly into Vancouver on a Friday night and we'd get together Saturday morning. When we were writing, it was very disciplined. We'd meet up at noon. We always started with a cup of tea and a sandwich. Then we'd play a game of backgammon. Then we'd go down to the studio and decide what we were going to do that day. We'd have pencils and blank pieces of paper, pick up our guitars and just noodle until inspiration struck. Some days nothing, some days magic happened. It was unpredictable, never the same twice."

Bryan Adams: "There's something that happens when you're writing songs. A fleeting moment while you're playing where you create something you didn't have two minutes ago and wouldn't have two minutes later. It's all about that one magic moment."

Henry Small: "Prism shared a manager with Bryan Adams, Bruce Allen. I knew Jim Vallance, and I tried to write with Bryan once. I can't say there was a great chemistry there."

Jim Vallance: "Every day, noon to midnight, we worked and worked at it, incessantly and seriously. I'm not sure I can even think of an impasse. Really, we'd set the template almost from that first day we got together in my basement. Best idea wins. There was no ego, no self-interest, no competition between us. We were very honest with each other. We trusted each other's opinions. It was always about writing the best song possible, and it was all about putting in the time. Norman Mailer said the same thing. He sat down at his typewriter every day from 9 a.m. till noon. That was when he wrote. Some days he got nothing, and some days it was brilliant. But he did it every day, and I think that's part of the ticket. Putting in the time and work."

Bryan Adams: "Let's say Jim and I would play together for an hour. Then I'd leave and Jim would sit and go through what we'd taped. He'd say, 'I think this one idea is really good, let's work on that tomorrow.'"

Jim Vallance: "Once we'd written something, we'd make a cassette and go for a drive. Just to hear it on the car radio. That was the acid test to know if it was going to work or not, literally as a radio song."

Henry Small: "I thought *Beat Street* was a better Prism album, artistically anyway, than *Small Change*. We hired Bobby Kimball, Timmy

Schmidt, and Bill Champlin from Chicago to come in and sing backgrounds. The producer, John Carter, was involved a lot with that. I didn't really care for Bobby Kimball. Those guys did do the background vocals, but that was in between going to the bathroom and snorting coke the whole time we were there. And Carter was paying them exorbitant fees. Carter also took a week to get the drum sound, maybe longer. What he was doing was using up the $250,000 budget. I didn't realize that at the time. I was a trusting soul. He was a company man, and he was doing what the company wanted him to do."

Jim Vallance: "By the third album in 1983, *Cuts Like a Knife*, we were more cognizant of who Bryan was as an artist. What worked with his vocal range, what our sound was. We were being influenced by all kinds of people, and players, and songs, and just growing and learning. It's a craft."

Al Cafaro: "With Bryan, it was all just really smart. He was going to get his record played, then his next record played. He was going to get his career exactly where he wanted it to be. He was very ambitious. Not overly so, he didn't telegraph it per se. But if you asked Bryan to do something, he did it. And he did it with a smile."

Jim Vallance: "Canada is a small market for selling records. It has a 35 million population, whereas the US is 350 million. So we were always hoping to make a break across the border. There are two cities, one in Canada and one in the US. They are literally almost the same city, but with a river and a bridge between them. Windsor in Canada, and Detroit in the US. It's actually called Windsor-Detroit. A DJ in Detroit heard 'Cuts Like a Knife,' the song, on the radio station from Windsor. That was how it snuck across the border, and from there it went exponential."

Al Cafaro: "I was the local New York promotions guy for A&M, and we got 'Cuts Like a Knife.' That was the first big single for Bryan. We went right for those AOR radio stations. It was not easy. By no means was it an automatic, but we got enough critical mass."

***

Henry Small: "Bruce Allen had a fight with the president of Capitol Records. The album was done. I'm rehearsing with a new band to go out on tour. Bruce walks into the middle of a rehearsal and says, 'We're not going on tour.' And walked out."

Jim Vallance: "The next thing Bryan was on tour opening for Journey. I went out for a bit to see him on that tour. It was certainly an education seeing Journey perform and which songs really resonated with the audiences. You're always absorbing as a songwriter. Journey was huge at the time, and Bryan wanted to be huge. That tour with them changed our writing and our approach to writing."

Al Cafaro: "Then you just hoped that you had follow-ups. The place you didn't want to be was without the opportunity to have a strong second hit. As it happened, Bryan just might have been the most successful artist we ever dealt with at A&M. It's shocking how many hits he went on to have."

Bryan Adams: "I remember calling my manager, Bruce Allen, and saying, 'Bruce, you're great. Selling a million records—it's amazing. Where's the money?' He told me there wasn't any. I was going back to paying the previous album off and for the tour support. I'd signed a really shitty record deal with a low royalty rate. So that's what happened with *Cuts Like a Knife*."

Henry Small: "My good friend John Carter, who I saw as something of a mentor, called me and said we needed to have a meeting. He came into the Capitol building in LA, sat down with me, and said, 'We've decided to drop Prism.' Out of that $250,000 budget, John said, 'We're going to offer you $5,000.' I had spent $28,000 on getting an airtight contract. There was no way they could do that. I said to John, 'Well, I guess that we have to go to court.' He said, 'Yes, you can go to court. But you won't be able to record or perform until it's resolved. We have a team of lawyers, and by the time you win, which you will, it will have taken years.' This is my friend. I settled for $10,000."

CHAPTER FORTY-FIVE

JOURNEY'S HIGHWAY RUN INTO THE MIDNIGHT SUN.

"There were the beginnings of the band having more difficulty getting along."

John Kalodner: "By 1983 that sound was the spirit of America. Big, fun, anybody could achieve anything, America at the top of its game. The Reagan era. The Rocky Balboa and Arnold Schwarzenegger movies, and that music. Those bands had bloomed and none more so than Journey."

Steve Perry: "The press, and especially *Rolling Stone*, decided to call us—and by us, I mean Foreigner, Journey, Styx—they called us faceless bands. They said we all sounded alike. To this day, I don't understand what that meant. We didn't sound alike... I've read three reviews in my entire career, and they were all so painful that I decided not to read them anymore."[1]

Steve Smith: "Having to follow *Escape* was a challenge. At the time, the phrase was 'platinum paranoia.' It was a twofold challenge. We wanted to have an album that sold well, but also that had critical success. In retrospect, I see that as a complete waste of effort and mental energy—trying to second-guess what the critics were going to like. We wanted to have hits plus 'rock credibility.' It doesn't make sense now, but somehow it did to us at the time."

Jonathan Cain: "As the [*Escape*] tour ended, we found ourselves in the studio to start recording *Frontiers*. Herbie had his unrelenting timetable."[2]

Herbie Herbert: "If Journey, Jon Cain, any of these guys, wanted to be really honest and say, 'Wow, what was the greatest thing Herbie Herbert ever afforded me as an artist?' They never had a record company executive step anywhere near them in the studio, in the songwriting process, or any part of the creative process. We completely controlled everything vertically: album covers, the content, the songs."[3]

Steve Smith: "We did have a lot of music from the rehearsals, and we ended up recording a lot of songs."

Jonathan Cain: "We already had 'Separate Ways' ready to go. During the tour, we discovered we needed an uptempo rock anthem...I wrote it on a foot-long Casio. Steve and I wrote the lyrics in the hotel the next day, [and] we were doing it at soundcheck on the third day."[4]

Steve Smith: "There were two songs, 'Ask the Lonely' and 'Only the Young,' that got dropped from the record. 'Back Talk' and 'Troubled Child' went on instead. At the time, I remember the conversations we had about those latter two songs having some kind of rough integrity to them. Whereas the tracks that got left off were thought to be too obviously hits. Herbie wanted 'Ask the Lonely' and 'Only the Young' to go on the record, but we, as a band, outvoted him. In retrospect, of course he was right."

Neal Schon: "We were in the studio and Mike Stone, our producer, said, 'I think you guys are missing a real big power ballad.'"[5]

***

Jonathan Cain: "Somewhere in the hum and steady rocking on a tour bus, I heard a tune in my dreams that woke me up. Finding a pen in the dark, I scribbled the words on a napkin, something I'd never done before. 'Highway run into the midnight sun.' The next day, I took the napkin and grabbed my $30 Casio keyboard. The rest of the lyrics flowed out of me."[6]

Neal Schon: "It didn't sound anything like what we made it sound like. It sounded like a beautiful country ballad. We ran through the song once, and I just free-formed my way through it. What you hear on the record is the second take we did."[7]

Jonathan Cain: "I'd never had a song rise so quickly inside me and take its full form in a matter of minutes. It was an anointed, supernatural thing to write it in a full-out thirty minutes."[8]

Neal Schon: "Steve wanted everybody to leave the studio—he wanted to have time with the song to experiment with it. So coming back into the studio and hearing what Steve did, I was like, 'Oh my God.'"[9]

Steve Lukather: "A power ballad? Big melodic piano ballad with crunchy power chords in the chorus and big harmonies. It's usually a love song of some sort. A big, echoey drum and quadruple-tracked vocals with nice, long reverbs. It's like having a great chocolate sundae. Maybe not with every meal, but it tastes good every once in a while."

Donald Roeser: "The power ballad was one of the more annoying vehicles of the time. Nothing comes to mind that I liked."

Billy Squier: "Clichés become part of your culture, and there are good power ballads. But a lot of them really aren't. They're very formulaic and they're pointed toward a very specific target audience. I had no interest in them."

Neal Schon: "'Faithfully' and 'Open Arms' probably get played more at weddings than any songs ever."[10]

Herbie Herbert: "I had this grand plan that I presented before the *Infinity* album. I said, 'Here's the title of all our albums—*Infinity, Evolution, Departure, Captured, Escape, Frontiers,* and *Freedom*. And here's our artwork.' When we got to *Frontiers*, Steve really wanted to change that. He fought like hell to change the art and the imagery. And it was our signature style. It was instantly recognizable."[11]

Steve Smith: "We could have had an album as popular as *Escape*, I think. But it was difficult to have perspective at that time in our career."

Herbie Herbert: "At which point the meetings degenerated into a pissing act between me and Steve Perry and his attorney, with all of the other members of the band watching like a tennis match. This is where I lost enormous amounts of respect for Neal Schon, Ross Valory, Jon Cain."[12]

John Kalodner: "There's a very interesting personality type. This is something I've never discussed with anybody but psychologists before, but this was always my theory. The leader of the band, usually the singer, has to have a combination of a highly developed superego, along with an incredible amount of self-doubt and insecurity. That is what creates the art in them, and the ability to go out and sing in front of 20,000 people a night. It's that mixture of super confidence and ego combined with insecurity and all the negative things that happen to people in their lives. That all meets in some place in their brain that causes this great creativity."

Herbie Herbert: "Journey could have been a polished Grateful Dead, and that was my model as a Deadhead."[13]

***

Steve Smith: "Herbie was a tremendous human being and quite a visionary. He helped set me up financially, so I could be free in my choices after Journey. I was conservative in my 'rock star' consumption. I didn't really indulge myself. I had a beautiful home, and I built a home recording studio, but it was all within my means. I drove conservative cars. I had a Volkswagen van and a Volvo station wagon. I never bought Ferraris or Lamborghinis."

Jonathan Cain: "This was the MTV era, so Journey played the game like everybody else... Steve Perry wasn't so sure about doing the videos. And when we showed up for the video of 'Separate Ways' in New Orleans, his girlfriend Sherrie Swafford was equally resistant after seeing the blonde who would star in the video with us."[14]

Neal Schon: "Our manager came to us and said, 'Look, we need to get a music video.' I give it a ten on the cringe scale. It's so silly, man."[15]

Steve Smith: "I don't remember the *Frontiers* tour as a glorious celebration."

Herbie Herbert: "During that tour, Perry was really upset for the most part with this ongoing success, and me continually being right about all these things."[16]

Jonathan Cain: "Steve's voice became so tired and worn out that it shut down, which forced us to cancel some shows. The doctor told Steve he had irritated his vocal cords. Steve didn't want to take steroids, he wanted to let it heal naturally."[17]

Steve Perry: "Everybody thinks singers are prima donnas. And to a degree I guess we are. But at the same time, the moment a singer gets one callus, he's finished. Singers live on the edge of not degrading their voice. It's the most difficult edge to walk... So it can make a singer a little crazy. It can make you live your life in a state of insecurity and fear."[18]

Jonathan Cain: "We could have played things a little differently... We should have given Steve more time to recover."[19]

Dennis Dries: "Look at Journey. They just ruin singers. I don't know why it was so important back then to sing everything so high. I guess it matched the music, but it was very difficult, and you had to be in shape. That era of music was not easy. Those songs were tough to sing."

Steve Perry: "When I try to sing those songs today... Oh my God. It's like baseball pitchers that throw at 98 mph. You know why they do that? Because they can."[20]

Steve Smith: "There were the beginnings of the band having more difficulty getting along. We always traveled in buses before that, but for the *Frontiers* tour we chartered a plane, a four-prop, not a jet. But Steve Perry didn't join us on the plane. He traveled in an RV, separate from us. There was some separation, and I can't speculate on the reasons for that, but we were together less during that tour."

Jonathan Cain: "I got divorced. Families started having an impact, people wanted to do different things. *Frontiers* was great. I call *Escape* and *Frontiers* the twins. But it became all-consuming. It couldn't sustain."[21]

Steve Perry: "And then Neal did his second [solo album]. And I said, 'Okay... I'm probably going to end up doing one.'"[22]

CHAPTER FORTY-SIX

DENNIS DEYOUNG'S WATERLOO.

> "That song 'Mr. Roboto'... That was about the dumbest idea ever."

Tommy Shaw: "You can only be on a honeymoon period with a band for so long. Eventually, things get in the way. One person might be making a lot more money than everyone else, or have more airplay than somebody else, and it starts to affect the chemistry of the band. You do your best to try and work through it. We went up and down, in and out."[1]

Dennis DeYoung: "And then in 1983 I tried making another concept album with *Kilroy Was Here*. Was it too much? Maybe."

James "JY" Young: "Dennis had this vision for an idea that none of the rest of us agreed with, and we battled about it for quite some time."[2]

Dennis DeYoung: "Coincidentally, I'm just now writing the *Kilroy Was Here* chapter in my book. It's the longest chapter. I'm paraphrasing here, but the chapter opens: 'Three things you never discuss at Thanksgiving dinner with Styx fans. Religion, politics, and *Kilroy Was Here*. Unless you like agida and the throwing of food.'"

***

James "JY" Young: "We all finally gave in to him. He believed in it, but none of the rest of us really did. We tried our best to make something out of what we had."[3]

Dennis DeYoung: "You might want to go back to 1982, 1983 and see what was happening in the music world. ZZ Top had put synthesizers on their music. I look at it like this. 'The problem's plain to see. Too much technology. Machines to save our lives. Machines dehumanize.' I wrote those lines in 1982, and I think to myself, 'Huh, that didn't suck.' Nobody was a dictator. How do you dictate to grown men? You can't."

Danny Kortchmar: "It's how it's been said, man. Protest songs make good protest, and lousy songs."

Dennis DeYoung: "I know what's wrong with *Kilroy Was Here* as an album. There's not enough rock 'n' roll on it. For an album that's about banning rock 'n' roll, you might want to have some. This would be a good idea. Tommy wrote two ballads for that record. *Tommy* wrote two ballads. Nobody told him to. They're good songs, too."

James "JY" Young: "Dennis was a strong-willed individual and had the most success as a writer and lead singer in the heyday. So when we were gonna go with his idea about this robot thing I said, 'We run the risk of really alienating our male audience.' And it all went bad."[4]

Dennis DeYoung: "You know, 'Mr. Roboto' was dismissed by so many people because it was so doggone catchy and clever."[5]

James "JY" Young: "Well, 'Mr. Roboto,' I was so against that song—because this thing is targeted at seven-year-olds."[6]

Al Cafaro: "How did it go? 'Domo arigato, Mr. Roboto.' Torture. It was like, 'What the fuck are you doing?' By the way, Derek Sutton, the manager, I understand, thought it was an insane move. And there was tension between Dennis DeYoung and the rest of the band."

Bob Pittman: "That song, 'Mr. Roboto,' it killed Styx. It was truly awful. I mean, that was about the dumbest idea ever. The first time we saw that video at MTV, it took your breath away. It was like, 'Oh my God, they're doing *what*?' Styx was a pretty cool group until that moment."

Les Garland: "You know 'Mr. Roboto' does stick in my mind. But I thought that the video was actually pretty clever, and my recollection is it was a big hit."

James "JY" Young: "The craziest thing is, it's the only single that Styx put out that has sold a million records. I refused to play it."[7]

Dennis DeYoung: "I didn't do this for people to hate what I'm doing. I didn't do it so people could say, 'Dennis DeYoung's a poo-poo face.' Quite the opposite... You'd think I'd invented the Coronavirus."[8]

Al Cafaro: "Then when we heard the *Kilroy Was Here* album at A&M, we knew we were fucked. Pure and simple, we were fucked."

James "JY" Young: "It cut our album sales in half because the male audience *was* absolutely alienated by 'Mr. Roboto.' Not all of them, but a large chunk. What that song did is it killed a whole lot of people's interest in our music."[9]

Dennis DeYoung: "For all the people that didn't like *Kilroy*... and thought 'Mr. Roboto' was almost as bad as spreading Ebola, I can't help them. It was *one song*."

CHAPTER FORTY-SEVEN

NIGHT RANGER BREAKS BIG. KANSAS AND RAINBOW BREAK UP.

"The record company...told us we had to airbrush the nipples off."

John Elefante: "Robby Steinhardt left the band before we started work on the next Kansas record, *Drastic Measures*. I don't know if I really want to get into the reasons for that. He's passed away, God rest his soul, and I just don't want to dig up any dirt on Robby."

Chuck Burgi: "AC/DC was being managed by a big company called Lieber-Krebs at the time, and they signed up Michael Bolton. Or Michael Bolotin as he'd been in Blackjack. I was asked to participate in Michael's first solo album as Michael Bolton [*Michael Bolton*, 1983]. That was a funny album, because we really didn't see much of Michael when the band was rehearsing. We spent all of our time running through these really elaborate arrangements. A couple of the songs ended up being hits. Michael would come in for a very brief period and sing them. He wasn't aloof, he just didn't spend much time with us. I don't know why."

***

Steve Lukather: "The Tubes' record company, Capitol, wanted the same team to help them to follow up 'Talk to Ya Later.' Besides Fee Waybill, who's a great cat, I'm pretty sure the other guys in the band weren't too pleased to have me at least back, but I played on every track on their *Outside Inside* album. One of the first things I came up with was the riff for the opening track, 'She's a Beauty.'"

Fee Waybill: "Foster goes, 'Let's meet with Lukather again and write another song.' We wrote 'She's a Beauty.' The same way. Two hours, we're done. I had written these lyrics already, but I didn't have a chorus. Another thing Foster would say in the studio, instead of saying it was a good take, he'd say, 'Beauty, eh?' I got 'She's a Beauty' out of that."[1]

Steve Lukather: "Foster, Fee, and I took it from there and it became this extravagant production, very Toto-esque. Foster also had Bobby Kimball do a backing vocal. It went on to be a huge hit for the band."

Fee Waybill: "[The rest of the band] went, 'Oh, you did it again, huh? Where was I?' Pride goes before the fall."[2]

Jack Blades: "People were making fun out of [Night Ranger] because we were a rock band. They were yelling out insults, like, '1975! Deep Purple!' But we took it as a compliment. The first album [*Dawn Patrol*, 1982] was very much a full-on, kick-ass American rock record...We fit right in there with Van Halen and Def Leppard. We sold a million. And right then, in the middle of a tour, our record company went bankrupt. And they owed us all that money on a million records."[3]

Eric Martin: "Sandy Einstein had managed me in a band called Kid Courage in 1978. I moved on to a band called 415 that Sandy also looked after. Sandy was working with Journey's management, just answering the phones and stuff, and he set up a meeting for us with Herbie Herbert. At this meeting, we asked Herbie for his help to get us a record deal, and he agreed to sign on as our co-manager with Sandy.

But he also told us, 'You're going to change your name to the Eric Martin Band. Because Eric is the principal songwriter.' We were sat right there in his office. The keyboard player was like, 'This is bullshit, man, I'm not dealing with this.' And Herbie goes, 'Don't let the door hit you on the ass on your way out.'"

John Elefante: "Right when I joined the band, things were changing. MTV was coming on the scene. There were no longer faceless bands. The record company wanted more singles. A video, and a single on MTV and at radio equaled sales. They wanted us to get away from the album-oriented stuff, ten-minute songs, and have three-and-a-half-minute songs. Mostly, they relayed that to our manager, but we got the hint. And you know, it was out of character for Kansas to do that, but it was me that was encouraged to try and come up with singles."

Chuck Burgi: "Next, I got asked to join Rainbow. I was friends with Joe Lynn Turner, we went way back. And I'd been a fan of Ritchie Blackmore's since high school, but I'd read enough about him in magazines to be apprehensive. Our first meeting, he was pretty cold. We played a bit, and he didn't even look at me, man. He was in one of those Blackmore moods. After about fifty minutes of jamming, he just unplugged, looked over, put his thumbs up, and left. Literally, got off the stage and walked out without a word. I went over to Joey, and I was like, 'What the fuck!' Joey said to me, 'Yeah, he's like that.'"

Joe Lynn Turner: "Especially with Rainbow, people didn't talk. They didn't confront each other. It was almost like you were walking on eggs all the time."

Eric Martin: "Herbie was a little bit like a father figure for me. He would say, 'No, no, shut up. This is what you need to do. You don't have a clue. I know what's best for you.' I had a big gap between my teeth. Herbie goes, 'You are going to fix your teeth.' I had my top two teeth pulled out and had to have veneers put in to close them together. Then he'd tell me, 'You look like shit. Get some new clothes.' I'd play him all these demos and he'd go, 'No, not good enough. Keep going.' He used to give me Journey demos. They'd write a song, go, 'Yeah, that's okay,' and stick it in a huge duffel bag full of tapes. Herbie would take a cassette out from this bag and instruct me, '*Don't* tell those guys that I gave you this, but this is how I want you to sound.' In the songwriting world, you're not stealing but you make something sideways."

Jack Blades: "Kelly wrote ['Sister Christian'] about his sister, whose name is Christy. She grew up in a small town in Oregon."[4]

Kelly Keagy: "She was sixteen and doing what was popular back then, which was driving up and down the streets, cruising and looking for guys. They called it 'motoring.' It was like out of *American Graffiti*. That time in your life when you're not a kid, but you're not fully adult either."[5]

John Elefante: "*Drastic Measures* became my record by default. Kerry only had three songs on that record. I didn't want to write the songs. I joined the band mostly to be with Kerry Livgren, to be alongside of a genius. When he wasn't writing, I was like, 'This really stinks, man. We need more Kerry.' For whatever reason, his head just wasn't in it."

Chuck Burgi: "It was so hard to do that *Bent Out of Shape* record with Rainbow. *So hard*. Ritchie was an even bigger asshole to me during the making of it. He was very short with me, not a nice guy. I thought he hated me. Musically, we were going up against Foreigner and all that stuff. And we had the one song, 'Street of Dreams.' I knew it was going to be a hit all along, and it ended up being the biggest Rainbow ever had on American radio. Every other song on that album, it was a case of, 'Let's do this *right now* because we're really behind.'"

Eric Martin: "Herbie got us a record deal with Elektra. A lot of money, and the big producer, Kevin Elson, who'd done all of the really good Journey records. We made the *Sucker for a Pretty Face* album at Studio

One in Doraville, Georgia. That room was famous for having hosted Lynyrd Skynyrd and the Atlanta Rhythm Section."

Jack Blades: "Kelly wrote the song as 'Sister Christy,' but when he sang it, we all thought he was saying 'Sister Christian.' I said, 'Dude, you should change it. "Sister Christian" is much cooler.' He said, 'You really think so? My sister's gonna kill me.'"[6]

Kelly Keagy: "The big drums, the big chorus…Sure, why not? But… we don't sit around going, 'Okay, time to write the power ballad.'"[7]

Jack Blades: "Kelly rocks way hard, man, but he's a natural when it comes to singing the ballads. He does them better than anybody."[8]

John Elefante: "Kerry Livgren quit, leaving me as the only accomplished songwriter left in the band. I begged him to stick around, I really did, to not let go of this good thing. And I didn't think I was good enough to continue and become the new Kerry. It would be like having to replace Tom Brady."

Eric Martin: "The album cover had my face on it. It was a stupid cover. The name 'Eric Martin Band' was so tiny, if you had bad eyesight, you wouldn't see it. Next to my face, there was the shadow of a girl. We'd actually got a cool shadow painting done of a naked girl, but the record company didn't like that. They told us we had to airbrush the nipples off."

Jack Blades: "When 'Sister Christian' hit we were selling out arenas, 10,000 to 15,000 people a night. It was a defining moment for us."[9]

Chuck Burgi: "Once we hit the road, Ritchie and I were suddenly best buds. We laughed together, we screwed around together, we just had the best time. But as it turned out, Ritchie and Roger Glover were already in negotiations for the Deep Purple reunion."

***

Joe Lynn Turner: "I knew about Purple re-forming, but Ritchie had always said we'd get back together after this interim. Rainbow was his baby."

Chuck Burgi: "I got one of those good news, bad news calls from the manager, Bruce Payne. The good news was I was going to be on retainer for another couple of weeks. The bad news was that Ritchie was off with Purple."

Joe Lynn Turner: "I just remember the manager separating us. He was telling Ritchie that all I wanted to do was a solo thing. Then he'd come over to me and tell me that Ritchie wasn't going to get Rainbow back together, so I could forget it. I knew it was over on the flight back from our last shows of the tour in Japan. But my low points only ever last for a couple of days. As my mom, bless her soul, used to tell me, when God closes a door, he also opens a window. So look for the window."

John Elefante: "My fondest memory of being with Kansas is of when the whole band came around to my parents' house and my folks cooked a big Italian meal. All the guys sitting around the dinner table. They were cracking jokes, and we were having a lot of fun. It was so Italian. My mom made big bowls of pasta with sausage and meatballs, garlic bread, and her famous chicken piccata. Kerry eats all his pasta, and he falls asleep on the couch."

Steve Lukather: "Much later on, Fee invited me to come out and play 'She's a Beauty' with the Tubes a couple of times at shows in LA. One of those nights, their guitarist, Bill Spooner, gave me a bunch of shit for not recalling a guitar part that by then I'd written many years ago and hadn't played since. I don't know what he expected me to say. I wrote his band a smash. You know, sorry."

Eric Martin: "Thanks to Herbie, we got all these great gigs, opening for everybody. Loverboy, Foreigner, Quarterflash, Billy Squier, Heart. We traveled all over the United States. We played with ZZ Top and Night

Ranger. Then we came home and got dropped by Elektra. The band dissolved around me."

Jack Blades: "'Sister Christian' was on the soundtrack of the movie *Boogie Nights*. In that scene in the drug dealer's house where everyone is freaked out on cocaine. Kelly and I saw it at the cinema with our wives. Both of us were sweating, because we swear, we had been in the same house in 1984. That was wild."[10]

CHAPTER FORTY-EIGHT

"LOVE IS A BATTLEFIELD" AND THE ART OF THE HIT.

"Why even open your mouth to sing if you have nothing to say?"

Mike Chapman: "When I talk about a hit song what I'm referring to is something that's groundbreaking. Something that is completely different. Alongside everything else that's out there, it shines."[1]

Desmond Child: "The thing is, I never think about trying to write a hit. That's like trying to think too much about how you ride a bicycle, and then you fall over. It's deadly to coming up with a hit, thinking that you're going to do it."

Pat Benatar: "Out of the blue [in 1983], one day we got a call from Chrysalis demanding we start work immediately on another album... I said, 'Fuck you.' The only way we could meet their deadline was record a live album. We decided to include two new songs on *Live from Earth*... We got 'Love Is a Battlefield' from our friend Holly Knight."[2]

Holly Knight: "I've been fighting my whole life for things that mattered to me. It started when I was a child, but as I got older, I was able to articulate in a more elegant and creative manner what was most important to me: independence, autonomy, expressing my own voice, anarchy in all its glory, and essentially telling people to fuck off in a clever way."[3]

Bill Champlin: "There's a fluke factor in every hit. Somewhere along the line, somebody trips and lands right in the middle of the clover. I don't think I've ever heard a really big record on the radio that didn't have a certain level of fluke factor. Take Michael Jackson and 'Beat It.' Getting Eddie Van Halen on that track was kind of throwing it at the wall and seeing what would stick and work. And nobody saw it coming."

David Paich: "David Bowie once related that John Lennon had told him, 'You've got to write from your heart, it's got to rhyme, and it's got to have a beat.' Those are the three things right there, and he's not far off. All the things the great Richard Perry used to tell us whenever we worked with him. It's got to have a verse, chorus, bridge, outro chorus. Basically, it's got to have structure."

Desmond Child: "I spent two years writing with Bob Crewe. He was the man who co-wrote all of the songs for the Four Seasons and with Kenny Nolan he co-wrote 'Lady Marmalade.' Bob taught me how to write in the Brill Building style, the Broadway style, which is to do anything you can not to have a soft rhyme. Have tight rhymes, especially on the choruses. The verses are a little more relaxed. Like, you can say 'enough' and 'love,' which don't rhyme. Nothing but 'dove' rhymes with 'love.' Also, before when I used to write, I would play chords and mumble aloud and hope I could use those mumbles to build a nest of words, like a bird. Bob told me, 'Why even open your mouth to sing if you have nothing to say?'"

Pat Benatar: "[Neil Giraldo] started fooling around with a brand-new drum machine. It was its own thing, danceable but still rock… [Chrysalis's] reaction wasn't good. They hated *everything*. And Mike Chapman [Holly Knight's co-writer] really hated it."[4]

***

Desmond Child: "When you're in that sacred circle of collaboration, my angle is to have the artist I'm working with spill their guts about what's going on in their life. Everything they say I write down, and something pops out as a title. You have to engage a public's imagination. A lot of artists don't understand this. If you're not feeling it as you sing it, no one else will. It's like with Meryl Streep. If a scene demands she cries, she has to make tears well up in her eyes, take after take. That's her job. I expect the same commitment from the artists that I work with."

Pat Benatar: "It didn't hurt that Bob Giraldi signed on to direct the video—fresh from doing Michael Jackson's 'Beat It'... The combination of the video and the song proved unstoppable, propelling 'Love Is a Battlefield' to the top of the charts."[5]

Desmond Child: "To Bob Crewe, music was always secondary. It was always about the hook."

Bill Champlin: "Some people think they have a formula, but it's like gambling. 'I've got a formula that'll make me win.' That's why there's so many pawnshops in Las Vegas."

Pat Benatar: "After it became a hit, [Mike Chapman] thought it was a classic."[6]

Mike Chapman: "There's a lot of hits out there, and they're not really hits. They're not *real* hit songs. [A hit has] got to be good. I'm talking about really, *really* good."[7]

Pat Benatar: "[And] I won a Grammy for 'Love Is a Battlefield,' my fourth."[8]

CHAPTER FORTY-NINE

THE WOES OF BOSTON AND HEART.

"A genius, but with every negative thing you could think of in his personality."

Los Angeles Times **news report:** "CBS Records sued Boston, claiming it was failing to deliver the requisite number of albums under a 1976 contract."[1]

Extract from a letter sent by Tom Scholz to Walter Yetnikoff, president of CBS Records, in 1983: "Apparently, some people at [CBS] feel I should be punished for my refusal to sacrifice quality and deliver a record that's compromised by haste. In fact, I will never foist a second-rate record on the public to fill CBS's pockets or my own."[2]

Tom Scholz: "Of all the entertainment businesses, including television and the movies, the music business is the worst of all of them. It attracts the lowest form of life in many cases."[3]

Paul Elliott: "This was your classic irresistible force meets immovable object battle between Tom Scholz and Walter Yetnikoff. Scholz was an obsessive and the lack of output from Boston, even now it's astonishing. The sheer level of tweaking away in his basement. The mad scientist of rock."

Barry Goudreau: "Was Tom difficult to work with?...He was a real perfectionist and he knew exactly what he wanted. And, you know, it was tough sometimes."[4]

Tom Scholz: "It doesn't matter what it is. If I'm cleaning out the kitchen—which I rarely do—I gotta do it right...It's just something that I have to do."[5]

Danny Kortchmar: "In the '60s and the mid-'70s, the lawyers didn't run the music business. People that actually loved music ran it. Like Elliot Roberts, David Geffen, even Irving Azoff. All those guys, they actually liked music, and they liked their artists. Then the lawyers came in, guys that didn't give a flying fuck about the music, the artists, or anything else. They realized there's money to be made here, and that's when everything got corporate."

Steve Lukather: "The music business itself was fucking cutthroat. It was a serious business, man. All the ha-ha-ha, and people snorting coke, the sex and champagne, and people being beautiful and fabulous, the sun's shining and 'Hotel California'? That's the whole BS story they sold everybody. The reality was that there was an undercurrent of, 'How much money are we generating from this? How much money can we get from off these clowns?'"

John Elefante: "I didn't realize this was a big business. And a lot of decisions were made on business grounds, not just on music. I was naïve enough to think decisions were going to be made on the music. Sometimes they were, and the band usually fought for that, but the business was always in the boxing ring with you. That was very odd to me."

***

Billy Squier: "Artists don't mean shit now. The business took over."

Tom Scholz: "There have been multiple times where I've spent months, at one point six months, completely recording a piece of music and then just going, 'Nope.' That happened several times. One of my worst characteristics is that I never know when to stop. Every single Boston album, after it was released, had revisions. I literally wouldn't stop until I got my head into something else that basically took over my life. I stopped recording a song when I thought there was literally nothing more that I could do to make it better. I could only make it worse."[6]

Steve Lukather: "The artist always ends up paying for the cost of everything. That's what people don't realize. They think we sold a million records and all of a sudden got a check for a million dollars. It doesn't go down that way, man. I *wish* it was that simple! No, man, they take every scrap of every hamburger you've ever put on the bill. It all comes off. You're working twenty hours a day for these guys. Then there's taxes. Oh, wow, did we ever find out about taxes the hard way when you get a lot of money when you're young."

Tom Scholz: "It was a landmark case. I never set out to be any sort of crusader when it came to cleaning up the record business, but somehow it ended up happening."[7]

John Kalodner: "I worked with Tom Scholz when I was at Sony Music, years later. I was putting together a Boston 'greatest hits' for him. I loved his music, but he was impossible to deal with on any level. So rigid. And paranoid."

Andrew McNeice: "Unfortunately, I've done an interview with Tom. It was so boring I never even transcribed it. He was just tone deaf."

John Kalodner: "Scholz was so paranoid that whenever I went to meet him in Boston, he would make me wait in the parking lot of this shopping center for him to pick me up in his stupid Honda car. He'd take me to his house, where he had his studio, and drop me back off at the same shopping center afterward. At the time, he was working on his first new song in maybe ten years and I'd managed to place it in the *Independence Day* movie. Thinking that it was going to be one of the biggest movies ever, which it was.

"He plays me the song, it's called 'Higher Power.' It has the potential to be great, but he had this girl he was seeing at the time. He'd put her into AA treatment, and in the middle of the song, he has her recite the 'Serenity Prayer' along with all of these other weird things. I begged him to take it out. But I'd say that I had the least influence in my professional career on Tom Scholz. Not only did he not fix any of the changes to the song I asked for, but he had four months to submit it, and ultimately, he didn't deliver it until the film was already out. It was awful, and all he ever did was bad-mouth me to the people in charge of Sony. Who, by the way, obviously knew he was pretty much off his rocker from all the experiences they'd had with him. For somebody who created one of the greatest records ever, he was beyond a disappointment. A genius, but with every negative thing you could think of in his personality."

Denny Carmassi: "Mark Andes [bass] and me had joined Heart for the tour they did for *Private Audition*. That was kind of a feeling-out situation, but it was a good time. Then we started on a new record with them. They'd got Keith Olsen in to produce it, but the Wilson sisters were still searching for what they wanted to do next."

Nancy Wilson: "We worked really hard on the *Passionworks* album, wrote all the songs between us. The trouble was, we worked with a producer who was kind of hitting bottom on his cocaine habit. So everything was really hard and difficult. We were trying not to get sucked into the cocaine of it all. But the songs and the production really suffered in the process."

Keith Olsen: "It was the '80s. Drugs were a way of life for the entire industry."[8]

***

Nancy Wilson: "The album came out. It entered the chart at, like, Number 2,000. I mean, it was nowhere to be found. And we were like, '*Shiiiiit!*' That was really hurtful. It hurts your feelings. Even if you have an ego trip going on, you still think you're doing something good and there's something you've worked so hard on, and then it goes and stiffs like that."

Ann Wilson: "After *Passionworks*, I partied. I'll just say it. I went home. I bought a house in Seattle, just for me and my friends. We lived a high life for a couple of years. It was a *lot of fun*. But it was not necessarily that creatively successful."

Nancy Wilson: "Me and Ann and our bestie Sue Ennis, who we always wrote with, we got together and decided to have a movie night where we could watch movies that would make us cry. So we watched *Terms of Endearment*, then the Spielberg *The Color Purple*, and *Steel Magnolias*. It was a three-pronged cryfest. We got out a big box of Kleenex and sat around in Ann's library crying for six-plus hours. We had some wine and a nice night. It actually felt better after we did that."

Ann Wilson: "The stuff we were writing in that era was just a little bit too self-important and self-absorbed. It wasn't about the songs it was about us. About *me*. That doesn't work."

CHAPTER FIFTY

YES AND GENESIS JOIN ASIA'S AOR TRAIL. GOING TRICKY.

*"They said I drank too much. True.
That I was arrogant. True."*

Steve Howe: "I will limit myself to three reasons for why things went wrong for Asia. One: the second album [*Alpha*, 1983] was done too soon. There was too much pressure from the label to repeat our success. Two: I love Canada, but we were not on home soil. And three: the levels of commercialism. It was a big mistake to think that suddenly we were a pop band."[1]

John Wetton: "Steve Howe—he was used to being treated like a superstar because of the Yes thing and he expected it to carry on with Asia."[2]

Hugh Padgham: "I loved Genesis, but I always thought it was a bit wishy-washy sounding. Especially the long songs. I think Phil Collins wanted them to be a bit more sort of ballsy."

Phil Collins: "It was always on the band's to-do list to have hit singles, to be played on the radio. Even before I joined, that was the premise of the band. I think we got better at knowing when to stop, and when to say, 'Okay, this song sounds great just like this.'"³

Hugh Padgham: I'd first got drafted in for *Abacab* in 1981, but only as engineer. That record was relatively successful, and we went to America to do overdubs. It was in that early '80s era when I became aware of FM radio and what it comprised. And Genesis was already beginning to break America. They'd had a minor hit out there with a song called 'Misunderstanding' on *Duke*, the record before *Abacab*. For my part, I was totally into making records that were sonically great, and I guess that just fitted in with FM radio."

Trevor Rabin: "I started sending out demo tapes. The irony is that I sent out all of the material that was going to end up on *90125*, like 'Owner of a Lonely Heart' and 'Changes,' and they were rejected. I've still got the letter from Clive Davis at Arista saying, 'While we feel your voice has Top 40 appeal, we feel ["Owner of a Lonely Heart"] is too left field for the marketplace today.'"⁴

Tony Kaye: "Trevor and I were sharing an apartment in Knightsbridge. Trevor had tapes...'Owner of a Lonely Heart' I thought was potentially a hit. He said, 'No, it's not.'"⁵

Trevor Rabin: "Chris Squire, me, and Alan White and Tony were rehearsing for nine months. It was under the name Cinema. So it was a fresh thing. There were no rules. We didn't quite know what we were doing."⁶

John Wetton: "I was expelled from [Asia] in a Machiavellian conspiracy. Management and the record company combined to oust me for 'personal reasons.' They said I drank too much. True. That I was arrogant. True. That I wasn't a team player. True. But did I deserve to be expelled from the group that I started? No. Would the public accept this blatant travesty? No."⁷

***

Carl Palmer: "I found working with [Wetton's short-lived replacement] Greg Lake really hard. Asia was not right for Greg... I never really wanted Wetton to be out of Asia."[8]

Hugh Padgham: "We were aware of what was going on in America. MTV was out, so suddenly we were able to hear, albeit on TV, what was currently going on. I don't remember ever having a conversation with Mike Rutherford or Tony Banks saying, 'Let's make this sound like it's going to be great on FM radio.' But there was a sense of momentum by then, I think. What was so strange was that Phil Collins's own solo career was going the same way, and his records got more and more successful."

Tony Banks: "I never really saw a big change in Genesis. It was a slow thing. We got better at the short stuff. In many ways it's more difficult to write a good simple song. I love a well-done single. There's a real art to that."[9]

Phil Collins: "The biggest difference between me and Peter [Gabriel] and Tony and Mike [Rutherford] is that basically they're a bit emotionally screwed up. They went to boarding schools, only saw their families on holidays, while I went to a regular school, went home every day. They would never put 'I love you' in a lyric, whereas I think nothing of it."[10]

Trevor Rabin: "Chris Squire said, 'How do you feel about Trevor Horn producing us?' I said, 'Who? The Dollar guy?' I was really apprehensive, and Tony Kaye wasn't into the idea at all."[11]

Tony Kaye: "I was not particularly enamored with Trevor Horn in a lot of ways. I think the feeling was mutual."[12]

Trevor Rabin: "I got on really well with Trevor. We had different ideas. He was very much, you know, 'Six o'clock, have a joint, and then have a listen.' But a great guy to work with."[13]

***

Trevor Horn: "I would never have been able to have had the input I had as producer on *90125* if I hadn't previously been in the band. At the time I took the job on, I was probably one of the most successful producers in the world. And I never would have worked with Yes again if I hadn't loved them, because they were a pain in the neck."[14]

Tony Kaye: "['Owner of a Lonely Heart'] was never rehearsed. It was never played. It was conceived at the end of recording the album. Trevor Horn says he's the one that found it, or at least recognized the potential."[15]

Trevor Horn: "They kept trying not to do 'Owner of a Lonely Heart.' One day, when I got to the studio, there was a deposition waiting for me, saying, 'We've all decided that we're not doing it.' I got on my hands and knees on the floor, pulled at everybody's trouser legs, and made a noise and shouted, '*Pleeease, pleeease* have one more go. Let me program the drums. It's got to be simple.'"[16]

Tony Kaye: "I left the band. I just left. I was getting tired of what it was becoming, and tired of London, and tired of Trevor Horn...I missed the finale of Jon Anderson coming back into the band and re-recording the vocals, and all of that."[17]

Trevor Rabin: "We'd finished the album when Jon came back. All the overdubs were done. Atlantic said that even though they felt very secure about the record, why didn't we get Jon Anderson in the band so we can call it Yes?"[18]

Trevor Horn: "There's no doubt Jon's voice is totally unique, and it finished it off. I walked out at the end over the final mixes. These things are complicated. Bands are difficult to work with."[19]

Hugh Padgham: "I think Tony Banks was always a little bit suspicious of Phil Collins and Hugh Padgham. Tony had this vibe that Genesis was his band."

***

Phil Collins: "I was just trying to write the best songs I could, but… Peter got all the credibility… And I got the money! Ha! I've never said that before, but that does sum it up."[20]

John Wetton: "I don't dwell on the past."[21]

John Kalodner: "Everything fell apart with Asia through alcohol. That was the downfall of that band. And there was nothing you could do to stop it. The implosion of that band was a huge letdown to me. The biggest of my career."

Tony Kaye: "Then they pulled me back in. What can you say? [*90125*] was a hit."[22]

Trevor Horn: "When I listen to that record now, I'm so glad I did it, because they were also fucking brilliant, you know?"[23]

Trevor Rabin: "Getting successful on that level was completely new to me. And I realized once the record had been out for a while, that it was new to everybody. Yes had never had a record like it. So we were all in the same boat in a sense."[24]

Tony Kaye: "The tour was shocking to everyone. At least 60 percent of the audience were just fans of 'Owner of a Lonely Heart.' It was odd. The entire front of the stage was young girls. For Yes, that was completely a phenomenon. It was great. Everyone was having fun. We had our own plane. We did anything we wanted to do."[25]

PART FOUR

NO BRAKES

CHAPTER FIFTY-ONE

IT CAME FROM NEW JERSEY...

"It was gonna happen. There was no question, not one moment of doubt."

Jon Bon Jovi: "[I had] your typical middle-class upbringing. It was very much a blue-collar childhood. No one I was best friends with or even buddies with were seeking higher education. It was the factory or service.[1]

"My first time onstage was a talent show in Sayreville, New Jersey. I sang 'Strutter' by Kiss, 'Johnny B. Goode,' and 'Taking Care of Business' by Bachman Turner Overdrive. I did not win."[2]

Richie Sambora: "There's a certain attitude that comes from New Jersey. A lot of it's down to being around a vast city like New York, which is a big melting pot of energy."

Jon Bon Jovi: "Tony [Bongiovi]'s a distant cousin. I'd never met him, but my dad asked him to come and see me perform. Tony told [my dad], 'The band's not very good, but your kid's got something going.' So after high school, in September 1980, I called him up and he allowed me to run errands in the studio."[3]

***

Joe Lynn Turner: "My father in his excellent wisdom said to me, 'If you're gonna build a house, you need a hammer. You better go for some voice lessons.' I couldn't find a good teacher until later on in life, one that resonated with me. He's a famous teacher. I sent Jon Bon Jovi to him. A guy named Martin Lawrence, he warmed up Caruso, Whitney Houston, and Michael Bolton. *Everybody.* He taught a technique like a bel canto. It's a pyramid shape, and diaphragm, and no breath in your lungs. I'm basically a baritone. I've got a very low voice. But everybody was singing up high. And in order to be in that rock medium, you had to sing high. He taught me the pyramid of the high notes and that's what got me where I needed to go. I remember Jon calling me up and saying, 'Man, I need a good voice teacher. Whaddya got?' We're both from New Jersey and I was the older guy. I said, 'Martin Lawrence and you'll bless the day I was born.' Worked like a charm. He gave Bon Jovi a great technique."

Tim Pierce: "When I went to New York to work on John Waite's record at the Power Station studio, Jon Bon Jovi was living in the apartment on the top floor. He was a really nice seventeen-year-old kid. His uncle Tony owned the Power Station, and he funded master demos, not an easy thing to do in that era. He heard me play on John's record and liked what I played and asked me to come back and do his demo."

Jon Bon Jovi: "It was gonna happen. I had the song ['Runaway']. There was no question, not one moment of doubt. None."[4]

Tim Pierce: "It just happened to coincide with me being back in New York with Rick Springfield. We did something like five nights at Carnegie Hall. So I also did master demos with Jon. I ended up doing all the guitars on 'Runaway.' Aldo Nova was the other guitar player, but they didn't keep any of his parts on that particular song. They probably tried to recut it for the first Bon Jovi record, but that version we did ended up on the record. It just was a magical thing. We all got full credit, and it was his first single."

Jon Bon Jovi: "I remember hearing ['Runaway'] on the radio in the car, and it made me want to roll the windows down and drive faster…

I wanted the police to pull me over so that I could say, 'That's me on the radio!'... So I get this song on the radio, and the quality of my band members I thought could be better, so I started seeking out the guys that I'd seen around. Dave [Bryan] was playing keyboards. Alec [John Such, bass] I'd recruited from a cover band, and Tico [Torres] was the best drummer I'd ever fucking seen. Alec got Richie over to see us. So when Richie shows up, he comes in the dressing room and we make small talk, and I like his presence."

John Kalodner: "Jon Bon Jovi was extremely talented. Him and Richie Sambora. Jon glowed with it, and especially when Richie Sambora was around, it made him even stronger."

Jon Bon Jovi: "What mattered was that these guys believed in something that I sold them. I said, 'This is my vision, and this is what I want to do.' And they went, 'Okay.' Tico was making records with Frankie and the Knockouts. Richie had his own band that he was just getting off the ground. Dave was gonna go to school and be a doctor. Alec was making a lot more money than the rest of us combined in a club band. So these guys were all doing great, and they went down to making no money, losing their wives and houses, to come into this band. Say today I was playing with Clapton, Jeff Beck, Elton, and Ringo. It might be nice, but it wouldn't be those guys who were in the garage with me."

Richie Sambora: "The 'Jersey Sound' seems to have come from Mitch Ryder and the Detroit Wheels, which had horns and that kind of thing. What we do is nothing like that. We just have that attitude. It's kind of like being aggressive and pigheaded about what you want to do. It's fucking honesty."

Jon Bon Jovi: "You've got to be somewhat influenced by your surroundings. You're an English guy. More than someone from New York or LA, I think it'd be easier for you to see that we're more like Phil Lynott and Thin Lizzy than Bruce Springsteen. What we do is a heavier, guitar-oriented storytelling."

***

Richie Sambora: "People in New Jersey just walk up and go, 'Hey, fuck you' to your face. If there's anything we bring from New Jersey, it's that you ain't got no time to bullshit. That comes out in our music, too."

Jon Bon Jovi: "The first record [*Bon Jovi*] came out in January '84. We made our first visit to the UK supporting Kiss. What a thrill. It was electra-glide. Our idea of the big time was if the record company would take us out to dinner."

Doc McGhee: "[As a manager], you want to work with acts who are driven to be the biggest band in the world. They want to perform in front of 20,000 screaming kids, and my job has always been to get them from where they are to that arena level."[5]

Jon Bon Jovi: "Our first video [for 'Runaway'] took three days to shoot, and we were only allowed to be there for one day. When we saw it there was silence. We knew we were dead."[6]

Doc McGhee: "When I was signing Bon Jovi, I brought them five Van Halen books and told them, 'This is who you could be—you can take over from Van Halen because they will implode.' It's the reason we chose a two-word band name: Bon Jovi. It was modeled on Van Halen. Then I showed them two magazines. *People*, which had a photo of an artist outside his house with his dog and his BMW car. Then a picture of David Lee Roth on the cover of *Rolling Stone* with three girls half-naked on the side of the bed looking disheveled, with a half-eaten pizza on the floor, and the headline, 'I Used to Have a Drug Problem, but Now I Can Afford It.' What were the kids going to gravitate to? The BMW or David Lee Roth? That's never changed."[7]

Tim Pierce: "Jon knew exactly what he wanted to do. At seventeen, he was absolutely focused on being a lead singer in a huge rock band. He had his eye completely on what he wanted."

CHAPTER FIFTY-TWO

MUTT LANGE WITH THE CARS AND DAVID FOSTER WITH CHICAGO: THE GREAT DICTATORS.

"We went a million dollars over budget."

Danny Kortchmar: "You know, at the time I didn't really think, 'Oh, this is a golden era!' Now, looking back on it, it was kind of like Liverpool in the '60s. All hell was breaking loose. Everybody was writing songs. You couldn't go anywhere without somebody grabbing you and going, 'Hey, listen to *this*!' It was all the time, everywhere. It was a beautiful time."

Bill Champlin: "Of all the records Chicago made, *17* more than anything was definitely in that ball game. Timing-wise, we got really lucky on a lot of stuff. At a certain point, one of the things David Foster was really good at was using a lot of classical devices. And they are devices. It's deeper than just minor and major keys, but minor is kind of sad sounding and major is kind of happy sounding, and diminished is, 'I'm not sure.' There are certain devices that a lot of good arrangers really know how to use, and hide, pretty well."

***

Alan Pasqua: "Everybody was fantastic. The producers were fantastic. The engineers were fantastic. The recording studios were fantastic. You had to be able to listen and react. The most successful records from that period, everybody was really listening and reacting to each other."

Steve Lukather: "It was a very tactile time. There was an energy, it was very intense. You were either in it, or you were out of it. You had to really fight to stay relevant, because everyone was trying to outdo and outrace you."

Elliot Easton: "In the Cars, we were in our own lane. We just did our thing. But of course, we were very aware of everything else that was going on."

Ric Ocasek: "I always wanted our songs to be pop. At the time, we needed a change. A change is always good."[1]

Elliot Easton: "When it came to the *Heartbeat City* album, it was mostly, I think, Ric who was thinking about a change of producer. At the time he worked with us, Roy Thomas Baker was the state of the art. You couldn't get a better or more complete producer. Then along comes Mutt Lange and it was a similar thing, he's the new, current state of the art. We chose Roy not so much for the bands he produced—none of us was a big Queen fan—but because of the sound of the records he made. Same with Mutt. It wasn't necessarily the groups he was producing, but their sound and the kind of widescreen production they'd got."

Bill Champlin: "On *17*, Humberto Gatica was way more careful about throwing echo, reverb, on stuff. He cut back on that, and everything else was dead on the money, it always was. The whole record sounded really good. I think he ended up getting all kinds of sonic awards for the record."

Robert Lamm: "I firmly believe that without David Foster at that time [Chicago] would probably have ceased to exist, at least as a mainstream band. That was, like, the right guy at the right time both for us and with radio. David really created a sound that incorporated the Chicago sound but turned out to be his sound."[2]

Bill Champlin: "A lot of times, David would have a different musician come in and play on stuff. Jeff Porcaro came in and played on 'What You're Missing.' Then Carlos Vega drummed on 'You're the Inspiration.' Danny Seraphine wasn't very happy about that. Matter of fact, he flipped out. David also played a lot of the Moog bass, because that's what was going on at the time. He made a lot of really right decisions in terms of how to put the music together."

Elliot Easton: "The funny thing about Mutt being so mysterious and enigmatic and nobody ever seeing him, he looked like a blond surfer dude from Malibu. He had a long, shaggy blond haircut. Vans sneakers, Levi's, and striped T-shirts. He was very sweet, and very nice, but really, he meant business. He was very, *very* exacting. To a level I'd never experienced before and haven't since. He went through engineers. Those guys would be under the mixing desk sleeping and until they couldn't do it anymore. He wore all of us out, and he was there in the studio for as long as any of us. That speaks to his stamina."

Bill Champlin: "Now, 'Please Hold On' was a pretty funky tune. David had been working with Lionel Richie. They'd kind of put a track together, but all they really had was a title. There was a scratch vocal, a lot of 'da-da, da-da' going on. James Carmichael, who was Lionel's producer, said it was too Black for the record they were going to do with Lionel. It was Lionel's first album after leaving the Commodores, and they wanted to cross him over. So David said, 'If it's too Black for Lionel, let me give it to Bill.' I knocked off some lyrics and we went in to cut it. To tell the truth, I'd been partying the night before and I was a mess. No sleep, I'd been looping it with the attitude adjustment powder, and I was crazier than a junkyard dog. Foster said, 'Let's just put down a scratch vocal. You're kind of shot.' Two or three lines in, he goes, 'Man, you're singing great!' It was kind of a falsetto thing. When they heard it, some of the guys in the band didn't even know who it was singing.

David talked everybody into leaving it on the record because it spread it out a little bit. It made the album more interesting."

Elliot Easton: "We were cutting 'Drive' and Mutt was saying that the LinnDrum was off in its own internal timing. He was moving around the Linn parts by literally a millisecond, going, 'Oh, the snare is off. Listen.' And we couldn't hear it. He claimed that Fender had fretted Ben Orr's bass inaccurately. He sent it to a guitar shop and had them tear out the frets, and re-fret it. Doing my guitar overdubs, he had me re-tune after every take, even if it was a two-note punch. To the point I said to him, 'Mutt, you take the guitar and tune it. I just can't take it anymore.'"

Bill Champlin: "It's not even so much about the vocals on 'Hard Habit to Break,' it's about the arrangement. I'd known [songwriter] Steve Kipner a long time. He'd written 'Physical' for Olivia Newton-John, and he sent this tune over to us. The second verse wasn't quite what it should have been. It needed to be much more the same as the first verse, certainly the way David was producing it. So I got Steve on the telephone and said, 'Steve, listen, can we leave this with you for a day or two?' He said, 'Give me one minute.' I was kind of on hold for a minute, and he came back on the line and said, 'How's this?' Boom, he'd nailed it in a minute. That's how good Kipner is."

Elliot Easton: "There's a certain timelessness about *Heartbeat City*, and a lot of it I think has to do with the lyrics. Ric always explored more of the dark side of the human condition. 'You're just what I needed, I needed someone to bleed.' 'Who's gonna hold you down when you shake? Who's gonna drive you home tonight?' It's universal things that guys and girls still go through. Not 'la-di-da' kind of stuff."

Robert Lamm: "Foster badly, still to this day, wants to be an artist and he'll never be an artist. So what he does, he makes records using artists, so that what he does can shine through using the artist as a synthesizer, if you will."[3]

***

Elliot Easton: "We went a million dollars over budget. The label was starting to get very concerned. But the result was a huge record and with all the hits that came off it. 'Drive' and 'Magic,' and all of those songs."

Bill Champlin: "CDs were starting to take off, and we had a great-sounding record. Once again, that fluke factor thing with our timing. We got lucky with the tour, too. We went out and the only other big tours that were on the road at the same time were Prince and the Jacksons with the *Victory* tour. People will probably bust me for saying it, but I got a feeling a lot of parents said to their kids, 'You can go see Chicago,' because it's white. They didn't want them in the parking lot or the building with a Black audience. I mean, I prefer Prince's music to Chicago's, between you and me, but I would say we got the white flight that year. Plus, we'd had a couple of big hits and Cetera was on his game, singing his brains out."

Elliot Easton: "All the effort was worth it. The blood and sweat that went into making *Heartbeat City*. Because we got an incredible record out of it, and it still stands."

Bill Champlin: "Absolutely, it felt like a boom time. We had our own Viscount plane. The tour ran for two and a half years. It just seemed to never stop. How much cake we came home with on the back end of those gigs was really great."

Elliot Easton: "Ben had sung 'Drive,' but naturally, journalists wanted to talk to the songwriter, which was Ric. And Ben didn't get that it was meaningless. Like, I was happy that anyone emerged from the band as a star and brought the whole thing up. You know, who cares? It made the band more popular. But Ben was really hurt by the management sort of grooming Ric away from the rest of us in a sense."

Bill Champlin: "I was just going, 'Wow, enjoy this while it happens because this kind of thing doesn't last for that long.' I mean, I was kind of hoping it would go on a little bit longer. But then Peter bailed out at the end of the tour."

Elliot Easton: "What we should have done after *Heartbeat City*, with 20/20 hindsight, is taken a break. After all the success we'd had, it was a fractured time in the band."

Steve Lukather: "What we've been talking about, that way of making records, it'll never happen again. The way that we lived and dealt with each other. The healthy competition. All of it, it's gone."

CHAPTER FIFTY-THREE

STEVE PERRY GOES SOLO.

"He said that I sandbagged him, that I fucked him."

Steve Perry: "I went to LA and in about three weeks, I wrote *Street Talk*."[1]

Randy Goodrum: "One day, I was at the kitchen table with one of my daughters, who was sitting next to me. I got a phone call, and my daughter said, 'Who's that?' I said, 'I think it's the lead guitarist with Aerosmith.' And she said, 'Joe Perry?' And I said, 'No, Steve Perry.' Then she ran into her room and tore off a Journey poster from her wall, and she showed it to me. She said, '*That's* Steve Perry.'"[2]

Steve Perry: "[I used] real musicians like Larrie Londin on drums, Bobby Glaub on bass, Michael Landau on guitar, Randy Goodrum on keyboards. I mean, amazing players. We're talking players who spent their youth reaching for the ability to perform with feel. And when these guys play, the performance is dripping with feel."[3]

Randy Goodrum: "I talked with Steve, who said he was looking for writers to work with him for his solo album. A musician friend of mine, Andy Newmark, had suggested me to Steve. So Steve said, 'I'd like to write a couple of songs with you for my solo record. When are you next coming out to LA?' I said, 'Tomorrow.' I got on the phone and booked a red-eye flight [from New York], and I showed up at 11."[4]

Steve Perry: "There were no computers back then. Everything you're hearing on the *Street Talk* record is absolutely performed in the studio and captured on a piece of tape."[5]

Randy Goodrum: "I wanted to bring him an idea to start a song, so the day before I flew to LA, I went to the piano and came up with this little vamp that I thought was a good thing to start with. Then I showed up at his house, and it was great meeting him. We went inside and I met his girlfriend Sherrie, and we went into this little songwriting room he had. I sat down at the piano and I started playing the vamp. He started singing along to it, and I immediately started writing down a draft of the lyrics. We worked on it all day, and by 11 p.m. we had the demo for 'Foolish Heart,' and it was killer."[6]

Steve Perry: "The feeling [of 'Foolish Heart'] was just basically one of being confused about falling back in love again because your heart wants to so bad, but your head says, 'Wait a minute, you've done this before, and it doesn't feel good.' It's just that real teeter totter of the head and heart conflict that I think everybody goes through."[7]

Randy Goodrum: "Over the next four days, Steve and I wrote four songs. 'Oh Sherrie' came at the end…Steve had written this new song, but he said he didn't like the lyrics, and he asked me for help. He gave me the track without lyrics, so I wrote and participated in the lyrics. It was the last song that was written for the album."[8]

Steve Perry: "Sherrie actually got tired and went to bed. And I don't know where it came from, just the words 'Oh Sherrie' came out, and the 'Hold on, hold on.' That's all we had for the entire chorus. We had no lyrics, no nothing. We had a bunch of mumbles on tape. Next thing I know, the song was almost finishing itself because it was such a personal song. I really needed someone with great lyric insight, like Randy Goodrum had, and he helped me to finish the lyrics on it."[9]

Paul Elliott: "I would rate *Street Talk* up there with the very best of what Perry's done with Journey. That record's an absolute masterpiece. The simplicity of what he did with it is beautiful."

Steve Perry: "I went for a whole different thing entirely. A different production sound, a different band sound, a different vocal register. Things that I used to do an awful lot before I joined Journey. I came from R&B."[10]

Herbie Herbert: "The one solo record that had come and done extraordinarily well, virtually the same time, was *Bella Donna*, Stevie Nicks. She did triple platinum, and we did more than double platinum in just America alone on Steve Perry's *Street Talk*."[11]

Steve Perry: "We just knocked the record out. It did pretty good."[12]

Herbie Herbert: "And I can tell you honestly, he denigrated me at every possible opportunity and said that I sandbagged him, that I fucked him."[13]

Eric Martin: "Steve Perry's attitude with Herbie was, like, 'I don't like you managing another band.' He wanted Herbie just to manage Journey. Exclusively. Herbie had other things going on. He had a company, Nocturne, that did the video screens at Winterland in San Francisco. Nocturne ended up doing video screens for Michael Jackson, David Bowie, U2. That's the genius of Herbie, and all the while still smoking pot and yelling and screaming."

John Kalodner: "My experience of working with Perry, after he got clean and sober in the mid-'80s, was that he also became very paranoid and suspicious. He was a perfectionist before then, but he became even more of one. He was really impossible to get to do anything."

Herbie Herbert: "With a guy like Steve Perry, everything is a hang-up to him. This guy is the farthest from a hippie you could imagine. Zero love."[14]

Jonathan Cain: "When I showed up for Steve's solo show at the Warfield in San Francisco, I was turned away because my name wasn't on the list. Herbie was supposed to take care of this for me... I wasn't going to buy a ticket."[15]

Steve Smith: "At the time, we had been working together so closely for six straight years that we all needed a break from each other to do some different things. With hindsight, we can see that Steve Perry having a very successful solo record changed the direction, and inner dynamics, of Journey."

Herbie Herbert: "Post Steve Perry's solo record, he had a gun to Journey's head."[16]

Steve Perry: "In my heart of hearts, I was never going to leave Journey. I had no desire to."[17]

Mike Baird: "I found out the real scoop through Steve Smith. Steve told me that Steve Perry didn't want to do another Journey album, because he'd had all of this success with 'Oh Sherrie' and his solo thing. He was dictating his own shit, not having to deal with other band members. Okay, I get that. But, dude, you've got a cash cow here that's filling stadiums. Why would you want to dump that?"

CHAPTER FIFTY-FOUR

A VIDEO KILLS BILLY SQUIER'S STAR.

"Well, now you had to be a fucking actor, too."

Bob Pittman: "There was a generation of young artists that intuitively got MTV. Those people were very visual. By the way, early '70s rock was not that. It was stand onstage, look very cool, don't move much. That's completely different from what these younger artists knew to do. Pat Benatar was there. She got it."

Martha Quinn: "Rick Springfield came in very early on. I asked him what his first impression of MTV was, and he said, 'Well, you actually, Martha. I walked in and thought, "Who is this twelve-year-old interviewing me?"'"

Elliot Easton: "Every new single required you to make a video. We went way back with MTV. Bob Pittman came to Boston before it launched. We went out to a restaurant with him, and he told us all about this new thing. It was a little abstract to me, I didn't quite get it. 'It's like radio with pictures, and the record companies are going to give us the videos for free because it's such amazing promotion.' And that all came true."

Martha Quinn: "A lot of the bigger artists were still saying, 'We're selling out arenas. We don't need MTV.'"

John Elefante: "I didn't like making videos. Acting out some dumb part. I just thought it was hokey. I mean, the kind of videos that I liked were Peter Gabriel's, but they cost a million dollars apiece to make. I don't think Kansas ever had that kind of surplus."

Billy Squier: "I didn't want to do videos. None of us did. We were musicians. Then I went ahead and made one for 'Rock Me Tonite,' and the backlash to that was dramatic."

Les Garland: "If you think about a video that might have hurt somebody's career, you think about Billy Squier's 'Rock Me Tonite.' The power of negative and positive. You know, 'I like the song, but boy, I hate the video.'"

Billy Squier: "What was so shattering about that video wasn't that it was a bad video, and certainly not a bad song. It's a great song. It was a hit song. That fiasco is a four-minute clip that completely upended my career through no intention of mine. It had nothing to do with Billy Squier as a singer-songwriter-guitar-player-performer, and yet I was completely subverted by that."

Les Garland: "I had friends that were involved at Billy's record company, Capitol, and I would be asked all the time what I thought, of course. I remember the first time I saw 'Rock Me Tonite.' I don't even know if I could find the words to describe it. I said something like, 'Is this really the best image you can present of this guy? Is this really what you're looking to do?' It went down in history as the video that destroyed this guy's career. I've heard that said countless times now, so I suppose it must be true."

***

Billy Squier: "The video misrepresents who I am as an artist. I was a good-looking, sexy guy. That certainly didn't hurt in promoting my music. But in this video, I'm kind of a pretty boy. And I'm prancing around a room. People said, 'He's gay.' Or, 'He's on drugs.' It was traumatizing to me. I mean, I had nothing against gays. I have a lot of gay friends."[1]

Martha Quinn: "I swear, I wish I could talk to Billy Squier. It wasn't even that bad. That's just one of those things that's of the moment. If I was Billy, I would go on a 'Rock Me Tonite' tour with a big bed and pink T-shirt and make that the center of my show. That whole thing was so overblown, and I feel bad about that because he's so talented, and his songs were so good."

Billy Squier: "Forget what I had to go through after that to keep myself together and keep afloat in the world, this is the power of that medium and it can work both ways. It can also make other people tremendously successful who have nothing to do with music. People who look good, who have more dancers and effects, who are creating props around who they are."

Bob Pittman: "Everybody went, 'Oh my God, MTV is hot.' But the thing you have to remember is, the product became a hit right away, but it was still not being widely distributed. In fact, it was a dismal financial failure. With advertising, we had a budget of doing $10 million the first year. Instead we did $500,000 in advertising revenue. The board of directors hired a guy named Drew Lewis, who had been Ronald Reagan's secretary for transportation, to come in and run Warner-AmEx. He was a tough guy. He got a meeting with us soon as he came in, and he goes, 'Hey Bob, they all love you here. But if you can't make MTV profitable by the end of the year, I'm going to shut it down.'"

Martha Quinn: "I'll tell you exactly when MTV really started to make a noise. When the 'I want my MTV' spots started to air."

Les Garland: "The Rolling Stones were on tour in Europe. I set up a meeting with Mick Jagger in Paris and took a camera crew along with me. I pitched him the idea, and he told me, 'The Rolling Stones don't do commercials. We did something for Atlantic Records once, but we got paid *a lot* for that.' I said to him, 'It's about the money. Is that what's at issue here? Tell you what I'll do.' I reached into my pocket, pulled out one American dollar, put it down in front of him, and said, 'How about if I pay you out of my own pocket?' Next day, I had Mick Jagger on film saying, 'I want my MTV.' As soon as it got out that I'd got Mick, bang! We got David Bowie, Tina Turner, Pat Benatar…"

Steve Lukather: "Pretty quickly, MTV became this juggernaut, a phenomenon. Then, all of a sudden, you had to be pretty to play in the music business. Those of us who had our heads in the books, learning music the hard way, practice and study, taking every shitty gig there was, paying dues and eating shit up? Well, now you had to be a fucking actor, too. The whole game changed."

David Spero: "The truest thing that was said? 'Video Killed the Radio Star.' It was so much more exciting to watch it happen than hear it happen."

Bob Pittman: "We turned musicians into celebrities. Some people thought that was terrible. Some people thought it was wonderful. Prior to MTV, unless you had a front-row concert seat, you had no idea what the artists looked like."

Elliot Easton: "There's this magical thing that happens if you're on television. It's like, 'Oh, I've seen you on TV!' Instant celebrity."

Steve Lukather: "The drag for us was that they would make us spend $100,000 on a stupid video on the false promise they were going to play it. We'd have to split those costs with Sony, and they would take that $50,000 as recoupable income from us. This business is not for the squeamish, man. See this white hair, I've fucking earned every single one of them."

***

Donald Roeser: "Blue Öyster Cult's 'Shooting Shark' video was pretty ambitious. I got to hug a goat in that one. I don't know why. It was supposed to be some kind of dream. The videos cost almost as much as the records to make, and in some cases more. Each of our videos was $150,000. It took the band well into the 1990s to recoup all of those expenditures."

Steve Lukather: "It's us playing on the Michael Jackson record, and on Stevie Nicks's record. I played the guitar solo on Olivia Newton-John's 'Physical,' for God's sake. I was on MTV every day. I just wasn't making any money from it."

Al Cafaro: "At first, MTV was novel and fresh and exciting. But I think it quickly became a negative. It took the experience off the music, and it made it so much more about novelty and the visualization of a theme. And in the process, of course, we basically built their business for free. They developed this multimillion-dollar business off the back of the record companies' product and the artists' creativity."

Les Garland: "You know, I did get that tossed at me a time or two. I really found it to be pretty laughable. It seemed ludicrous to me. Why would we pay you to break your artist? Nobody paid us 15 percent of their royalties once they became successful, and I never had the nerve to come and ask for that."

Billy Squier: "I had a precious relationship with FM radio. All those records I heard I created my own story to. MTV stopped people from listening to music, and now they were watching it instead."

Steve Lukather: "Then it got dirty like it always does. Come on, man. You've seen the mobster movies. They're based upon reality. All I can say is it was a very expensive, and a really weird time to be a part of."

Billy Squier: "In the wake of 'Rock Me Tonite,' I tried to make subsequent videos play more to what I thought were my obvious strengths, which was performance based. It didn't really make a difference. The ship had sailed."

Steve Lukather: "You want me to tell you exactly how corrupt it at all was and what was going on? Man, I'd end up in a fucking pine box."

Billy Squier: "If I weren't that big at the time, no one would have cared. It's not really a silver lining, but it's the best I can get."

CHAPTER FIFTY-FIVE

CHASING THE MIGHTY DOLLAR.

"It's about how far you're prepared to go to make it."

Desmond Child: "My relationship with Paul Stanley continued. We kept writing together. Kiss had taken their makeup off, and I did a song with him called 'Heaven's on Fire' for their *Animalize* album [1984]."

Bruce Kulick: "I got the call to help out on *Animalize*. I'd actually auditioned for Kiss before, when Ace Frehley left the band. But I had facial hair then, and Gene Simmons hated that."

Desmond Child: "I had no relationship with Gene Simmons. I never had anything to do with him."

Bruce Kulick: "It was always a very intense dynamic between Paul and Gene. Paul had a keen sense of wanting to have big, competitive hit songs. And once the makeup came off, Gene kind of felt awkward. Paul had to steer the ship, and I never felt that was a bad thing at all. Paul's very driven."

***

Paul Stanley: "Look, subtlety is not in our name. If you think you're going to spend your hard-earned money and see some guy with an acoustic guitar sitting on a rug singing about saving the whales, you're at the wrong show."[1]

Bruce Kulick: "We played Cobo Hall in Detroit on the *Animalize* tour. Detroit was really important to Kiss, of course, and the MTV cameras were there. Gene, being Gene, knew Diana Ross very well. They'd dated for a while, and she was with us backstage. I was having a little trouble with the laces to my Reebok sneakers, and Diana Ross helped me to tie them. That there's a memory."

Desmond Child: "Paul was interested in buying a Bentley. I went down with him to the Bentley place, and they'd got a Bentley Arnage T, all black, looking like something the Queen Mother would've driven around in the back of. It was the sport model, so the seats had cross-patched leather. The fittings were walnut. Everything about it was perfection. By the time we left the place, I'd bought the Bentley, and Paul still had his Mercedes. Everybody who ever even looked at me in that car, I'd give them a $20 tip. Like, Sinatra would always hand $100 bills out. I couldn't do that much, but I could stretch to $20 bills."

Barry Goudreau: "I went through a real dry period [after leaving Boston]. Three years went by from the time I did the solo album to the time I did the *Orion the Hunter* album. I was sort of adrift."[2]

Pat Benatar: "Our record company were upset with the *Tropico* album. It *only* sold one and a half million records, and that's not enough. You've gotta sell five million each time."[3]

John Waite: "My marriage was falling apart so I wasn't seeing my wife, and I was living in New York. I was very good friends with Nina [Blackwood, MTV VJ], and I met another girl I wound up getting engaged to. 'Missing You' is an amalgam of three different people. Each girl played a large part in the song."[4]

***

John Parr: "I got a publishing contract with a little company called Carlin Music. They'd send my tapes out to the people of the day—Rod Stewart, Diana Ross. Meat Loaf was the first bite I got. He heard a couple of my songs and called me. A month later, I was living with him in Connecticut."

Patty Smyth: "We knew Jon Bon Jovi, because he was living above the Power Station. Scandal didn't have a guitar player yet. So, Jon pretended to play guitar in our 'Lyin' on You' video, which actually got us the record deal."[5]

John Waite: "['Missing You'] was kind of made up on the spot over somebody else's chord changes. I hadn't got a clue what I was going to do. I just heard the backing track and asked if I could sing over it. Me and this guy were writing this other song. I even used the Babys' 'Every Time I Think of You,' one of our big singles, to get me going."[6]

John Parr: "Meat Loaf was unique, larger than life. He had a reputation for being tough, but he was a sweetheart. He was a family guy, but he was also going through a very rough time. He'd just filed for Chapter 13 bankruptcy when I arrived in Connecticut. He'd signed a terrible deal with *Bat Out of Hell*, and he was $2 million in debt. We'd be working on a song and the bailiffs would come into the house and nick all his stuff."

Patty Smyth: "I was just so happy to get a record deal and have people believe in me. I grew up without a dad, so these were older guys who wore suits. To me they seemed like professionals, and I thought they knew what they were doing. Since I was a woman, they would weigh in on a lot more stuff than they would have with a dude."[7]

John Parr: "I was signed to Atlantic by Ahmet Ertegun and Doug Morris. Being the son of a Turkish diplomat, Ahmet knew all of these exotic people. I'd be out with him, and he'd go, 'Oh, this is the king of wherever.' He was the ultimate rock 'n' roller, too. A big cigar, a girl on each arm, and everything else that goes along with that. I mean, I was privileged enough to be at the sharp end of that real rock 'n' roll era."

John Waite: "That whole first chorus came about in one unbroken stream of word association... It's about being in love and being at a crossroads, and being in denial, and being in the sort of half-world of something being over. That terrible calmness, where you've stepped outside of that circle, and you don't ever get back in."[8]

Patty Smyth: "Mike Chapman brought us 'The Warrior.' I knew the song was a hit, and I knew I could sing the shit out of it."[9]

John Parr: "Atlantic put the money up and we went straight down to Criteria Studios in Miami. Stephen Stills was recording in the other room, so it was like I was in the big league. I had a very clear vision of what the *John Parr* album was going to be like. A blend of Foreigner, the Art of Noise, and a bit of blue-eyed soul. 'Naughty Naughty' wasn't even going to be on the record. It was just a riff I had that we used to warm up with in the studio. The Bee Gees also had a studio in Miami. They lent me a Fairlight [digital synthesizer and sampler], and I spent a couple of days at Criteria with it smashing the song up."

John Waite: "Every time I hear the word 'demographic,' I want to throw up. The music business—it's just fucking ridiculous... There's something primal about music, obviously. People respond to that, and you can't feed them prepackaged stuff."[10]

Patty Smyth: "I wanted to do a live video instead of some dumb warrior-esque video. I was unrecognizable because I had so much crap on my face and all these crazy costumes. I just got frustrated. I didn't feel like I was coming through."[11]

John Parr: "We came out with 'Naughty Naughty' in November '84. People loved the song, but it was tough going. At the time, the record companies were what they called 'triple bonusing' at radio. That meant they'd give their independent pluggers a triple bonus for getting a song playlisted at a major station. Well, Atlantic was the exception to the rule and weren't triple bonusing. And I was going up against Bruce Springsteen and Bryan Adams. 'Naughty Naughty' would be 109 on the chart one week, 94 the next, then 90. It made heartbreakingly slow progress, but over a six-month period it reached the Top 30, and what it did do was set the tone."

Barry Goudreau: "I was really pleased with *Orion the Hunter*. It felt good. We toured on that album opening for Aerosmith. It was when they first got back together, but before they had dried out. I'm telling you, that was a wild time. We would do a 20,000-seat venue and they would only have sold 500 tickets. Once Aerosmith had done their soundcheck, the local radio station would go on air and tell everyone that they'd shown up at the venue. Then there would be a walk-up that would sell out the place."[12]

Pat Benatar: "The record company start going, 'Well, what about Madonna?' Well, what about her? I taught her how to wear fucking tights, man. Please let her do it for a while."[13]

John Waite: "[After 'Missing You' was a hit] I was able to go back home and not feel like a loser, you know. My parents were really proud. I could go to the pub, and it was, like, people sending pints of Guinness over. It was very sweet."[14]

John Parr: "The thing is, it's about how far you're prepared to go to make it. And I was prepared to go to the end of the Earth."

CHAPTER FIFTY-SIX

TOTO, SURVIVOR, AND THE TALE OF TWO NEW VOICES.

"You fill your head full of your own shit."

Steve Lukather: "Bobby Kimball's state of mind made Jeff reluctant to tour. Bobby had deteriorated to the point he wasn't capable of bringing it every night. Our managers should've held everything up and gotten him into rehab. Paich, though, had gotten a handful of great songs together and so we set ourselves to work on our next album at his home studio, The Manor. We managed to get just one good track out of Bobby, on a song called 'Lion,' and that was painfully extracted over a period of weeks."

Jim Peterik: "It proved hard to follow the *Eye of the Tiger* album, and we labored over [1983's] *Caught in the Game*. Dave [Bickler], in particular, struggled. He had nodes on his throat and had a tough time in the studio. Following that album, we knew we needed a facelift. It was a very hard decision to let Dave go, but he took it well. There were no hard feelings. He knew he would need two years off to repair his throat after surgery, and we did what we had to do."

Steve Lukather: "In general, we had a hard time with just getting

Bobby to turn up to the sessions. He would disappear for days at a time. When he did show up, more often than not he wouldn't have a voice to do anything with, and we ran into a brick wall. Bobby was not an evil man, but blow is a very addictive drug, and it had changed him."

Bobby Kimball: "There were some personality problems between some of the guys, and about three-quarters of the way through that record, I was asked to leave the band. I told the guys I wouldn't call them to come back. I didn't want to be where I was not welcome by everyone."[1]

Steve Lukather: "It was Jeff who finally pulled the plug on him. Even after a thousand warnings, Bobby didn't see it coming. He was stunned. It was tragic. It was also a body blow for us as a band. We were at the height of our career, and it really knocked us off course. To be fair to Bobby, some of the songs were written in impossible keys, and he was ridden hard. It might have been Steve Porcaro that said, 'We had a racehorse, and we ruined it.'"

Jimi Jamison: "I was in a band called Cobra who were a lot heavier than Survivor. So I came out of a heavy metal band, and was thrown into a pop-rock band, which was a bit of a culture shock to me in the beginning."[2]

Jim Peterik: "We held auditions here in Chicago. When Jimi came to town, we knew at once he was the guy. His voice just rang out. He was also an amazing guy. Very humble. Southern charm."

Jimi Jamison: "I did a lot of jingles singing before I got into Survivor. I was in the studio every day from 8:30 a.m. until 7:30 p.m. at night. It really taught me a lot about how to work the microphone. My first audition with those guys, I hit the note in 'Eye of the Tiger.' It's a high C, and I'd never before hit a note that high in my life."[3]

David Paich: "We had to go through the whole audition thing. That was hard. We went through a bunch of people and didn't find anybody."

***

Steve Lukather: "We offered Richard Page the gig, but he declined. His own band Mr. Mister had just signed to RCA."

Richard Page: "I knew those guys, [but] I wanted to do stuff on my own. I was honored and flattered, just couldn't do it."[4]

Henry Small: "I got asked to join Toto. Unfortunately, I had a manager at the time, Terry Powell, who had signed Toto to Columbia, and I guess they'd had a falling-out. I was told I'd be getting $10,000 a week, plus royalties for anything that I wrote. Then they found out about Terry, and that was the end of that. I went from having a party, because this was a great offer, to... I was crushed, obviously, and embittered."

Fergie Frederiksen: "I was in Frankfurt recording with Ricky Phillips and Tim Pierce. I got a phone call at the studio, and someone asked if I'd like to try out for Toto."[5]

Steve Lukather: "Fergie had sung backing vocals with Survivor and at the time was fronting a band called Le Roux. He was male-model handsome and sang super-high."

Jim Peterik: "Of all our albums, *Vital Signs* is probably my favorite. Nine songs, no duds. We were reunited with Ron Nevison, which was really a blessing. Ron had a way of knowing exactly what was needed. He wasn't a musician, but he *knew* music."

Fergie Frederiksen: "Probably half of the [*Isolation*] album was already written, and the other half was written when I arrived. I co-wrote 'Endless,' too, but didn't get credit."[6]

Steve Lukather: "God bless Fergie, but it was hard for him in the studio, it really was. We were asking a lot from him."

David Paich: "When I get in the vocal booth, everybody struggles.

I set such a high bar. I learned that perfectionism from working with guys like Seals & Crofts and Steely Dan. I would watch both of them fine-tune the vocals to the point they were perfect. So I used to put everybody through the grinder trying to get ours to be perfect."

Jim Peterik: "We played Jimi 'Broken Promises,' and he couldn't hit the high note the first time. I said to Frankie, 'We better lower this a half step.' Jimi looked at me and said, 'Aw, give half a man a chance!' He gave it another shot, and he nailed it. Jimi liked a challenge."

Steve Lukather: "I feel that Fergie was maybe pushed unfairly, and then we became impatient too quickly. We reacted in a panic. But it also was painfully obvious that *Isolation* didn't sound like the work of the band that had made *IV*."

Jim Peterik: "The best songs write themselves. I wrote most of 'The Search Is Over' in the car. It took me three hours to write. I'd got my little tape recorder with me, and I was driving around. I never would have come up with that modulation had I been sitting at a piano. Sometimes a thought will come into your head, and you just have to capture it right then, or else it's gone. You can't do it consciously."

Jimi Jamison: "When we recorded that song, it was just Ron and me in the studio one night. He whipped out a bottle of wine and we proceeded to get drunker than a couple of hobos."[7]

Jim Peterik: "I'd really like to be remembered for a bunch of songs, but I think 'The Search Is Over' is *the one*. Sometimes magic happens. I love those stories people tell you when they recognize you on the street. How 'The Search Is Over' was their prom song."

David Paich: "Once more, we'd felt we were bulletproof. We thought we could put any lead singer in there with us and make a hit record. We found out, when we shipped a whole bunch of records, that the retailers were very upset and disappointed that we didn't give them *Toto V*."

***

Steve Lukather: "Before we even finished the record, we'd been booked a major arena tour of the US. We spent $350,000 of our own money on pre-production and rehearsals, and then ticket sales were slow to nonexistent. We lost our shirts. To look out at a 10,000-seat arena and see a quarter that number of people was brutal."

John Parr: "I opened for Toto on that tour. I used to travel with Steve Lukather and Jeff Porcaro. That was the naughty bus, and we just had a ball."

Steve Lukather: "Between us in the band, a lot of blame went on. Fergie took the brunt of it, which wasn't fair."

Fergie Frederiksen: "It wasn't quite working out. There was nothing I could do about it. I'm not an R&B singer and never will be."[8]

Steve Lukather: "We fired our booking agents in a rather shitty way, but really, we were trying to pass the buck. People were obviously waiting for us to serve up the next 'Rosanna' or 'Africa.' Shit, if it was that easy, I'd be working from out of my own space shuttle by now."

Jim Peterik: "We were out on the road with REO. Frankie and I were at poolside in LA, and we got a call from Stallone. 'Hey, you guys gotta do it again.' This time we didn't have the benefit of working from a rough cut of the movie. He sent us the script for *Rocky IV*, and we cut 'Burning Heart' on a break from the tour back in Chicago. It was just a little studio, but it was available and cheap."

Dennis DeYoung: "Irving Azoff called me up and said, 'You wanna try to write a song for this David Lynch movie, *Dune*? They're looking for one.' Okay. So I read the book. No idea what it was about. Got through 150 pages and thought, 'I hate that.' But I got the idea. Deserts. Moons. About a month later, Azoff called again and said, 'They got somebody else to do it.'"

***

Steve Lukather: "Two movie things were offered to us. *Footloose* and *Dune*. David Lynch's offer was for us to write the whole score. Being artsy-fartsy fuckheads, when I heard the words 'David' and 'Lynch' I was sold. The score was pretty much Paich's baby, but we all jumped in and wrote for it. David Lynch would sit with us while we were recording the music. He wore the exact same clothes every day: khaki pants, a white shirt buttoned up to the neck, and a brown fleeced flying jacket. This was in the middle of summer, 100 degrees in the shade, but he didn't appear to sweat. I ate lunch with him every day for three months and also in the exact same place—Bob's Big Boy, a '50s-style diner in Burbank. Every day, without fail, Lynch had a Bob's cheeseburger."

Jim Peterik: "There's a moment in time for every successful band when all the gears click, and that was ours. Frankie and I were on a roll. Jimi was flawless with his pitch and phrasing. I knew with whatever I wrote, he could sing it."

Steve Lukather: "*Footloose* became the Number One hit movie in the country, and the soundtrack album sold ten million copies. We were invited to the premiere of *Dune* and hid under our seats with embarrassment. It'd been sold to us as the next *Star Wars*. We were salivating. Like, we were going to win Academy Awards and be made gazillionaires. You fill your head full of your own shit."

CHAPTER FIFTY-SEVEN

DON HENLEY AND CYNDI LAUPER MAKE "BOYS OF SUMMER" AND "TIME AFTER TIME."

"You can't go to school and learn to sing soulful."

Danny Kortchmar: "I'd kept on writing and coming up with grooves for Henley. The *Building the Perfect Beast* record in 1984 was the next step, the next way to go, I thought. The great thing about working with Don was, if I made a primitive demo at home, put it on a cassette, and played it for him, he would say right away, 'I can do something with that.' Boom, we're done. We'd go in the studio and start work on the track that same night, or the next day, right away. The idea that you could write a piece and have one of the greatest singer-songwriters ever, period, go, 'Yeah, let's do it.' There's nobody there to tell us what to do. Nobody telling us we've got to hurry up. Nothing. We did it our own way. There's no budget with Don, no time constraint, we do what we want. Because of that we were able to experiment and try different things. Throw stuff away that didn't work. It was a very creative experience."

***

Cyndi Lauper: "To all the songs [on *She's So Unusual*], I thought we should have our own sound. It was raw, but I wanted it to be modern. This was the time, and you only get one shot at a first impression, right?"[1]

Rob Hyman: "We spent months in our little studio in Philly. Then Rick [Chertoff, producer] said, 'The record sounds great but we could use one more song.' The door is closing, the budget's closing, time is short, no pun intended. Cyndi and I sat at the piano one night after the session. Everybody else went out to dinner, and we didn't."[2]

Danny Kortchmar: "What Don usually does is pop a cassette of a song in his car, drive around, and start singing along with it while it's playing. 'Boys of Summer' was a demo track sent to Don by Mike Campbell from Tom Petty and the Heartbreakers. He listened to it, loved it, started singing along to it."

Don Henley: "It was one of those great, rare moments where I got so inspired by the track that Mike Campbell had given me that it just sort of wrote itself. It came just screaming out of me. And I was jumping up and down in the car 'cause I knew I had something there."[3]

Danny Kortchmar: "When we started to work on it, Mike was there. Great guy, very creative. Don had loved his demo so much that he wanted Mike to duplicate it. It was on a cassette, so now we've got to get it over to multitrack, and so Don can sing to it. Mike has got to duplicate everything on the track, and Don is meticulous about that. He wanted *exactly* what was on the tape. Mike was able to re-create a lot of it, he had the drum part and the keyboard part going. But there was one lick, the one that starts the song off, Don had him play that lick thirty times. Don would sit there and go, 'No, one more. No, once again.' Mike's not used to that. He's already played it as far as he's concerned. I'm sure the Heartbreakers didn't work like that, but that was Don's choice."

Don Henley: "People I work with will tell you that I'm not very demonstrative, at least until most of the pieces fall into place. I liked the percussion Mike had created with the melodies. I liked the guitar sounds a lot, and the synthesizer lines. All the layers merged into a texture that was really evocative."[4]

Cyndi Lauper: "We were able to take real-life things, real things that were happening, things that people said, things that people did, and put them right in ['Time After Time']. You know, 'Lying in my bed, I hear the clock tick, and I think of you.' Not for nothing. And if you're writing and you put something very real in it, then someone listening is going to feel something very real."[5]

Rob Hyman: "We just caught lightning…Most of the instrumentation was first, second take. I keep telling people, 'The record you hear is the demo.'"[6]

Danny Kortchmar: "I came in late with the synths and just added to what Mike had already put down. It was one of those horrible-looking Roland guitar synths. That piece of gear was so finicky and difficult to manipulate that we had to keep punching in all the time. It would keep glitching and we'd freak out, but it was one of the first successful uses of that thing."

Don Henley: "I had mixed emotions about the new electronic instruments."[7]

Cyndi Lauper: "['Time After Time'] was just a working title. And every time I tried to pull it out, everything fell apart. The melody was catchy and hypnotic. The rhythm was hypnotic. My vocal was hypnotic. The songs had to be not just hit songs. Because I didn't want that. I wanted them to be deep. I wanted you to get the chills when you heard them. I wanted it to be like, 'Wow!'"[8]

Don Henley: "My inspiration [for the lyrics] came from the Dylan Thomas poem, which begins, 'I see the boys of summer in their ruin.' It was a gift. It came from the mysterious place that lyrics sometimes come from. I'd been stuck on the bridge section, couldn't get the words, the melody. One afternoon, I was driving on Interstate 405, somewhere south of Sunset, the cassette of the track blaring through the sound system. I looked to my left and there it was: a 1979 Cadillac Seville with a 'Deadhead' sticker on the back. It just struck me as ironic, paradoxical, with a little touch of nostalgia, and it went right into the song."[9]

Danny Kortchmar: "There were a couple of notes that I encouraged Don to hit. But I didn't force him to do it. He forced himself. Nobody is harder on Don than Don. He's unbelievably good. And I'll tell you why. He's got soul. He grew up playing in soul bands in Texas. He grew up on Black music and soul and R&B bands. He has a fantastic high tenor voice. A soulful voice, I should say, which is why he can get his message over."

Don Henley: "We recorded the whole song in whatever key it was written in, and I did it, and I said, 'This is not quite right. We've got to take this up half a step.' And they all looked at me like, 'You're nuts! What's the matter with you?' And I said, 'No, believe me, it'll be a lot better.' So we did it all over again and they went, 'Geez, you're right.'"[10]

Danny Kortchmar: "Some guys can do it, and some guys can't. Don can do it. It's just that simple. You've got to have the physical equipment for it. Then you've got to have the mind for it. Then you've got to have the soul. Because without those elements, you've got nothing. It's not enough just to hit high notes, it's got to mean something. It's God-given. You can't go to school and learn to sing soulful. They don't teach you that in school."

Don Henley: "I learned in the Eagles, from way back, that putting the song in the right key is very important. You have to get it up high enough so that it has a sense of urgency, so that your voice cuts through."[11]

Andrew McNeice: "Oh, absolutely, 'Time After Time' is a classic melodic rock song. I'm also a diehard fan of Rob Hyman's band, the Hooters, so they'd got me there from the start."

Rob Hyman: "The video really drove it home. Cyndi was perfect for that medium as well. All the planets aligned."[12]

Cyndi Lauper: "I was very angry, too. Because I felt like, 'You bastards put me through so much just to write this fucking song, and now you think it's the best thing ever.' I was always being told, 'You're not a good writer.'"[13]

Danny Kortchmar: "I knew 'Boys of Summer' was great. Did I know it was a hit? No. I'm not Mr. Hit Producer. I've never in my life said, 'That's a hit!' Because I don't know. I know what I love."

Don Henley: "The song is forty years old now. It's just another reminder that life is short but it's very wide."[14]

Danny Kortchmar: "Don actually fired me three or four times during the course of the three albums we made together. He would fire me by mail. And then I'd get another letter from him saying, 'All is forgiven. It's okay. Come on, let's go back to work.' One occasion, it was my wife's birthday and a bunch of us went out to dinner. We all put our credit cards down to pay for the meal. Next day, Don sends me a letter. He wrote, 'That was a low move. You should have paid for dinner. Expecting everyone to pay...' I didn't expect everyone to pay, they just threw their cards on the table. But he was right, I should have said, 'No, no, I got this.' But I didn't. As for that being a reason to get fired from a musical project? *Mmmmm*, that's a stretch. So I sent him a letter back even nastier than the one he'd sent me. Six weeks go by, and then we went back to work."

CHAPTER FIFTY-EIGHT

STYX COMES UNDONE.

"There was such a lack of self-awareness."

Tommy Shaw: "We tried to keep that lineup together, but it wasn't meant to be."[1]

James "JY" Young: "We changed management as a result of [*Kilroy Was Here*]. It was a financial disaster. It alienated probably half our fan base. Dennis insisted on firing the manager that had managed us to this great success."[2]

Tommy Shaw: "We had gotten comfortable with our dysfunctional way of dealing with each other by complaining to our manager who would try to smooth things over."[3]

Dennis DeYoung: "Okay, here's the number one problem with *Kilroy Was Here* above everything else. Throw everything else out. What the music was like, whose big idea it was. It was the fact that Tommy Shaw quit. We had a stadium tour booked in 1984. I'd promised JY for his support for *Kilroy*... that I would do it, and Tommy quit the band to pursue his own solo career and that ended Styx. And it took us all by shock."

***

Tommy Shaw: "I would say there were underlying situations to that. We had worked nonstop for years, never taking a significant amount of time off."[4]

Dennis DeYoung: "They were so mad—*they*—that they wanted me to simply replace Tommy and carry on. JY wanted me to plug somebody else in for the tour. There was such a lack of self-awareness. 'How does that work? Do you know who Tommy is? Do you even know how this thing works? Have you been watching?' I didn't want to have the responsibility of selling Styx without this guy. I wanted to be in the band with Tommy. And do you know who JY wanted to be in the band? The guy from Stray Cats. What's his name? Brian Setzer. He's great, a wizard, but I talked to Brian. I said to him, 'You want to be in Styx? You're great, but the critics like you. Why would you get in this fucking band?' So I said no, and I waited. I thought Tommy would do a solo album and he'd come back."

Tommy Shaw: "I overestimated my own ability to make [*Girls with Guns*, 1984]. I had to rely on others. At the time, my vision was probably a little bit blurred."[5]

Dennis DeYoung: "I never wanted to do a solo album of my own. I only did one because Tommy had quit the band. I had the title *Desert Moon* from the *Dune* movie. After I got passed over on that I said, 'Well, what else could the song be?' I wrote it on the theme that you can't go home again. That's the song. The 'Desert Moon' is that place in your memory that you want to go back to, and you can't. That song had a great fucking video, too. It might even be better than the song. It captures a moment in time. The essence of the '80s is right there, the loss of innocence. Blah-blah-blah."

Tommy Shaw: "Back then, I had no idea what I was doing."[6]

Dennis DeYoung: "If Styx does it, how big a song is 'Desert Moon'? It was Top 10 for me, so it's going to be Top 3 at least. That should have been *our* next album. It's a good record, but I wanted to be in a band. I took my solo career very seriously, but it was almost like a hobby."

Tommy Shaw: "In hindsight, if we'd been better able to communicate with each other it's possible we might not have had such an acrimonious split. But then again, the personalities were what they were."[7]

Dennis DeYoung: "This gigantic void was there for the next six years. I didn't tour any of my solo records. I didn't want to. I didn't want to be 'Dennis DeYoung.' I wanted to be Dennis DeYoung in Styx. I still see myself that way to this day. I wanted to be your favorite guy in Styx. And if I wasn't, it was Chuck, or Tommy, or JY, okay? We're on the same fucking team. As I've gone through my life and with that in mind, it's always impressed upon me, 'You ain't so much. You've worked with people you thought were more talented than you, but it happened to you.' And the only thing I can put that down to is dumb stupid luck and the willingness not to ever give up. That's not to say I don't have an ego, but there's nothing wrong with that if it's used properly. And it's got to be big. You don't get to have this whole wall over here of platinum and gold discs from being a shrinking violet."

CHAPTER FIFTY-NINE

REO THROW AWAY THE OARS, FOREVER.

―⚮―

"There are times when even I gag on it."

Kevin Cronin: "There was a girl, of course. When I met her, she was dating one of my friends, so it was off-limits. But I definitely felt the thing with her, and we became friends. I entered the friend zone. About a year later, they broke up, and it was like, 'Well, now what's your excuse?' I realized that I was afraid to expose those feelings. I was afraid of being rejected. That was what the song was about in a nutshell. I started it in about 1973. I wrote the verses, but I couldn't write the chorus. I wrote a number of horrible choruses. I was like, 'Okay, I'm going to file this, and I'm going to wait.' The truth is, I hadn't lived the chorus yet. Finally, about twelve years later, I had a cathartic day. I literally was on the floor of my bedroom, crying and sweating. I went and got my lyric notebook, and the very first line of the song is, 'I can't fight this feeling any longer.' And I was like, '*That's* what this song is about.' It was right there all this time, hiding in plain sight. Music is an amazing thing. Without it I would never have survived, and songwriting has been my savior."[1]

***

Bruce Hall: "We didn't make it out of the Midwest by being a ballad band. We rock. We rock hard. [But] we've been successful with ballads, and we can write a love ballad better than anybody."[2]

Kevin Cronin: "The kind of songs we write are like folk songs. I look at them like electrified folk songs. All my songs I write on acoustic guitar, and then I bring them to the band, and they crank it up."[3]

Gary Richrath: "I think 'Can't Fight This Feeling' is the best song he's ever written. I do. The problem is, he's written it on a piano or an acoustic guitar, and he doesn't hear in his head a Marshall amp or a Les Paul in there. And I do."[4]

Paul Elliott: "It's a great song, but you just can't help but smile whenever you hear the chorus."

Kevin Cronin: "In my defense of my overuse of the rhyme, I wrote that chorus in fifteen minutes. It just appeared there on the paper."[5]

Paul Elliott: "I mean, come on. It goes, 'I can't fight this feeling anymore. I've forgotten what I started fighting for. It's time to bring this ship into the shore. And throw away the oars, forever.' When I interviewed Kevin Cronin, I had to ask him if he thought he'd possibly over-egged it just a little bit there."

Kevin Cronin: "There are times when even I gag on it. But it was a sitting duck—I couldn't resist. It sounded like a hit, so I went for it."[6]

Neal Doughty: "From that time on, radio only wanted that type of power ballad from us. They would always call us up and ask, 'Where's the ballad?'"[7]

Kevin Cronin: "It's just one of those songs that gets into people's bloodstreams. Over here, everybody knows it. The people who were in high school or college when it was first released and now work in television, movies, and advertising companies. It's a song that keeps popping up."[8]

Neal Doughty: "You can't complain. We wouldn't be working today if it wasn't for those big ballads."[9]

Kevin Cronin: "We've all gone through moments of insecurity. I remember this one day, kind of just thinking, 'Wow, there's people who at this point in their lives have been doctors or schoolteachers, or just occupations that really have an impact. Scientists discovering new things! And here I am, a frickin' singer in a rock band.' I was feeling kind of like, 'Oh boy. What have I contributed to the world? How have I made the world a better place?' Then I thought, 'Well, wait a minute. These hardworking people that make the world go round, we kind of make their lives more fun. Without us, they'd be really bored and probably wouldn't do as good a job.' Then I felt a little better."[10]

CHAPTER SIXTY

BRYAN ADAMS AND *RECKLESS*.

---

*"I figured if I could remember it, and
I could sing it, so could anybody."*

Bryan Adams: "I never really cared what anybody else thought about me. I didn't have the time to worry if I was being undervalued. I just had to keep going because the alternative of washing dishes was no good. I had no choice, I had to do it. And luckily, I had another record in me after *Cuts Like a Knife*."

Jim Vallance: "Bryan took a significant amount of time away from touring to make time for the writing. We were certainly aware of other bands that were making records, and other genres. We always tried to sit down together and write good songs, and sometimes we did. And by that time, 1984, we really had learned about our craft."

Bryan Adams: "I thought the songs Jim and I were writing were exciting. The litmus test for us was always to put a song on in the car and see how it sounded. If it was good enough for me, it was good enough full stop. Never again did my record company ever show up and try to tell me what to do."

Jim Vallance: "We knew what we were doing. *Reckless* was a premeditated, well-considered album that came from a lot of hard work and thought. We probably wrote twenty songs to get the twelve that ended up on the record."

Bryan Adams: "I've never really thought of myself as a good singer, or a good guitarist. I've made the best of what I could with the three chords that I knew. When it came to the songs, I figured if I could remember it, and I could sing it, so could anybody. However, simple is difficult. I really must give credit to Jim. Great teacher. Always would be there to help me filter out the shite. Take 'I Need Somebody' off *Reckless*. It was just a jam that was sitting on a cassette tape until Jim picked it out for us to work on."

Jim Vallance: "We knew we were doing our best work at that moment in time. That this was as good as we could do. We were happy, we were pleased."

Bryan Adams: "I remember listening to the first take of 'Run to You,' which is the one you hear on the record, and thinking, 'Fuck, this is great.'"

Jim Vallance: "Writing the lyrics to 'Summer of '69,' we literally sat across from each other with blank sheets of paper in our laps. I couldn't from all these years later tell you which line was written by who. Bryan would write a line. I would write a line. It was like a game of tennis, back and forth. By the end of the day, the blank sheets of paper were full of lyrics and, as with any song, you kind of marvel at it. It's a somewhat autobiographical song. I can't speak for Bryan, but we consciously decided to write a song about our schooldays and our first bands and girlfriends. I was thinking about the first band I was in at thirteen, and Betty Donaldson, who was my first big crush when I was fifteen. It wasn't her mother's porch, but it was someone else's porch I was standing on. That song is close to my heart. It's a little more my story, and Bryan's story, too."

Bryan Adams: "People have always talked about that everyman thing with me. As I said, it's about making music that everybody can sing. Isn't that the joy of it? And *everyone* can sing 'Summer of '69.' That's also the magic of it."

Jim Vallance: "We'd finished the song, and it was titled 'Best Days of My Life.' We left it like that for weeks and weeks, and then we came back to it one day, and we thought it was not finished. 'Summer of '69' was a better title and it was just one line of lyric, three lines into the song. So we just took that phrase and shoehorned it into another couple of spots in the song and changed the title. Miraculously, it worked. It elevated the song immeasurably."

Paul Elliott: "The truth of the matter is, Bryan Adams wrote 'Summer of '69' because he wanted his own version of Bob Seger's 'Night Moves.' Every possible teenage fantasy is right there in 'Night Moves.'"

Bryan Adams: "I was such a huge Tina Turner fan. I used to go and see her in the clubs before *Private Dancer* happened for her and when she was still trying to get back on her feet. Back in 1982, Tina was coming to Vancouver, and just for a laugh, Jim and I wrote a song for her called 'Lock Up Your Sons Cuz Tina's in Town.' Terrible song. I managed to wangle my way backstage at her show. She'd just played this tremendous set, and I saw her coming down the hallway, they'd wrapped her in a blanket. As she went by me, I said, 'Miss Turner, I've written a song for you.' I handed her this cassette tape, and she said, 'Thank you very much,' and disappeared into the night.

"The real fun came in 1984 when I got a call from the producer John Carter. A sweet guy. He said, 'Man, I'm producing Tina Turner. Do you have a song for her?' We were finishing up *Reckless* in New York and I told him I didn't, but maybe Tina would sing on one of my songs. I sent him 'It's Only Love.' Never heard back. So, fast forward...*Reckless* is mixed, done. I'm back in Vancouver, and I hear that Tina is coming to town again, this time to open a show for Lionel Richie. I got a message to her manager, asking if she'd have time to record this song for my album. And I got a call back saying Tina wanted to meet me.

I'm backstage in Vancouver once more, so nervous, and Tina is coming down the hallway again but this time she has that big wig on. I could hear her saying, 'Where is he? Which one is he?' Someone said to her, 'He's the scrawny little shit over there in the corner.' She came over and said to me, 'I love that song.'

"She recorded it with us the next day. It was only when we were in the studio I realized 'It's Only Love' was in my pitch. It wasn't really made for her. I'm twenty-four, and I had to go into the room and say to her, 'Tina, it's not really working with you singing my melody. Why don't you sing this…' And I started to sing, pretending to be Tina Turner. After that, she just went off in the booth and did her thing. When she'd said her goodbyes, I turned to Bob Clearmountain, who was my co-producer, and said, '*Tell me* you got that.' We ran the tape back and there it was, a sensational moment."

Al Cafaro: "There are just a few times in your career, if you're lucky, when someone presents you with something and you go, 'Oh wow!' When you just *know it* right away. *Reckless* was one of those times. It was ecstasy when we got handed that record. Super exciting."

Jim Vallance: "You never really know, you can't predict."

Bryan Adams: "There was a lot of pressure to put 'Heaven' out as the first single, because it was easy, and people were playing it already. I didn't care what anybody else said, I was determined 'Run to You' would come out first. Never regretted it."

Al Cafaro: "With *Reckless*, it was so clearly going to be a record that would live on the radio for a year, eighteen months, or more, and as you rolled out all these singles. I mean, people were just *dying* when they heard it."

Jim Vallance: "The album went to Number One, and then 'Heaven' went to Number One. That was enormously thrilling. Bryan was touring with Journey, I think, and we were both keeping a close eye on the charts, week to week. It was, like, Number 89, then 72, then 58… Then it gets up into the twenties and the teens. It's like watching a horse race and you're rooting for your horse to win. Bryan and I were on the phone almost daily. I was in Vancouver, and I said to him, 'Gosh, if it goes to Number One, I'll jump on an airplane, fly to wherever you are, and we'll celebrate.' It went to Number One, and Bryan was in Cleveland. So I jumped on a plane, and we clinked our glasses in Cleveland. That moment was magical."

Bryan Adams: "Throughout my career, I've always pushed myself to be with people that are better than me. I consider myself to be extremely average, but when I put myself with good people, they get good things out of me."

Jim Vallance: "I'm grateful for having been a part of *Reckless*, and for having had the success we had in that period of time. Our hard work paid off. I sometimes forget how hard I worked in the '80s. That success was earned."

CHAPTER SIXTY-ONE

FOREIGNER SENDS IN THE CHOIR.

"It's the one song I'll be remembered for long after I'm dead and gone."

Mick Jones: "Every album in the making has its challenges. *Agent Provocateur* was one where we began writing and experimenting in the studio. I didn't want to repeat the formula of *4*, so there was never a question of working with Mutt Lange again. I started off the record collaborating with a New York engineer, Frank Filipetti, who'd worked with Billy Joel and Carly Simon. Frank was first rate, but I found it difficult to get back into the swing of things. My wheels weren't rolling. When I at last did get some clarity back, I decided to have Trevor Horn produce the record with us. He'd just come off making *90125* with Yes, which had been very successful both commercially and creatively."

Lou Gramm: "I asked [my co-writer] Bruce Turgon to come in with me and help me play 'Midnight Blue' for Mick as an idea for the new album. Bruce had an acoustic guitar. He played the chords, and I sang a verse and a chorus. Mick goes, 'Pretty good. Let me see the guitar.' Bruce gave him the guitar, and he tried to figure out the chords and the voicings, and you could see he was getting frustrated. Bruce took the guitar and showed him the fingering and stuff like that. That didn't help the situation. That got him enraged. Somebody was showing *him*? And he says, 'Well, it's pretty good. Let's forget that, though.'"[1]

Mick Jones: "We began in New York with Trevor, then the project was shifted to London. It became apparent pretty quickly that Trevor's focus wasn't in line with mine, and things went awry. The fact was, working with Yes had left him pretty much frazzled and, really, he wasn't in a fit state to take anything else on. The sessions broke down. Trevor and I mutually agreed to part ways."

Lou Gramm: "A waste of time and money."[2]

Mick Jones: "We'd flown all our gear over to London at great cost. That made it impractical for us to move again, so were stuck fast in the old Island Records studios, SARM West in Notting Hill. I started to make calls, desperate to find us another producer. The late Alex Sadkin's was one of the first names to pop up. Alex was producing a Thompson Twins album, and he'd also done Bob Marley's *Survival* and a bunch of Grace Jones records. I duly gave Alex the job of helping me steer *Agent Provocateur*. That was an error on my part."

Lou Gramm: "When Mick and I finally resumed writing, I began worrying about the direction the band was headed... A sentiment shared by Rick Wills. Mick didn't seem to care."[3]

Mick Jones: "Alex had a softer approach to making records than we were known for, and I think ended up feeling a bit impotent. It fell back to me to make all the decisions. To be honest, I wasn't at the top of my game either and so a sort of vacuum developed into which all our ideas got lost. The hardest thing to do was keep everyone focused. We were writing and recording at the same time. Not the best way to make an album. There were always last-minute changes to tracks which led to frustration among the band members. We did at least have one saving grace. On *4*, I'd observed what Thomas Dolby was doing on his

Jupiter-8, which at that time was a cutting-edge keyboard. I'd gone and bought myself a Roland Jupiter-8, and I got the guy from our local music store in London to come round to my apartment and show me how to work it."

Lou Gramm: "Mick would stay up nights playing with the sounds. Thereby the songs we wrote were keyboard songs. At the eleventh hour he would put a little guitar part on it. I told him face-to-face, 'We're going to lose our rock audience.'"[4]

Mick Jones: "At the very beginning of the sessions, I was fiddling around on the Roland, and I came up with the opening chords to a song. Once I'd got the vocal line set, I'd played Trevor my backing track. He'd immediately enthused, 'That's a Number One.' After that, I also came up with a chord progression for strings on the Roland. It was simple in its shape, but it's such a memorable melody because it's so easy to remember."

Lou Gramm: "A lot of the keyboard songs were ballads. I started to dislike being involved with the band."[5]

Mick Jones: "The most profound moment of making 'I Want to Know What Love Is' was when we had the choir come in. Originally, I'd wanted Aretha Franklin to do a duet with Lou."

Lou Gramm: "The day that Mick and I were supposed to work on my lead vocal for the song happened to be the same day the choir came in. So Mick started working with them."[6]

Mick Jones: "I hadn't experienced a choir since I was eight or nine, and in the church choir. I'd certainly never been surrounded by thirty or forty voices, which was the case with the New Jersey Mass Choir."

Lou Gramm: "That was very interesting, but the clock was ticking, and we had no real vocal on that song. I told Mick that I was going to take the other engineer and go in the smaller studio next door and work on the lead vocals, and he was okay with that, which surprised the heck out of me. Because usually, any vocal that I did, he wanted to be there. He wanted to interject his little, 'Can you do this, Lou?' 'Can you do that, Lou?' He felt the choir and how they sang was so important, and 'I Want to Know What Love Is' was his baby. He told me, 'Go ahead and sing the song.' I'm walking in there thinking, 'Who is this guy? This is not the Mick I know.'"[7]

Mick Jones: "We did a couple of takes to warm up and get everybody into it, but it wasn't happening. It needed a little more finesse. The conductor came over to me and said, 'Hey man, there's something missing and we're just gonna see if we can find the vibe this time.' He went and got everyone in a circle, me included, and my mother, who was there that day, and asked us to say the Lord's Prayer together. And, phew, it blew my fucking mind. I was in this circle of soulful people and thinking about it still brings tears to my eyes. We did it in one take after that."

Lou Gramm: "When we played the vocal track to Mick, he was very moved. I got no criticisms."[8]

Paul Elliott: "There's an emotional power to so many of those songs from that era. They're about love, or heartbreak, in its many forms. And what's more important in your life when you're eighteen years old than finding and falling in love with someone? It's a heady combination unless you're emotionally stunted. 'I Want to Know What Love Is'? Yes, I did. All the yearning that's in there, and what could be more powerful than having it sung by Lou Gramm?"

Lou Gramm: "I love the song, but it pigeonholed us into something that we were not... I think ultimately it did substantial damage to our rock reputation."[9]

Paul Elliott: "There's also the history of Atlantic Records in that song. Mick Jones didn't write it for just a rock audience."

***

Mick Jones: "When we were close to wrapping with Alex, Ahmet Ertegun paid a visit to the studio. Ahmet was very much into his soul and gospel, so I wanted to play him the finished track. We went and sat in this little mix room, just him and me, and I turned the lights down and rolled the tape. I'll always remember, during the second chorus I risked looking over at him and he had tears rolling down his cheeks. That I had brought the fabled Ahmet Ertegun to tears with a song was a profound achievement for me."

Lou Gramm: 'During the negotiations for the percentages for '…Love Is,' I wrote down 'Mick 60, me 40.' He immediately became indignant. His sheet read, 'Me 95, Lou 5.' I was pissed beyond belief."[10]

Eric Martin: "I first met Mick Jones at the Sunset Marquis hotel in Los Angeles, and we had a couple of drinks together. We tried to write a couple of songs. We got together in a little studio. I was playing piano, and he was on guitar. Lou Gramm was there, too. Mick was kind of phasing Lou out at the time. Lou came into the room. Mick and I are in the middle of writing a song. Lou goes [one finger], 'Ding, ding, ding…' on the piano, and walks away. And Mick says to me, 'Ah, fuck, we're going to have to give him 15 percent for that. He never takes no for an answer.' It was kind of sad."

Lou Gramm: "He wouldn't budge…His hard-line stance cost me millions of dollars."[11]

Mick Jones: "We got the album done, but it wasn't easy."

Lou Gramm: "[Mick and I] had a very good friendship. But after the 'I Want to Know What Love Is' thing happened, it was different. I knew what he did to me was wrong and it was dishonest. He made a fortune, and I got nothing, and no credit from peers. It was, 'The Mick Jones mega-touch—he did it again.'"[12]

***

Mick Jones: "Although I was proud of '... Love Is,' because of it we were also accused of having gone soft. That, in turn, had a more damaging knock-on effect. Lou kind of jumped on that very specific criticism as a way of telling me he didn't want to sing that style of song ever again. And I think the little coterie of advisors he'd gathered around him by then were already bumping him toward doing his own thing."

Lou Gramm: "We barely spoke to each other on tour."[13]

Mick Jones: "The album itself was another massive success for us, but I've never been satisfied with it as a whole. There were personal reasons for that as well, which are private. All I will say is, I wish that I'd had a bit more control over my own behavior at that point. Then it might have been a period of greater creativity for the band."

Lou Gramm: "After the *Agent Provocateur* tour, we were supposed to take a three- or four-week break and then begin work on a new album. But that tour was so exhausting that Mick decided he was going to take his wife on a boat cruise around the world. We didn't see him for almost five months. Maybe it was six months."[14]

Mick Jones: "People started to say we'd lost our way. I've a certain few regrets in my personal life. Nothing I could say musically, except for the fact that it was such a pity we never really did make a proper follow-up to *4*."

PART FIVE

DON'T STOP BELIEVIN'

CHAPTER SIXTY-TWO

HEART'S REINVENTION AND RESURRECTION.

"I was kind of the Farrah Fawcett of rock for a minute there."

Nancy Wilson: "After *Passionworks*, we had to do *something*. We were a little desperate after the big turkey."

Ann Wilson: "We met a guy named Don Grierson, who at the time was the head of A&R for Capitol Records. He really believed in us. He believed that with the right songs, Heart could be reanimated and brought back. He said to us, 'If you give me the opportunity to go out fishing for some songs for you, and you write some songs too, I bet you we could have a hit record.'"

Nancy Wilson: "Our accountants were like, 'God, you're in trouble.' So we were like, 'Okay, we'll go get dressed up.'"

Ron Nevison: "I loved Heart, so I went up to Seattle to interview for the job [of producing them]. I had a great time with them. I loved the songs they had, but I didn't think they had any that could be a big hit single.

So I grabbed a song that was sitting on Don Grierson's desk called 'If Looks Could Kill' that was headed to Tina Turner. I thought it would be a good one for Ann Wilson to sing."[1]

Nancy Wilson: "The songs had started to all sound kind of the same, and bands to look sort of the same. The guys and the girls all had the same blond hair, like I did. The same spandex. The mind expansion of the 1960s and '70s had turned into the ego-expanded, cocaine-driven 1980s. The whole stylistic movement was just so different. And kind of unfamiliar and foreign to us as a little band from Seattle that made it big out of the apple-growing capital of the United States. We were not sophisticated. We were not LA people. We were not New York people. It was not a fit."

Ron Nevison: "[Ann and Nancy Wilson] didn't like the label interfering, just like John Waite didn't when I was doing the Babys' stuff."[2]

Ann Wilson: "We didn't take [to using outside songwriters] too well. We took it as a personal affront...It was a big blow to our artistic ego. They were right. The times were a-changing again, and the type of perspective we had in our songs, it was old news."[3]

Ron Nevison: "My manager, Michael Lippman, managed Bernie Taupin and he gave me a cassette with 'These Dreams' on it."[4]

Ann Wilson: "I thought 'These Dreams' was a remarkable song."

Ron Nevison: "Grierson brought in 'What About Love.'"[5]

Jim Vallance: "That was a song I'd written for another band back in 1982, and they rejected it. It just sat there on a shelf for three years until it was brought to Heart's attention. I'd completely forgotten about it."

Ron Nevison: "I remember playing 'What About Love' at Nancy's house for the first time. She went down the stairs to cry because she didn't like it. What she was really offended by was how the demo sounded. It was really wimpy. I said to them that they should record it and try to make it their own. Ann goes in to record it, and it's amazing."[6]

Nancy Wilson: "Those songs we did make our own. They were beautiful songs that we still like to do today. So we did escape with something meaningful from that time."

Denny Carmassi: "Making a record with Ron was interesting. He ran a really tight ship."

Ron Nevison: "Look, I was brought in by the label and management to get the job done, and that meant I sometimes had to lead them kicking and screaming into the charts. What can I say? It is what it is."[7]

Ann Wilson: "I'll tell you what, the *Heart* album [1985] was actually fun to do. And Don Grierson was proved to be right."

Denny Carmassi: "I mean, I knew it was a good record. But I'd no idea that it'd do *that* good."

Steve Fossen: "I was happy they were successful. At that exact same time, it just so happened that the industry was switching from vinyl to CD. So when everybody went to the store to buy the *Heart* CD, they were also replacing their vinyl copies of *Dreamboat Annie* and *Little Queen*. We all benefited."

Jim Vallance: "They had a huge hit with 'What About Love.' Out of the blue one day, it ended up at the top of the charts. You just never know. You do your best work and then it's out of your hands."

Mike Fisher: "It wasn't my vision for Heart, that's for sure. I felt like they were a copy band, but with Ann as the lead vocalist. It didn't seem nearly as good as the original to me, but who's to say I'm right."

Steve Fossen: "It wasn't the kind of music I'd have liked to have done, and I was happy to be out of it. I heard stories from Howard Leese, so I kind of knew what the dynamics in the band had gotten to be like."

Denny Carmassi: "Ann would probably have the final say on whatever decisions were being made, but it was more of a democratic situation. We were a pretty tight group there for four or five years."

Nancy Wilson: "I always had a joke with myself, that I'd know I was a success when I heard a Heart song in an elevator. You know, 'That's when I'm gonna know I've truly made it.' And it happened. I heard 'These Dreams' in the grocery store. You feel worthy. Like you've worked really hard to do something that's connected to people. That has helped. Music is the ultimate healer in my opinion. It always helped me to survive my life. That's what it's really there for, it's the landscape of your emotional growth and your life."

Ann Wilson: "The whole '80s makeover look we got given was theater. The big hair and the wild clothes. Having wanted to be a fashion designer myself at one point, to have stylists heaping clothes on me was great. I just loved it."

Nancy Wilson: "It was a new era. The fashion was changing. MTV was there and pushing the agenda on rock bands to have the big hair and the look and the image-making machinery in place more than the songs. In our consciousness, we felt hemmed in by the image-making. But we did okay. We got through it. We put on the fun costumes and the jewelry."

Denny Carmassi: "The videos were a real grind, though, man. You'd sit around a lot, and you're running on no sleep, and they'd call you at 3 a.m. to come and do a shot. The shoots would last two or three days, and it was hard work. It's like a form of insanity."

Nancy Wilson: "Yeah, I became a poster girl. I was kind of the Farrah Fawcett of rock for a minute there. I didn't feel like that was who I am.

I'm a musician first and I've got more to offer than some saucy-looking image of me."

Marty Callner: "I featured Nancy Wilson [in the video for 'Never'], who had never been featured in a video before. Everybody told me how much they loved her tits in that video."[8]

Les Garland: "Well, there's always been this component of sexual attractiveness in advertising and promotion. It's always been around, hasn't it?"

Bob Pittman: "Sadly, that was of the moment. I mean, it wasn't unique to MTV or the music business. That was reflective of society at the time. As people got a little more culturally aware, it looks awful when you look back. At the moment, everybody was looking cool and hip. By the way, the guys had big hair, too."

Ann Wilson: "The dignity of women was at a low ebb. I've never seen it at a lower ebb, in fact, and I've been around a while now and through different eras of feminism, no-feminism. That was really a low point for women. And yet, there was an attitude of, 'This is okay because it's only theater.' But the message that was sent out is one we're still recovering from."

Les Garland: "I go back to my own culpability. I didn't create music videos. I didn't make them. We were just the gallery that showed them. Certainly, that came with a responsibility. We had standards. We created a Standards and Practices Committee. If a video was a little too questionable, something we should or shouldn't touch, they would rule on it. And also, if we detected a huge hate factor among our audience for something, it came off the wall immediately. Can I think of something in terms of the presentation of women that hit that mark? No, I can't right now."

Nancy Wilson: "I figured, okay, this is survival and I'll be a poster girl for this if I get to go out and play my guitar. I'll be fine with that. It got a little out of hand a couple of times, but who cares? It was indelibly emblazoned in the minds of many men, so I'm glad for that. I can't complain."

Mick Kleber: "Ann Wilson's weight was a big issue... Each video presented a challenge. There were a lot of different tactics that were used, with technology and lighting. You didn't have to be a genius to figure out that we were sort of hiding her in different ways... They stretched the video in post-production to make her appear slimmer. As for me, I'd been in the Marines before working for Capitol, so I said, 'Why don't we just get her in shape?'"[9]

Ann Wilson: "Everyone in those MTV years was objectified to death. *Everybody*. You were expected to look like a model and be a dancer and an actor, and sing. Wow. To be a quadruple threat when you're just a person from Seattle who played in bar bands. It was really hard."

Denny Carmassi: "The tour was a lot of fun. I had a good time, you know."

Nancy Wilson: "Being onstage was our escape. It's like the feeling of being on a roller coaster and going chink-chink-chink up to the top of the track and that's the moment the lights go down when you're at the top. The ride is about to start and next thing you know you're gonna be hurtling through space. I've been there before and I like going on that roller coaster, but I never feel casual or cavalier about it, ever. It's a big moment."

Ann Wilson: "That's when everything's okay. That's when the nerves go away. You have to just relax, strap in, and enjoy the ride."

Denny Carmassi: "Did I have any particular extravagances? Oh boy, how do I answer that?"

***

Ann Wilson: "Oh, it was definitely excessive. Everything that era was made out to be, it was. There was never enough of anything, including money. It was a very materialistic time."

Nancy Wilson: "You're kind of going like, 'Wow, I can afford to take a long shower again now!' I didn't have to cancel all of my magazine subscriptions or scrimp and save every penny like we'd had to do for a while there. We toured nonstop and made more money than we'd ever done before. You could afford stuff. You were able to pamper yourself and treat yourself to things."

Ann Wilson: "Everything being said, I totally enjoyed our success. I loved being up on the big stages and riding around in private planes. And just being entertained in these lavish ways. *All* of it."

CHAPTER SIXTY-THREE

STARSHIP PLAYS THE MAMBA.

"Oh, you're shitting me, that's the worst song ever."

Mickey Thomas: "Rock music was moving over more to the Top 40 singles chart with the advent of MTV. That's when we realized that we may have to shake it up and reinvent the band. First, we morphed into Starship. Next came the *Knee Deep in the Hoopla* album in 1985, and that certainly changed things for us."

Les Garland: "The legendary Jefferson Starship house in San Francisco. Posted on the wall was a company memo to the staff. 'Effective immediately: the use of cocaine on premise is strictly prohibited... until after 4 p.m.' That's how wild it was back then."

Mickey Thomas: "It was 1978 when I decided I'd accomplished just about everything I could with being pretty much a sideman in the Elvin Bishop Band. I set out to record a solo album, but out of the blue, I got a phone call from Paul Kantner about joining the Jefferson Starship. It'd been like a soap opera with relationships in the band. Grace Slick and Marty Balin had both left. Then the drummer John Barbata got in a horrible car crash and broke both his legs. I went over to meet with them at Kantner's house. They told me their vision of what their new musical direction would be, which was quite different. We jammed a rough version of 'Jane,' and it was like a lightbulb went on over my head and I thought, 'Wow, this might actually work!'

"The second album I did with Jefferson Starship was *Modern Times* in 1981. We were working at the Record Plant in Sausalito, and Grace was living right up the road in Mill Valley. She just kind of started dropping in. Toward the end of making that album, we decided it'd be kind of cool if we were to sing something together. We did a duet on a song called 'Stranger,' the last one we recorded for *Modern Times*. Our voices had a great blend, and off the cuff, she said, 'Hey, it looks like you guys are having a lot more fun now than what was going on in the band when I left.' She'd gone to rehab and straightened her personal life out, and that's what led to her segueing back into the band. Like everybody else I only ever heard all the wild stories about Grace. We used to have a sick little joke between us. I would tell her, 'If you ever fall off the wagon call me up, 'cause I want to party with you.'"

Grace Slick: "I was such an asshole for a while, I was trying to make up for it by being sober, which I was all during the '80s, which is a bizarre decade to be sober in."[1]

Mickey Thomas: "The process leading up to *Knee Deep in the Hoopla* was difficult. Kantner decided to quit the band. It was never dull with us. Paul just wasn't on board with the musical direction we were wanting to go off in. It got to be pretty confrontational with him. He left the group, but didn't think the rest of us should continue either. Part of the legal appeasement process with him that ensued was us having to retire 'Jefferson' and shorten the name to Starship. It didn't really bother us because most people referred to the band as just Starship anyway. It was also symbolic of the change coming.

"On ... *Hoopla*, we wanted to try using some outside writers. I was working a lot with a guy named Martin Page. Martin had brought in some songs for us, one of them being 'We Built This City.' He'd written the music for it and Bernie Taupin had done the lyric. Right off the bat it really intrigued me, but the original demo was leaning more toward Peter Gabriel. The bass line was along the lines of 'Shock the Monkey.' Then, of course, the lyric I thought was fantastic. It's so multilayered."

Bernie Taupin: "The original song was a very dark song about how club life in LA was being killed off and live acts had no place to go. A producer named Peter Wolf—not the J. Geils Peter Wolf, but a big-time pop guy and Austrian record producer—got hold of the demo and totally changed it."[2]

Mickey Thomas: "Peter came in as our new producer, and with that whole new way of making records with samples and sequencers. It was a fresh start for us. There wasn't really a chorus to the original song. That whole anthemic 'We built this city' part didn't exist. With Peter and Dennis Lambert, the executive producer, we got around the piano in the studio and came up with it. That chorus is probably the reason the song became such a huge hit, but also why it's taken its lumps over the years. Sometimes it gets in the way of people actually listening to the verses and the lyrics and what the song is all about. That's always kind of tickled me. I always think to myself, 'Did you ever take the time to actually listen to the lyrics? Do you know who wrote them? Because he's pretty good.'"

Les Garland: "I was dear friends with Starship's manager, Bill Thompson. MTV was roaring, but I had some free time, and I buzzed out to San Francisco to visit my buddy Bill. Saturday morning, we were going to play golf and Bill said, 'The band is in the studio at the Record Plant in Sausalito. They want me to bring you by.' Over we go to the studio. The band had been working all night long, and the producer Peter Wolf was still on the board. Bill says, 'Let's play a few songs for Gar.' I don't remember the first song. I guess I didn't get excited. The next song is 'We Built This City.' As it ended, I looked up and I go, 'That is a huge hit right there.'

"Peter told Bill the song wasn't done yet, and that he'd an idea to put a radio DJ's voice in the bridge. Bill says, 'Well, Garland could probably do a demo for you. Garland used to be a DJ.' Sure, I was glad to. I go out to the car, opened the trunk, pulled out one of my golf clubs, started up a joint, smoked a little pot, and came rolling back into the studio ready to go. Peter wanted to play the song again for me a couple of times, but I told him that wouldn't be necessary, I'd got it. I didn't have any idea what I was going to say, but he rolled the tape, and I just started in, 'Riding across the Golden Gate Bridge on another…' Whatever it is I said, it came to me at that moment. That was it, the first and only take."

Mickey Thomas: "We set out to make a really commercial album, and it was really fun to do. We wanted to have hit singles. Everybody was happy and having fun together."

Grace Slick: "I like to write my own stuff or have the band members write their own stuff, and we weren't doing that. I was in my forties and I remember thinking, 'God, this is just awful.'"[3]

Mickey Thomas: "All I know is that after … *Hoopla*, a lot of people wanted to grab Peter Wolf to produce their records. Sonically, it was such a great record. 'Sara' was kind of closer to what people expected of Starship. It's a little more somber, a breakup song. But we were really taking a big chance with that whole record. We rolled the dice and reinvented the band, and it worked."

Les Garland: "Two months later, I'm in my office in New York and my assistant buzzes to tell me she has an attorney from RCA Records on the phone. Starship and management had decided they wanted to use my voice on the song. I turned all the money I got from it over to the T. J. Martell Foundation for cancer research. I did it as a favor to my friends, not for the money. I sent the band a telex. 'Dear members of the Starship, I want to thank you for backing me up on my worldwide smash.' They got such a kick out of that."

Mickey Thomas: "The night 'We Built This City' went to Number One was jubilant. We were in the middle of our tour in Kalamazoo,

Michigan, and we had quite the party. I called up Bernie Taupin. He was on the West Coast, so it was still a little bit early in the evening for him, whereas we were well into our beer and wine and everything else. He answered and I said to him, 'Bernie, now more than ever, people are gonna ask me just what does "Marconi plays the mamba" mean?' He didn't miss a beat. He said, 'Well, I have no fucking idea, mate, but it sounds good, doesn't it?'"

Grace Slick: "I was trying to make it up to the band by being a good girl. 'Here, we're going to sing this song "We Built This City."' Oh, you're shitting me, that's the worst song ever. I could do it. I could get it up and imitate myself, but that doesn't feel right."[4]

Mickey Thomas: "The next couple of years were almost a blur, and 'We Built This City' sort of became the poster child for what was going on in music that a lot of people didn't particularly care for. This idea that rock 'n' roll was being homogenized or disinfected. Because of the history of our band with Jefferson Starship and Jefferson Airplane, the stakes were a little bit higher for us, too. People looked at it as a sellout. We were going to change the world, and look at us now, we were *just* a Top 40 band. That's how it went.

"We performed 'We Built This City' live at the Grammys in 1986. That wasn't very comfortable. All of your peers are in the audience. Sting was sitting in the front row center. As I was singing, he was giving me this weird look. Like he didn't like me, or something. I was thinking, 'He must hate this song.' I only realized later that I was wearing the same jacket as he had on. That's probably what pissed him off."

Grace Slick: "I felt like I'd throw up on the front row, but I smiled and did it anyway. The show must go on."[5]

CHAPTER SIXTY-FOUR

JOHN PARR: MAN IN MOTION.

"Good guys win in the end.
That's the story."

John Parr: "David Foster had loved 'Naughty Naughty,' and that's what got me 'St. Elmo's Fire.' I was on tour with Toto when Foster called. He told me he was doing his first film soundtrack, and he wanted me to come over and write a song for it with him. The guys in Toto know David very well, but I wasn't up to speed with just how gigantic he was in the business. I mean, just then he was one of the four biggest producers on the planet. I was in the shape of my life, though. I'd been singing that first album on the road, which was a killer to do, so I was like Arnold Schwarzenegger with steroids down my throat.

"Foster and me, just the two of us, went into this little studio in LA, Lighthouse Sound. Foster turned up fried, and said he was too tired to write anything new. He gave me this song he already had to sing. To be honest, it was a piece of crap. I said that I thought we could do better and persuaded him to go into the control room with me and try to work something up with a piano and drum machine. He agreed to give it half an hour. We wrote another song in that time, but I insisted we could still do better. 'St. Elmo's Fire' was the third thing we did that day. All in an hour. Then we recorded the backing track and everything else in a couple more days.

"I'd written the main melody, and Foster had done an incredible production, but I was struggling with the lyric. I hadn't seen the film, fortunately. Foster said to me, 'Look, this has nothing to do with the film, but a young boy came by the studio last week in a wheelchair. He's trying to go round the world to raise money for spinal injury research.' That was Rick Hansen. Rick was a Canadian, like David, and he'd been paralyzed in a pickup truck accident when he was fifteen.

"Foster put a local news video item on for me. It was a film of Rick wheeling out from Vancouver with three men and a dog waving him off as he goes. He'd got a spare wheelchair on the roof of his relief vehicle, a bucket, and not much else. The local police had put him on the B roads because they didn't want him holding traffic up. In my hotel room that night, I wrote my dream. That Rick did it. That he crossed mountains and deserts and made it around the world. Of course, that's what happened and that's what the song became about, this boy in a wheelchair.

"I knew Columbia Pictures wouldn't swallow that, so I made sure they thought the pair of wheels in the lyrics were Demi Moore's from the film, and the line 'just once in his life a man has his time' was for when Emilio Estevez gets the girl. But they're not, they're Rick's. That's also why I insisted on the song being subtitled 'Man in Motion,' because that was the name Rick gave to his attempt.

"After I'd done my lead vocal on the Sunday, I went into the bathroom in the studio and just fell to my knees. I knew I'd been given something. Wherever it had come from, and whether you're religious or not, I knew I'd been blessed in that moment with my performance and with what Foster and I had written. I knew it was something very special. It's not me. It was given to me, lightning in a bottle. I'd also had twenty years of heartache and frustration, so *I was* that guy in the wheelchair, trying to overcome. I know how cornily romantic that sounds, but it's the truth. I think that's what people get when they hear the song, too. Good guys win in the end. That's the story.

"The cast of the film appeared in the video we shot for the song. They were the Brat Pack, the hottest thing on the planet in 1985. The film's director, Joel Schumacher, came down and they rebuilt this huge set from the movie. The film was long wrapped, and they were about to burn the set, but they were able to re-create the bar from the film for us. None of the cast wanted to be back there on the set. You can see that in the video. Anyway, we became pals. Demi Moore's played onstage with me, so has Rob Lowe.

"The truth is, my record company, Atlantic, didn't like the song and so they didn't promote it. It was the work of Columbia Pictures that made it take off the way it did. Atlantic didn't hate the money, I'm sure, but they didn't want their little leather-clad rocker singing this mainstream song. It didn't even go on my next album. That became the history of me. I went on to have songs in *The Running Man* with Schwarzenegger and *Three Men and a Baby*, the biggest movies at the box office, and they were never even released in America. It was incredibly frustrating, but that's really why it all came to an end for me.

"For me, the high point was playing the song at Rick's return home, as he wheeled back into Vancouver. On that occasion, people were lining the streets and brass bands played him along. Foster and I played 'St. Elmo's...' as he wheeled into BC Stadium. We'd raised $18 million for spinal research with the song at that point. Today, that figure stands at over $375 million. The song has helped change human history. People with the same spinal injury Rick had, if they're lucky and get treatment early, can walk again. Forty years later, the song continues to be special. People have had the opportunity to hear it on its own terms and to simply like it. There's no intellect to it.

"So many people tell me now how they wish they'd lived through that era. To me, there's a big similarity between the '60s and the '80s. The bar was very high. Standards were high. You had all these bands and artists coming out, and you knew you had to punch your weight just to be heard. The records we made back then just sounded bigger. Larger than life."

CHAPTER SIXTY-FIVE

CAUTIONARY TALES.

―∽―

"There's no accountability, except for the fact you might die."

Pat Benatar: "Of all our albums, [1985's] *Seven the Hard Way* cost the most to make and sold the least... I was stunned, but not surprised. We'd made a record we had no business making."[1]

Bruce Kulick: "I was thrown into the creative process between Paul and Gene on Kiss's *Asylum* album. I had four co-writes on that record. There I am writing with Desmond Child, which was a real thrill. I saw firsthand that he could bring out the best of Paul."

Pat Benatar: "The record company was—if you look up 'dick' in the dictionary, their faces will be there. They are so sickening. It made my life so difficult. I'd just had a baby. I didn't know what the hell I was doing... No one cared. No one had any sympathy that your life was totally changed. No one looked at you as a human being, no one looked at you as a woman, no one looked at you as a person. And it was just horrendous. It was an awful record and there were probably two songs on there that belonged there."[2]

***

Desmond Child: "When I was having all of this success later on, Gene came out with a press release that said, 'Kiss is not using outside writers. In fact, we've put guards at the door to keep Desmond Child out.' I was so hurt. I called Paul and said, 'Why would he attack somebody who's put money in his pocket? Who's been nothing but supportive. There are so many haters of Kiss, why doesn't he go after them?' Paul told me, 'I can't control Gene. He says whatever he wants.' But he was sitting next to him, and he didn't defend me. Later that day, there was a message on my answer machine. It was from Gene. Four words. 'Hi. It's Gene. Sorry.' Click. I think that's the only apology Gene Simmons has ever given to anyone."

Pat Benatar: "[Chrysalis] got exactly what they deserved: shit."[3]

Bruce Kulick: "Touring with Kiss, everything was first class...It's all there for you, and unfortunately, there's no accountability, except for the fact you might die. Not a bad job, though. There's nothing more exciting than having girls show you their boobs, you know what I mean?"

Jon Bon Jovi: "The second [Bon Jovi] album [*7800° Fahrenheit*] didn't set the world on fire, but we did the best we could with our limited knowledge of any aspect of record making...Let's not be too harsh, it sold okay—750,000 record sales in America—so the curve was still going upward."[4]

Fee Waybill: "When we got to the [*Love Bomb*] record, we sat down with David Foster and he said to the guys, 'What I want to do is write four songs with Fee and Lukather and me, so we'll have three choices for a follow-up to the first single. And you guys can do whatever you want for the other side—you can produce it, you can write it, whatever you want to do.' And the band went, 'No.' The record company's going, 'Don't fire David Foster.' The management company's going, 'Don't do it.' Everyone said, 'No, don't do it.' And they went ahead and did it."[5]

Richard Page: "Mr. Mister was one of a handful of bands that had two

Number One hits off a Number One album [*Welcome to the Real World*]. The other ones, of course, are the Beatles and just a couple more. It's strange that a band with our short duration of success was in that league."[6]

Fee Waybill: "That's why I ended up quitting the Tubes... They fired David Foster and went to Todd Rundgren and made that third record on Capitol Records, and it was straight to the dumper."[7]

Richard Page: "The real pressure comes after you've sold a multiplatinum album. After *Welcome to the Real World*, that's when the pressure hit and they were like, 'Okay, well where's the "Broken Wings" and where's "Kyrie"? Let's keep this going.' It's hard to top that."[8]

Michael Bolton: "I was thirty-four when I had my first hit record. Until that time I just kept struggling."[9]

Bruce Kulick: "Michael didn't have good luck with doing the rock stuff. I did all the guitars for his *Everybody's Crazy* solo record in '85. That whole record is wonderful, but it wasn't very successful. It didn't do what Michael wanted, but people at least still believed in him."

Joe Lynn Turner: "I did a solo album, *Rescue You*, with Roy Thomas Baker. We were on the moon with that record. It's still a great record. What a production! The sound is so rich and crisp and powerful. I was writing with Al Greenwood, who had that whole Foreigner background. Brilliant. To this day, 'Endlessly' is still very popular as a wedding song. There's a lot of good songs on there. And Roy's a pretty crazy guy."

Chuck Burgi: "Joey, back then, I thought was as great a singer as Lou Gramm, or any of those other guys. He just wasn't really taking care of himself vocally. When we did his solo record... Ah, man, it just breaks my heart. He had that aspect to his personality that we called 'The Reverend.' The Reverend came out under a special combination of usually blow and vodka."

***

Eric Martin: "My first solo album [*Eric Martin*, 1985] had that AOR sound to it, but with R&B overtones. Danny Kortchmar was my producer. We were recording at Record One on Hollywood Boulevard. Don Henley was in the next-door room. Danny would work on Don's record in the afternoon, and then when Don went home, he'd bring all of these guys over to the smaller studio to work on my record. The Section guys. There was Waddy Wachtel, Ricky Marotta, Stan Lynch, Steve Lukather, Paul Shaffer from the Letterman show on organ. Stevie Nicks popped her head in a bunch of times. Henley would occasionally come into our studio and be a grumpy-ass motherfucker. I'd go, 'Hey Don, my name's Eric Martin.' And he'd be like, 'Uh, no. I don't care.'"

Joe Lynn Turner: "It was a tight, kick-ass band I had. We opened for Loverboy. Kicked the shit out of them. We toured with Pat Benatar. The vixen of rock had just become a mom, and she didn't want us to have any alcohol or girls in our dressing room. It was like being in a convent. Neil Giraldo was cool. He'd sneak into our dressing room to get a drink. Eventually, we got thrown off the tour. We got thrown out of Tyler, Texas, touring with Night Ranger. My bass player, Barry Dunaway, he had a stripper girlfriend, and she was quite the thing. During 'Sister Christian,' she came onstage in almost nothing. Just veils and what have you. Kelly Keagy is singing the song. It's about his sister, so this was like a sacrilegious act. Man, he got pissed off. The mayor's son was in the front row, and somebody threw a monitor at him. The next day, the Tyler police were all over us. They let us go, but we had to take a private plane belonging to Hulk Hogan to the next show in Fort Worth. The Hulk-man came along with us for the ride. I mean, it was nuts."

Chuck Burgi: "Oh my God, Night Ranger was in their heyday of partying and doing blow. Joey used to ride in their bus and stay up all night being The Reverend. He'd show up with them to the gigs and have no voice left."

Joe Lynn Turner: "Falling in love was my greatest extravagance. With all the wrong faces and places. Ex-wives. Two so far. The houses. The cars. That's a horse you don't ride anymore. It's like doing the drugs before you've paid the dealer. A big lesson right there. Divorce is a curse."

Chuck Burgi: "You know, Joey was his own worst enemy. I couldn't be doing it with him anymore, so I upped and left his band. I love him to death, but eventually I wanted to love him from afar."

Eric Martin: "I wrote a song called 'Just One Night' for my record with Neal Schon. It's a beautiful, huge, epic song. One of my best vocals ever. Lukather played the guitar on it. That *Eric Martin* album cost a lot of money. There was a lot of cocaine. I was 'The Kid' to these guys. When it came time to do the overdubs, they'd go, 'Right, kid, we're gonna put you in a cab and we're gonna do a bunch of blow.' There'd be twenty-five of these guys in the room, all of these big-name cats just hanging out. They spent a thousand dollars a pop on just sushi. The record didn't do well, but I had a blast making it."

CHAPTER SIXTY-SIX

VAN HAGAR.

"Eddie was so fucking good, I hated him."

Eddie Van Halen: "When I was, like, twelve or thirteen, a German shepherd jumped through the screen door and bit me. It hurt like a motherfucker. So my dad said, 'Have a shot of vodka, Ed. This will make you feel better.' And he gave me a Pall Mall to smoke. I started drinking and smoking all in one day, right there and then...Listen, my dad played until he died. I think it's something you're born with. You're either rock 'n' roll, or you're not."[1]

Steve Lukather: "Paich brought the first Van Halen record into the studio when we were making *Toto*. He told me, 'You have *got* to hear this guy.' And he played me 'Eruption.' My jaw hit the floor. Eddie Van Halen, man, he was extraordinary. He was funky, soulful, had unbelievable timing. Eddie was so fucking good, I hated him."

Eddie Van Halen: "[David Lee Roth] was always into roller skating and jogging. Hey, that's fine. But he would bang on everybody's door at eight, nine in the morning, going, 'Come on, get your ass out of bed, come roller skating.' I'm going, 'Fuck you, man, I just got to sleep.' And he's saying, 'Well, man, you live wrong.' We were very, very different people."²

David Lee Roth: "Poor little Eddie Van Halen. Struggled to survive a continuing onslaught of platinum records and Lamborghinis. Poor little Eddie. Forced to live a lie. They just couldn't get their asses out of bed. They usually couldn't get through rehearsals for a two-week period without an argument."³

Martha Quinn: "David Lee Roth was so smart. He's the most charismatic person you ever want to sit across from. It was just take-your-breath-away."

Eddie Van Halen: "[Roth] wasn't showing up for rehearsal. He'd call me and say, 'Oh, I don't feel so good today, man—tell the guys I don't think I'll be making it.' And he'd be at the office, doing interviews for his solo thing. After a couple of weeks of that, I just laid it on the line. I said, 'What's going on here? Do you want to do a record or not?' And he said no. He wanted to make his movie. And he actually asked if I'd write the music for it."⁴

Eric Martin: "Eddie Van Halen gave me a call. That came about through Danny Kortchmar. Eddie told Danny he was looking for a singer, and Danny told him, 'Oh man, I've got this kid, he'd be perfect for you.' We talked for a long time on the phone. All the while, Eddie's obviously asking me to come and sing and jam with him. I'm so excited, I can't believe it. But I didn't have confidence back then. *At all.* And I thought to myself, 'Holy shit…David Lee Roth! I'm gonna step in the clown shoes of David Lee Roth!' I went to LA, and I bragged a little bit. 'I'm going to go see Eddie Van Halen tomorrow over at his 5150 studio in Coldwater Canyon.' I talked too much. It was raining that next morning, and I felt a fake cold coming on. I totally shit the bed and chickened out. This was the Led Zeppelin of America, and I didn't feel suited. I didn't have *it*."

***

Patty Smyth: "Who the heck knows what would've happened if I had joined Van Halen? I was probably heavily hormoned out because I was eight months pregnant, so there was a state of mind I was in of how I need to take care of myself. But I regretted turning [Eddie] down. For a long time I regretted it. I was like, 'Oh man, I would've made so much money.' I never said anything about it for years. I got a call from Ed, and he was like, 'Look, I'm not saying that I asked you to join because I don't want Sammy Hagar to look like [he was] second choice.' And I was like, 'Okay.' So I never spoke about it after that."[5]

John Kalodner: "I suggested that Sammy Hagar go with Van Halen. He was perfect for Van Halen. Eddie was used to a star who was not very easy to get along with, and Sammy Hagar was."

Sammy Hagar: "I had a good career going. I was wealthy, I was eating in the finest restaurants and wearing the finest fucking clothes. I was driving Ferraris. I was becoming a little too sophisticated—it was killing my music. Whereas those guys were living a completely different lifestyle. These guys had cigarette butts and empty beer cans and whiskey bottles everywhere... Eddie comes walking out with a pair of sunglasses, jeans with holes in them, just out of bed, cracking a beer, and smoking a cigarette. Alex was still drunk. Mike hadn't even been home. I'm looking at these guys, then I'm looking at myself in a suit, and I go, 'I look like a fucking idiot. This is a real rock 'n' roll band.'"[6]

Eddie Van Halen: "I'd written 'Jump.' [Roth's] going, 'Hey, nobody wants to see you play keyboards.' That was Roth's trip... When Sammy joined the band, I was free to do what I wanted. I didn't have anyone saying, 'No, you can't do that.'"[7]

Mick Jones: "I'd known Sammy Hagar for years. In fact, I believe it was Sammy and John Kalodner who championed my cause to Eddie and Alex Van Halen. As their producer on the *5150* album [1986], I knew from the time of hearing the basic backing tracks that my main task would be to find a spot for Sammy to be in, because they already sounded so powerful. Essentially, it came out as the 'fuck you, David Lee Roth' album."

Sammy Hagar: "The record company weren't confident. They were saying we should name the band Van Hagar, just in case it goes wrong. They could always go back to Van Halen and not take the whole band down."[8]

Mick Jones: "I had to navigate the shenanigans. Eddie, and Alex in particular, were going through a rough period with each other and things could erupt between them at any time. The presence of their father really would not help. He'd come over to the studio and incite them to fight. He would stir up one against the other and then sit back and watch as his sons beat the shit out of each other. It seemed to give him some sort of perverse pleasure, and neither Eddie nor Alex ever held back."

Sammy Hagar: "Eddie's talented, and he's a sweet, wonderful, heart guy. But he's got some demons."[9]

Mick Jones: "The track I was most proud of was 'Dreams.' I pushed Sammy over the top on that one. Laying down his lead vocal, he almost passed out from the exertion."

Alan Pasqua: "The phone rang one morning at 2 a.m. I said, 'Hello.' This familiar voice shouted back at me, 'Pasqua! It's Sammy Hagar. Look, I think most keyboard players suck. But you suck the least.' He wanted me to get up, get dressed, and go put down a keyboard overdub on one of their tracks. If it had been 'Jump' I would've been there in a minute, but I told him absolutely not and went back to bed."

Sammy Hagar: "We didn't let the label in the studio. We made the whole *5150* record, and then we invited Mo Ostin, one of the greatest record company presidents in history, down. We played 'Why Can't

This Be Love' live, right there for them. And after we'd done, Mo Ostin raises his finger in the air and says, 'I smell money!'"[10]

Mick Jones: "*5150* turned out to be a really good record, and their first US Number One."

Sammy Hagar: "It went platinum faster than any album in Warner Brothers' history."[11]

Mick Jones: "I wasn't asked back. Eddie, like me with the Foreigner records, probably viewed *5150* as the end of our relationship. Also, I think he resented a little bit the fact I'd helped them to get to that pinnacle. Or at least, that was how it appeared to me in the aftermath. For a time there, Eddie went into a different place. He had such a God-given gift, but like most people that are incredibly blessed, he paid a price for it in other areas of his life. Most often you find that deep down these kinds of virtuoso people are very spiritual and they just can't handle the burden of what they're able to do, or the acclaim that they're given. They turn elsewhere for ammunition."

Sammy Hagar: "Until it turned bad, it was the greatest thing on the planet."[12]

CHAPTER SIXTY-SEVEN

JOURNEY COMES BACK TOGETHER, BREAKS APART.

"When we turned over the leash of the project to Steve Perry, we sold our souls to the devil."

Mike Baird: "See, a lot of people don't get this. My piece in the pie really is inconsequential. The lead singer is always the key. You might have the best band in the world, and the best song, but if you don't have a singer to pull it off, it ain't going anywhere. It just isn't."

Jonathan Cain: "There's the happy, carefree guy I met during the *Departure* era, the singer who walked the walk and talked the talk... Then there's the guy six years later, reserved, and cautious... The weight of the world in his head and heart."[1]

Mike Baird: "Steve Perry said to his bandmates in Journey, 'I'll do another album with you guys. But only if I call all the shots.'"

Steve Smith: "There were a lot of changes that had happened by the mid-'80s. Technology had developed. The Linn drum machine was in use, and people were able to program drumbeats, bass parts, and keyboard parts with computers. Jonathan and Steve, and to some extent Neal, wrote a lot of the music using the new technology. And Steve, Jonathan, and Neal changed the structure of the publishing. They no longer wanted to use Weed High Nightmare Music, which up until then had shared the publishing equally among the band members. They wanted to publish the songs that they wrote themselves. All of the *Raised on Radio* record was written before we went into the studio to make it. Ross Valory and I were completely left out of the creative process."

Eric Martin: "Herbie gave me a demo of the song 'Once You Love Somebody.' He goes to me, 'This is what I want you to do.' My girlfriend, Stacey, who worked at Macy's, she had Neal Schon come in the store. Stacey goes to Neal, 'Oh, I just heard your cassette. Herbie gave it to Eric, and he's going to write a song. Blah-blah-blah.' Totally got in trouble for that. I had to drive to the Record Plant, walk into the studio, Steve Perry and Neal Schon are there, and I go, 'Sorry.' They were like, 'Fuck, what were you thinking?' Yelling at me."

Mike Baird: "Steve Smith told me, 'When we turned over the leash of the project to Steve Perry, we sold our souls to the devil.' His words not mine. There was a lot of animosity there."

Steve Smith: "At that point, I didn't have the studio drumming chops that I later developed. I wasn't able to come up to the standard needed to play that music without rehearsing, without ever having played with a click track or a quantized keyboard. That was all new for me. It was a difficult time."

Jonathan Cain: "I never stopped to think that Ross and Steve might have a problem doing it this way... We went about it the wrong way."[2]

Herbie Herbert: "They call me over to Sausalito for a band meeting on the waterfront. I'm sitting there with Neal Schon, Jon Cain, and Steve Perry. They inform me, 'We're struggling, and Steve doesn't feel right about the recording.' And I go, 'All the tracks are finished!' 'Yeah, he doesn't like them. He wants to replace Smith and Valory.' Replace Smith and Valory? Over my dead body. That turned out to be a brutal mistake. It wasn't Journey. It was lame."[3]

Ross Valory: "It was pretty evident that the majority of the players wanted to take a different direction, a different approach in style, and that was their prerogative. It's so long ago. There's no judgment at this point. It was probably a wrong move, but it was a short move."[4]

Steve Smith: "There was a decision that for the band to move forward they wanted to have the ability to hire whomever they wanted to play drums and bass. They wanted Ross and I to 'retire' from the band. I don't remember the language exactly, but basically, we were fired."

Herbie Herbert: "I forced [Perry] to pay them as if they were on the tour and everything. He wanted to divide and conquer."[5]

Andrew McNeice: "Herbie was a gem. A very intelligent guy and he wasn't beholden to anybody to behave himself. He was Herbie Herbert, and he could say whatever he liked. Even people he knew and loved, like Neal Schon, he didn't tiptoe around. He once said to me, 'Neal's not the sharpest knife in the drawer.' That's one of his business partners and lifelong friends."

Steve Smith: "Steve Perry wound up being producer on that album. Eventually, he used the same rhythm section as he'd had on his *Street Talk* album. I ended up on just three songs. I recorded more but was replaced by Larrie Londin. Ross isn't on any of it. I was very upset at the time. I was hurt."

Mike Baird: "I heard another story. Steve Perry and Larrie Londin were good friends. And after that record they weren't good friends. From what I heard from Larrie, God rest his soul, he told me, 'We were in there doing *Raised on Radio*, and Steve's trying to tell me what he wants to have me play.' The straw that broke the camel's back is Perry goes, 'Let me show you.' He sat down at Larry's drum kit. Larry goes, 'Fuck you, I'm out of here,' and left, and that was the end of their relationship."

Neal Schon: "Herbie wanted to call the album *Freedom* because he always came up with these one-word titles. Steve fought him and got his way."[6]

Herbie Herbert: "Perry's a tough nut to figure. One time he phoned me at my house and just went nuts about 'Be Good to Yourself' having been the first choice of single off *Raised on Radio*. And I said, 'It's a great song, it's a great production, it's a great sound, it's Journey.' That was the problem. It sounds too much like Journey. Well, too many of the other songs sounded too much like a glorified Steve Perry solo record."[7]

Steve Perry: "I think [*Raised on Radio*, 1986] was an amazing accomplishment. That album was a very adventurous departure, dare I say… You'll see an exploration of grooves and changes and vocal styles and harmonies and choruses that were different from anything that came before. I was proud of it because I thought we needed to grow."[8]

Steve Smith: "There is a particular chemistry that works in a band. You can replace certain members, and even replace them with better players, but it may not equal the sum of the parts. The sound will be different. Sometimes there's a fragile balance with personalities that are in a group. With the five of us, with Ross and myself, there was an equilibrium that took place where it balanced out the personalities somehow. Taking us away from the equation altered the inner dynamics of the personalities. They definitely had a lot of trouble after that."

Steve Perry: "That album did not do as well as the rest."[9]

Mike Baird: "We call it 'Lead Singer Syndrome.' It's no different than acting and actors. In general, they're not who you think they are. It's perception from seeing them in a TV show, or a movie. You meet them in person and go, 'Uh, they're the dullest fucking person I've ever met.' Put them in front of a camera and all of a sudden, it's like, boom! It's the same thing with singers. For the most part, they're more introverted personalities than outgoing personalities. They're more subdued. But you get them in front of a microphone, and it's zero to 60 in one point five seconds."

Joe Lynn Turner: "Man, I hate being a singer. Guitar is so much more fun. You can play drums drunk. Everybody's looking at you and judging you when you're the singer. You can feel all the knives coming at you from the guys in the front row and their girlfriends are all in love with you. It's a difficult job."

Steve Smith: "I moved on from the hurt and the pain. I went to therapy and worked my way through it, to the point I could see it was a good thing for me to leave the band. It was enough. There is a Taoist quote: 'It's enough to know when enough is enough.' Steve Perry, shortly after the *Raised on Radio* period, called me. We got together and he apologized for what he felt were bad decisions on his part. We've become pretty good friends over the years, so that's all water under the bridge."

Steve Perry: "My mother had died during the making of *Raised on Radio*. I came home, took care of that, went back, finished the vocals and stuff, and before I know it, we're on tour... I hadn't really addressed or dealt with anything pertaining to that loss."[10]

Steve Smith: "Here's the thing with being in a band. You want to have hits on the radio. You want to play sold-out concerts. And you want to make a lot of money. Let's say you do all of that. Then what?"

Mike Baird: "The *Raised on Radio* tour? I didn't know what I was getting into. I knew they'd called in Randy Jackson to play bass. And they didn't want to use Larrie Londin for the tour, even though they liked Larry. I mean, I was obese, but Larrie made me look skinny. Their concern was, 'We'll get out on the road, and this guy will have a heart attack.'"

***

Jonathan Cain: "We were now a trio performing with session artists. Few people knew how broken our lead singer was. His relationship with Sherrie had deteriorated...but that wasn't the main reason. Nor was it the price of fame...Neal and I had no idea how physically and emotionally exhausted he had become."[11]

Mike Baird: "I got the call from Steve Perry on my birthday. So I went down to rehearse with them a couple of times, but without being offered the job. Next thing I hear is they've hired this young guy instead of me. But then Jonathan Cain calls. He goes, 'We want to know if the door's still open...for you to come play with us again?' I go, 'You're out of your fucking mind.' After all the shit I'd gone through. I told him I wanted x amount of dollars wired into my bank account, and a contract. 'Okay, fine.' So I was dealing with Herbie over the contract, and they put money in my account."

Neal Schon: "I loved touring. I was ready to go, go, go."[12]

Mike Baird: "The tour was great. We traveled first class everywhere. And they were a class act every night, just amazing. My life at the time was not great. It was a horrible time for me. I'd made a wrong choice in marriage, and I allowed this woman to make my life miserable. I only brought her out once during the tour. We were in Hawaii for a week or two, and we were doing two shows. She had a couple of her friends also come out to visit and hang with us. I wound up leaving the hotel and staying with them, because I didn't want to go back to the room. Before she left, I told her, 'When I get home, I want a divorce.'"

Steve Perry: "I remember by the end of the tour feeling musically, emotionally, vocally toasty, and telling the manager, 'I just don't want to stay out there and keep doing this. Can't we stop?' And eventually I had to say, 'Look, don't book any more shows after October.'"[13]

Neal Schon: "In the middle of a tour, he just pulled out."[14]

***

Steve Perry: "The passion for music had left me. I could not find the honest passion for singing. Because of that, I was stepping into some other, dare I say, party behaviors to augment my frustrations. My voice was also suffering. Everything was starting to suffer for me. Certainly, drinking and drugs were part of it, of course. I mean, that came with the times."[15]

Jonathan Cain: "I knew it was over. Not just the tour, but the band… We had only played forty concerts. Herbie took the liberty to book fifteen more shows, only to have Steve immediately pass on them. His response had been, 'I'm done.'"[16]

Steve Perry: "The point is we were toast… I felt like we should just stop. So I did."[17]

Neil Schon: "It was sort of left at a hiatus. And it was based around Steve giving us a call and saying, 'Okay, I'm fine now, I'm ready to go.' And it just didn't happen."[18]

Herbie Herbert: "Steve Perry, I don't think he appreciates what he had at all. Or he wouldn't have given it up so easily."[19]

Tim Pierce: "The thing about Steve Perry is, he kept hold of every dollar he ever earned. So at a certain point, he never had to make any choices that were based on earning money."

CHAPTER SIXTY-EIGHT

HIGHWAY TO THE DANGER ZONE...

"Everybody at Moroder's studio became a drug addict."

Steve Lukather: "All of a sudden, to have a song featured in a blockbuster movie was a very good career move."

Les Garland: "I'm in my office one day and the head of Paramount Pictures, who I didn't know, is on the line calling. He says, 'Our movie is *Flashdance*. You're playing the clip from our film, and you blew the box office up.' Boom! We opened the gates for movie advertising on MTV that day."

Bob Pittman: "Now, *Flashdance* was a terrible movie that they couldn't figure out what to do with. And the guy that produced it said, 'Hey, MTV's hot. Let's just cut it up and make it look like a big music video.' Everything afterward began to be fast cut. Scripts got shorter. *Miami Vice* came along. Michael Mann will tell you that he was very much influenced by MTV with that show."

***

Phil Collins: "I was asked to write a song for the movie *Against All Odds*. It was basically like saying, 'Here's $10 million. Would you want it?' ['Against All Odds'] was written around the time of 'In the Air Tonight,' but I discarded it. I had actually written the lyrics before I saw the film. When I think about the movie, the first thing that comes to mind is the size of Rachel Ward's breasts. I thought they were fantastic."[1]

Bryan Adams: "I refused all the many soundtrack offers in the 1980s. I hadn't wanted to do *Footloose*. Then I didn't want to do *Top Gun*."

Steve Lukather: "Columbia was putting together the soundtrack for *Top Gun* with Giorgio Moroder."

John Kalodner: "The *Top Gun* producers, Don Simpson and Jerry Bruckheimer especially, they were great to work with. Unlike one of the greatest directors, Steven Spielberg, who knew shit about music and didn't know how to use it, or didn't care about it, Jerry Bruckheimer knew everything about music."

Kenny Loggins: "Giorgio Moroder wrote 90 percent of 'Danger Zone.' I came in and made some chord changes, substitutions and additions, a couple of melodic lines here and there, some lyrics, but not much… It established me as a movie guy."[2]

Giorgio Moroder: "I did 'Danger Zone,' and they liked it. Then Jerry Bruckheimer said they needed something slow for the romantic scenes with Tom Cruise and Kelly McGillis."[3]

Steve Lukather: "Paich and I went along to an advance screening of the film. We were told Don Simpson and Jerry Bruckheimer were looking for a love song, and so we went back to The Manor that same day and wrote 'Only You,' which I sang."

John Crawford: "[Berlin was] working with Giorgio Moroder on our music, and at the same time he had been hired by Columbia Records to do the entire soundtrack for the *Top Gun* movie, so he was working on 'Take My Breath Away.'"[4]

Steve Lukather: "Simpson and Bruckheimer came out to Paich's place to listen to what we had. The first thing Simpson said to us was, 'Who's got the Ferrari outside?' He had the same car as me and was kind of pissed I had one, too. We played them 'Only You' and they're like, 'Uh, it's okay. We'll get back to you.' They split, and they ended up going with the fucking annoying sound of Berlin and 'Take My Breath Away.'"

Giorgio Moroder: "My Ferrari was parked behind the studio, with brake trouble. One day a guy, Tom Whitlock, came by and said he could fix it. Later he said: 'Oh and, by the way, I'm also a lyricist. If you ever need some words.' He wrote the words for 'Danger Zone' and 'Take My Breath Away.'"[5]

Henry Small: "I get a call from my friend Richie Zito. He says, 'Giorgio Moroder has heard something you sang with Tommy Whitlock, and he wants to sign you to a contract for a movie called *Top Gun*.' I'd written some stuff in the studio with Tommy. I was excited about it, but I had just gotten out of this contract with Capitol, and I was destroyed by what they had done to me. Giorgio wanted me to co-write and have equal billing. Tommy got the job because he was smart enough to sign Giorgio's contract. I didn't."

John Kalodner: "I'd signed Berlin. Terri Nunn was incredibly talented. Jerry Bruckheimer and the music supervisor for the movie wanted Berlin to do the song. But Terri Nunn didn't like the song. And so I kind of forced her to sing 'Take My Breath Away.'"

John Crawford: "Giorgio asked Terri to come in and sing the demo of it, so basically 'Take My Breath Away' had nothing to do with Berlin at all. I never heard the song until I went to the premiere of the movie."[6]

Terri Nunn: "John Crawford hated it… Giorgio was a great writer and such a talent. I was all in for him. He could have farted, and I would have sung it. But John's like, 'I'm not doing this. Fuck this guy. This is not our song.' The record label jumped in and said, 'You're doing this. You need all the help you can get.'"[7]

Henry Small: "Everybody at Moroder's studio became a drug addict. *Everyone.* I mean, they had bowls of cocaine all over the place. They had three control rooms. Every time you'd go in to record anything, there was literally a bowl of blow with straws stuck in it on the console. All those guys had to go to rehab."

Terri Nunn: "At first, nothing happened, and our manager said: 'Terri, if this goes Top 10, I'll get a mohawk.' It went to Number One around the world, so MTV came and filmed our manager getting a mohawk."[8]

John Kalodner: "After it became a worldwide hit, Terri did some bad press about it, saying she didn't like the song, and I had forced her to do it. I don't think she appeared in a TV show or a movie again ever. I'm sure that Jerry Bruckheimer worked his magic on getting back at her unnecessary comments. Terri was a lovely person, beautiful and talented. It just was one of those things. Everybody makes mistakes. That was a big mistake that she made."

Terri Nunn: "It opened the door to the world for me, and still does, to this day. It's the gift that keeps giving. It's a song that keeps going."[9]

Joe Lynn Turner: "Movies? Let me tell you something. You wanted to make money? TV and radio jingles. When you sang those things that was like in perpetuity, residual money. I owe Michael Bolton to this day for turning me on to that. He'd been the Gillette guy, the Budweiser guy, but he was getting out of it and was off on his own career. Michael introduced me to his jingle agent, Susan Hamilton, and told me I was going to make a fortune. All of a sudden, I was the new kid in town. The fast gun. The fast voice. I became pretty much the prince of jingles. When I next saw Michael, I said to him, 'Man,

I gotta thank you. I've gotten two houses out of that stuff.' A hell of a time, man."

Henry Small: "With all due respect, Tommy Whitlock was a really nice guy, but he wrote lyrics that were...*uh*. Anyway, he made $35 million out of *Top Gun* and got a Grammy for doing it. Have you met someone as stupid as me before? Watching Tommy and Giorgio get their Grammy for 'Take My Breath Away,' that hurt. I'm sitting in Kamloops, British Columbia, going, 'Oh my God,' and I started to tear up. My wife at the time said, 'What's wrong with you? Look what you have.' That's why she's an ex-wife. Yes, I had a couple of kids, and that's wonderful. But it didn't satisfy any creative accomplishment. It just didn't."

CHAPTER SIXTY-NINE

EUROPE CALLING.

"We sang in Danish, and Danish is not a pretty language."

Dennis Dries: "Melodic rock was always strong in the UK and parts of Europe. Japan, too. This kind of music is just more appreciated over there."

Joey Tempest: "I learned to play guitar and piano from copying the stuff I heard on the radio. Deep Purple, Led Zeppelin. In the late '70s, Sweden was not open yet for bands singing in English. There were a few local radio stations, though, that would play hard rock. I'd met John Norum by then and we had a band. We went to some big-name record labels around Stockholm with our early demos. They all said, 'Well, if you sing in Swedish maybe. Or have shorter hair and turn down the guitars.' None of them would touch us."

Mike Tramp: "I was a kid from Copenhagen when I joined Mabel in 1976. They were ten years older than me and already a professional band. I could play some campfire guitar, but I knew nothing. Apart from one thing. I knew I couldn't be two things. I couldn't be the street kid from the neighborhood that I came from, and at the same time the singer in a band. It was all or nothing."

Steve Overland: "After the *Boston* album came out, I discovered lots of other American bands. I got really into Hall and Oates, the Eagles, and later on Journey. Those kinds of bands took over my listening. It's how I learned about harmonies and how to do vocal arrangements."

Joey Tempest: "A girlfriend of mine sent in our tape to a national battle of the bands competition. It was being run by the biggest newspaper in Sweden together with Thomas Erdtman, who became our manager. Eighty bands got chosen to compete from something like four thousand tapes that were sent in. The final was broadcast on TV. And we won."

Mike Tramp: "In 1978, Denmark had been absent from the Eurovision Song Contest for many years. Mabel was in the middle of recording our second album and our record company came in, not caring about the future of the band but just instant gratification, and said, 'You should do Eurovision.' We'd already written a song, 'Boom Boom.' It sounded very close to '39' by Queen, and we got to represent Denmark in the final in Paris. We sang in Danish, and Danish is not a pretty language. We finished sixteenth out of twenty."

Joey Tempest: "I remember listening to Deep Purple's *Made in Europe*. Looking at the album cover and thinking, '*That* could work.' I had to get the guys drinking before I could present our new band name to them. When I thought they were drunk enough, I told them our name was Europe. They just went quiet. A few more beers and they were like, 'That's fucking great, man!'"

Mike Tramp: "We signed a contract with Warner Bros. in Spain. So we escaped Denmark and moved to Madrid. Van Halen were on the same label as us, and they came to town to promote their *Diver Down* album in 1982. Since I spoke Spanish, I was sent to the airport to pick them up and look after them. The first guy I met was David Lee Roth. He'd got these big sunglasses on. He just stared at me and barked, 'Who the fuck are you? Have you got a joint?' I was in his hotel room one day, and he was listening to New York disco music. That really confused me. This was my rock 'n' roll hero."

Steve Overland: "I was in a band called Wildlife with Simon Kirke from Bad Company. We were signed to Led Zeppelin's label, Swan Song, by Ahmet Ertegun. The album we made [*Wildfire*, 1983] was a hard-edged blues-rock record, but with the American-style harmonies. I'd watch all of the videos on MTV and think, 'I *need* to go there.' It was the place be."

Mike Tramp: "That was when Foreigner's *4* came into my life. I discovered it in a record store in Madrid. Instantly, I was like, 'Holy shit, you can have hard rock guitar *and* great melodies!'"

Joey Tempest: "The second Europe album we made in ABBA's studio in Stockholm. They were nice to us. We wanted to sing in English. Swedish is a limited language. It's stark, to the point. We had more words, more expressions to play with in English. You can paint a picture easier, and it sounds better. Slowly, we found our way out of Sweden, and in 1985, we signed with Epic Records in New York."

Mike Tramp: "An American guy offered to manage us. So we changed our name to Lion and moved to New York. By that time, I was writing all of the songs and had taken over the band. The rock clubs in New York were on fire. We played a gig at a club called L'Amour in Brooklyn with another band, Dreamer. Their guitarist was Vito Bratta. We met in the dressing room. I was sat there with my Danish boys, thinking we were the shit. Vito came in and asked if he could plug into our little rehearsal amp. For the next hour, we sat listening to him play with our jaws in our laps. I knew instantly, '*That* is the guy I need to be with.' He came over to where I was living in Queens, and that first night we wrote a song together, 'Broken Heart.'"

***

Joey Tempest: "I was working on the demos for our third record. I had one song already, 'Rock the Night.' And the title for another. 'The Final Countdown.'"

Mike Tramp: "For me, it was not an option to go back to Denmark. Failure was not an option. I didn't care where I was living. Bless the '80s, because it was 80 percent girls at every rock club. It wasn't so difficult to find a bed to sleep in."

Steve Overland: "After Wildfire, my brother Chris and I got signed by Brian Lane, who managed Yes and Asia. We were living in Brian's house in London, and he put us on a retainer. I got a call one day from Pete Jupp, a drummer who'd very briefly been in the first incarnation of Wildfire. Pete told me he was forming a melodic rock band with a bass player he knew, Merv Goldsworthy, and were Chris and I interested in joining them. We agreed to do a four-track tape together, put it out there, do one showcase, and if nothing happened, we'd all go back to what we were doing rather than waste time trudging around trying to get this thing off the ground."

Joey Tempest: "The intro to 'The Final Countdown' dated back to when I was seventeen. I wrote it on a keyboard I'd borrowed from a kid at high school. The chord sequence came to me one night. It was just a one-minute piece, meant as an intro to us coming onstage, and it'd sat in a drawer ever since. The other guys got to hear it when we were working on the third album and told me I should build something around it. I went home, put my Oberheim keyboard on, and found a tempo for the piece that would fit a verse. The lyrics were probably inspired by Bowie's 'Space Oddity.' I had a thought that the song could be about us leaving a dying Earth."

Steve Overland: "Meat Loaf's management heard our tape and asked us to open for him in Europe on his *Bad Attitude* tour. We had no name for the band, not enough songs for a set, nothing, but we went out and did arenas in Germany with Meat Loaf. After that, we got offered two record deals. We became the first UK band signed to Portrait Records, so we were on the same label as Heart. And then we needed a name fast. It was Merv who suggested FM, because it sounded American."

Mike Tramp: "Vito and I were obviously inspired by Eddie and Dave with Van Halen, but as songwriters we were a bit different, more melodic. We started White Lion in a fucking freezing basement in an industrial area of Brooklyn."

Joey Tempest: "We went to Switzerland to record the album with Kevin Elson, Journey's producer."

Steve Overland: "There was so much money around at that time to make records. No such thing as a budget. It was just a case of, 'Where do you want to go? Have this. Have that.' Judas Priest's drummer, Dave Holland, had this fantastic studio on Ibiza. So we went there for six weeks in the summer to make *Indiscreet* in 1986."

Mike Tramp: "We did the *Fight to Survive* album in Germany. We were signed to a massive deal with Elektra Records. We finished the record, shot the album cover, and then we got a phone call from our manager. Elektra had decided they didn't want to release the album. We got to keep the advance. So we had $300,000 in the bank, but we were heartbroken."

Joey Tempest: "First of all, 'The Final Countdown' started to climb the chart in Holland. And in those days, Holland was a key territory. If you got on Radio Veronica in Holland, you knew something was going on. From there, it spread all over Europe."

Steve Overland: "I came up with the riff to 'American Girls.' It was from all those chord progressions the American bands were doing. I mean, I'd sat down and learned those songs. That processed, thin guitar sound they had was so great. I guess we just became instinctively Americanized."

Mike Tramp: "We got the part of a band in a Tom Hanks movie, *Money*

Pit. The director, Richard Benjamin, wanted us dressed up as gigantic flies. Vito goes, 'So, no one will see our faces?' 'Not really.' The stage they built for the shoot was like a gigantic foam tongue. We were meant to be jumping around inside of a venus flytrap. Every time we jumped up, the drum kit would flip over. I cry whenever I watch *Spinal Tap*, because to me it's not a joke. It's fucking reality."

Joey Tempest: "The success was bittersweet in a way, because John Norum quit the band. He wanted to do other stuff. There were personal things, too, maybe with the manager and in his private life. You'd have to ask him."

Steve Overland: "Obviously, we needed a ballad. We felt like we had to have one of those big ones, like Heart's, so we sat down and consciously wrote 'Frozen Heart.' That became the song that kicked it all off for us."

Mike Tramp: "We managed to get the first album licensed in Japan. It got well reviewed in *Kerrang!* magazine in the UK, and we began to get an almost underground following in the UK, and in Germany and Italy. There was a little more talk going on about the band, and in 1986, we started on a new record."

Joey Tempest: "That was an amazing period. As a guy from a suburb of Stockholm, to be in one of the biggest bands on the planet. We were doing stadiums all over Europe. We had Number One records wherever we went in the world. Security, bodyguards, helicopters, everything. There were a *lot* of distractions. Quite a bit of wild partying going on with some members in the band. But the thing is, we survived. We were sensible, I'd say. Like, when I got my first big royalty check, I bought a new BMW. Nothing too extravagant."

Mike Tramp: "Vito and I had written this song. We were driving back from rehearsal one day, the two of us in my car, listening to it on the car stereo. We knew we were measuring up against Journey, Foreigner, Cheap Trick, all the great bands out there at the time, and the tape was distorting. But we just looked at each other and went, '*What* a fucking song!' That was 'Wait.'"

Joey Tempest: "To actually walk down the street today and hear 'The Final Countdown' as a ringtone, that's strange. There was a version these guys from Morocco did, playing it on logs. I was so young when I wrote it, and I have to pinch myself still."

CHAPTER SEVENTY

A PRAYER FOR BON JOVI.

"I am the wizard, and I wave my magic wand, and suddenly they're the greatest they can ever be."

Paul Elliott: "Jon Bon Jovi working with Desmond Child? The exact same thing as Def Leppard and Mutt Lange. Naked ambition."

Danny Kortchmar: "Jon Bon Jovi was a striver. Even after he'd made zillions of dollars and had hit after hit. Henley, the same thing. He was in the Eagles, for Christ's sake. Where else do you go? But he wasn't finished yet. He wanted to create more music. Same thing with all these guys."

Desmond Child: "Because of my success with Kiss, I got interest from Bon Jovi. Bon Jovi had been the opening act for Kiss in Europe. Jon gave me a call. He and Richie were thinking of writing songs for other people, because they'd seen what Bryan Adams had done with Tina Turner. I went to write with them, and I had a title in my back pocket. 'You Give Love a Bad Name.' I interpolated a song I'd written for Bonnie Tyler, 'If You Were a Woman and I Was a Man,' that was popular in Europe. Used the same melody, because I knew it was a hit melody. And Jon had a song he'd written that was meant for someone like Loverboy called 'Shot Through the Heart.' 'Shot through the heart and you're to blame,' it went. I added to that my, 'You give love a bad name.' We wrote our song, and then they decided they were not going to pitch it to Loverboy, or whoever. That was the start of a great creative relationship."

Steve Overland: "My brother Chris and I later on went and wrote with Desmond up in Bearsville. He was fantastic. A great guy, and very clever. He has a weird way of working. He tells you he 'knows what the kids want to hear.' The 'whoa-whoa' stuff is all him. That's what he comes up with. He's got a grand piano in his studio. You'll sit down with him, and he'll start banging out a couple of notes on the piano. Just two. Basically, he'll give you hooks. Then you go away and write the song. And it's true, he does know what sells. He can almost hear what the crowd is going to do when you play the song live."

Desmond Child: "Bob Crewe taught me the tension of opposites. To make titles so intriguing that people would want to see what the song is about. 'You Give Love a Bad Name.' How can love be bad? 'Heaven's on Fire.' Why is heaven on fire? It goes on and on. All of that helps to build a hit song."

Jon Bon Jovi: "We rehearsed all of the material for *Slippery When Wet* at a studio in New Jersey."

Desmond Child: "The story in 'Livin' on a Prayer'? 'Gina works the diner all day.' That's Maria Vidal working at Once Upon a Stove in New York. And I was Tommy, who she 'brings home her pay for love.' Jon had his own story going on, too. He had friends in high school, Bonnie and Joe, who'd got married young and had really hard times and struggled. He never said that when we were writing the song, but he's claimed since that he had Bonnie and Joe in the back of his mind. Then again, Richie says he always thought about his own parents struggling. New Jersey, working class, it's never easy. I understood that from living in the projects. My mother was always borrowing $20 from this person or that one, trying to put gas in the car. The 'it doesn't make a difference' line actually came from the commune. It was something Bill Barber would always say. You know, with whatever else he was pontificating."

Jon Bon Jovi: "It came to life when we got in the room and developed the bass line. That's when it popped."[1]

Desmond Child: "The music and genre of the music is secondary to the story. It's whatever helps to tell that story. I focus always entirely on the story, what is it and then what goes with it in context with the artist and what they're capable of performing. Anything that doesn't fit with that picture, I try to strip away as I work with them and to help them to achieve their fullest potential. I was gifted with a kind of empathy and creative imagination. I'm the wizard, and I wave my magic wand, and suddenly they're the greatest they can ever be."

Jon Bon Jovi: "If we all just sit around saying the world sucks, what's left? You could do something really miniscule. You could wake up in the morning and maybe say 'Hi' and smile at somebody. They're gonna take that attitude away, and maybe not go home and beat their wife. As small a spark as you can do, at least you're making the effort."

Desmond Child: "It's amazing being in a writing session and all of a sudden—pop! Oh my God, that's the line, or the melody. Like when we were working on 'Livin' on a Prayer' and we thought we had the chorus, with the 'Hold on to what we've got.' I said, 'You know what, let's push on. Let's write another chorus on top of that.' Then we're singing, 'We're halfway there...' and Richie was looking for his harmony. So he went, 'Whoa-whoa.' I said, 'Let's make that the harmony.' It was by accident. I mean, magical things can happen. It's the chemistry of elements that ignite the creative process."

Steve Overland: "The first question Desmond asked us was, 'What do you want to write, guys?' Well, 'Livin' on a Prayer' will do. He said, '*Everybody* wants to write "Livin' on a Prayer."'"

***

Desmond Child: "That song has had so many meanings for so many people. I've gotten so many letters. People that have said it got them through cancer. That it got them through a bad relationship, or hard economic times. One guy wrote this amazing letter. He said he was getting ready to kill himself. He had been drinking, and he pulled his car up to the middle of the bridge. He jumped out of the car with the radio still on, the door open. He started to climb up to the rail, and 'Livin' on a Prayer' comes on the radio. He could hear it from the car. It was his favorite song. He got back into the car. By the time it got to the modulation, he drove home. So Bon Jovi saves lives."

Jon Bon Jovi: "With 'Wanted (Dead or Alive),' I'd always wanted to do an acoustic track with that kind of a Clint Eastwood approach. All rock 'n' rollers have a nomadic, cowboy sort of existence. We come to a town, try to pick up women, take the money, and you don't see us again."

Richie Sambora: "We were *this* close to one another, and we were on edge, man. Through the machine drudging you on and pushing you forward all the time, there was all this edginess that was happening between us. All this shit we'd either said or thought."

Desmond Child: "Jon and Richie were so different from each other. Richie was talkative and gregarious, laughing, and full of joy. Jon always had many things on his mind. He was the boss, and he was thinking about the touring schedule, or the bus that broke down. He's kind of a Pisces, very pensive, and he always seemed to me to be a little bit down. The two of them created one person. They were like twins. I have twins. One's one way, the other's the other way. Together, they can work a room and get the best girls. The two of them, Jon and Richie. That's what made the magic."

Jon Bon Jovi: "Once the songs had been arranged and worked out, we invited in a lot of kids we'd met in a local pizza parlor to listen to them. When the album was finished, I gave a cassette to my younger brother,

Anthony, and told him to play it for all his friends at school to get their reaction. To me, it's always important to know what the fans think."

John Kalodner: "The first time I ever saw Jon, it was right before *Slippery When Wet* came out in August 1986. I just couldn't believe what he looked like and his presence. Just the aura he put out and the aura around him. You just knew he was going to be one of the biggest artists ever."

Jon Bon Jovi: "And then this bitch just took off. That was the last time anyone saw us for four years. We were orbiting. The machine starts to roll."

Joey Tempest: "We met Bon Jovi for the first time in England doing *Top of the Pops*. We were Number One with 'The Final Countdown' and 'Livin' on a Prayer' was at Number Seven."

Steve Overland: "FM opened up for Bon Jovi on their UK tour. All of a sudden, *Slippery When Wet* had gone to Number One all over the world and they were flying. They were shell-shocked, too. They hadn't expected it. They were the biggest band in the world. The audiences were full of women. That was an amazing tour to do."

Jon Bon Jovi: "At twenty-five your thought process is, 'I want credibility! I want the critics to like this!'...We're on the cover of *Rolling Stone*. And the first thing the girl talks about is, 'Your hair looks nice. Will you take your shirt off for me? Got any tattoos?'"[2]

Steve Overland: "They worked hard for it, too. They gave 150 percent every night. They made sure that when they left that stage every night, there was nobody in the audience that didn't believe they deserved what they'd become."

Danny Kortchmar: "I don't recall any of these guys ever patting themselves on the back and going, 'Oh, I'm rich, I've made it.'"

***

Desmond Child: "That song has had so many meanings."

Jon Bon Jovi: "This was the American dream realized. It was important to understand that. There are better players, better singers, and better songwriters, but when I turned around onstage and looked at these guys, I remembered our first rehearsal space, which was just a little storefront in New Jersey. It was hard to believe where we were."

Richie Sambora: "When I look back through all the supernova of Bon Jovi's success, it's lucky we're still alive. People just don't realize how dangerous this business actually is, how detrimental it can be to your state of mind. There's no rule book for that shit."

Jon Bon Jovi: "Look at any picture of us by 1987. We were physically and mentally burned. All the people around us were telling us we had to go on. I had a beard, sunglasses, my voice was completely shot. They're shooting me up with steroids, but no, you had to go to work. We trudge on, glad to be there, not realizing that we were burned. You'd think that someone around us would have mentioned it."

CHAPTER SEVENTY-ONE

THE BIG SHORT.

"I saw a lot of money being spent on records that just didn't need to be spent."

Tom Scholz: "Making music is very frustrating sometimes, but there are times when it is quite sensational. When things happen for me with the music I'm working on, it makes everything worthwhile. I have sacrificed an awful lot, but the music is very rewarding. Other than the people in my life, the art is the most important thing."[1]

Bill Champlin: "I saw a lot of money spent on records that just didn't need to be spent. There's an old joke. 'Hey, you guys spent all your money on blow for this album, so you're gonna have to mix in fast-forward.' I saw a hell of a lot of time being wasted."

Tom Scholz: "The *Third Stage* album was done under very difficult circumstances."[2]

Steve Lukather: "We hurried into the studio to make *Fahrenheit* in 1986, but we had a glaring problem with Fergie Frederiksen. He would get very nervous, and not be able to stay in tune. One take after another,

Fergie would struggle but to no avail. Jeff would be throwing up his hands and Paich sat slumped over the console. It was costing us time and money. Eventually, the record company began to ask what the hell was going on."

Henry Small: "I went to England in 1986 to work with John Entwistle of the Who on his solo album, *The Rock*. I liked John. He was a gentleman, but it was very loosey-goosey. He had his own studio in his mansion. But there was no order... I thought I was going to there for three weeks, tops. Six months later... There was a lot of cocaine going on. John had a bar in his house, and a guy serving the drinks. Somebody was always going missing or would have a hangover. The engineer would be off on a bender for three days."

Mike Baird: "Richie Zito, who's a friend, was producing the *Can't Hold Back* album for Eddie Money. He calls me up and asks me up to the sessions in Marin County. The first day, we get in the studio, we're setting our gear up, and we're almost done when Eddie shows up. He's still doing tons of drugs and whatever. I didn't have an issue with him, but Richie and Eddie were going at each other off the bat."

Henry Small: "But God, to be in London at the weekends and go to Bootleggers for a night, and until ten o'clock in the morning. It was a private club. John would get us in. We'd all be drinking and doing whatever. Prince came in one night with two huge bodyguards with Egyptian headgear on. I also remember being at Jeff Beck's girlfriend's birthday party. I was sat next to Barbara Bach and Ringo Starr. Bill Wyman was sitting over there with his girlfriend who's about fifteen, and his son is with the girl's mother who he's dating. It was a whole different thing... I talked to John not long before he passed. I said to him, 'John, where's the money for the album we did?' I had to beg, borrow, and steal just to get myself back home."

Brad Delp: "Tom and I only see each other when it's time to work...[3] I certainly consider us friends but, for whatever reason, we never really socialized all that much. That may speak as much about me as it does about him."4

Tom Scholz: "Who really wants to work virtually by himself for six years? It's something that no one in his right mind would do. I was by myself most of the time. I didn't even spend much time with my family. Brad was there for the vocals about 10 percent of the time. And I had Jim [Masdea] there working on parts with me sometimes. But for the most part I was in the studio alone, working constantly."5

Bill Champlin: "Peter Cetera had wanted out of Chicago for a good period of time, but him going really threw a wrench in the works. If he'd stayed for one more album, we'd probably have been doing baseball stadiums. I don't blame him. There was so much resentment within the band from all the attention he was getting. And something felt wrong making the *18* album. The reason, I think, was that David Foster kind of felt he'd lost his guy. Peter's replacement, Jason Scheff, did okay, I thought, considering he came out of nowhere. But he needed a little more coaching than Peter ever did. Peter's a pretty major singer."

Steve Lukather: "We'd found ourselves back at square one, so we had no option but to let Fergie go. I think he knew it was coming. The most painful thing was that Fergie was one of the nicest cats you could ever hope to meet. So we chickened out and had our managers deliver the bad news."

Fergie Frederiksen: "I left under distressed terms, which is a shame, but I don't have anything bad to say about those guys."6

Brad Delp: "I do think of Tom as a special person. I'm not one to throw the term 'genius' around and apply it to anyone. I think Tom certainly had an ingenious approach to making music."7

Tom Scholz: "There's a song on *Third Stage* called 'To Be a Man.' It was an unusual arrangement with an unusual chorus with lots of key changes. And I knew that those chords came from a piece of music, but I had no idea what it was. About ten years ago, I finally heard the piece of music, and it was a Beethoven piece."[8]

Eddie Money: "I called Ronnie Spector and said, 'I got this song that's truly amazing and it's a tribute to you. It would be so great if you did it with me.' I could hear clinking and clanking in the background. She said, 'I'm doing the dishes, and I gotta change the kids' bedding. I'm not really in the business anymore, Eddie. Phil Spector and all that, it was a nightmare...' But then she came and did 'Take Me Home Tonight.' She was even better on a cheap bottle of wine and some crappy grass, I gotta tell you."[9]

Mike Baird: "Eddie had specific ideas about what he wanted, and they weren't necessarily the best ideas. Richie would have to wrangle him in, get him to focus, which is what producers are supposed to do. Eddie wound up living literally five minutes from my house, so we would hang. We became friends. We'd always argue in the studio, but I could reason with Eddie. He was great to work with, besides it always being a bloodbath."

Bill Champlin: "I wish I'd have jumped sooner than I did. Those last five years I was with Chicago was sheer marking time. I was angry with myself and with what had become the battery for the band, which was just money. When your band is starting to make its decisions in a boardroom, where bankers and real estate guys make decisions... A band should make its decisions in a cheap pizza parlor with three-two beer and greasy-assed pizza. That's where Chicago started. Go back there for a minute."

Steve Lukather: "We had loads of people come in to audition to be our new singer. Between us, we even had a brief conversation about where Bobby Kimball might be. The answer was out on the road using our name to sell tickets. We immediately scratched him off the list. For my part, I lobbied hard for Eric Martin, and so we had him fly down from San Francisco."

***

Eric Martin: "I was *in* Toto, dude. I hung out with them for a week, ten days. I got too comfortable. We went to see Jeff Porcaro's dad play at this jazz club. We were crammed in this red leather booth. We had a carafe of wine. And, man, they were pouring the wine, and I was drinking it. Lukather drank, too, but he wasn't too far in his cups. He was so funny. He could do a funny-ass Sammy Davis Jr. impersonation. I thought I was funnier because I'd had a couple of glasses of wine in me. I was joking around, and Jeff probably wanted to talk to me in a more serious light. Maybe I was sarcastic."

Steve Lukather: "Poor Eric proceeded to get plastered and then rub Jeff the wrong way."

Eric Martin: "Jeff stepped outside, and I never saw him again. Each of the other guys went out to talk to Jeff, and then they left, too. It was Luke who came back into the club and said to me, 'We're gonna vote on it, man.' Two weeks later, he called me and said, 'It's a no.'"

Steve Lukather: "Jeff described him as being like a little kid. To me, it was really hard on Eric."

Eric Martin: "Years later, I went to a NAMM show with Luke. By then, he *was* in his cups. I'm having to help him across the floor, and he's saying to me, 'Hey, man, just get me back to the hotel safely.' Luke was in dire straits back in the day, and he cleaned himself up. Anyway, we're a mess. And we're walking across the street, and David Paich comes toward us. Luke goes, 'Hey, Paich, this is the guy that got away.' Paich goes, 'I know, I know...' And I'd wanted to be in that band so bad."

Steve Lukather: "Out of the blue, Joseph Williams's name popped up. Steve and I knew Joe from high school. He came along to The Manor and nailed everything Paich threw at him. Paich was ecstatic."

***

Tom Scholz: "I was very happy with the [*Third Stage*] album and the way it was finished. I got to say what I wanted to say with it."[10]

Paul Elliott: "Eight years later, Tom Scholz makes *Third Stage* for another record label, MCA, and it goes straight in at Number One. It's a total fuck-you. You've got to admire him, really. He would not concede. It was art to him and he's a genuine artist. I have huge admiration for him on that level. Although you wouldn't want to be in a band with him."

Steve Lukather: "*Fahrenheit* turned out being a hell of a record. Joe Williams sang his ass off. Don Henley came in and sang on a tune, 'Lea.' We had Miles Davis play on the last track on the album, 'Don't Stop Now.'"

David Paich: "Oh, man, Miles Davis. That was a trip."

Steve Lukather: "It was arranged that Miles would come over to Paich's place. At 10 p.m. precisely, the gateway bell rang out. Now, in the hallway of his house, Paich had mounted a stuffed German shepherd dog in an attack position. When the front door opened, it'd be like this great snarling beast was about to leap out and take a bite out of you."

David Paich: "When I got married in '83, my in-laws had given me this stuffed dog as a wedding present. Whenever we'd go on the road, I'd stand it in front of the window, just to fuck with people."

Steve Lukather: "Miles knocks on the door. He's with his producer, Tommy LiPuma. He's in a red leather suit, huge dark glasses on, his hair long. The instant the door swings open, he jumps back as if he's been shot. We'd all seen Paich's dog so often we took it for granted. We start shouting, 'Whoa, Miles, the dog's a fake!' Miles walks into the hall, crouches down, lifts his glasses up over his eyes, and peers intently at the dog. Then he says, 'I got some shit on me make that thing come back *aliiive*.' That broke the ice."

***

David Paich: "No one could get Miles Davis to play on their records. He didn't do session work for anybody. Jeff had a charcoal, pen-drawn sketch that Miles liked. He said to Jeff, 'I'll trade you a solo for that piece of art right there.' That's what went down, no attorneys, no record company people, no contract."

Steve Lukather: "Here he was, the hippest of cats, hanging out with the whitest motherfuckers in Hollywood. There isn't anybody on Planet Earth hipper than Miles Davis. I'm good enough for Miles, but not for Jann Wenner and all those other morons? Give me a fucking break, man. And that wound up being the last thing people heard on the *Fahrenheit* record. Miles's horn blazing off into echo."

Bill Champlin: "The other guys in Chicago would like to erase Peter, Foster, and me from their history completely. I mean, going right back to when we did *17*, even the management was suggesting we shouldn't play those songs on the tour. It started to get to me more and more. The original guys didn't dig me because they couldn't give themselves the credit for what we'd achieved."

Tom Scholz: "The touring in '78 and '79, I had a horrible time. They were very draining. With some trepidation, in 1987 I agreed to try again."[11]

Barry Goudreau: "Brad left Boston. He wasn't a partner when he went out on the *Third Stage* tour. He was a hired hand essentially."[12]

Brad Delp: "I never really left. I de facto removed myself."[13]

Tom Scholz: "It was the best tour of my life. It sold. We were able to play some things we had never been able to before. We did everything."[14]

Steve Lukather: "*Fahrenheit* gave us a bunch of hit songs. We went on tour around Europe and that was a sellout smash, too. We were back on track. We couldn't possibly have known that after that we were going to be hit by one hammer blow after another."

CHAPTER SEVENTY-TWO

AEROSMITH MAKES *PERMANENT VACATION* AND THE YEAR OF ROCK.

"It was as obvious we needed to revamp our thinking as the balls on a dog."

Andrew McNeice: "It was 1987 when rock basically went mainstream. That was when there was an explosion. You'd had *5150* and *Slippery When Wet*. Then along comes Aerosmith, Whitesnake, Def Leppard… And of course, the records they were making were all absolutely melodic rock."

Steven Tyler: "When we'd climbed out of the hole we were in, got back together and made the *Done with Mirrors* album in 1985, it was… really uncomfortable."

Joe Perry: "That record sounded good to me at the time, but we were holding back. The basic songs were good, and we *were* cleaning up our act personally. What was missing was the edgier stuff. That was because of the way the band was at the time. We were afraid to step on each other's toes. We needed to work out a new paradigm. And that took us another couple of years of being out on the road."

John Kalodner: "Steven Tyler is, I think, the most talented person I've ever worked with. He could do anything. Him and Joe Perry just needed to be... Well, first of all their manager, Tim Collins, cleaned them up from drugs and alcohol. Then they needed to have some other songwriting influences. Guys like Desmond Child and Jim Vallance who could spur these great ideas that came out of them."

Desmond Child: "Tyler and Perry, another pair of opposites. Steven was the gregarious one with the big smile, the big mouth, and hyper. Joe was pensive. Always with his head down, kind of looking sideways with his arms crossed."

John Kalodner: "The lead singer and the lead guitarist or main songwriter. That's who you focus on. Steven and Joe. We used to call the other guys in the band 'The L. I. Three.' The Less Important Three. That really pissed them off."

Joe Perry: "Our personalities are so different I can't believe Steven and I ever bumped into each other. Somehow, there's magic there. I mean, I didn't put an ad in the paper going: 'Wanted—guy that loves life, scuba diving, and shooting guns, but also has visions of being a rock star and is looking for someone to argue with half the time.' You can't plan for that stuff."

John Kalodner: "They also needed a new producer. And to be away from any distractions to make *Permanent Vacation*. So I sent them up to Vancouver where Bruce Fairbairn worked."

Joe Perry: "It was as obvious we needed to revamp our thinking as the balls on a dog. That being said, none of us liked the whole idea of bringing in outside writers at first. We had to be dragged kicking and screaming to it. But ultimately, we realized it was going to bring new energy to the table and part of what was going to keep us going."

Steven Tyler: "We got the riff first off for 'Dude (Looks Like a Lady).' We bought a sampling machine and put it in the rehearsal hall. This thing grabbed sound bites like an answering machine. So we nicked a piece of Joe's guitar, and it was fucking great. Fun. I love to bastardize our own songs. It's a thing. Then Desmond came along and wrote some lyrics. And I thought they sucked."

Desmond Child: "The first day, I walked into this big airplane hangar where they had their tour setup. Steven came up to me and said, 'Hey, come with me.' We didn't even say hello. I hadn't said one word. They were working on this backward guitar thing. Then Steven started singing: 'Cruising for the ladies...' They stopped and he said, 'What do you think?' I said, 'That's really bad.' Those were the first words out of my mouth. Joe Perry was looking at me sideways. I said, 'I don't think Van Halen would put that on the B-side of their worst record.' Just to try to break the ice. They did not laugh. Then Steven kind of sheepishly said, 'Well, originally, I was singing, "Dude looks like a lady."' And Joe said, 'But we don't know what that means.' I said, 'Okay, stop right there. *I* know what that means.'"

Steven Tyler: "I'd never really worked with somebody of Desmond's... ilk. I was intimidated. I didn't know how to say to him, 'This sucks.' Like I would with Joe."

Desmond Child: "I asked Steven where he'd come up with that phrase. He told me they were at this bar on the shore. It was almost empty, but for them and their roadies. They were all in the program, so they were drinking soda. At the end of this long bar there was this vision of loveliness. Big bouffant, platinum mullet hair, porcelain skin, black fingernails, and jewelry. Very curvy body from behind. They were drawing straws over who was going to go over and say hello. 'She' turned around... And it's Vince Neil from Mötley Crüe. That's when Steven said, 'Ooh, that dude looks like a lady.' I said to them, 'That's a hit title. Let's just tell the story.' So, 'Walked into a bar on the shore. Her picture graced the grime on the door. She was a long-lost love at first bite.' That last one was Steven's line. It makes no sense. It means *nothing*, but Steven loved it. The second verse is where it all comes together. He doesn't run away. He says, 'Never judge a book by its cover, or who you gonna love for your lover?' I mean, that was very progressive. And that song ended up being a sensation. It really brought them back."

Steven Tyler: "One of the secrets is to overwrite. You've got to get twelve songs on an album, so write twenty-five. To get the best out of those you've got to look at the list and go, 'Can you imagine playing this live?' Before it's even a finished song."

Desmond Child: "Then we wrote 'Angel' and 'Heart's Done Time.'"

Joe Perry: "Desmond doesn't write songs with anybody else like he did with us. Because he loves to do ballads."

Steven Tyler: "I love ear candy. Put the headphones on and that shit whizzes past. Close your eyes and you go on a bit of a trip. Not to say we haven't done the commercial slop. Like 'Angel.' That's real commercial. But we wrote a bunch of other songs with Desmond that are so fucking unlike anything else he's written. There's no telling what you can do or accomplish if you don't care who gets the credit. It's all about fun and good times. I mean, throw me a fish. I don't care where it comes from."

Joe Perry: "You never really know what the record sounds like until you can lay it all out on the car stereo and play it a couple of times."

John Kalodner: "*Permanent Vacation* was a huge hit record. And Aerosmith acknowledged what I'd done for them, but just a little bit and begrudgingly. Tyler used to say in interviews that the songs were his children, and I'd killed his kids."

***

Steven Tyler: "These songs *are* your kids, and you throw them out into the water. The ones that swim back are the hits. The ones that drown, you're supposed to look the other way while these fucking things die. I take a lot of pride in my stuff, maybe too much. I was devastated when there's something I'd sweated over and John Kalodner comes in and goes, 'That sucks.'"

John Kalodner: "He really didn't like me telling him to make his lyrics more radio accessible. They could be way too X-rated. A lot of the commercial things that they were capable of, and that Bruce Fairbairn was capable of, I had to keep pushing them toward all the time. And they kept wanting Tim Collins to fire me. I got no thanks, but that wasn't unusual. That's just how it is."

Mike Baird: "Neal Schon and Jon Cain produced 'Sittin' on the Dock of the Bay' for Michael Bolton's *The Hunger* record. I got the call to play on it from Jon. I show up, and I say to Michael, 'Okay, what's the tempo?' And he goes, 'I don't know. You set it.' How do you make *that* song better than it was? But I heard the version we did just the other day and, you know what, it actually sounds pretty damn good. He was a very talented cat, obviously."

Michael Bolton: "I like to think that class is a part of everything I do. I'm a class act."[1]

Bruce Kulick: "*The Hunger*? That's a good record. Michael had taken some time off and rebranded himself. He wisely adjusted from wanting to be a rock star to being a blue-eyed soul singer that your mother loves. He did that quite well, right? There was suddenly a new maturity and command to his voice. The confidence in it was so much different."

Mike Tramp: "To me, *Pride* in 1987 is the first White Lion album. That was when we became a band. My memory is of the happiness of that, and of the chase before the catch. It was the high point."

***

Bruce Kulick: "Ron Nevison was our producer on Kiss's *Crazy Nights* album. Absolutely, he knew how to make big hits in an era where that's what radio wanted. Paul Stanley saw what Nevison had done with other contemporary acts, and he schmoozed him. Gene Simmons was more, 'I don't like this guy.' That's what was going on. And we ended up with more of a Ron Nevison record than a Kiss one. Samples on the drums, too many keyboards."

Paul Stanley: "Those albums [Kiss] did in the '80s sold very well, but the problem was, we weren't leading anymore. We were following."[2]

Bruce Kulick: "Writing with both Gene and Paul for that record was very hard. I had to be a diplomat. There were a whole set of approaches I needed, and a game I had to play. I'd use my own instinct, too. There were some hiccups even still. If I failed with an idea with Gene, Paul wouldn't want to have anything to do with it. Gene was a little easier. I could present him with a whole concept, a chorus and a verse, and if he liked it, boom, we were working on it. Paul very clearly wanted to get his stamp on it. It was a wonderful opportunity, but also a gigantic mountain to have to climb. 'Crazy, Crazy Nights' was a huge single in Europe. In America, the record didn't quite take off."

Mike Tramp: "We got on the Kiss *Crazy Nights* tour for a month and a half. That's probably the worst tour they ever had. They were struggling to sell tickets. It wasn't a party backstage. Not a great environment overall. We barely spoke, apart from on the first night of the tour in Jackson, Mississippi. We were doing our soundcheck, and Gene appeared at the other end of the arena. He made his way over to me like Clint Eastwood, one slow step at a time. He gets within earshot, and he says to me, 'Mike Tramp. That's a cool name.' Then he turned back around and slowly walked off again."

CHAPTER SEVENTY-THREE

IN THE STILL OF THE NIGHT...

"A new adventure. Whitesnake and the Temple of Doom."

Neil Murray: "Whitesnake was a blues-based British hard rock band. And we were riding on a pretty successful wave, certainly in Britain and Europe and Japan. I had great admiration for David Coverdale's vocal ability and his charisma and his stage presence. He changed a lot as a person over time. Initially, he was more down-to-earth, let's say, one of the lads."

David Coverdale: "The point is, Whitesnake couldn't go any further in Europe. We were doing sellout tours and smashing records for attendances and *still* only breaking even or losing money. Then America beckoned."[1]

Neil Murray: "David signed up with management in LA in 1985. From there, everything started working more in the direction that the record company, Geffen, and John Kalodner were planning on."

David Coverdale: "It was a new adventure. Whitesnake and the Temple of Doom."[2]

***

Neil Murray: "Up to then, we'd only had a little bit of contact with Kalodner. The general attitude we got in the band was that David was really the only important person as far as Geffen was concerned. The more sort of old guard, the ex–Deep Purple guys like Jon Lord and your blues-rockers, could be eliminated. The vague feeling was, 'There's a huge gap in the market for a Led Zeppelin for the '80s.' In terms of the influence of the music going on at the time, certainly it was Journey and Foreigner. David was quite slow to move in that direction. He was stubborn and often had to take quite a long time to shift."

John Kalodner: "It was incredibly difficult. David was very *kind of* motivated to make it. He'd made these pretty good records but had not been very successful except in England."

Neil Murray: "Kalodner certainly had that typical American kind of thing where it seems like they know everything. And it all had to fit with how business was in the States, and not really giving a hoot about the rest of the world."

Al Cafaro: "In 1987, if you were an artist, you could get signed to a record company, and no one in the world need care about you or your music, except for one person at a record company who had the clout to make it happen. You didn't need to have an audience. You could come into the record company, and you would be handed over to teams of people. Artist development people. Product management people. Creative services people. Artists and repertoire people. All of these people would hold your hand through the entire process. It was a full concierge service. We had the staff to do this. Artists ended up having big careers, because we had people at the record company who knew what to do, and they were smart enough to listen."

John Kalodner: "I told David that his band wasn't strong enough and that he needed a great co-writer, which was John Sykes. I told him he needed a whole new band if he was going to be a star in America. I think he always resented that. That's just what happens, because you're forcing these people to do something kind of against their will. But I knew that he was a star, as a singer and a personality."

Neil Murray: "Certainly, John Sykes was an exciting guitar player and more of a hooligan element than had been in the band previously. It's a complicated thing explaining how John was in terms of his personality and fitting in with other people. I mean, John was very money-oriented, it has to be said."

John Sykes: "David? I don't believe he had any clue what we should sound like. I was the person who began the project by telling David we had to focus on breaking America."[3]

David Coverdale: "I wanted Whitesnake to be leaner, meaner, and more electrifying. It was simply my choice as an artist. The reason I invited John Sykes into the band was to actually afford that transition. It was all about the Americanization of Mrs. Coverdale's little boy."[4]

John Sykes: "We started work on the [1987] album in the spring of 1985. David and I headed to a place called Le Rayol in the south of France. We rented a villa there. I had lots of riffs and ideas for songs, recorded onto cassettes. One of the first songs we worked on was 'Still of the Night.'"[5]

David Coverdale: "When my mother died, I was going through some stuff at her house and found some early demo cassettes. One of them was a song that Ritchie Blackmore and I had been working on [together in Deep Purple], which was the basic premise of what would become 'Still of the Night.' I took it as far as I could then gave it to Sykes-y when we were in the south of France. He put the big guitar hero stuff on there."[6]

Neil Murray: "David would often not come up with the finished lyric and melodies until way into the recording process. He needed to have a finished structure to put himself on top of, as it were. Going back to what I said about John, he certainly wasn't in any rush to give me credit for anything I might have contributed to the songwriting. I can point to a couple of things that were certainly my ideas, but sadly I didn't get credited."

David Coverdale: "Recording 'Here I Go Again' for the second time wasn't my idea. I very rarely like to go back on any level. I can't even reverse my car I hate going backwards so much. Of course, John Sykes fucking hated it."[7]

Neil Murray: "John had no interest in the blues. For *1987*, we re-recorded both 'Here I Go Again' and 'Crying in the Rain' from the *Saints and Sinners* album of 1982, and John almost prevented us from doing that. Because he hadn't been part of the writing of either song. There had to be some form of financial inducement for him to do anything. It made him difficult to deal with at times."

John Kalodner: "Then David began to have sinus problems. We had a doctor, Joe Sugarman, operate on him, but he was still having difficulties."

John Sykes: "David used every excuse possible to explain why he didn't want to record his vocals. I honestly think he suffered from nerves. His voice was fine until the red light came on, and it was time for him to record."[8]

Neil Murray: "They went to Compass Point with Journey's producer, Mike Stone. David tried out thousands of different microphones. None of those recordings was ever used. David tended to be a bit of a hypochondriac. You never really knew whether he had actual vocal problems, or if it was more psychosomatic. I'll give him the benefit of the doubt, but then again, he's so used to rewriting history."

John Kalodner: "Finally, I took him to Keith Olsen. Keith wasn't a particularly stable or pleasant person at the time. But he was able to coax these incredible vocals from him, like he'd done with Sammy Hagar and Lou Gramm."[9]

John Sykes: "With Keith on board, we finally got things done."[10]

Neil Murray: "I think Kalodner would've liked us to have used Keith Olsen from the start. But our experience with Keith was that it was all a bit kind of clean and clinical. Not quite as rock 'n' roll as we would have liked. They were also spending so much money. That had a very negative effect on myself and our drummer, Aynsley Dunbar, because we stopped getting paid. Aynsley, quite correctly, took that as being, 'See you.' Whereas my position was much more ambivalent. And I wasn't given the impression I was out of the band."

John Sykes: "It began with Aynsley. Once the drum parts were done, David suddenly wasn't answering or returning Aynsley's calls."[11]

Neil Murray: "John definitely wanted to have Mike Stone mix the album. Geffen and maybe David wanted Keith Olsen. John was very upset about that. That's when the power struggle between David and John came to a head. David didn't want John there when the mix was being done. John felt that it was his right. So John flew over to LA to confront David at Keith Olsen's studio."

John Sykes: "I went down to the studio where David was still recording his vocals to confront him. Honest to God, he ran away. Got in his car and hid from me. I chased him and shouted at him. All he did was wind the window down a quarter of inch and bleat, 'It wasn't my doing. Geffen made me do it.' I haven't spoken to him since then."[12]

Neil Murray: "It was silly from John's point of view to chuck it away like that. On the other hand, it might have been inevitable. If it hadn't happened then, it might well have happened six months later. I heard

I'd been fired from a music journalist. I didn't even know about Rudy Sarzo replacing me, or the new lineup with Tommy Aldridge, Vivian Campbell, and those guys, until I saw the video for 'Still of the Night.' If you look at the video, you can't really even tell that it's not John Sykes or me."

John Kalodner: "I felt bad about that, because Neil Murray is a great guy. But David Coverdale wanted to be a star."

Neil Murray: "Like everybody else, I didn't know about Tawny Kitaen either until I saw the videos for 'Here I Go Again' and 'Is This Love' with her and David. He'd had a sort of LA girlfriend when we were making the album. Sometimes I thought she was possibly not a good influence. Other times I thought David wasn't being particularly gentlemanly with her."

David Coverdale: "Yorkshire lads shouldn't marry American actresses. I woke up from the nightmare… a few million dollars later."[13]

Neil Murray: "You can't take everything David says in interviews as gospel. His version of events is always going to make him look like the good guy. If something goes wrong, there's always an excuse."

John Kalodner: "David has said some very negative things about me on the internet. The fact is, he'd been struggling for five, six years on the route he was going, and I made him the big star he should've been. I'm proud of that."

Neil Murray: "After the *1987* album was so successful, Aynsley and me had to resort to lawyers. Finally, at the end of 1988, I did get a payment. It was enough for me to put a down payment on a flat, which I then had to sell a couple of years later because I was so stony broke. If I blame people, it would be a combination of David and John Kalodner, and to an extent John Sykes as well."

John Kalodner: "I loved that period. It was the greatest. Everything about it."

Neil Murray: "Have I listened to *1987* very much? Mostly not. It's been slightly depressing reading through my old diaries from that time. Putting myself back in that frame of mind. But what do I know? It sold ten million copies."

CHAPTER SEVENTY-FOUR

DEF LEPPARD POUR SOME SUGAR ON.

"It started to spread like wildfire through strip clubs across the States."

Al Cafaro: "No one else was more responsible for the sound of that era than Mutt Lange. There was no one like him. He was just incredible."

Joe Elliott: "It was difficult to do it twice. But unmanageable? No. Straight off the *Pyromania* tour, we did six months of writing with Mutt in Dublin."

Phil Collen: "One of the reasons we went to Ireland was due to taxes."[1]

Joe Elliott: "In August of 1984, we went over to Holland to actually start recording *Hysteria*. It didn't help that from then on, we had all of these hand grenades thrown in our path. First off, there was Mutt saying he couldn't carry on with us. He'd only just then finished with the Cars, and he was worn out."

***

Phil Collen: "We had a very short list of producers. We ended up with Jim Steinman."[2]

Joe Elliott: "To this day, I can't figure out why our management suggested Jim Steinman. Because he's not a producer. *Bat Out of Hell* was produced by Todd Rundgren if you look at the fucking credits. Steinman wrote it. So they thought we needed a song doctor? Okay, fine, I was into that if the guy could come up with any ideas. But every idea Jim Steinman came up with was so anti–Def Leppard, it was completely wrong."

Jim Steinman: "One of the first conversations I had with [them] was in Dublin. I was so excited to be in Dublin and I said, 'This is great for me. I'm finally in the land of James Joyce and Yeats... You guys feel that at all?' And they said, 'No, we haven't had a chance to meet any of the local musicians.' It was like that from beginning to end, one absurdity after another."[3]

Phil Collen: "We thought we'd got the Ferrari. In reality, we'd got a secondhand Ford Cortina."[4]

Jim Steinman: "Def Leppard was interesting in the way a scientist finds a strange sort of insect interesting. Listen, I did four months of hell with those guys in Holland. Nice kids, even though they're a bit faceless. It's like Peter Sellers in *Being There*. It's all behind them. They have planners and programmers and people who package them."[5]

Joe Elliott: "Steinman lasted four, five weeks and then we had to get rid of him. It was a rudderless ship. Nigel Green came back. He was a familiar face as Mutt's engineer. He'd worked with us on *High 'n' Dry* and parts of *Pyromania*. It was kind of like when a football manager leaves, and his assistant takes over. There's an initial couple of months where it runs fine, momentum carries you through, but you're missing the cherry on the top. By the end of 1984, we had some backing tracks, but they were just all right. They weren't brilliant. Fine for another band, but we'd set a level for ourselves that now we couldn't possibly go below. Then Rick had his accident during the Christmas break."

Rick Allen: "My girlfriend at the time and I were on a winding country road, having a nice drive near Sheffield. This Alfa Romeo came round a corner and went blazing past. As I continued on, I realized this Alfa had slowed, so I would catch up. For three or four miles, every time I tried to pass, he would speed up... Finally, I kind of lost my cool and put my foot down... Suddenly, this long corner revealed itself and, at a certain point, it was too late. I lost control."[6]

Phil Collen: "Steve Clark and I were in Paris that night. We got a message that Rick had severed his arm."[7]

Rick Allen: "As the car rolled, the seatbelt came undone and took my left arm. The arm stayed in the car, and I disappeared through the sunroof... What saved my life is I tensed up, so I didn't bleed out... I was in a coma for two weeks. During that time, they reattached the arm. Everything seemed to be going okay. Then, unfortunately, probably because I lost my arm in the middle of rural England in a farmer's field, I ended up getting a really bad infection. That's when they decided to take the arm completely, which obviously I didn't know about because I was in a coma."[8]

Joe Elliott: "I remember the phone call from our manager Peter Mensch. He said, 'Are you sitting down?' When he said, 'Your drummer's had a car crash and he's lost his arm,' there's no way for you to process that information. It doesn't make any sense. I just burst into tears."[9]

Phil Collen: "We drove up from London, and we had no idea how he was going to be, or how he was going to react to us... We went into his room, and he was all bandaged up, and he came over and hugged us, as if nothing had happened. He said, 'Hey guys, how are you doing? I've got this all figured out and I've been practicing on the edge of the bed on the pillow. I'm going to use my left leg instead of my left arm.'"[10]

***

Joe Elliott: "Within eight or nine days, he started telling us, 'I think I've figured a way around it.' And of course, we thought it was just the morphine talking. But he was back on a drum kit within three months."[11]

Rick Allen: "I was able to put things on the electronic drum kit in different places. I could put a kick drum where I could play it with my right hand...It made me think outside the box."[12]

Joe Elliott: "Eventually, in March 1985, Mutt said that he was happy to come back. Very cleverly, he came over to Holland and didn't say, 'Right, we're going to start from scratch.' That would have killed us. What he did was, he said, 'Okay, let's add some guitars to this and that song.' And over a couple of weeks, he'd just lose the original tracks and none of us would notice."

Phil Collen: "As soon as he came back into the fold, everything fell into place. He raised everything to a whole new level."[13]

Joe Elliott: "I went down to the sauna in the hotel one day and they were playing 'Burundi Black.' It was the drum rhythm that struck me. I asked the owner of the hotel if I could borrow his cassette of the song, took it into the studio, and got our engineer to make me a loop of the drum part. That became the embryonic version of 'Rocket.' I put some chords on it and gave it to Mutt. And I'd always wanted to do a name-check song, like 'Friday on My Mind.' So, we just ended up naming everybody whose records we bought as kids. 'Pour Some Sugar on Me' came about the same way. By accident."

Billy Squier: "We all learn from and borrow from each other. If Def Leppard borrowed 'Pour Some Sugar on Me' from 'The Stroke,' they're welcome to it."

Joe Elliott: "We'd toured with Billy Squier. Did we take that song from him? Not really. '...Sugar' was inspired by 'Walk This Way' and Run-DMC with Aerosmith. It was also the first time that we had the chorus come to us first. I've learned since, that's so much the easiest way to write a song. If you've got a great chorus, the verses and bridges will follow naturally. There's eleven different guitar parts on 'Hysteria' itself. It's completely orchestrated. Why? Because that's what the big boys do."

Phil Collen: "We got a mix [of the finished album] on a cassette. Steve and I took it back to this little house we had on the lake, and we played it all the way back. We looked at each other and said, 'Fuck, we couldn't have done anything better. We're so happy with it, if no one buys it then we don't care.'"[14]

Joe Elliott: "In England, [*Hysteria*] was an absolute instant success—straight in at Number One. But in America it was a real slow burner… By Christmas, we'd only sold just over two and a half million copies. Which is relatively successful for most folk, but considering we had to sell about four million to break even, it was an absolute disaster for us."[15]

Phil Collen: "It wasn't a good business move. We'd spent $5 million, or whatever it was, on a record."[16]

Joe Elliott: "It was 'Pour Some Sugar on Me' that took *Hysteria* to the next level. When we were recording it, I remember Mutt saying, 'We've got to make this sound sexy.' A year later, it started to spread like wildfire through strip clubs across the States. After that, it had a life of its own. It's become our 'Radar Love,' our 'Free Bird.' It's the one song that gets played in every karaoke bar in America every night. Then 'Love Bites' followed it as a Number One single."

Andrew McNeice: "I worshipped Def Leppard. Absolutely worshipped them. I reckon I sold them forty copies of *Hysteria* just from playing it around school. Mates would go, '*What's this?!*' And they'd go off and buy their own copy."

***

Joe Elliott: "We shipped four million albums in three months. Even Taylor Swift would struggle to do that nowadays."

Billy Squier: "To be honest, I don't think the Def Leppard records hold up as well as mine today. Great when they came out, but they sound a little bit dated to me now."

Joe Elliott: "Mutt would tell us, 'This is *not* about making a record that you're going to go out and tour. This is about making a record that people will put on for the rest of their lives. One that doesn't get old.' He told us to make our *Rumours*, our *Hotel California*. And he was preaching to the choir. We were all on board with it. We dreamed in 1977 that we would be the biggest band in the world, and we became it eleven years later."

CHAPTER SEVENTY-FIVE

END DAYS.

"The cracks started to become holes in the ground."

Lou Gramm: "I'd some songs written already, and I went in and recorded my first solo album [*Ready or Not*, 1987] and released it. I was touring with Steve Miller when I got the call from Mick. He goes, 'Listen, it's time for us to work on a new album. Can you remove yourself from the tour and come home?' I said, 'Honestly, I could do that, Mick. But I learned from you that when you have an album release, you do anything and everything you can to have it heard by as many people as you can.' He did not like that answer."[1]

Mike Jones: "Lou said to me, 'I don't want to become a crooner.' Well, you know, there's nothing wrong with being Frank Sinatra. I mean to say, when he said crooner, he meant a singer of ballads."

Lou Gramm: "Mick was so angry, he went and talked to Ahmet Ertegun and convinced him that if *Ready or Not* was a huge success I would be gone from the band. [Atlantic] pulled all of the publicity and salespeople out from under the album."[2]

***

Mick Jones: "It's difficult when the focal point of a band decides to go off and do a solo album. It's shocking for the rest of the group, and nine times out of ten it never really works. Do you know how many copies Mick Jagger sold of his first two solo albums? Not a lot. And they still won't accept it. But that's ego."

Ann Wilson: "By *Bad Animals* we were getting tired of it all, because Heart was touring so extensively. The incredible costumes and theater makeup was fun, but then you try taking it out into the sweaty country where it's 100 degrees onstage and you're dancing around in stiletto heels. We got tired."

Denny Carmassi: "My most vivid memory of making *Bad Animals* is Ann walking out because she didn't want to sing 'Alone.'"

Ann Wilson: "I think 'Alone' was pretty stunning. That was before Pro Tools. We were still doing everything analog. I just went in there… Most of the time I preferred to wait until the track was all there, and then go in and just be inspired. Because the vocal would be more 'live' and have more fire to it."

Denny Carmassi: "I don't know how that song happened in the end. I wasn't involved in persuading her to sing it. But she sang the shit out of it."

Mick Jones: "*Inside Information* was an even more difficult record to make than *Agent Provocateur* had been."

Lou Gramm: "I contributed very little to it other than vocals."[3]

Mick Jones: "Lou would drive down from where he lived in the country and be in and out of the studio in a flash. He literally sang just what he was required to and left. I think he'd have preferred it if he could've done his parts by telephone. He was completely divorced from us. It's amazing the record even got made. To be honest, Lou wasn't completely to blame either. Toward the end, I suppose it had gotten to be me exclusively running the show. Back then, though, I was convinced that my way was the right way."

Jimi Jamison: "They put poor Lou Gramm through the mill. He had to sing those songs and sometimes you could tell he was just barely making it to the note. But he was such a great singer and delivered it so great, you overlooked that. Back in those days everybody was writing everything with such a high pitch. They really didn't have to be doing that."[4]

Mick Jones: "Well, you know, making them sing at the very top of their range is part of the instruction manual for keeping lead singers in check. I would push Lou hard with his voice, but then, I also knew he had the capacity to handle it. Due to the circumstances, *Inside Information* turned out not being a very good record. Lou and I could be the best of friends on occasion, but I always had a feeling that he didn't entirely trust me and that hurt a lot. I believed I'd done so much for him by putting him in the position in Foreigner in the first place and essentially making him a star."

Denny Carmassi: "All of us in Heart had problems with drugs and alcohol at that point. Everybody got through, but it didn't help the band situation. There were personalities within the band who weren't getting along. We were under a lot of pressure, and drugs and alcohol don't help anyone to be clear-minded when making decisions and with interactions in the group. The cracks started to become holes in the ground."

Ann Wilson: "People couldn't really tell us what they were missing. They liked the new stuff. They liked 'These Dreams,' because it was pop music, and it carried them away. But there was something at the very soul of the music we were doing that wasn't Heart. They were other people's songs to a large degree. It wasn't our words we were singing, it was somebody else's."

Denny Carmassi: "There was a real sense of accomplishment until we had to make the same record again three times. The stories are all the same, at least in my experience. It worked for a while, but like all bands, from the minute you join the clock is ticking down. Until there's no more time left."

Kevin Cronin: "[REO] wasn't having the same kind of success that we had in the early '80s, and that freaked some of us out. You expect every record is gonna sell ten million copies."[5]

Jack Blades: "Things got kind of weird for [Night Ranger]."[6]

Eric Martin: "I'd done this song 'Eyes of the World' for a movie, *Iron Eagle*. Basically, it was a poor man's *Top Gun*, but it made me some money and got me off my dad's couch. Because I was still living with him. Then in 1987, I did another solo record for Capitol Records called *I'm Only Fooling Myself*. I didn't write one thing on that album. Don Grierson got all these songwriters in for me, just as he'd done with Heart. The whole record was AOR, but with some R&B to it as well. Pretty much they were grooming me to be the next Michael Bolton. That sounds a little smarmy, but I knew Michael, and he wasn't smarmy."

Kevin Cronin: "Fame and the riches that come with it can also bring out the demons in people. There was plenty of collateral damage that came with our success."[7]

Jack Blades: "I fell into a trap, personally, of trying to write songs that I thought people would like, instead of writing what was in my soul. It was the beginning of the end… Plus, there was a lot of drinking and, uh, chemicals involved. That made everyone uptight. We were all severely medicated at that point."[8]

Eric Martin: "My record didn't sell. I got to feel as if I were cursed. I had a royalty check come through. Holy shit, it was for $50,000. Turned out to be a mistake. My publishing went under the name of Martunes. And wouldn't you know it, Celine Dion's husband also published as

Martunes. The check was meant for him. Everything felt like it was going downhill."

Trevor Rabin: "When an album comes out and it's so successful, and the process of making it has been so peculiar, you then realize that you have a bunch of guys that have never really worked together apart from being onstage. I didn't really know Jon Anderson at all. The record company—who had no idea what had gone down during the recording of *90125*—suggested Trevor Horn again. Tony said, 'No way.' But it became clear that Trevor was going to do it, and that wasn't going to work well with Tony."[9]

Tony Kaye: "It was just an odd situation with Trevor Horn, who probably still hated me… We spent an awful lot of time and money recording *Big Generator*."[10]

Trevor Rabin: "We had an offer to record the album at a castle in Italy, and I thought that was a good idea. Unfortunately, it was a bit of a party period, so very little was achieved. In terms of writing together, there was no cohesiveness whatsoever, and the atmosphere between certain people was very toxic. To cut a long story short, a friend of mine from South Africa, Paul DeVilliers, came in to help finish the recording in California. In the end, I went into Sunset Sound in LA and said, 'Just leave me alone, and let me finish it.' It was the only option we had to get a completed album."[11]

Tony Kaye: "It took a long time and way too long to capitalize on what had gone before."[12]

Elliot Easton: "What the Cars should've done after *Heartbeat City* is taken a break. Not rushed into another record. But after the experience of *Heartbeat City*, the general feeling in the band was, 'Let's make the next one fast and cheap, because that was crazy, and surely we don't have to go through that again.' Ric hadn't been writing as much. So a lot of the songs on *Door to Door* were left over or rejected from the previous five albums. Ric was also producing, so there was no sort of buffer. The whole atmosphere was different. There was a hostility there. Things were not great in the band. Ben Orr was in kind of a funny place at the time. He was isolating. Everything had been building up to a head between him and Ric. It was a fractured period. Greg Hawkes [keyboards] was promised a co-production credit. When we finally got to see the finished record, that Spinal Tap moment where you have the box of records with the plastic on them in your hands... Greg flipped it over and saw, 'Produced by Ric Ocasek.' Just that. And he cried."

Ric Ocasek: "The *Door to Door* tour was the first tour we did that wasn't fun. Some people took buses, some people took planes. Nobody talked."[13]

Elliot Easton: "Then we went on the road, and it kept getting worse. The tour was not selling like we had before. Ben had his own bus while the rest of us flew. He was doing the Elvis number, covering up the windows of his bus with aluminum foil. Word had it he had a gun with him. He was very unhappy. He had a dark side, Ben, God bless him. Everything kind of ground to a halt at the Mississippi. We never made it out to the West Coast because the promoters were just taking a bath. Even the Boston Garden wasn't sold out. That was really more or less the end."

Ric Ocasek: "I was like, 'This has to stop. And I'm not going back to this again.' I held out for twenty-three years."[14]

Mickey Thomas: "Starship did a Diane Warren song, 'Nothing's Gonna Stop Us Now,' in between albums. It was something we had fun with and didn't really expect too much of, and then it became such a huge hit."

Diane Warren: "That song wasn't really written as a duet, it just turned out when Starship did it—it was Grace Slick and Mickey Thomas—you had the female and male vocal and it really worked...I want all my songs to be forever songs. Are you gonna sing them in karaoke bars? You know what I mean?"[15]

Mickey Thomas: "Suddenly, we'd had three Number Ones in the course of eighteen months, and from then on, everyone was expecting nothing but male-female love song duets from Mickey and Grace. That wasn't how Grace or I saw it going. That wasn't how we wanted to be identified as Starship, but we were trapped by the success of that one song."

John Kalodner: "In 1987? I made a big record with Cher."

Desmond Child: "John Kalodner hired me to try to bring Cher back after she had not made a record for eight years. Nobody believed in her, but it worked. She exploded back with the *Cher* record. One of her many comebacks."

John Kalodner: "Personally, I was really sorry I ever worked with her."

Desmond Child: "Cher was my idol when I was a little kid. I wasn't sure whether I wanted to be her, or to sleep with her, but I was just fascinated with her, and I still am. She was like Cleopatra, a queen, and that was how she conducted herself. To her, I was just another crew member. And her whole life, she'd had crews of people work with her. I may as well have been in catering, or something. I wasn't special to her, but I knew I had to conquer her to get the album done. So I started being strong with her. And she didn't like being controlled. That kind of tension, I guess it didn't bode well for us to have an ongoing personal relationship. She's only ever given me one compliment. She told me I had beautiful lips. That's Cher."

John Kalodner: "Altogether, she was a huge disappointment to me. I mean, Cher turned out to be a really terrible person."

CHAPTER SEVENTY-SIX

AFTERMATH.

"I don't think that anyone was completely
able to get away without having any pain."

Joe Elliott: "New Year's Eve 1987. I can tell you exactly what was going on with Def Leppard. At midnight, we were onstage in Orlando, Florida. We'd arranged to go on at 10 p.m. so we could bring the New Year in. I'll tell you what I remember about that night the most. Susannah Hoffs from the Bangles came out to see us. *Whoa!*"

Les Garland: "That era truly was the heyday of good times. I cannot lie, there were moments of extravagance certainly. Excess, boom and bust, all of that. And it was fun. That's the most important thing, I think. That it was so much *fun*. A bunch of like-minded people having a blast. What a concept, you know?"

Tim Pierce: "It *was* a boom time, but nobody knew it at the time. We just thought it would last forever. All the billboards were music stars. All the Rolls-Royce cars were driven by music stars. The business of music was huge. Budgets were unlimited. Even the people who were playing sessions on records had ranch houses with horses."

***

Mike Tramp: "Everybody wanted to be on that train. Nobody was going to show up and say, 'Ah, we'll stay home and be miserable.' Everybody wanted to be part of everything. We were a bunch of cocks running around trying to outdo each other. It was the way the business worked, and it got to be too much."

Al Cafaro: "The music business was still booming. But a big, *big* part of that was from off people replacing their vinyl and cassettes with CDs. The industry was peaking. Superficially, it was in really good shape. But a lot of things were not being anticipated that should have been."

Bruce Kulick: "By 1987, 1988, the Sunset Strip was really hopping. Guns N' Roses, Mötley Crüe, Ratt… The hair metal bands and all that scene."

Joey Tempest: "We played the Budokan in Tokyo in 1988. Two nights. That was huge for us. The next night after us, Guns N' Roses played Budokan. We went to see them, and you could literally see the shift. Musically, it was in the same kind of ballpark, but it was the difference in attitude. They had hardly any lights. They didn't have a set list. It was so loose. It almost felt like a reaction to what bands like ours were doing."

Jon Bon Jovi: "We'd gotten off the road from the *Slippery…* tour in October 1987. We took three weeks off, no more, then ran straight in and started on the *New Jersey* album. Within one more year, we were back on the road again. Look at the inner sleeve of *New Jersey*. The last thing I wanted to do was be me. I had my back to the camera, a long coat down to my ankles, hiding as much of my body as I can. My hair's as long as it can possibly be."

Jim Vallance: "*Into the Fire* in 1988 was not the record that could, or should, have followed *Reckless*. Bryan and I lost our way. *Reckless* was such a big record we didn't quite know how we would top it. The thought was, maybe we shouldn't try to do a better one, maybe we should try to do a different record. We got a little too inside our own heads. We abandoned what had worked for us in the past, which was lyrics about relationships, boys and girls. And we started writing about topical things like the First World War, Native American issues, and politics. It was a chore because we were so far outside our comfort zone."

Jim Peterik: "It was a pretty scary time. Our very last album, *Too Hot to Sleep* [1988], it was a really strong record, but it got buried. The tides were turning. After that, that was it—lights out."

Jim Vallance: "Compared to *Reckless*, *Into the Fire* was, I hate to use the word disappointment, but it was back down the other side of the hill. It didn't sell as well or get played on the radio as much."

Rick Nielsen: "We were doing the [*Lap of Luxury* album, 1988]. The record company, and the management, and the record producer, they were coming up going, 'Hey, we got this one great song for you.' 'The Flame' was about the tenth, 'This is great for you.' That's when I almost left the band."[1]

Eddie Money: "Everybody really likes 'Walk on Water,' and I hate singing, 'Na-na-na-na-na-na-na-na-na.' I feel really silly singing the song. You try doing that for thirty years in a row. It was supposed to be a horn part, but the horn player never showed up, so I had to do it with my mouth."[2]

Ann Wilson: "We were over it. We needed another break. But those were great times. I go down as being famously sort of anti-'80s, but I'm not really. There was some great music that happened then."

Jim Vallance: "I don't have the fondest memories of that particular time. Bryan and I were burned out. We'd spent ten or eleven years, two guys in a room with no windows, twelve hours a day, and we needed a break. It was like a marriage that had run its course. We parted ways. For the next five to ten years, we barely ever saw each other or spoke, and we certainly didn't write together."

Kevin Cronin: "By the end of 1989, my working relationship with Gary Richrath had deteriorated. And that was the spark—the core of the band."[3]

Richie Sambora: "The best way I can equate it is, it's like you're surfing, and you get caught up in this big wave. With us, we were caught up for four years and, I swear to God, the last note of the last show of the *New Jersey* tour in Mexico City was the first time I got out of the water. It was like, 'Where am I? Who am I? How am I?'"

David Bryan: "You stop feeling. We were charred, singed, ashes, soot."

Kevin Cronin: "Gary was the personification of a rock guitar player. He had this thing about him. He walked in the room, and it was like, 'Okay, this kid's a star.' Unfortunately for Gary, drugs got a hold of him. It brought Gary down, and it ruined a great artist and a great person. There was nothing anybody could do about it."[4]

Jon Bon Jovi: "When we got off that stage in Mexico City, we were all loaded, drinking a lot. We just split. Everybody got on a plane and said, 'See ya.'"

Mike Reno: "There is a moment, a point when things become redundant because you're too famous, or you're too wealthy, or too popular, or people start to get jealous. It happens. We were pretty tired by then. I started to lose interest, from being pushed so hard. I rebelled by not putting so much effort into it."[5]

Billy Squier: "There are people who will shift with the landscape, and not necessarily in a bad way. Those are people who have a good support base in terms of management and label. People that can steer and help them to take advantage of things that are going on. That can happen.

But for a lot of us, it's sort of like with silent pictures. What happened to the silent movie stars who couldn't transition to talkies. They either didn't want to or weren't competent to do it. It wasn't their field. If I wanted to be a video star, I guess I could have put in the work and done it. But I didn't."

Mick Jones: "By the end of that decade, we definitely weren't the taste of the day, that's for sure. But to try and change direction, become more quote-unquote modern? I wouldn't have known how to do that."

Derek Oliver: "I went to work at Atlantic Records in New York in the late '80s. By then, if you had a melodic rock band, people just wouldn't even touch it. I signed some AOR bands to Atlantic. That was almost suicidal. You couldn't get them arrested."

Mickey Thomas: "We made one more Starship album in the '80s, *Love Among the Cannibals*. My all-time favorite Starship album, but the musical landscape was starting to change. We wrote a song with Mutt Lange, 'I Didn't Mean to Stay All Night.' Mutt produced it for us, too. I thought, 'Man, this is going to be huge.' And it just didn't happen. Maybe it sounded too much like Def Leppard, but that was a great disappointment to me."

Al Cafaro: "We signed an AOR band to A&M called Giant. They were managed by Bud Prager, who managed Foreigner. Bud was an excellent manager, and the Giant record [*Last of the Runaways*, 1989], we thought it had all of the attributes of that music. We bet that it was going to be that kind of big record for us. And it was a miserable failure. We were two years too late to the party."

Derek Oliver: "If even Journey would have arrived then, fully formed, people wouldn't have given them the time of day."

Mick Jones: "The glam bands started to turn a lot of our audience off. That's when people really started to make the shift toward country music to replace classic rock. They sought a more peaceful, gentler alternative that wasn't that much divorced from rock or pop."

Al Cafaro: "The principal guy in Giant was Dan Huff. A brilliant guitar player and an incredible singer. He's gone on to have a very big career in Nashville as a producer."

Steve Lukather: "We had a couple of years there of just hanging on by our fingernails. There were three years, man, where it could have gone either way. It was scary. You're only ever as good as your last hit record. You're only as good as the last dime that you made for this guy in the suit."

Joey Tempest: "In the 1990s, some of the guys in Europe had to go and get work at Arlanda Airport in Stockholm."

Ann Wilson: "My lowest ebb would have been in the 1990s, when I was recovering from the 1980s. I just wanted to be alone and stay in the house and watch movies. I don't think that anyone was completely able to get away without having any pain. I know I wasn't."

Kevin Cronin: "There was always the glimmer of hope in the back of our minds that at some point the five of us would go out and do three weeks of shows, just in the Midwest or something."[6]

Ann Wilson: "I pulled out of it. I've some really good friends. I have these little red flags that wave in my brain when I get to a certain point. Like with anxiety, or depression. At a certain point, I realized that I needed something, so I started studying meditation. I learned the basic techniques. I can definitely do myself tremendous good by knowing how to stop and be still and be mindful. It's really saved me a lot of times."

Kevin Cronin: "Gary passed away in August 2015. I still think of him almost every day and find it shocking when it dawns on me that I will never see him again."[7]

***

Denny Carmassi: "I did a tour with Foreigner in 2002. That was when Lou had come back into the fold for a spell. I thought it'd be fun, because I knew both Mick and Lou. But they just didn't get along together. The two of them couldn't stand to be in the same room with each other. It was a drag to be around."

Steve Perry: "I didn't sing in those years. I didn't write music. I must have gained fifty or sixty pounds. I got a butch haircut. I just said, 'I'm going to just become a plump kid in my hometown again.' I'd already lived the dream of dreams and didn't know how I could come close to being anything like what I was before."[8]

Jonathan Cain: "I could never understand why Steve Perry seemed to be in recluse mode, hiding somewhere. When you're one of the greatest voices of all time, you should be onstage where you belong."[9]

John Kalodner: "Perry went on a solo tour in the mid-'90s. Then at least, he could still sing live just like he did on record. Anyway, he got maybe a throat virus, but he couldn't sing for a week or two. He had to cancel a bunch of shows. He did go back out, but he was scarred from singing again just from those few days when he was ill and couldn't do it properly. I used every trick I knew to try to get him to go out again with Journey, and he just wouldn't do it."

Steve Perry: "I've had a very big love-hate relationship with fame. I think it led eventually to my isolation propensities. One of the things I discovered when I was going into therapy when I left the group was that there's a hunger in me from when I was younger—because I felt this invisibility in me that happened when my family split up. I used to isolate in this garage. There was something safe about that. People don't become performers unless they want to be seen... Then it gets to the point where you don't want to do it anymore."[10]

CHAPTER SEVENTY-SEVEN

RESURRECTION.

"I always believed. I told the guys, 'Listen, we're going to get the last laugh. I'm telling you.'"

Dennis DeYoung: "All that time ago, the thought that anyone would be interested today in what I had to say, or had done? It would've been unfathomable, unbelievable to me. But then again, the sphincter was so much tighter then, too."

Steve Lukather: "I always believed. I told the guys, 'Listen, we're going to get the last laugh, I'm telling you.' But who knew this fucking music would last this long? And now we've got three generations coming along that are digging it."

***London Evening Standard* article, February 26, 2021:** "Journey's 'Don't Stop Believin'' has reached one billion streams on Spotify—a milestone previously only achieved by Queen's 'Bohemian Rhapsody.'"[1]

***Forbes* headline, January 3, 2024:** "Journey's 'Don't Stop Believin'' Is Officially the Biggest Song of All Time."[2]

***

Total streams for Journey's "Don't Stop Believin'" on Spotify as of February 27, 2025: 2,306,256,597.

David Chase: "I was driving on Ocean Park Boulevard, near the airport, and I saw a little restaurant. It was kind of like a shack that served breakfast. And for some reason I thought, 'Tony [Soprano] would get it in a place like that.' Why? I don't know. That was, like, two years before [the final episode of *The Sopranos* aired]."[3]

Neal Schon: "I could never have imagined it was going to be the blackout scene in the last episode."[4]

David Chase: "No matter what song we picked, I wanted it to be a song that would have been from Tony's high school years, or his youth... There were three songs in contention for the last song, and 'Don't Stop Believin'' was the one that seemed to work the best. I think it's a very good rock 'n' roll song."[5]

Steve Perry: "Of the three songwriters, I was the one that was holding out on approving that song—only because I did not want to see the whole family get whacked...I just wanted to know, 'So, what happens?' But because it was the last one, it was all hush-hush and very tight. I didn't say okay from my side until I got some qualification of, how is it used? The Thursday before it airs on Sunday night, my publisher calls and she says, 'Okay, you have to swear not to tell anybody...' She tells me how it ends. She did not tell me they went to black. I, like the rest of country, when it went to black went, 'What happened to my TV?' It was really brilliant."[6]

David Chase: "I directed the scene to fit the song...I felt that [Tony and Carmela] had taken the midnight train a long time ago. That is their life. It means that these people are looking for something inevitable. Something they couldn't find...They took the midnight train going anywhere. And the midnight train, you know, is the dark train."[7]

***

Steve Perry: "I'm looking at it very simply. *Tony Soprano thinks Journey's cool!* And look at the choices he had. He could've picked Tony Bennett—the greatest voice! And he picks *Journey*. It was really intense."[8]

David Chase: "When I hear 'Don't Stop Believin',' when I see Meadow running towards the restaurant... It still gets me to this day."[9]

Neal Schon: "It just rocketed the tune to a whole different spectrum."[10]

Jonathan Cain: "I think every song has a destiny. When it was first released in 1981, 'Don't Stop Believin'' didn't get played on the radio—it only made Number Nine and then it was gone. But it has lasted and lasted. It's a song that gives you permission to dream... Everybody is still looking for that window of hope and opportunity and possibility. That's universal. That's never going to change."[11]

Neal Schon: "Then *Glee* happened. I was terrified by that, because I thought it was a teenybopper show, not so cool for us. Little did I know that it would open up a younger generation to our music."[12]

Steve Perry: "When this 'Don't Stop Believin',' the biggest song of all-time article came out, I was so emotionally stunned. To be part of such a moment made me reflect on my parents. By that I mean, though I lost them both years ago, I was so happy for them because they are truly the reason this is happening."[13]

Steve Lukather: "Here's the thing. As it turns out, they're good songs. Old school. Guys sitting in a room. Songs that started out with a piano or a guitar. 'What do you think of this?'"

Steve Smith: "When you get right down to it, it's the actual performance recorded by the entire band, played by all the members, that's what lives on. That's what's true if it's Frank Sinatra with the Count

Basie Big Band on 'Fly Me to the Moon,' or Pink Floyd recording *Dark Side of the Moon*. The overall band performances are timeless, indelible."

Steve Lukather: "This 'Africa' craze. *Stranger Things* on Netflix started it. That, and the song also being featured on *Grand Theft Auto*. 'Africa' has just gone on from there and morphed into this *thing*. That band Weezer covered it as a joke, as a fuck-you to us, and it blew up for them. Now they have to play our song forever. So ha-ha. It's this monster that keeps growing. Our golden carrot."

David Paich: "When we go out and play 'Africa' live today, we break down to the audience and have them sing the song. It's our closing song. I look at all these people covering it. These TikTok things and on YouTube. There are 138 different variations of that song at last count. It's really a phenomenon to me."

Steve Lukather: "Right now, today, our shit's gone through the fucking roof. We're at almost four billion streams in total. It's been great for business, man. We're wailing. We're starting to get a little love for the first time. We've become part of pop culture. I've twice been a character on *South Park*. There's even such a thing as a Toto bidet. I just happen to have one in my house, and nothing cleans my prune like one of those bad boys."

Bryan Adams: "They tell me 'Summer of '69' has been streamed a billion times now. Nice. I don't even think about it."

John Kalodner: "Going to a store, or the gym, I'll sometimes hear ten records in a row that I've been involved with. That's the most rewarding thing that's ever happened to me, because they've stood the test of time. People still love them."

Mick Jones: "'I Want to Know What Love Is' is the one. That's the song I'll be remembered for long after I'm dead and gone. That might sound pretty melodramatic, but it'll be something that my kids will hopefully be proud of."

Phil Ehart: "All of a sudden, it's 'classic rock,' so here comes Journey again, here comes Styx, and here comes Kansas. One thing that strikes me is the young age of our audience now. The TV show *Supernatural* adopted 'Carry On My Wayward Son' as its unofficial theme song, and millions of these younger people that are watching the show hear the song."[14]

Desmond Child: "My music has reached billions of people. 'Livin' on a Prayer' has already got to a billion plays on Spotify. 'You Give Love a Bad Name,' too. How many billion people are there on Earth? Eight billion? So that means, even if you didn't buy one of those songs specifically, you'll have heard them in a restaurant, or a cab, or a store. Even out in the jungles."

Danny Kortchmar: "I hate to say this, but music today isn't as good as it was back then. It just isn't."

John Kalodner: "If you listen to the records of that era against the shit that comes out nowadays, the shit that comes out nowadays sounds like it was recorded on a Casio Game Boy. Unless I'm missing something."

John Parr: "I always think of the '80s—*my* '80s—as the American decade. The fact is, back then we were selling as many records as McDonald's was selling hamburgers. The purity of those great records. Toto *IV* is a masterpiece. So is Foreigner *4*. And they'll be recognized as such once everybody's got their head out of their arse."

Steve Lukather: "That is a period of time that will never come back. Because once everyone had a home studio, and a computer and sequencers to do everything, you don't have to put in that intense five, six hours a day of practice as a kid. It's a lost art. You're talking to a dinosaur right here, man. We're the last of a breed."

***

Ann Wilson: "Heart got inducted into the Rock and Roll Hall of Fame in 2013. They wanted to induct the original, first lineup of the band. That's the rule. It turned out fine."

Steve Smith: "Journey was inducted in 2017. When it came up, I didn't take it that seriously or know what to make of it really. But actually, taking part in the ceremony, it felt really good. It was an honor."

Mick Jones: "Foreigner was inducted in 2024. It's nice to have been recognized by your peers. Why did it take so long for us to be nominated? I really haven't thought about that."

Lou Gramm: "I certainly am still a fan. When one of the songs comes on, then I crank it up. They still sound good to me."[15]

Ann Wilson: "I don't think I'd change anything even if I could. Every decision that was made was made for a good reason. Music has meant everything to me. It's my religion. It's the thing that keeps me interested in life. It's the thing I think about every day. It's like a river running through my soul."

Steven Tyler: "What do 'normal' fucking people know? They're the ones that said 'don't,' and we said 'do.' They said 'can't,' and we said 'can.' They said 'fu,' and we said 'ck.' Music is about writing your feelings down. That's *it*."

Tom Scholz: "I have sacrificed an awful lot, but the music is rewarding. And I'm not speaking of the financial aspect, or the fame, or anything like that. I'm just talking about the music itself."[16]

Steve Smith: "Am I proud of Journey? Yes, I am. Definitely. Do I think Journey's one of the greatest rock bands ever? No. It's not Led Zeppelin or the Beatles. But I think it was a very good band and the best of its era."

***

Neal Schon: "We've just got done selling out three years of arenas, and the band is firing on all cylinders right now. When we play 'Don't Stop Believin'' live I'm in my Ferrari."[17]

Joe Elliott: "Taylor Swift literally grew up with Def Leppard. Her mum was a huge fan of the band, and she was born in 1989. She was listening to *Hysteria* in the womb."

Sammy Hagar: "I still have more fun than anybody on the planet. My mind still works. My voice still works. My dick still works. My heart is still good, and I got a memory. I'm rich and famous, and I got a beautiful family. Dude, if you see me going around with a bad look on my face, hit me on the shoulder and say, 'Aren't you Sammy Hagar?' And I'll say, 'Oh yeah, you're right!'"[18]

Joe Elliott: "It might not make the front page of the *New York Times*, but there's an enormous amount of respect for this band within the industry. But do I give a shit? No. For the last six years, we've gone out and played stadiums. We've had a Top 10 album in five different decades. We mean something to people. So job done."

Bryan Adams: "My greatest accomplishment? Paying my rent."

Dennis DeYoung: "I've got a piano upstairs. A 1980 Yamaha grand. It's got good songs in it. That's why I bought it. I could write more of those songs today, but I've made the decision to say, 'You know, I think I've said what I needed to say.' It may be time to let somebody else say something. The music business is pretty much unrecognizable to us old farts. It's hard to imagine that there ever was an Oz. But I was there, and I clicked my ruby slippers together, and magic did happen."

Steve Lukather: "I've put forty-seven fucking years into this band. Endurance, man. And I'm not a greedy motherfucker. The house doesn't need to be too big. I haven't got ten cars. I'm not trying to cover up a micro-penis. But we're doing all kinds of crazy shit these days. Selling out shows, making tons of bread, having a laugh. So I have to wear glasses, and I've got grandma hair. Laugh all you want. I'm almost fifty years in. How many motherfuckers can say that? I'm living my best life right now."

ACKNOWLEDGMENTS

This book simply would not have been possible without the contributions of these good people: my representatives on Earth, Matthew Hamilton and David Dunton; publishers par excellence Ben Schafer and Andreas Camponar; Carolyn Kurek and Cassie DeNicola at Hachette; copy editor Roland Ottewell; Teams Hachette and Constable; Sian Llewellyn at *Classic Rock*; everyone who spoke and shared their memories with me in the compiling of *Raised on Radio*; and most especially, and always, my beloved Denise, Tom, and Charlie. My deepest gratitude to them all.

Thank you, thank you, to the music-makers. *Raised on Radio* was written to the following soundtrack:

Journey—"Separate Ways (Worlds Apart)"
Heart—"If Looks Could Kill"
Def Leppard—"Rocket"
Foreigner—"Cold as Ice"
REO Speedwagon—"Take It on the Run"
Survivor—"Eye of the Tiger"
Toto—"Hold the Line"
Billy Squier—"The Stroke"
Boston—"Peace of Mind"
Pat Benatar—"Love Is a Battlefield"
Eddie Money—"Two Tickets to Paradise"
Quarterflash—"Harden My Heart"
Rainbow—"Since You Been Gone"
John Waite—"Missing You"
Steve Perry—"Oh Sherrie"
Van Halen—"Why Can't This Be Love"
Bon Jovi—"Runaway"
Journey—"Any Way You Want It"

Blue Oyster Cult—"Burnin' for You"
Don Henley—"The Boys of Summer"
The Cars—"Drive"
Bryan Adams—"Summer of '69"
Toto—"Africa"
Pat Benatar—"Hit Me with Your Best Shot"
Cheap Trick—"Surrender"
Asia—"Heat of the Moment"
Def Leppard—"Photograph"
Bon Jovi—"Livin' on a Prayer"
Heart—"What About Love"
Foreigner—"Urgent"
Boston—"More Than a Feeling"
Journey—"Don't Stop Believin'"

NOTES

CHAPTER ONE: When, why, and how it all began, and for the greater part on a February evening in 1964.

1   From *Steve Perry: A Singer's Journey* by Laura Monica Cucu (2006).
2   From "Steve Perry: 'Music Really Saved My Life'" by Dave Ling, Classic Rock, August 2014.
3   From "Tom Scholz Interview—Boston/More Than a Feeling," posted by T Grace, YouTube, October 11, 2015.
4   From "Steve Perry: 'Music Really Saved My Life.'"
5   From "Lou Gramm—Foreigner," interviewed by Paul Stephenson, *VRP Rocks—Classic Rock Interviews*, Apple Podcasts, April 8, 2024.
6   From "Cheap Trick Takes a Giant Step" by Jim Farber, *Circus*, July 6, 1978.
7   From "Backstage Pass: Meet REO Speedwagon's Gary Richrath," *Goldmine*, December 22, 2008.
8   From "Rick Springfield: Hollywood Rock Icon" by Christine Montanti, *Park Magazine NY*, Fall 2023.
9   From "An Interview with Tommy Shaw" by A. J. Charron, Guitar Noise, 2024.
10   From "Bruce Hall of REO Speedwagon Interview," *Glide Magazine*, August 19, 2023.
11   Courtesy of Dave Ling.

CHAPTER TWO: Journey, REO Speedwagon, Styx, and Kansas lift off.

1   From "James 'JY' Young Looks Back on 50 Years of Styx" by Matt Wardlaw, Ultimate Classic Rock, June 17, 2022.
2   From "Chuck Panozzo—The Guitar Player Interview" by Tom Mulkern, *Guitar Player*, July 1981.
3   From "James 'JY' Young Interview" by Marc Parker and Melissa Benefield Parker, *Smashing Interviews Magazine*, September 10, 2021.
4   From "Chuck Panozzo—The Guitar Player Interview."
5   From "REO's Neal Doughty: Back on the Road Again" by Jeb Wright, Classic Rock Revisited.
6   From "Inventing David Geffen," PBS interview, June 10, 2009.
7   From "Backstage Pass: Meet REO Speedwagon's Gary Richrath," *Goldmine*, December 22, 2008.

8   From "REO Speedwagon's Big Breakout" by James Henke, *Rolling Stone*, March 19, 1981.

9   From "REO Speedwagon's Big Breakout."

10   From "REO Speedwagon: We Thought Every Album Would Sell 10 Million Copies" by Paul Elliott, Classic Rock, November 22, 2019.

11   From "REO Speedwagon Makes Its Way" by John Swenson, *Rolling Stone*, October 5, 1978.

12   From "REO Speedwagon Will Dedicate Every Show to Late Guitarist Gary Richrath 'Probably Forever'" by Gary Graff, *Billboard*, September 17, 2015.

13   From "Inventing David Geffen."

14   From "REO Speedwagon: After the Ninth Album You Don't Throw the TV Set Out of the Window" by Sandy Robertson, *Sounds*, November 10, 1979.

15   From "Castles Burning: The Herbie Herbert Interview" by Matthew Carty, 2001.

16   From "Journey to the Centre of the AORth" by Sylvie Simmons, *Kerrang!*, October 1981.

17   From "Journey: No Longer an Uphill Road" by John Swenson, *Rolling Stone*, June 1, 1978.

18   From "Journey's Bassist Ross Valory Opens Up About the Band's Saga—And His Adventurous Solo Album" by Andy Greene, *Rolling Stone*, March 14, 2024.

19   From "Gregg Rolie's Musical Journey" by Joe Matera, *Mixdown*, March 2002.

20   From "From Triumph to Nowhere and Back: The Story of Kansas, in Their Own Words" by Dave Ling, Classic Rock, May 18, 2023.

21   From "Steve Walsh Interview," posted by Lad Voc, YouTube.

22   From "Even Though They've Sold 10 Million Albums in the USA to Date, Kansas Are a New Wave Band" by Sylvie Simmons, *Sounds*, January 12, 1980.

23   From "Jeff Glixman: Past the Point of Know Return!" by Jeb Wright, Classic Rock Revisited.

24   From "Interview: Steve Walsh" by Gary James, Get Ready to Rock, 2003.

25   From "REO Speedwagon's Big Breakout."

26   From "REO Speedwagon Makes Its Way."

27   From "REO Speedwagon Makes Its Way."

28   From "Reo Speedwagon," *The Big Interview with Dan Rather*, AXS TV, 2019.

29   From "Styx," *The Big Interview with Dan Rather*, AXS TV, 2018.

30   From "Styx," *The Big Interview with Dan Rather*.

31   From "James 'JY' Young Looks Back on 50 Years of Styx."

32   From "Tommy Shaw: Under the Influence" by Jay S. Jacobs, Pop Entertainment, April 11, 2007.

CHAPTER FOUR: From a basement in Boston.

1   From "Fran Sheehan Interview" by Michael Hill, thirdstage.ca, 1998.
2   From "The Big Interviews: Barry Goudreau" by John Beaudin, Rock History Music, 2021.
3   From "Boston Takes Over" by Cameron Crowe, The Uncool.
4   From "'I've Spent Six Months Making a Recording of a Song That I've Thrown Out': Tom Scholz on the Secrets of Boston's First Album" by Ken Sharp, Classic Rock, July 4, 2022.
5   From "Boston Takes Over."
6   From "'I've Spent Six Months Making a Recording of a Song That I've Thrown Out.'"
7   From "Jim Masdea Interview" by John Beaudin, Rock History Music, 2021.
8   From "Boston Takes Over."
9   From "Fran Sheehan Interview."
10 From "March 1999 Interview" by Pär Winberg, archived at Melodic.net.
11 From "The Big Interviews: Barry Goudreau."
12 From "Boston's Tom Scholz Remembers Bradley Delp," *Rolling Stone*, March 13, 2007.
13 From "Boston Takes Over."
14 From "Boston Shows, Myths, and Truths," letter by Tom Scholz, reproduced at Steve Hoffman Music Forums, May 1, 2009.
15 From "Fran Sheehan Interview."
16 From "'I've Spent Six Months Making a Recording of a Song That I've Thrown Out.'"
17 From "Classic Rock Revisited Presents an Exclusive Interview with… Brad Delp of Boston" by Jeb Wright, thirdstage.ca, July 2003.
18 From "'I've Spent Six Months Making a Recording of a Song That I've Thrown Out.'"
19 From "The Big Interviews: Barry Goudreau."
20 From "'I've Spent Six Months Making a Recording of a Song That I've Thrown Out.'"

CHAPTER FIVE: The makings of Toto.

1   From "Toto: A Growth Industry for Modern People" by Sandy Robertson, *Sounds*, March 10, 1979.
2   From "Episode 244—Boz Scaggs," *Sodajerker* podcast, 2023.
3   From "Episode 244—Boz Scaggs."

CHAPTER SEVEN: Vindication of the "mad scientist."

1   From "'I've Spent Six Months Making a Recording of a Song That I've Thrown Out': Tom Scholz on the Secrets of Boston's First Album" by Ken Sharp, Classic Rock, July 4, 2022.
2   From "How Boston Flew So High and Fell So Far" by Derek Oliver, Classic Rock, June 23, 2020.

3   From "Jim Masdea Interview" by John Beaudin, Rock History Music, 2021.
4   From "Boston: Heaven Is a Reel-to-Reel Tape" by Chuck Miller, thirdstage.ca, June 8, 2012.
5   From "'I've Spent Six Months Making a Recording of a Song That I've Thrown Out.'"
6   From "Classic Rock Revisited Presents an Exclusive Interview with... Brad Delp of Boston" by Jeb Wright, thirdstage.ca, July 2003.
7   From "'I've Spent Six Months Making a Recording of a Song That I've Thrown Out.'"
8   From "Jim Masdea Interview."
9   From "'Mad? Some People Think So...' Tom Scholz: Boston's Reluctant Boffin" by Paul Elliott, Classic Rock, December 17, 2014.
10 From "Classic Rock Revisited Presents an Exclusive Interview with... Brad Delp of Boston."
11 From "Tom Scholz Interview—Boston/More Than a Feeling," posted by T Grace, YouTube, October 11, 2015.
12 From "Classic Rock Revisited Presents an Exclusive Interview with... Brad Delp of Boston."
13 From "Boston Takes Over" by Cameron Crowe, The Uncool.
14 From "Jim Masdea Interview."
15 From "Tom Scholz Interview—Boston/More Than a Feeling."
16 From "'Mad? Some People Think So...' Tom Scholz: Boston's Reluctant Boffin.'"
17 From "Classic Rock Revisited Presents an Exclusive Interview with... Brad Delp of Boston."
18 From "'I've Spent Six Months Making a Recording of a Song That I've Thrown Out.'"
19 From "The Big Interviews: Barry Goudreau" by John Beaudin, Rock History Music.com, 2021.
20 From "Tom Scholz of Boston—The Vinyl Guide Interview Ep297 & Ep298," YouTube, August 27, 2021.
21 From "Boston Takes Over" by Cameron Crowe, The Uncool.com.
22 From "Boston Stranglehold" by Geoff Barton, *Sounds*, January 29, 1977.
23 From "'I've Spent Six Months Making a Recording of a Song That I've Thrown Out.'"
24 From "The Big Interviews: Barry Goudreau."
25 From "Just Another Band Out of Boston..." by Hugh Fielder, *Sounds*, September 29, 1979.
26 From "Classic Rock Revisited Presents an Exclusive Interview with... Brad Delp of Boston."
27 From "The Big Interviews: Barry Goudreau."
28 From "Classic Rock Revisited Presents an Exclusive Interview with... Brad Delp of Boston."

29 From "'I've Spent Six Months Making a Recording of a Song That I've Thrown Out.'"
30 From "The Big Interviews: Barry Goudreau."
31 From "'I've Spent Six Months Making a Recording of a Song That I've Thrown Out.'"

CHAPTER EIGHT: Three Brits and three Americans.

1 From *Juke Box Hero: My Five Decades in Rock 'n' Roll* by Lou Gramm with Scott Pitoniak (Triumph Books, 2013).
2 From *Juke Box Hero*.
3 From "Lou Gramm—Foreigner," interviewed by Paul Stephenson, *VRP Rocks—Classic Rock Interviews*, Apple Podcasts, April 8, 2024.
4 From "Lou Gramm: It's Urgent!" by Jeb Wright, Classic Rock Revisited.
5 From "Lou Gramm—Foreigner."
6 From "Lou Gramm—Foreigner."

CHAPTER NINE: The advent of Sammy Hagar and the Babys; further adventures of REO and Styx; Kansas and Blue Öyster Cult strike gold…

1 From the film *John Waite: The Hard Way*, written and directed by Mike J. Nichols (Real Moon Films, 2022).
2 From *Red: My Uncensored Life in Rock* by Sammy Hagar (It Books, 2011).
3 From "Well Worth the Waite" by Ken Sharp, Pop Entertainment Archives, July 24, 2013.
4 From "Sammy Hagar Interview: Diamond Dave, the Van Halens, and a Long Life in Rock" by Dave Everley, Classic Rock, October 16, 2020.
5 From the film *John Waite: The Hard Way*.
6 From "A Conversation with John Waite" by Michael Cavacini, MichaelCavacini.com, June 6, 2014.
7 From *Red: My Uncensored Life in Rock*.
8 From the film *John Waite: The Hard Way*.
9 From *Red: My Uncensored Life in Rock*.
10 From the film *John Waite: The Hard Way*.
11 From "Revved Up Rocker Gary Richrath" by Jim Schwartz, Guitar Player Vault, November 2015.
12 From "After the Ninth Album You Don't Throw The TV Set Out of the Window" by Sandy Robertson, *Sounds*, November 10, 1979.
13 From "Revved Up Rocker Gary Richrath."
14 From "Dennis DeYoung: Gazing Back in Time!" by Ralph Chapman, Classic Rock Revisited.
15 From "Rock Legend Kerry Livgren Interview," *Topeka High News*, YouTube, 2018.
16 From "Kansas," *The Big Interview with Dan Rather*, AXS TV, 2018.
17 From "From Triumph to Nowhere and Back: The Story of Kansas, in Their Own Words" by Dave Ling, Classic Rock, May 18, 2023.

18 From "Kansas," *The Big Interview with Dan Rather*.
19 From "From Triumph to Nowhere and Back."
20 From "Kansas," *The Big Interview with Dan Rather*.
21 From "Jeff Glixman: Past the Point of Know Return!" by Jeb Wright, Classic Rock Revisited.com.
22 From "From Triumph to Nowhere and Back."
23 From "Jeff Glixman: Past the Point of Know Return!"
24 From "From Triumph to Nowhere and Back."
25 From "Kansas," *The Big Interview with Dan Rather*.
26 From "Jeff Glixman: Past the Point of Know Return!"
27 From "Rock Legend Kerry Livgren Interview."
28 From "Kansas on Reviving 'Leftoverture'" by Steve Smith, *Rolling Stone*, September 8, 2016.
29 From "Rock Legend Kerry Livgren Interview."

CHAPTER TEN: The second band on Atlantic Records to go platinum.

1 From "Lou Gramm Interview on Early Years, Writing & Recording with Foreigner, and Career Highlights," Curtin Call, YouTube.
2 From *Juke Box Hero: My Five Decades in Rock 'n' Roll* by Lou Gramm with Scott Pitoniak (Triumph Books, 2013).
3 From "Lou Gramm Interview on Early Years, Writing & Recording with Foreigner, and Career Highlights."
4 From "Screamin' and Steamin'" by Steve Gett, *Kerrang!*, May 6–19, 1982.
5 From *Juke Box Hero*.
6 From "Screamin' and Steamin'."
7 From *Juke Box Hero*.

CHAPTER ELEVEN: Trouble with the Wilshires.

1 From "Heart's Ann and Nancy Wilson: Our Life in 15 Songs" by Richard Bienstock, *Rolling Stone*, July 12, 2016.
2 From "Heart's Ann and Nancy Wilson: Our Life in 15 Songs."
3 From "Heart's Ann and Nancy Wilson: Our Life in 15 Songs."
4 From "Heart's Ann and Nancy Wilson: Our Life in 15 Songs."

CHAPTER TWELVE: The price of making it.

1 From "Classic Rock Revisited Presents an Exclusive Interview with… Brad Delp of Boston" by Jeb Wright, thirdstage.ca, July 2003.
2 From "Boston Takes Over" by Cameron Crowe, The Uncool.
3 From "The Big Interviews: Barry Goudreau" by John Beaudin, Rock History Music, 2021.
4 From "Classic Rock Revisited Presents an Exclusive Interview with… Brad Delp of Boston."
5 From "Boston Takes Over."
6 From "Boston Takes Over."

7   From "The Big Interviews: Barry Goudreau."

8   From "REO Speedwagon Frontman Kevin Cronin Speaks Out on Legacy...," *San Francisco Examiner*, July 7, 2011.

9   From "Revved Up Rocker Gary Richrath" by Jim Schwartz, Guitar Player Vault, November 2015.

10 From "REO's Neal Doughty: Back on the Road Again" by Jeb Wright, Classic Rock Revisited.

11 From "REO Speedwagon: The Prairie Dog Has His Day" by Sylvie Simmons, *Sounds*, May 2, 1981.

12 From "REO's Neal Doughty: Back on the Road Again."

13 From "REO Speedwagon Frontman Kevin Cronin Speaks Out on Legacy..."

14 From "Revved Up Rocker Gary Richrath."

15 From "Jeff Glixman: Past the Point of Know Return!" by Jeb Wright, Classic Rock Revisited.com.

16 From "From Triumph to Nowhere and Back: The Story of Kansas, in Their Own Words" by Dave Ling, Classic Rock, May 18, 2023.

17 From "Jeff Glixman: Past the Point of Know Return!"

18 From "Rock Legend Kerry Livgren Interview," *Topeka High News*, YouTube, 2018.

19 From "Kansas," *The Big Interview with Dan Rather*, AXS TV, 2018.

20 From "Jeff Glixman: Past the Point of Know Return!"

21 From "From Triumph to Nowhere and Back."

22 From "Eddie Money," *The Big Interview with Dan Rather*, AXS TV, 2018.

23 From "Eddie Money: Rock's Rodney Dangerfield Endures" by Jason Newman, *Rolling Stone*, April 25, 2018.

24 From "Eddie Money," *The Big Interview with Dan Rather*.

25 From "Rediscovering Paradise: Eddie Money Plays It Straight and Takes Control" by Toby Goldstein, *Creem*, February 1983.

26 From "After the First Couple of Years the Darkness Descended" by Dave Ling, Classic Rock, November 26, 2023.

27 From "Ron Nevison (Producer, Engineer: Led Zeppelin, KISS, Heart)" by Carlos Ramirez, No Echo, October 24, 2014.

28 From "After the First Couple of Years the Darkness Descended."

29 From "Ron Nevison (Producer, Engineer: Led Zeppelin, KISS, Heart)."

30 From the film *John Waite: The Hard Way*, written and directed by Mike J. Nichols (Real Moon Films, 2022).

31 From "Cheap Trick," *The Big Interview with Dan Rather*, AXS TV, 2019.

32 From "Cheap Trick: Light of the Trick" by Tom Cox, *Uncut*, August 1977.

33 From "Cheap Trick," *The Big Interview with Dan Rather*.

34 From "Cheap Trick's Conquest of Japan" by Wayne Robins, *Newsday*, May 20, 1979.

35 From "Cheap Trick Find Heaven" by Daisann McLane, *Rolling Stone*, June 14, 1979.

CHAPTER THIRTEEN: Styx pulls back the curtain.

1   From "Can Styx Save America" by Sylvie Simmons, *Kerrang!*, September 1981.
2   From "Can Styx Save America."
3   From "Styx," *The Big Interview with Dan Rather*, AXS TV, 2018.
4   From "James 'JY' Young Dishes on All Things Styx" by Martin Popoff, *Goldmine*, June 12, 2012.
5   From "The Story Behind the Album: The Grand Illusion—Styx" by Paul Elliott, Classic Rock, July 7, 2017.
6   From "Dennis DeYoung: The Songwriter Interview" by Rob Sanford, *Songwriter* magazine, August 1980.
7   From "Dennis DeYoung: Speaking the Truth" by Jeb Wright, Classic Rock Revisited.
8   From "Styx and Their Long Fall from Grace" by Derek Oliver and Geoff Barton, Classic Rock, December 3, 2015.
9   From "Styx and Their Long Fall from Grace."
10 From "Styx and Their Long Fall from Grace."

CHAPTER FOURTEEN: In which Toto find their voice.

1   From "Bless the Rains: Inside Toto's Slow Fall and Surprise Resurrection" by Andy Greene, *Rolling Stone*, November 20, 2020.
2   From "Bobby Kimball—30 Days Out Interview," archived at Bobby Kimball.com.
3   From "Bobby Kimball—30 Days Out Interview."
4   From "Bless the Rains: Inside Toto's Slow Fall and Surprise Resurrection."

CHAPTER FIFTEEN: The man with the golden throat.

1   From "Journey's Bassist Ross Valory Opens Up…" by Andy Greene, *Rolling Stone*, March 14, 2024.
2   From "Herbie Herbert: One Man's Journey" by Andrew McNeice, Melodic Rock, March 2008.
3   From "Foolish, Foolish Throat: A Q&A with Steve Perry" by Alex Pappademas, *GQ*, May 29, 2008.
4   From "Robert Fleischman: The Forgotten Singer Who Was Sacrificed for Steve Perry" by Neil Daniels, Classic Rock, August 28, 2018.
5   From "Herbie Herbert: One Man's Journey."
6   From "The Most Joyous and Romantic of Journey According to Neal Schon" by Devon Ivie, *Vulture*, July 5, 2022.
7   From "Robert Fleischman: The Forgotten Singer Who Was Sacrificed for Steve Perry."
8   From "The Most Joyous and Romantic of Journey According to Neal Schon."
9   From "Robert Fleischman: The Forgotten Singer Who Was Sacrificed for Steve Perry."

10   From "Start Believin': The Story of Journey's 'Infinity' Album" by Derek Oliver, Classic Rock, August 24, 2018.

11   From "Herbie Herbert: One Man's Journey."

12   From "Robert Fleischman: The Forgotten Singer Who Was Sacrificed for Steve Perry."

13   From "Steve Perry Interview" by Neely Tucker, Library of Congress, April 13, 2022.

14   From "Steve Perry Interview."

15   From "Herbie Herbert: One Man's Journey."

16   From "Journey's Bassist Ross Valory Opens Up…"

17   From "Herbie Herbert: One Man's Journey."

18   From "Steve Perry: A Legend Finds Peace" by Andrew McNeice, Melodic Rock, May 7, 2014.

19   From "Herbie Herbert: One Man's Journey."

20   From "Start Believin': The Story of Journey's 'Infinity' Album."

21   From "Start Believin': The Story of Journey's 'Infinity' Album."

22   From "Foolish, Foolish Throat: A Q&A with Steve Perry."

23   From "Foolish, Foolish Throat: A Q&A with Steve Perry."

24   From "The Most Joyous and Romantic of Journey According to Neal Schon."

25   From "Castles Burning: The Herbie Herbert Interview" by Matthew Carty, 2001.

26   From "Foolish, Foolish Throat: A Q&A with Steve Perry."

27   From "The Most Joyous and Romantic of Journey According to Neal Schon."

28   From "Foolish, Foolish Throat: A Q&A with Steve Perry."

29   From "The Most Joyous and Romantic of Journey According to Neal Schon."

30   From "Steve Perry: A Legend Finds Peace."

31   From "Gregg Rolie's Musical Journey" by Joe Matera, *Mixdown*, March 2002.

32   From "Start Believin': The Story of Journey's 'Infinity' Album."

33   From "Castles Burning: The Herbie Herbert Interview."

34   From "Steve Perry Looks Back on Touring with Van Halen" by Andy Greene, *Rolling Stone*, October 19, 2020.

35   From "Truth About Evolution: Journey's Road" by Michael Goldberg, *Crawdaddy*, April 1979.

36   From "Castles Burning: The Herbie Herbert Interview."

37   From "Start Believin': The Story of Journey's 'Infinity' Album."

CHAPTER SIXTEEN: Boston and Foreigner follow up.

1   From "The Big Interviews: Barry Goudreau" by John Beaudin, Rock History Music, 2021.

2   From "'Mad? Some People Think So…' Tom Scholz: Boston's Reluctant Boffin" by Paul Elliott, Classic Rock, December 17, 2014.

3   From "Lou Gramm: It's Urgent!" by Jeb Wright, Classic Rock Revisited.
4   From "Lou Gramm Interview on Early Years, Writing & Recording with Foreigner, and Career Highlights," Curtin Call, YouTube.
5   From "Lou Gramm Interview on Early Years, Writing & Recording with Foreigner, and Career Highlights."
6   From "Boston Takes Over" by Cameron Crowe, The Uncool.
7   From "The Big Interviews: Barry Goudreau."
8   From "Classic Rock Revisited Presents an Exclusive Interview with… Brad Delp of Boston" by Jeb Wright, thirdstage.ca, July 2003.
9   From "'I've Spent Six Months Making a Recording of a Song That I've Thrown Out': Tom Scholz on the Secrets of Boston's First Album" by Ken Sharp, Classic Rock, July 4, 2023.
10   From "Lou Gramm: It's Urgent!"
11   From "Does Keith Olsen Really Believe This Stuff, Or What?" by Alan di Perna, *Musician*, November 1988.
12   From "How Boston Flew So High and Fell So Far" by Derek Oliver, Classic Rock, June 23, 2020.

CHAPTER SEVENTEEN: Styx surge; REO stall; the Babys bust up.

1   From "We've Had to Circle the Wagons Many Times as a Band" by Jerry Ewing, Classic Rock, September 1, 2021.
2   From "REO Speedwagon: We Thought Every Album Would Sell 10 Million Copies" by Paul Elliott, Classic Rock, November 22, 2019.
3   From "Bruce Hall of REO Speedwagon Interview," *Glide Magazine*, August 19, 2023.
4   From "REO Speedwagon: We Thought Every Album Would Sell 10 Million Copies."
5   From "James 'JY' Young Dishes on All Things Styx" by Martin Popoff, *Goldmine*, June 12, 2012.
6   From "Styx," *The Big Interview with Dan Rather*, AXS TV, 2018.
7   From "Tommy Shaw: How I Wrote 'Blue Collar Man'" by Joe Bosso, *Guitar Player*, February 23, 2021.
8   From "Interview: James 'JY' Young from Styx" by Tina Whelski, *The Aquarian*, April 24, 2013.
9   From "Tommy Shaw: How I Wrote 'Blue Collar Man.'"
10   From "Styx and Their Long Fall from Grace" by Derek Oliver and Geoff Barton, Classic Rock, December 3, 2015.
11   From the film *John Waite: The Hard Way*, written and directed by Mike J. Nichols (Real Moon Films, 2022).
12   From "After the First Couple of Years the Darkness Descended" by Dave Ling, Classic Rock, November 26, 2023.
13   From "After the First Couple of Years the Darkness Descended."
14   From "Ron Nevison: Rock and Roll Dreams Come True" by Jeb Wright, Classic Rock Revisited.

15   From "After the First Couple of Years the Darkness Descended."
16   From "Journey to the Centre of the AORth" by Sylvie Simmons, *Kerrang!*, October 1981.
17   From the film *John Waite: The Hard Way*.
18   From "After the First Couple of Years the Darkness Descended."
19   From "Life Lessons with John Waite" by Ken Sharp, Rock Cellar, June 13, 2022.
20   From "After the First Couple of Years the Darkness Descended."
21   From "Tommy Shaw: Under the Influence" by Jay S. Jacobs, Pop Entertainment, April 11, 2007.

CHAPTER NINETEEN: Toto birth "Hold the Line"; Cheap Trick take Japan.

1   From "Toto: Losing the Studio Tan" by Colin Irwin, *Melody Maker*, March 10, 1979.
2   From "Catching Up with Cheap Trick's Rick Nielsen, 35 Years After 'At Budokan'" by Melissa Locker, *Time*, May 3, 2013.
3   From "Cheap Trick," *The Big Interview with Dan Rather*, AXS TV, 2019.
4   From "Cheap Trick," *The Big Interview with Dan Rather*.
5   From "Cheap Trick," *The Big Interview with Dan Rather*.
6   From "Catching Up with Cheap Trick's Rick Nielsen, 35 Years After 'At Budokan.'"
7   From "Cheap Trick's Conquest of Japan" by Wayne Robins, *Newsday*, May 20, 1979.
8   From "Catching Up with Cheap Trick's Rick Nielsen, 35 Years After 'At Budokan.'"
9   From "Catching Up with Cheap Trick's Rick Nielsen, 35 Years After 'At Budokan.'"
10   From "Cheap Trick," *The Big Interview with Dan Rather*.
11   From "Eddie Money: Rock's Rodney Dangerfield Endures" by Jason Newman, *Rolling Stone*, April 25, 2018.

CHAPTER TWENTY: Rainbow makes "Since You Been Gone."

1   From *Sounds*, July 28, 1979.
2   From *Sounds*, July 28, 1979.
3   From *Sounds*, July 28, 1979.
4   From "Ritchie Blackmore: The Lost Interview" by Neil Jeffries, Classic Rock, June 9, 2016.
5   From "Ritchie Blackmore: The Lost Interview."
6   From "Ritchie Blackmore: The Lost Interview."
7   From "Ritchie Blackmore: 'I'm Not a Guy Who Likes Jamming and Having Fun…'" by Michael Hann, *Guardian*, May 25, 2017.
8   From "Ritchie Blackmore: 'I'm Not a Guy Who Likes Jamming and Having Fun…'"

9   From "Ritchie Blackmore: 'I'm Not a Guy Who Likes Jamming and Having Fun…'"

CHAPTER TWENTY-ONE: Portrait of a young woman in a men's urinal and the damage done.

1   From *Juke Box Hero: My Five Decades in Rock 'n' Roll* by Lou Gramm with Scott Pitoniak (Triumph Books, 2013).
2   From *Juke Box Hero*.
3   From "Technology: Roy Thomas Baker" by Mark Blake, Classic Rock, July 16, 2014.
4   From "Lou Gramm—Foreigner," interviewed by Paul Stephenson, *VRP Rocks—Classic Rock Interviews*, Apple Podcasts, April 8, 2024.
5   From "Foreigner: Mass-Appeal Rock in a Post-Golden Age" by Kurt Loder, *Rolling Stone*, October 5, 1981.
6   From *Juke Box Hero*.
7   From "Lou Gramm—Foreigner."
8   From "Lou Gramm—Foreigner."

CHAPTER TWENTY-TWO: Michael Bolton and Blackjack: the AOR supergroup that never was…

1   From "Michael Bolton" by Sian Pattenden, *Smash Hits*, March 21, 1990.
2   From "A Conversation with Michael Bolton," BMI.com.
3   From "Michael Bolton."

CHAPTER TWENTY-FOUR: Kiss do disco with Desmond Child.

1   From "Paul Stanley: My Life in 10 Kiss Songs" by Paul Brannigan, Classic Rock, December 14, 2021.
2   From interview with Steve Jones on *Jonesy's Jukebox*, KLOS-FM.
3   From "Paul Stanley: My Life in 10 Kiss Songs."
4   From interview with Howard Stern on *The Howard Stern Show*, SiriusXM.
5   From interview with Steve Jones on *Jonesy's Jukebox*.
6   From interview with Steve Jones on *Jonesy's Jukebox*.
7   From interview with Howard Stern on *The Howard Stern Show*.

CHAPTER TWENTY-FIVE: The birthday present that went to Number One.

1   From "Styx," *The Big Interview with Dan Rather*, AXS TV, 2018.
2   From "James 'JY' Young Dishes on All Things Styx" by Martin Popoff, *Goldmine*, June 12, 2012.
3   From "Styx," *The Big Interview with Dan Rather*.

CHAPTER TWENTY-SIX: There's something about Patricia.

1   From "Pat Benatar: This Year's Model" by Steve Pond, *Rolling Stone*, October 16, 1980.
2   From "Nervous Tension" by Steve Gett, *Kerrang!*, November 4–17, 1982.

3   From "Pat Benatar: This Year's Model."
4   From "Pat Benatar and Neil Giraldo," *The Big Interview with Dan Rather*, AXS TV, 2015.
5   From "Pat Benatar on Neil Giraldo, 'Heartbreaker,' Being a Badass" by Ed Masley, *Arizona Republic*, September 19, 2023.
6   From "Pat Benatar and Neil Giraldo," *The Big Interview with Dan Rather*.
7   From "Pat Benatar and Neil Giraldo," *The Big Interview with Dan Rather*.
8   From "Pat Benatar and Neil Giraldo," *The Big Interview with Dan Rather*.
9   From "Pat Benatar and Neil Giraldo," *The Big Interview with Dan Rather*.
10 From "Pat Benatar and Neil Giraldo," *The Big Interview with Dan Rather*.
11 From "An Interview with Pat Benatar" by Jancee Dunn, *The Believer*, May 1, 2003.
12 From "Neil Giraldo Remains Pat Benatar's Musical Voice" by Michele Derrough, *Glide Magazine*, May 28, 2013.
13 From "Pat Benatar: This Year's Model."
14 From "Neil Giraldo Remains Pat Benatar's Musical Voice."
15 From "Pat Benatar on Neil Giraldo, 'Heartbreaker,' Being a Badass."
16 From "Neil Giraldo Remains Pat Benatar's Musical Voice."
17 From *Between a Heart and a Rock Place: A Memoir* by Pat Benatar with Patsi Bale Cox (William Morrow, 2010).
18 From "Song Summit 2010: In Conversation with Mike Chapman," YouTube.
19 From "Pat Benatar: This Year's Model."

CHAPTER TWENTY-SEVEN: Journey finds its missing link.

1   From "Journey: The Platinum Game Plan" by Ben Fong-Torres, *Rolling Stone*, June 12, 1980.
2   From "Steve Perry: A Legend Finds Peace" by Andrew McNeice, Melodic Rock, May 7, 2014.
3   From "Herbie Herbert: One Man's Journey" by Andrew McNeice, Melodic Rock, March 2008.
4   From "Herbie Herbert: One Man's Journey."
5   From "Gregg Rolie's Musical Journey" by Joe Matera, *Mixdown*, March 2002.
6   From "A Conversation with Neal 'Vortex' Schon" by Michael Cavacini, MichaelCavacini.com, September 26, 2015.
7   From "Gregg Rolie's Musical Journey."
8   From "Castles Burning: The Herbie Herbert Interview" by Matthew Carty, 2001.
9   From "A Conversation with Jonathan Cain" by Michael Cavacini, Michael Cavacini.com, July 5, 2014.
10 From "After the First Couple of Years the Darkness Descended" by Dave Ling, Classic Rock, November 26, 2023.
11 From "A Conversation with Jonathan Cain."

12 From the film *John Waite: The Hard Way*, written and directed by Mike J. Nichols (Real Moon Films, 2022).
13 From "Jonathan Cain: Believin' Now… More Than Ever Before" by Jeb Wright, Classic Rock Revisited.
14 From "Castles Burning: The Herbie Herbert Interview."
15 From "Gregg Rolie's Musical Journey."

CHAPTER TWENTY-EIGHT: The trouble with Boston, Heart, Kansas, Pat Benatar, Cheap Trick…

1 From "Affairs of the Heart" by Sylvie Simmons, *Sounds*, July 5, 1980.
2 From "Steve Walsh Interview," posted by Lad Voc, YouTube.
3 From "From Triumph to Nowhere and Back: The Story of Kansas in Their Own Words" by Dave Ling, Classic Rock, May 18, 2023.
4 From "An Exclusive Interview with Barry Goudreau" by Jeb Wright, Classic Rock Revisited, October 2023.
5 From "March 1999 Interview" by Pär Winberg, archived at Melodic.net.
6 From "The Big Interviews: Barry Goudreau" by John Beaudin, Rock History Music, 2021.
7 From *Red: My Uncensored Life in Rock* by Sammy Hagar (It Books, 2011).
8 From "March 1999 Interview."
9 From "The Big Interviews: Barry Goudreau."
10 From "Pat Benatar: This Year's Model" by Steve Pond, *Rolling Stone*, October 16, 1980.
11 From "Cheap Trick: Light of the Trick" by Tom Cox, *Uncut*, August 1997.
12 From "Cheap Trick," *The Big Interview with Dan Rather*, AXS TV, 2019.
13 From "Cheap Trick: Light of the Trick."
14 From "Eddie Money," *The Big Interview with Dan Rather*, AXS TV, 2018
15 From "Ron Nevison: Rock and Roll Dreams Come True" by Jeb Wright, Classic Rock Revisited.
16 From "Rediscovering Paradise: Eddie Money Plays It Straight and Takes Control" by Toby Goldstein, *Creem*, February 1983.
17 From "How Boston Flew So High and Fell So Far" by Derek Oliver, Classic Rock, June 23, 2020.
18 From "The Big Interviews: Barry Goudreau."
19 From "How Boston Flew So High and Fell So Far."
20 From "An Exclusive Interview with Barry Goudreau."
21 From "Cheap Trick," *The Big Interview with Dan Rather*.
22 From "From Triumph to Nowhere and Back: The Story of Kansas, in Their Own Words."
23 From "Steve Walsh Interview," YouTube.
24 From "Jeff Glixman: Past the Point of Know Return!" by Jeb Wright, Classic Rock Revisited.
25 From "Steve Walsh Interview," Lad Voc.

26   From "Pat Benatar: Fire and Loathing" by Pete Makowski, *Sounds*, September 12, 1981.

27   From "Pat Benatar: This Year's Model."

CHAPTER THIRTY: Canada calling.

1   From "'The Audience Threw Lighters, Bottles, Ice Cubes and Coins. We Managed Four Songs Before Being Booed Off': The Rollercoaster Story of Loverboy" by Derek Oliver, Classic Rock, December 22, 2023.

2   From "Loverboy's Mike Reno Is Still 'Lovin' Every Minute of It,'" *Goldmine*, December 24, 2012.

3   From "'The Audience Threw Lighters, Bottles, Ice Cubes and Coins. We Managed Four Songs Before Being Booed Off': The Rollercoaster Story of Loverboy."

4   From "Mike Reno: The Invisible Rock Star of Loverboy" by Dennis Hunt, *Los Angeles Times*, April 10, 1986.

5   From "Mike Reno of Loverboy Offers His Best Advice…" by Katherine Yeske Taylor, *American Songwriter*, February 2, 2021.

6   From "Loverboy Remember Their First Kiss…" by Bob Ruggiero, *Houston Press*, December 22, 2020.

7   From "Loving Every Minute of It" by Jeb Wright, Classic Rock Revisited.

8   From "'The Audience Threw Lighters, Bottles, Ice Cubes and Coins. We Managed Four Songs Before Being Booed Off': The Rollercoaster Story of Loverboy."

9   From "'The Audience Threw Lighters, Bottles, Ice Cubes and Coins. We Managed Four Songs Before Being Booed Off': The Rollercoaster Story of Loverboy."

CHAPTER THIRTY-ONE: "Keep On Loving You" and the perks of being a radio programmer.

1   From "REO Speedwagon: The Prairie Dog Has His Day" by Sylvie Simmons, *Sounds*, May 2, 1981.

2   From "REO's Neal Doughty: Back on the Road Again" by Jeb Wright, Classic Rock Revisited.

3   From "REO Speedwagon Will Dedicate Every Show to Late Guitarist Gary Richrath 'Probably Forever'" by Gary Graff, *Billboard*, September 17, 2015.

4   From "Reo Speedwagon," *The Big Interview with Dan Rather*, AXS TV, 2019.

5   From "The 10 Best REO Speedwagon Songs" by Kevin Cronin, Classic Rock, May 11, 2016.

6   From "Revved Up Rocker Gary Richrath" by Jim Schwartz, Guitar Player Vault, November 2015.

7   From "The 10 Best REO Speedwagon Songs."

8   From "Revved Up Rocker Gary Richrath."

9   From "The 10 Best REO Speedwagon Songs."
10 From "Reo Speedwagon," *The Big Interview with Dan Rather.*
11 From "Revved Up Rocker Gary Richrath."
12 From "REO Speedwagon: We Thought Every Album Would Sell 10 Million Copies" by Paul Elliott, Classic Rock, November 22, 2019.
13 From "Reo Speedwagon," *The Big Interview with Dan Rather.*
14 From "The 10 Best REO Speedwagon Songs."
15 From "REO Speedwagon: The Prairie Dog Has His Day."
16 From "REO's Neal Doughty: Back on the Road Again."
17 From "REO Speedwagon's Big Breakout" by James Henke, *Rolling Stone*, March 19, 1981.
18 From "REO Speedwagon: We Thought Every Album Would Sell 10 Million Copies."
19 From *Hit Men* by Frederic Dannen (Vintage, 1991).
20 From "REO's Neal Doughty: Back on the Road Again."
21 From "REO's Kevin Cronin: Rolling with the Changes" by Jeb Wright, Classic Rock Revisited.com.

CHAPTER THIRTY-TWO: Clocking in at the hit factory.

1   From "7 Questions with Loverboy's Paul Dean..." by Joe Matera, *Guitar World*, July 6, 2023.
2   From "Mike Reno: The Invisible Rock Star of Loverboy" by Dennis Hunt, *Los Angeles Times*, April 10, 1986.
3   From "Paul Dean and Loverboy Are Set for a 'Rock 'n' Roll Revival'" by James Wood, *Guitar World*, August 16, 2012.
4   From "'The Audience Threw Lighters, Bottles, Ice Cubes and Coins. We Managed Four Songs Before Being Booed Off': The Rollercoaster Story of Loverboy" by Derek Oliver, Classic Rock, December 22, 2023.

CHAPTER THIRTY-THREE: New adventurers in AOR...

1   From "Rick Springfield Says Misdeeds of His Youth Would've Landed Him in Prison" by Julius Miller, *Los Angeles Magazine*, July 25, 2023.
2   From "Rick Springfield Gets to the Heart of New Album 'Automatic'" by George A. Paul, *Rock Cellar*, August 17, 2023.
3   From "The Fee Waybill Interview" by Ira Kantor, Vintage Rock, 2022.
4   From "Worry, Be Happy: Rick Springfield Discusses New Memoir" by Vanessa, *National Post*, October 20, 2010.
5   From "The True Story of the Rick Springfield Song That Turned Him Into a Superstar" by Dave Ling, Classic Rock, August 23, 2023.
6   From "Fee Waybill Interview" by John Beaudin, *Rock History Book* podcast, June 27, 2022.
7   From "Are You Ready to Rick?" by Annene Kaye, *NME*, September 10, 1983.
8   From "Worry, Be Happy: Rick Springfield Discusses New Memoir."

CHAPTER THIRTY-FOUR: Foreigner makes 4.

1   From "Lou Gramm—Foreigner," interviewed by Paul Stephenson, *VRP Rocks—Classic Rock Interviews*, Apple Podcasts, April 8, 2024.
2   From "Ed Gagliardi and Al Greenwood Interview" by Gary James, Famous Interview, July 15, 2022.
3   From "Foreigner: Mass-Appeal Rock in a Post-Golden Age" by Kurt Loder, *Rolling Stone*, October 5, 1981.
4   From "Foreigner: Mass-Appeal Rock in a Post-Golden Age."
5   From "Foreigner: Mass-Appeal Rock in a Post-Golden Age."
6   From "Screamin' and Steamin'," by Steve Gett, *Kerrang!*, May 6–19, 1982.
7   From "Lou Gramm: It's Urgent!" by Jeb Wright, Classic Rock Revisited.
8   From "Lou Gramm: It's Urgent!"
9   From "Lou Gramm: It's Urgent!"
10 From "Lou Gramm: It's Urgent!"
11 From *Juke Box Hero: My Five Decades in Rock 'n' Roll* by Lou Gramm with Scott Pitoniak (Triumph Books, 2013).

CHAPTER THIRTY-FIVE: Strangers waitin', up and down the boulevard…

1   From "A Conversation with Jonathan Cain" by Michael Cavacini, MichaelCavacini.com, July 5, 2014.
2   From "Journey to the Centre of the AORth" by Sylvie Simmons, *Kerrang!*, October 1981.
3   From "Steve Perry of Journey: 'Things Happened to Me as a Child…'" by Kate Mossman, *New Statesman*, September 26, 2018.
4   From "Jonathan Cain: Believin' Now… More Than Ever Before" by Jeb Wright, Classic Rock Revisited.
5   From "The Most Joyous and Romantic of Journey According to Neal Schon" by Devon Ivie, *Vulture*, July 5, 2022.
6   From "Herbie Herbert: One Man's Journey" by Andrew McNeice, Melodic Rock, March 2008.
7   From "The Most Joyous and Romantic of Journey According to Neal Schon."
8   From *Don't Stop Believin'* by Jonathan Cain (Zondervan, 2018).
9   From "Steve Perry Interview" by Neely Tucker of the Library of Congress, April 13, 2022.
10 From "'I Have Stood on Stage During Some Difficult Situations': Journey's Jonathan Cain on Band Animosity" by Dave Ling, Classic Rock, July 21, 2024.
11 From "Steve Perry Interview."
12 From "Journey's Jonathan Cain: Still Believin' in Music and Other Higher Powers" by Bob Ruggiero, *Houston Press*, May 1, 2008.
13 From "Steve Perry Interview."
14 From "Jonathan Cain: Believin' Now… More Than Ever Before."

15   From "Castles Burning: The Herbie Herbert Interview" by Matthew Carty, 2001.
16   From "The Return of the Voice" by Paul Elliott, Classic Rock, January 15, 2019.
17   From "Herbie Herbert: One Man's Journey."
18   From "Steve Perry: A Legend Finds Peace" by Andrew McNeice, Melodic Rock, May 7, 2014.
19   From "Herbie Herbert: One Man's Journey."
20   From "Castles Burning: The Herbie Herbert Interview."
21   From "Foolish, Foolish Throat: A Q&A with Steve Perry" by Alex Pappademas, *GQ*, May 29, 2008.

CHAPTER THIRTY-SIX: The revolution will be televised.

1   From *I Want My MTV: The Uncensored History of the Music Video Revolution* by Rob Tannenbaum and Craig Marks (Plume, 2011).
2   From *Between a Heart and a Rock Place: A Memoir* by Pat Benatar with Patsi Bale Cox (William Morrow, 2010).
3   From *Between a Heart and a Rock Place*.
4   From "REO Speedwagon: We Thought Every Album Would Sell 10 Million Copies" by Paul Elliott, Classic Rock, November 22, 2019.
5   From "Loverboy's Mike Reno Is Still 'Lovin' Every Minute of It," *Goldmine*, December 24, 2012.
6   From "Eddie Money," *The Big Interview with Dan Rather*, AXS TV, 2018.
7   From "Ron Nevison: Rock and Roll Dreams Come True" by Jeb Wright, Classic Rock Revisited.

CHAPTER THIRTY-SEVEN: Quarterflash and their one-hit wonder.

1   From "Interview with Marv Ross of Quarterflash" by Gary James, Classic Bands.com.
2   From *Living a Vocal Life: A Podcast for Singers* with Valerie Day, November 29, 2023.
3   From "Interview with Marv Ross of Quarterflash."
4   From *Living a Vocal Life: A Podcast for Singers*.
5   From "Interview with Marv Ross of Quarterflash."
6   From *Living a Vocal Life: A Podcast for Singers*.
7   From "Interview with Marv Ross of Quarterflash."
8   From *Living a Vocal Life: A Podcast for Singers*.
9   From "Interview with Marv Ross of Quarterflash."
10   From *Living a Vocal Life: A Podcast for Singers*.
11   From "Interview with Marv Ross of Quarterflash."
12   From *Living a Vocal Life: A Podcast for Singers*.
13   From "Interview with Marv Ross of Quarterflash."
14   From *Living a Vocal Life: A Podcast for Singers*.

15   From "Marv Ross: Old School Retro 80s Interview," Rediscover the '80s, May 13, 2001.
16   From *Living a Vocal Life: A Podcast for Singers*.
17   From "Marv Ross: Old School Retro 80s Interview."
18   From *Living a Vocal Life: A Podcast for Singers*.
19   From "Marv Ross: Old School Retro 80s Interview."
20   From *Living a Vocal Life: A Podcast for Singers*.
21   From "Marv Ross: Old School Retro 80s Interview."
22   From "Marv and Rindy Ross Scored Pop Stardom with Quarterflash..." by Douglas Perry, OregonLive.com, November 13, 2021.
23   From "Interview with Marv Ross of Quarterflash."
24   From *Living a Vocal Life: A Podcast for Singers*.
25   From "Interview with Marv Ross of Quarterflash."
26   From *Living a Vocal Life: A Podcast for Singers*.
27   From "Marv Ross: Old School Retro 80s Interview."

CHAPTER THIRTY-NINE: Chicago, Asia, and the fine art of reinvention.
1   From "John Wetton Interview," *Kickin' It Old School* blog, May 1, 2011.
2   From "Eastern Promise" by Steve Gett, *Kerrang!*, April 22–May 5, 1982.
3   From "John Wetton Interview."
4   From "Prog Still Lives Inside the Four of Us..." by Dave Ling, Classic Rock, September 6, 2023.
5   From "Eastern Promise."
6   From the film *David Foster: Off the Record*, directed by Barry Avrich (Bell Media Studios, 2019).
7   From the film *David Foster: Off the Record*.
8   From the film *David Foster: Off the Record*.
9   From the film *David Foster: Off the Record*.
10   From "Prog Still Lives Inside the Four of Us..."
11   From "I Really Didn't Expect the Scale of the Success" by Dave Ling, Prog, February 24, 2023.
12   From "Prog Still Lives Inside the Four of Us..."
13   From the film *David Foster: Off the Record*.
14   From "I Really Didn't Expect the Scale of the Success."
15   From "John Wetton Interview."
16   From "Prog Still Lives Inside the Four of Us..."
17   From "Prog Still Lives Inside the Four of Us..."
18   From "I Really Didn't Expect the Scale of the Success."
19   From "John Wetton Interview."
20   From the film *David Foster: Off the Record*.

CHAPTER FORTY: It's the thrill of the fight...
1   From "Survivor's Frankie Sullivan Talks 'Eye of the Tiger' at 40" by Ron Hart, *Billboard*, June 16, 2022.

2   From "Ron Nevison: Rock and Roll Dreams Come True" by Jeb Wright, Classic Rock Revisited.
3   From "Jimi Jamison: Reaching Out" by Nick Muller, Melodic Rock, August 6, 2007.
4   From "Survivor's Frankie Sullivan Talks 'Eye of the Tiger' at 40."
5   From by Saks Nikas, Rock Pages.gr, October 25, 2021.
6   From "Survivor's Frankie Sullivan Talks 'Eye of the Tiger' at 40."

CHAPTER FORTY-ONE: Assorted ups and downs in '82: sex addiction and alopecia included.

1   From "Heart to Heart" by Sylvie Simmons, *Sounds*, May 29, 1982.
2   From "REO's Neal Doughty: Back on the Road Again" by Jeb Wright, Classic Rock Revisited.
3   From "Nervous Tension" by Steve Gett, *Kerrang!*, November 4–17, 1982.
4   From "Rick Springfield Reveals Battle with His Sexual Appetite" by *Access Hollywood*, Today.com, October 19, 2010.
5   From "Sammy Hagar Interview: Diamond Dave, the Van Halens, and a Long Life in Rock" by Dave Everley, Classic Rock, October 16, 2020.
6   From "A Conversation with John Waite" by Michael Cavacini, MichaelCavacini.com, June 6, 2014.
7   From "Ritchie Blackmore's Rainbow: Seeing Is Believing" by Garry Bushell, *Sounds*, December 4, 1982.
8   From "Rick Springfield Reveals Battle with His Sexual Appetite."
9   From "Sammy Hagar Interview: Diamond Dave, the Van Halens, and a Long Life in Rock."
10   From "Pat Benatar: This Year's Model" by Steve Pond, *Rolling Stone*, October 16, 1980.
11   From the film *John Waite: The Hard Way*, written and directed by Mike J. Nichols (Real Moon Films, 2022).

CHAPTER FORTY-TWO: Def Leppard and Mutt Lange catch fire.

1   From "Steve Perry: A Legend Finds Peace" by Andrew McNeice, Melodic Rock, May 7, 2014.
2   From "Mike Shipley: Def Leppard and Mutt Lange…" by Jake Brown and Larry Crane, *Tape Op*, March/April 2017.
3   From "Mike Shipley: Def Leppard and Mutt Lange…"
4   From "Def Leppard's Joe Elliott: We Had This Inner Demon of Pop Wanting to Come Out" by Michael Hann, *Guardian*, August 8, 2018.
5   From "Def Leppard's Joe Elliott: We Had This Inner Demon of Pop Wanting to Come Out."
6   From "Phil Collen on Def Leppard's 'Pyromania'" by Richard Bienstock, *Metal Edge*.
7   From "Phil Collen on Def Leppard's 'Pyromania.'"
8   From "Phil Collen on Def Leppard's 'Pyromania.'"

9   From "Phil Collen on Def Leppard's 'Pyromania.'"
10   From "Ron Nevison: Rock and Roll Dreams Come True" by Jeb Wright, Classic Rock Revisited.
11   From "Phil Collen on Def Leppard's 'Pyromania.'"
12   From "Q Prime's Burnstein and Mensch on... Staying on Top for 33 Years" by Jem Aswad, *Billboard*, March 29, 2016.
13   From "Phil Collen on Def Leppard's 'Pyromania.'"
14   From "Phil Collen on Def Leppard's 'Pyromania.'"

CHAPTER FORTY-THREE: Excess—almost—all areas.

1   From "An Interview with Dennis DeYoung" by Michael Cavacini, *The Aquarian*, October 5, 2016.
2   From "REO Speedwagon: We Thought Every Album Would Sell 10 Million Copies" by Paul Elliott, Classic Rock, November 22, 2019.
3   From "Reo Speedwagon," *The Big Interview with Dan Rather*, AXS TV, 2019.
4   From "Reo Speedwagon," *The Big Interview with Dan Rather*.

CHAPTER FORTY-FIVE: Journey's highway run into the midnight sun.

1   From "Foolish, Foolish Throat: A Q&A with Steve Perry" by Alex Pappademas, *GQ*, May 29, 2008.
2   From *Don't Stop Believin'* by Jonathan Cain (Zondervan, 2018).
3   From "Herbie Herbert: One Man's Journey" by Andrew McNeice, Melodic Rock, March 2008.
4   From *Don't Stop Believin'*.
5   From "The Most Joyous and Romantic of Journey According to Neal Schon" by Devon Ivie, *Vulture*, July 5, 2022.
6   From *Don't Stop Believin'*.
7   From "The Most Joyous and Romantic of Journey According to Neal Schon."
8   From *Don't Stop Believin'*.
9   From "The Most Joyous and Romantic of Journey According to Neal Schon."
10   From "The Most Joyous and Romantic of Journey According to Neal Schon."
11   From "Castles Burning: The Herbie Herbert Interview" by Matthew Carty, 2001.
12   From "Castles Burning: The Herbie Herbert Interview."
13   From "Herbie Herbert: One Man's Journey."
14   From *Don't Stop Believin'*.
15   From "The Most Joyous and Romantic of Journey According to Neal Schon."
16   From "Castles Burning: The Herbie Herbert Interview."
17   From *Don't Stop Believin'*.

18   From "Foolish, Foolish Throat: A Q&A with Steve Perry."
19   From *Don't Stop Believin'*.
20   From "Music Really Saved My Life…" by Dave Ling, Classic Rock, August 2014.
21   From "Journey: The Great Escape" by Jon Hotten, Classic Rock, July 19, 2019.
22   From "Foolish, Foolish Throat: A Q&A with Steve Perry."

CHAPTER FORTY-SIX: Dennis DeYoung's Waterloo.

1   From "We've Had to Circle the Wagons Many Times as a Band" by Jerry Ewing, Classic Rock, September 1, 2021.
2   From "Styx," *The Big Interview with Dan Rather*, AXS TV, 2018.
3   From "Styx," *The Big Interview with Dan Rather*.
4   From "Styx Guitarist James 'JY' Young: Yes, They Will Do 'Mr. Roboto' on Tour" by Ed Maseley, *The Republic*, azcentral.com, 2019.
5   From "A Conversation with Dennis DeYoung" by Bruce Fagerstrom, *Magnet*, June 10, 2020.
6   From "James 'JY' Young Looks Back on 50 Years of Styx" by Matt Wardlaw, Ultimate Classic Rock, June 17, 2022.
7   From "James 'JY' Young Looks Back on 50 Years of Styx."
8   From "Dennis DeYoung: Styx Should Do One Last Tour for the Fans" by Andy Greene, *Rolling Stone*, March 19, 2020.
9   From "Styx Guitarist James 'JY' Young: Yes, They Will Do 'Mr. Roboto' on Tour."

CHAPTER FORTY-SEVEN: Night Ranger breaks big. Kansas and Rainbow break up.

1   From "Fee Waybill Interview" by John Beaudin, *Rock History Book* podcast, June 27, 2022.
2   From "Fee Waybill Interview."
3   From "The Rise, Fall, and Porn-Assisted Resurrection of AOR Heroes Night Ranger" by Paul Elliott, Classic Rock, December 16, 2023.
4   From "The Rise, Fall, and Porn-Assisted Resurrection of AOR Heroes Night Ranger."
5   From "Night Ranger—The Band Who Invented the Power Ballad" by Joe Bosso, Classic Rock, October 8, 2016.
6   From "The Rise, Fall, and Porn-Assisted Resurrection of AOR Heroes Night Ranger."
7   From "Night Ranger—The Band Who Invented the Power Ballad."
8   From "Night Ranger—The Band Who Invented the Power Ballad."
9   From "The Rise, Fall, and Porn-Assisted Resurrection of AOR Heroes Night Ranger."
10 From "When You Cut Us, Night Ranger Oozes Out" by Dave Ling, Classic Rock, August 18, 2021.

CHAPTER FORTY-EIGHT: "Love Is a Battlefield" and the art of the hit.

1   From "Song Summit 2010: In Conversation with Mike Chapman," YouTube.
2   From *Between a Heart and a Rock Place: A Memoir* by Pat Benatar with Patsi Bale Cox (William Morrow, 2010).
3   From "'80s Hitmaker Holly Knight Reveals Her Reasons for Writing" by Martin Kielty, Ultimate Classic Rock, December 2, 2022.
4   From *Between a Heart and a Rock Place*.
5   From *Between a Heart and a Rock Place*.
6   From *Between a Heart and a Rock Place*.
7   From "Song Summit 2010: In Conversation with Mike Chapman."
8   From *Between a Heart and a Rock Place*.

CHAPTER FORTY-NINE: The woes of Boston and Heart.

1   From "Short Takes: Leader of Boston Wins Lawsuit," *Los Angeles Times*, March 21, 1990.
2   From "'Mad? Some People Think So…' Tom Scholz: Boston's Reluctant Boffin" by Paul Elliott, Classic Rock, December 17, 2014.
3   From "'Mad? Some People Think So…' Tom Scholz: Boston's Reluctant Boffin."
4   From "The Big Interviews: Barry Goudreau" by John Beaudin, Rock History Music, 2021.
5   From "I've Spent Six Months Making a Recording of a Song That I've Thrown Out" by Ken Sharp, Classic Rock, October 2006.
6   From "Tom Scholz of Boston—The Vinyl Guide Interview Ep297 & Ep298," YouTube, August 27, 2021.
7   From "'Mad? Some People Think So…' Tom Scholz: Boston's Reluctant Boffin."
8   From "Keith Olsen: Producer, Engineer, Classical Artist and Industry Advocate" by Andrew McNeice, Melodic Rock.

CHAPTER FIFTY: Yes and Genesis join Asia's AOR trail. Going tricky.

1   From "I Really Didn't Expect the Scale of the Success" by Dave Ling, Prog, February 24, 2023.
2   From "Asia: Continental Drift" by Sylvie Simmons, *Creem*, April 1986.
3   From "How Genesis Journeyed from Pioneering Prog to Eighties Superstardom" by Chris Roberts, Classic Rock, March 2012.
4   From "Trevor Rabin's Challenging Road to Yes" by Stephen Lamber, Prog, November 28, 2023.
5   From "Tony Kaye on His Years with Yes" by Andy Greene, *Rolling Stone*, February 11, 2021.
6   From "Trevor Rabin Looks Back on Yes' Classic '90125' Album Turning 40" by David Chiu, *Forbes*, November 13, 2023.
7   From "John Wetton Interview," *Kickin' It Old School* blog, May 1, 2011.

8 From "Asia: Continental Drift."
9 From "Tony Banks: 'Genesis Never Really Changed'" by Grant Moon, Classic Rock, June 1, 2022.
10 From "Phil Collins Beats the Odds" by Rob Hoerburger, *Rolling Stone*, May 23, 1985.
11 From "How Yes' '90125' Became a Triumph" by Stephen Lamber, Prog, January 24, 2024.
12 From "Tony Kaye on His Years with Yes."
13 From "Trevor Rabin Looks Back on Yes' Classic '90125' Album Turning 40."
14 From "Trevor Horn on Fronting Yes" by Jonny Sharp, Prog, April 9, 2024.
15 From "Tony Kaye on His Years with Yes."
16 From "Trevor Horn on Fronting Yes."
17 From "Tony Kaye on His Years with Yes."
18 From "Trevor Rabin's Challenging Road to Yes."
19 From "Trevor Horn's Highs and Lows" by Daryl Easlea, Prog, October 4, 2023.
20 From "Phil Collins: From Genesis to Resurrection" by Mark Blake, Prog, February 26, 2016.
21 From "John Wetton Interview," *Kickin' It Old School*.
22 From "Tony Kaye on His Years with Yes."
23 From "Trevor Horn on Fronting Yes."
24 From "Trevor Rabin Looks Back on Yes' Classic '90125' Album Turning 40."
25 From "Tony Kaye on His Years with Yes."

CHAPTER FIFTY-ONE: It came from New Jersey...

1 From "'I Wish I Had Enjoyed Success More': Jon Bon Jovi on Megahits, Marriage..." by Safraz Manzoor, *Guardian*, June 7, 2024.
2 From "Jon Bon Jovi Masterminded One of the Biggest and Biggest Selling Bands of His Era..." by Paul Brannigan, Classic Rock, July 23, 2024.
3 From "'I Wish I Had Enjoyed Success More': Jon Bon Jovi on Megahits, Marriage..."
4 From "'I Wish I Had Enjoyed Success More': Jon Bon Jovi On Megahits, Marriage..."
5 From "Kiss and Tell: The Doc McGhee Story" by Gordon Masson, *IQ*, May 11, 2023.
6 From "I'm the Poster Boy for Marriage" by Oliver Burkeman, *Guardian*, May 26, 2006.
7 From "Kiss and Tell: The Doc McGhee Story."

CHAPTER FIFTY-TWO: Mutt Lange with the Cars and David Foster with Chicago: the great dictators.

1 From "He's Never Done a Band Like Us; He's Done a Lot of Heavy Metals" by Bill DeMair, Classic Rock, April 4, 2024.

2   From "Interview with Robert Lamm and Jimmy Pankow" by Debbie Kruger, DebbieKruger.com, March 4, 1999.
3   From "Interview with Robert Lamm and Jimmy Pankow."

CHAPTER FIFTY-THREE: Steve Perry goes solo.

1   From "Foolish, Foolish Throat: A Q&A with Steve Perry" by Alex Pappademas, *GQ*, May 29, 2008.
2   From "Hall of Fame Songwriter Randy Goodrum Talks About His Classic Hits…" by Dale Kawashima, *Songwriter Universe*, June 22, 2022.
3   From "Steve Perry: A Legend Finds Peace" by Andrew McNeice, Melodic Rock, May 7, 2014.
4   From "Hall of Fame Songwriter Randy Goodrum Talks About His Classic Hits…"
5   From "Steve Perry: A Legend Finds Peace."
6   From "Hall of Fame Songwriter Randy Goodrum Talks About His Classic Hits…"
7   From "Dick Clark Interview—November 1996" by Dick Clark, For the Love of Steve Perry.
8   From "Hall of Fame Songwriter Randy Goodrum Talks About His Classic Hits…"
9   From "Dick Clark Interview—November 1996."
10 From "Steve Perry Interview on Street Talk," posted by saboteur716, YouTube.
11 From "Herbie Herbert: One Man's Journey" by Andrew McNeice, Melodic Rock, March 2008.
12 From "Foolish, Foolish Throat: A Q&A with Steve Perry."
13 From "Herbie Herbert: One Man's Journey."
14 From "Castles Burning: The Herbie Herbert Interview" by Matthew Carty, 2001.
15 From *Don't Stop Believin'* by Jonathan Cain (Zondervan, 2018).
16 From "Castles Burning: The Herbie Herbert Interview."
17 From "Foolish, Foolish Throat: A Q&A with Steve Perry."

CHAPTER FIFTY-FOUR: A video kills Billy Squier's star.

1   From *I Want My MTV: The Uncensored History of the Music Video Revolution* by Rob Tannenbaum and Craig Marks (Plume, 2011).

CHAPTER FIFTY-FIVE: Chasing the mighty dollar.

1   From "Q&A: Kiss' Paul Stanley" by David Marchese, *Spin*, July 23, 2010.
2   From "An Exclusive Interview with Barry Goudreau" by Jeb Wright, Classic Rock Revisited, October 2023.
3   From "Lunch with Benatar" by Lydia Lunch, *Spin*, September 1985.
4   From "Life Lessons with John Waite" by Ken Sharp, Rock Cellar, June 13, 2022.

5   From "Interview with Patty Smyth" by Gary James, Classic Bands.
6   From the film *John Waite: The Hard Way*, written and directed by Mike J. Nichols (Real Moon Films, 2022).
7   From "Interview: Patty Smyth," Cryptic Rock, January 10, 2008.
8   From "A Conversation with John Waite" by Michael Cavacini, MichaelCavacini.com, June 6, 2014.
9   From "Rock/Pop Star Patty Smyth Returns…" by Dale Kawashima, *Songwriter Universe*, October 6, 2020.
10 From "A Conversation with John Waite."
11 From "Interview: Patty Smyth."
12 From "An Exclusive Interview with Barry Goudreau."
13 From "Lunch with Benatar."
14 From the film *John Waite: The Hard Way*.

CHAPTER FIFTY-SIX: Toto, Survivor, and the tale of two new voices.

1   From "Bobby Kimball—30 Days Out Interview," archived at BobbyKimball.com.
2   From "Jimi Jamison: Reaching Out" by Nick Muller, Melodic Rock, August 6, 2007.
3   From "The Popdose Interview: Jimi Jamison of Survivor," Popdose, December 18, 2012.
4   From "Richard Page Interview" by Melissa Parker, *Smashing Interviews Magazine*, November 28, 2010.
5   From "Interview with Fergie Frederiksen" by Mick Burgess, Metal Express Radio, December 29, 2011.
6   From "Interview with Fergie Frederiksen."
7   From "Jimi Jamison: Reaching Out."
8   From "Interview with Fergie Frederiksen."

CHAPTER FIFTY-SEVEN: Don Henley and Cyndi Lauper make "Boys of Summer" and "Time After Time."

1   From "The Breakdown: Cyndi Lauper, Rob Hyman Recall Making of 'Time After Time'" by Brittany Spanos, *Rolling Stone*, June 21, 2021.
2   From "The Breakdown: Cyndi Lauper, Rob Hyman Recall Making of 'Time After Time.'"
3   From "Don Henley in Conversation" by Bud Scoppa, *Record*, 1986.
4   From "It Was a Gift…" by Bill DeMair, Classic Rock, March 20, 2024.
5   From "The Breakdown: Cyndi Lauper, Rob Hyman Recall Making of 'Time After Time.'"
6   From "The Breakdown: Cyndi Lauper, Rob Hyman Recall Making of 'Time After Time.'"
7   From "It Was a Gift…"
8   From "The Breakdown: Cyndi Lauper, Rob Hyman Recall Making of 'Time After Time.'"

9   From "It Was a Gift..."
10 From "Don Henley in Conversation."
11 From "Don Henley in Conversation."
12 From "The Breakdown: Cyndi Lauper, Rob Hyman Recall Making of 'Time After Time.'"
13 From "The Breakdown: Cyndi Lauper, Rob Hyman Recall Making of 'Time After Time.'"
14 From "It Was a Gift..."

CHAPTER FIFTY-EIGHT: Styx comes undone.

1   From "We've Had to Circle the Wagons Many Times as a Band" by Jerry Ewing, Classic Rock, September 1, 2021.
2   From "Styx," *The Big Interview with Dan Rather*, AXS TV, 2018.
3   From "Tommy Shaw: Under the Influence" by Jay S. Jacobs, Pop Entertainment, April 11, 2007.
4   From "Styx," *The Big Interview with Dan Rather*.
5   From "Tommy Shaw: Under the Influence."
6   From "Tommy Shaw Interview" by Rick Huisseune, Melodic.net, August 6, 2006.
7   From "Tommy Shaw: Under the Influence."

CHAPTER FIFTY-NINE: REO throw away the oars, forever.

1   From "Reo Speedwagon," *The Big Interview with Dan Rather*, AXS TV, 2019.
2   From "Bruce Hall of REO Speedwagon Interview," *Glide*, August 19, 2023.
3   From "An Interview with REO Speedwagon Vocalist Kevin Cronin: A Speedwagon Summer" by Andrea Seastrand, *The Aquarian*, June 18, 2014.
4   From "Gary Richrath Interview," MTV, 1984.
5   From "REO Speedwagon: We Thought Every Album Would Sell 10 Million Copies" by Paul Elliott, Classic Rock, November 22, 2019.
6   From "REO Speedwagon: We Thought Every Album Would Sell 10 Million Copies."
7   From "Something Else! Interview: Neal Doughty, of REO Speedwagon" by Donald Gibson, Something Else!, May 28, 2012.
8   From "REO Speedwagon on Not Knowing What John Lewis Was..." by John Earls, *NME*, November 19, 2019.
9   From "Something Else! Interview: Neal Doughty, of REO Speedwagon."
10 From "An Interview with REO Speedwagon Vocalist Kevin Cronin."

CHAPTER SIXTY-ONE: Foreigner sends in the choir.

1   From "Dream Gig to Dirty Deal: Lou Gramm on Leaving Foreigner & Mick Jones' Greed!" Backstage Pass Rock-News, YouTube.

2 From *Juke Box Hero: My Five Decades in Rock 'n' Roll* by Lou Gramm with Scott Pitoniak (Triumph Books, 2013).
3 From *Juke Box Hero*.
4 From "Lou Gramm—Foreigner," interviewed by Paul Stephenson, *VRP Rocks—Classic Rock Interviews*, Apple Podcasts, April 8, 2024.
5 From "Lou Gramm—Foreigner."
6 From "Lou Gramm Interview on Early Years, Writing & Recording with Foreigner, and Career Highlights," Curtin Call, YouTube.
7 From "Lou Gramm Interview on Early Years, Writing & Recording with Foreigner, and Career Highlights."
8 From "Lou Gramm Interview on Early Years, Writing & Recording with Foreigner, and Career Highlights."
9 From "Lou Gramm on Foreigner's Long-Awaited Rock Hall Induction" by Andy Greene, *Rolling Stone*, April 24, 2024.
10 From *Juke Box Hero*.
11 From *Juke Box Hero*.
12 From "Lou Gramm—Foreigner."
13 From "Lou Gramm—Foreigner."
14 From "Lou Gramm Interview on Early Years, Writing & Recording with Foreigner, and Career Highlights."

CHAPTER SIXTY-TWO: Heart's reinvention and resurrection.

1 From "Ron Nevison (Producer, Engineer: Led Zeppelin, KISS, Heart)" by Carlos Ramirez, No Echo, October 24, 2014.
2 From "Ron Nevison (Producer, Engineer: Led Zeppelin, KISS, Heart)."
3 From "Heart," *The Big Interview with Dan Rather*, AXS TV, 2015.
4 From "Ron Nevison (Producer, Engineer: Led Zeppelin, KISS, Heart)."
5 From "Ron Nevison (Producer, Engineer: Led Zeppelin, KISS, Heart)."
6 From "Ron Nevison (Producer, Engineer: Led Zeppelin, KISS, Heart)."
7 From "Ron Nevison (Producer, Engineer: Led Zeppelin, KISS, Heart)."
8 From *I Want My MTV: The Uncensored History of the Music Video Revolution* by Rob Tannenbaum and Craig Marks (Plume, 2011).
9 From *I Want My MTV*.

CHAPTER SIXTY-THREE: Starship plays the mamba.

1 From "Jefferson Airplane's Grace Slick on Aging Rock Stars..." by Mickey Stanley, *Vanity Fair*, June 15, 2012.
2 From "An Oral History of 'We Built This City'..." by Rob Tannenbaum, *GQ*, August 31, 2016.
3 From "Jefferson Airplane's Grace Slick on Aging Rock Stars..."
4 From "Jefferson Airplane's Grace Slick on Aging Rock Stars..."
5 From "An Oral History of 'We Built This City'..."

CHAPTER SIXTY-FIVE: Cautionary tales.

1 From *Between a Heart and a Rock Place: A Memoir* by Pat Benatar with Patsi Bale Cox (William Morrow, 2010).
2 From "An Interview with Pat Benatar" by Jancee Dunn, *The Believer*, May 1, 2003.
3 From "An Interview with Pat Benatar."
4 From "'I Wish I Had Enjoyed Success More': Jon Bon Jovi on Megahits, Marriage..." by Safraz Manzoor, *Guardian*, June 7, 2024.
5 From "Fee Waybill Interview" by John Beaudin, *Rock History Book* podcast, June 27, 2022.
6 From "The Popdose Interview," Popdose, August 11, 2010.
7 From "Fee Waybill Interview."
8 From "The Popdose Interview."
9 From "A Conversation with Michael Bolton," BMI.com.

CHAPTER SIXTY-SIX: Van Hagar.

1 From "Eddie Van Halen: Balancing Act" by David Wild, *Rolling Stone*, April 6, 1995.
2 From "Van Halen Without David Lee Roth: Can This Be Love?" by David Fricke, *Rolling Stone*, July 3, 1986.
3 From "It's Only Roth 'n' Roll," *Spin*, April 1986.
4 From "Van Halen Without David Lee Roth: Can This Be Love?"
5 From "Patty Smyth on Turning Down Van Halen" by Rachel Bradsky, *Stereogum*, July 23, 2020.
6 From "Sammy Hagar Interview: Diamond Dave, the Van Halens, and a Long Life in Rock" by Dave Everley, Classic Rock, October 16, 2020.
7 From "Unabridged, Original Transcript: Eddie Van Halen in Conversation" by Shaun Baxter, 1995.
8 From "Sammy Hagar Interview: Diamond Dave, the Van Halens, and a Long Life in Rock."
9 From "Sammy Hagar," *The Big Interview with Dan Rather*, AXS TV.
10 From "Sammy Hagar Interview: Diamond Dave, the Van Halens, and a Long Life in Rock."
11 From *Red: My Uncensored Life in Rock* by Sammy Hagar (It Books, 2011).
12 From "Sammy Hagar Interview: Diamond Dave, the Van Halens, and a Long Life in Rock."

CHAPTER SIXTY-SEVEN: Journey comes back together, breaks apart.

1 From *Don't Stop Believin'* by Jonathan Cain (Zondervan, 2018).
2 From *Don't Stop Believin'*.
3 From "Castles Burning: The Herbie Herbert Interview" by Matthew Carty, 2001.
4 From "Journey's Bassist Ross Valory Opens Up..." by Andy Greene, *Rolling Stone*, March 14, 2024.

5   From "Herbie Herbert: One Man's Journey" by Andrew McNeice, Melodic Rock, March 2008.

6   From "Neal Schon Interview on Journey's New Album" by Melissa Ruggieri, *USA Today*, July 8, 2022.

7   From "Herbie Herbert: One Man's Journey."

8   From "Steve Perry: A Legend Finds Peace" by Andrew McNeice, Melodic Rock, May 7, 2014.

9   From "Steve Perry: A Legend Finds Peace."

10   From "Foolish, Foolish Throat: A Q&A with Steve Perry" by Alex Pappademas, *GQ*, May 29, 2008.

11   From *Don't Stop Believin'*.

12   From "Foolish, Foolish Throat: A Q&A with Steve Perry."

13   From "Foolish, Foolish Throat: A Q&A with Steve Perry."

14   From "Foolish, Foolish Throat: A Q&A with Steve Perry."

15   From "Steve Perry," *The Big Interview with Dan Rather*, AXS TV, 2019.

16   From *Don't Stop Believin'*.

17   From "Foolish, Foolish Throat: A Q&A with Steve Perry."

18   From "Foolish, Foolish Throat: A Q&A with Steve Perry."

19   From "Castles Burning: The Herbie Herbert Interview."

CHAPTER SIXTY-EIGHT: Highway to the danger zone…

1   From "Phil Collins: My Life in 15 Songs" by Andy Greene, *Rolling Stone*, February 29, 2016.

2   From "The Soundtrack King Kenny Loggins Looks Back…" by Todd Gilchrist, A.V. Club, August 23, 2022.

3   From "How We Made 'Take My Breath Away'" by Dave Simpson, *Guardian*, November 16, 2020.

4   From "Remember *Top Gun's* 'Take My Breath Away' in 1986!…," The Shortlisted, April 1, 2022.

5   From "How We Made 'Take My Breath Away.'"

6   From "Remember *Top Gun's* 'Take My Breath Away' In 1986!…"

7   From "Berlin's Terri Nunn on 1986's 'Take My Breath Away'" by Lily Moayeri, *Spin*, July 4, 2023.

8   From "Berlin's Terri Nunn on 1986's 'Take My Breath Away.'"

9   From "Berlin's Terri Nunn on 1986's 'Take My Breath Away.'"

CHAPTER SEVENTY: A prayer for Bon Jovi

1   From "Jon Bon Jovi Interview," *PBS NewsHour*, April 27, 2024.

2   From "I'm the Poster Boy for Marriage" by Oliver Burkeman, *Guardian*, May 26, 2006.

CHAPTER SEVENTY-ONE: The big short.

1   From "'Mad? Some People Think So…' Tom Scholz: Boston's Reluctant Boffin" by Paul Elliott, Classic Rock, December 17, 2014.

2   From "Back Talk: Tom Scholz of Boston" by Mike Mettler, Sound & Vision, July/August 2008.

3   From "Classic Rock Revisited Presents an Exclusive Interview with… Brad Delp of Boston" by Jeb Wright, thirdstage.ca, July 2003.

4   From "March 1999 Interview" by Pär Winberg, archived at Melodic.net.

5   From "Patience Pays Off for Boston Fans" by Dennis Hunt, *Los Angeles Times*, July 19, 1987.

6   From "Interview with Fergie Frederiksen" by Mick Burgess, Metal Express Radio, December 29, 2011.

7   From "March 1999 Interview."

8   From "Tom Scholz Talks Influences…" by Jim Sullivan, thirdstage.ca, April 16, 2017.

9   From "'Take Me Home Tonight': The 1986 Comeback for Ronnie Spector and Eddie Money" by Tina Benitez-Eves, *American Songwriter*, March 21, 2024.

10   From "Back Talk: Tom Scholz of Boston."

11   From "Back Talk: Tom Scholz of Boston."

12   From "The Big Interviews: Barry Goudreau" by John Beaudin, Rock History Music, 2021.

13   From "Classic Rock Revisited Presents an Exclusive Interview with… Brad Delp of Boston."

14   From "Back Talk: Tom Scholz of Boston."

CHAPTER SEVENTY-TWO: Aerosmith makes *Permanent Vacation* and the Year of Rock.

1   From "Michael Bolton" by Sian Pattenden, *Smash Hits*, March 21, 1990.

2   From "Legacy: Paul Stanley" by Mark Blake, Classic Rock, July 16, 2014.

CHAPTER SEVENTY-THREE: In the still of the night.

1   From "And Then There Was One?" by Dante Bunutto, *Kerrang!*, April 2–15, 1987.

2   From "And Then There Was One?"

3   From "John Sykes Interview" by Malcolm Dome, *Rock Candy*, June–July 2017.

4   From "How David Coverdale Americanised Whitesnake" by Dom Lawson, Classic Rock, October 17, 2022.

5   From "John Sykes Interview."

6   From "How David Coverdale Americanised Whitesnake."

7   From "How David Coverdale Americanised Whitesnake."

8   From "John Sykes Interview."

9   Courtesy of Dave Ling.

10   From "John Sykes Interview."

11   From "John Sykes Interview."

12 From "John Sykes Interview."
13 From "How David Coverdale, Tawny Kitaen, and MTV Turned Whitesnake into Megastars" by Jon Hotten, Classic Rock, May 12, 2021.

CHAPTER SEVENTY-FOUR: Def Leppard pour some sugar on.

1 From "Behind-Scenes Drama Made Def Leppard's 'Hysteria' Live Up to Its Name," *Goldmine*, December 11, 2013.
2 From "Behind-Scenes Drama Made Def Leppard's 'Hysteria' Live Up to Its Name."
3 From "Jim Steinman: Melody Maker Interview" by Martin Kelly, Ultimate Classic Rock, April 8, 2021.
4 From "The Story of Def Leppard's Jim Steinman Sessions" by Paul Elliott, Classic Rock, April 8, 2021.
5 From "Jim Steinman: Melody Maker Interview."
6 From "Def Leppard's Rick Allen on the 1984 Corvette Accident That Took His Arm" by Jim Clash, *Forbes*, November 21, 2021.
7 From "Behind-Scenes Drama Made Def Leppard's 'Hysteria' Live Up to Its Name."
8 From "Def Leppard's Rick Allen on the 1984 Corvette Accident That Took His Arm."
9 From "Joe Elliott Remembers How He Reacted When Rick Allen Lost His Arm" by Rafael Polcaro, Rock and Roll Garage, January 13, 2020.
10 From "Behind-Scenes Drama Made Def Leppard's 'Hysteria' Live Up to Its Name."
11 From "Joe Elliott Remembers How He Reacted When Rick Allen Lost His Arm."
12 From "Def Leppard's Rick Allen on the 1984 Corvette Accident That Took His Arm."
13 From "Behind-Scenes Drama Made Def Leppard's 'Hysteria' Live Up to Its Name."
14 From "Behind-Scenes Drama Made Def Leppard's 'Hysteria' Live Up to Its Name."
15 From "We've Soaked into People's DNA: Joe Elliott of Def Leppard Speaks" by Aug Stone, *The Quietus*, September 25, 2013.
16 From "Behind-Scenes Drama Made Def Leppard's 'Hysteria' Live Up to Its Name."

CHAPTER SEVENTY-FIVE: End days.

1 From "Lou Gramm Interview on Early Years, Writing & Recording with Foreigner, and Career Highlights," Curtin Call, YouTube.
2 From "Lou Gramm: It's Urgent!" by Jeb Wright, Classic Rock Revisited.
3 From *Juke Box Hero: My Five Decades of Rock 'n' Roll* by Lou Gramm with Scott Pitoniak (Triumph Books, 2013).

4   From "Jimi Jamison: Reaching Out" by Nick Muller, Melodic Rock, August 6, 2007.
5   From "REO Speedwagon: We Thought Every Album Would Sell 10 Million Copies" by Paul Elliott, Classic Rock, November 22, 2019.
6   From "The Rise, Fall, and Porn-Assisted Resurrection of AOR Heroes Night Ranger" by Paul Elliott, Classic Rock, December 16, 2023.
7   From "REO Speedwagon: We Thought Every Album Would Sell 10 Million Copies."
8   From "The Rise, Fall, and Porn-Assisted Resurrection of AOR Heroes Night Ranger."
9   From "Trevor Rabin's Challenging Road to Yes" by Stephen Lamber, Prog, November 28, 2023.
10   From "Tony Kaye on His Years with Yes" by Andy Greene, *Rolling Stone*, February 11, 2021.
11   From "Trevor Rabin's Challenging Road to Yes."
12   From "Tony Kaye on His Years with Yes."
13   From "Out of the Garage: Ric Ocasek on Reuniting the Cars" by David Fricke, *Rolling Stone*, February 17, 2011.
14   From "Out of the Garage: Ric Ocasek on Reuniting the Cars."
15   From "Diane Warren: How I Wrote 'I Don't Want to Miss a Thing,' 'If I Could Turn Back Time' and 'Nothing's Gonna Stop Us Now'" by Dave Fawbert, Shortlist, July 26, 2016.

CHAPTER SEVENTY-SIX: Aftermath.
1   From "Cheap Trick," *The Big Interview with Dan Rather*, AXS TV, 2019.
2   From "Eddie Money: Rock's Rodney Dangerfield Endures" by Jason Newman, *Rolling Stone*, April 25, 2018.
3   From "REO Speedwagon: We Thought Every Album Would Sell 10 Million Copies" by Paul Elliott, Classic Rock, November 22, 2019.
4   From "Reo Speedwagon," *The Big Interview with Dan Rather*, AXS TV, 2019.
5   From "'The Audience Threw Lighters, Bottles, Ice Cubes and Coins. We Managed Four Songs Before Being Booed Off': The Rollercoaster Story of Loverboy" by Derek Oliver, Classic Rock, December 22, 2023.
6   From "Reo Speedwagon Will Dedicate Every Show to Late Guitarist Gary Richrath 'Probably Forever'" by Gary Graff, *Billboard*, September 17, 2015.
7   From "A Note from Kevin Cronin," REOSpeedwagon.com, January 20, 2016.
8   From "Steve Perry Still Believes" by Andy Greene, *Rolling Stone*, October 5, 2018.
9   From "A Conversation with Jonathan Cain" by Michael Cavacini, MichaelCavacini.com, July 5, 2014.
10   From "Steve Perry," *The Big Interview with Dan Rather*, AXS TV, 2019.

CHAPTER SEVENTY-SEVEN: Resurrection.

1 From "Journey's 'Don't Stop Believin' Becomes Second Ever Classic Tune to Reach One Billion Spotify Streams" by Naomi Ackerman, *London Evening Standard*, February 26, 2021.

2 From "Journey's 'Don't Stop Believin" Is Officially the Biggest Song of All Time," *Forbes*, January 3, 2024.

3 From "'The Sopranos' Creator David Chase Finally Explained Tony's Fate" by Brady Langmann, *Esquire*, November 3, 2021.

4 From "The Most Joyous and Romantic of Journey According to Neal Schon" by Devon Ivie, *Vulture*, July 5, 2022.

5 From "David Chase Breaks Down the Final Scene of 'The Sopranos'" by John Hendrickson, *Esquire*, October 1, 2021.

6 From "Steve Perry," *The Big Interview with Dan Rather*, AXS TV, 2019.

7 From "David Chase Breaks Down the Final Scene of 'The Sopranos.'"

8 From "Foolish, Foolish Throat: A Q&A with Steve Perry" by Alex Pappademas, *GQ*, May 29, 2008.

9 From "'The Sopranos' David Chase on His Favourite Scenes From the Show" by Ben Travis, Empire, March 14, 2024.

10 From "The Most Joyous and Romantic of Journey According to Neal Schon."

11 From "'When The Sopranos Used It, My Phone Blew Up': Journey on Don't Stop Believin' Culture" by Henry Yates, *Guardian*, August 5, 2024.

12 From "'When The Sopranos Used It, My Phone Blew Up': Journey on Don't Stop Believin' Culture."

13 From Instagram post by Steve Perry, March 19, 2024.

14 From "Kansas on Reviving 'Letfoverture'" by Steve Smith, *Rolling Stone*, September 8, 2016.

15 From "Lou Gramm—Foreigner," interviewed by Paul Stephenson, *VRP Rocks—Classic Rock Interviews*, Apple Podcasts, April 8, 2024.

16 From "'Mad? Some People Think So...' Tom Scholz: Boston's Reluctant Boffin" by Paul Elliott, Classic Rock, December 17, 2014.

17 From "'When The Sopranos Used It, My Phone Blew Up': Journey on Don't Stop Believin' Culture."

18 From "Sammy Hagar Interview: Diamond Dave, the Van Halens, and a Long Life in Rock" by Dave Everley, Classic Rock, October 16, 2020.

INDEX

Abacab, 297
ABBA, 204, 398
Abbey Road, 149
Abrams, Lee, 3, 48, 49, 50, 52, 58, 190, 191
AC/DC, 79, 208, 234, 281
Adams, Bryan, 180–86, 268–71, 327, 345–49, 403, 443–45, 452, 455; *Cuts Like a Knife*, 270–71, 345; early music influences, 11, 14, 180–81; and Mutt Lange, 260, 261; *Reckless*, 345–49, 443–44; soundtracks, 392
Adams, Conrad, 180
Aerosmith, 416–21, 432–33
"Africa," 2, 5, 6, 234–35, 238, 332, 452
Against All Odds (movie), 392
Agent Provocateur, 350–55, 436
Agents of Fortune, 72
Ahern, Paul, 54, 58
Airey, Don, 135, 202
Alien Project, 108–9
Allen, Bruce, 203, 269, 271
Allen, Rick, 431–32
Allman Brothers, 119, 147
"All Right Now," 63
"Alone," 436
Alpha, 296
Anderson, Jon, 299, 439
Andes, Mark, 294
"Angel," 419
Animalize, 323–24
Animals, the, 49
"Any Way You Want It," 167–68
AOR (album-oriented rock), 2–6, 49
Armstrong, Neil, 223
Arquette, Rosanna, 232
Art of Noise, 326

Asher, Dick, 190
Asia, 241–45, 296–300
"Ask the Lonely," 273
Audio Visions, 175
Axis: Bold as Love, 167
Azoff, Irving, 19–20, 21, 292, 332

"Babe," 159–61
"Baby Hold On to Me," 90
Babys, the, 70, 91, 120–22, 168–69, 253, 360
Bach, Barbara, 410
Bachman Turner Overdrive, 186, 303
Bad Animals, 436
Bad Attitude, 399–400
Bad Company, 146, 398
Baird, Mike, 46–47, 200–201, 203, 205, 253, 316, 384–90, 410, 412, 420
Baker, Roy Thomas, 5, 75, 111, 140–41, 308, 376
Balin, Marty, 366–67
Ballard, Russ, 136–37, 202, 205
Banks, Tony, 298, 299
Barbata, John, 366–67
Barber, Bill, 158, 405
"Barracuda," 83–84
Barry Goudreau, 172–73
Bat Out of Hell, 145, 325, 430
"Beat It," 238, 289, 290
Beatles, the, 11–13, 14, 26, 49, 155–56, 189
Beat Street, 269–70
Bébé le Strange, 171
Beck, Jeff, 60–61, 72, 305, 410
Bee Gees, 326
"Be Good to Yourself," 387
Bella Donna, 315

Belushi, John, 154
Benatar, Pat, 162–65, 252, 255, 324, 327, 377; *Crimes of Passion*, 173, 175; "Love Is a Battlefield," 288–90; MTV, 223–24; *Seven the Hard Way*, 374–75
Benjamin, Richard, 401
Bent Out of Shape, 284
Berlin, 392–93
Bernstein, Cliff, 225, 261–62
"Best Days of My Life," 347
Bickler, Dave, 151, 152, 248, 328
"Big Beat, The," 178
"Billie Jean," 236
"Birthday Blues," 15
Blackjack, 144–49, 281
Blackjack, 147–48
Blackmore, Ritchie, 134–38, 202, 254, 283, 424–25
Black Sabbath, 61
Black Sheep, 64–65
Blackwood, Nina, 324–25
Blades, Jack, 282, 284, 285, 287, 438
Blair, Lou, 183
"Blue Collar Man," 119–20
Blue Öyster Cult, 61, 72, 197, 198, 321
"Bohemian Rhapsody," 140, 449
Bolan, Marc, 12
Bolton, Michael, 144–49, 281, 304, 376, 394–95, 420
Bon Jovi, Jon, 5, 303–6, 325, 375, 403–8, 443, 445
Bonnet, Graham, 135–38, 202
Bono, 105
Boogie Nights (movie), 287
Booker T. and the M.G.'s, 39
Boomtown Rats, 114
Boston, 78, 128, 172–74; *Don't Look Back*, 113, 115, 116; follow-ups, 113–17; formation of, 4–5, 38–43; signing of, 54–62; *Third Stage*, 409–15; touring, 86–89, 117; woes of, 291–94
Boston, 3–4, 55, 58–62, 397

Botnick, Bruce, 89
Bowie, David, 12, 289, 315, 320, 399
Boylan, John, 55, 57, 229
"Boys of Summer," 5, 335–37, 338
Bratta, Vito, 398, 400–402
Breakfast in America, 148
"Break It Up," 207–8
"Bringin' On the Heartbreak," 197, 225
Brock, Tony, 121
"Broken Heart," 398
"Broken Promises," 331
"Broken Wings," 376
Bruckheimer, Jerry, 392–93
Bryan Adams, 186
Bryan, David, 305, 445
Buckingham, Lindsey, 114, 175
Buddy Miles Express, 44
Building the Perfect Beast, 334
Burgi, Chuck, 50, 281–86, 376–78
"Burundi Black," 432
Busey, Gary, 154

Cafaro, Al, 51, 116, 429, 443; Boston, 58; Bryan Adams, 270–71, 348; Giant, 446–47; MTV, 321; Mutt Lange, 423; Styx, 95, 161, 279–80
Cain, Jonathan, 1–3, 316, 420, 448; the Babys, 121, 168–69; Journey, 213–17, 273–77, 384–90, 451
"Calley Oh," 179
Callner, Marty, 363
Campbell, Glenn, 339–41
Campbell, Mike, 335
Campbell, Vivian, 427
Canada, 180–86
"Can't Fight This Feeling," 342–44
Can't Hold Back, 410
Can't Wait, 177
Carlos, Bun E., 91–92
Carmassi, Denny, 69–70, 294, 361–65, 436–38, 448
Carmichael, James, 309
"Carry On Wayward Son," 73, 453

Index

Cars, the, 308–12, 429, 439–40
Carter, John, 204–5, 270, 271, 347
"Casey Jones," 39–40
Casey, Steve, 51
Cat Women of the Moon (movie), 163
Caught in the Game, 328
Cetera, Peter, 240, 243, 311, 411
"Chain Gang," 10
Champlin, Bill, 234, 270; Chicago, 240–44, 307–12, 411, 412, 415; David Foster, 201, 204, 240–43, 307–12; Pat Benatar, 289–90; Toto, 47, 104
"Change" (Waite), 255–56
"Changes" (Rabin), 297
Chapman, Mike, 163, 165, 288, 289, 290, 326
Charles, Ray, 44
Chase (band), 151
Chase, David, 450–51
Cheap Trick, 79, 91–92, 92, 131–33
Cheap Trick at Budokan, 133
Cher, 44–45, 441
Chertoff, Rick, 335
Chicago, 240–45, 245, 307–12
Chicago 16, 242, 243
Child, Desmond, 266, 441, 453; Aerosmith, 417–20; Bon Jovi, 403–7; early music influences, 14–15; Kiss, 155–58, 323–24, 374–75; Pat Benatar and "Love Is a Battlefield," 288–90; "You Give Love a Bad Name," 403–4, 453
Chouinard, Bobby, 178
Clapton, Eric, 13, 20, 21, 72, 147, 305
Clark, Dick, 237
Clarkin, Tony, 74
Clark, Steve, 431
Clearmountain, Bob, 348
Cobain, Kurt, 198–99
Cobra, 329
Cocker, Joe, 44, 64, 70
"Cold as Ice," 75–76
Collen, Phil, 259, 260, 262–63, 429–34

Collins, Phil, 296–97, 298, 300, 392
Collins, Tim, 417, 420
Colvin, Shawn, 13
"Come Sail Away," 95
Completion Backward Principle, The, 201
Cooke, Sam, 10
Cooper, Alice, 70–71
Corby, Mike, 120–21
Cornerstone, 159
Costello, Elvis, 201
Cougar, Johnny, 141
Coverdale, David, 422–28
Crawford, John, 392–93
Crazy Nights, 421
"Crazy on You," 34
Cream, 49
Creedence Clearwater Revival, 14
Crewe, Bob, 289, 290, 404
Crimes of Passion, 173, 175
Cronin, Kevin, 71–72, 87, 119, 187–92, 265, 438, 445, 447; "Can't Fight This Feeling," 342–44; formation of REO, 20–21, 23–24; "Keep On Loving You," 189–90, 192; MTV, 221, 225
Cropper, Steve, 103
Cruise, Tom, 392
"Crying in the Rain," 425
Crystal Ball, 71–72, 93–96
"Crystal Ball," 26, 71, 72
Curulewski, John, 25
Cuts Like a Knife, 270–71, 345

Daisley, Bob, 134, 137
Danger Zone, 172
"Danger Zone," 392–93
Dark Side of the Moon, The, 118–19, 129, 452
Davidson, John, 115
Davis, Clive, 297
Davis, Miles, 414, 415
Davis, Sammy, Jr., 44
Dawn Patrol, 282

Index

Dean, Jimmy, 10
Dean, Paul, 183–86, 196–97, 199, 203
"Death Alley Driver," 254
Deep Purple, 14, 20, 134, 135, 282, 285–86, 396, 397, 423, 424
Def Leppard, 5, 59, 195–99, 257–63, 429–34, 446, 455
Delp, Brad, 5, 39–40, 41–42, 55–56, 60, 86–87, 115, 172–73, 410–11, 415
Departure, 166, 275, 384
Derosier, Mike, 81, 83, 125, 251
Derringer, Rick, 163
Deserters, the, 29–30
"Desert Moon," 332–33, 340–41
DeVilliers, Paul, 439
DeYoung, Dennis, 122, 159–61, 264, 267, 449, 455; *Crystal Ball*, 71, 72, 93–97; *Dune* (movie), 332–33, 340; early music influences, 11, 14, 17–19; Foreigner, 78, 79; formation of Styx, 17–19, 24–26, 61; *The Grand Illusion*, 93–96, 118–19; *Kilroy Was Here*, 278–80, 339–41; *Paradise Theatre*, 196; *Pieces of Eight*, 118, 119–20, 159–61; surge of Styx, 118–20
Diamond, Neil, 47
Dickinson, Angie, 217
Diddley, Bo, 231–32
Difficult to Cure, 202
Dion, Celine, 439
"Dirty Laundry," 236
"Dirty White Boy," 141
"Disco Inferno," 111
Diver Down, 233, 397–98
Dog and Butterfly, 123–25
Dolby, Thomas, 208–11, 257–63, 351–52
Donaldson, Betty, 346
Done with Mirrors, 416–17
"(Don't Fear) the Reaper," 72–73
"Don't Give Up On Us," 78
"Don't Let Me Down," 189
Don't Look Back, 113, 115, 116
Don't Say No, 196

"Don't Stop Believin'," 2, 3, 5, 6, 215–16, 217, 449–52, 455
"Don't Stop Now," 414
Doobie Brothers, 79, 103–4
Door to Door, 440
Double Vision, 113–17, 139–40, 143–44
"Double Vision," 80
Doughty, Neal, 19, 87–88, 187–92, 252, 265, 343–44
Douglas, Jimmy, 77
Dowd, Tom, 147
Downes, Geoff, 241, 244, 245
Down to Earth, 134–35
Down Two Then Left, 46
Drastic Measures, 281, 284
Dreamboat Annie, 33, 35, 361
"Dream Police," 91–92
"Dreams," 382
Dries, Dennis, 53, 167, 168, 217, 277, 396
"Drive," 310, 311
Droubay, Marc, 153
"Dude (Looks Like a Lady)," 418–19
Dunaway, Barry, 377
Dunbar, Aynsley, 109, 426, 428
Dune (movie), 332–33, 340
Dunn, Donald "Duck," 103
"Dust in the Wind," 88

Eagles, the, 5, 24, 60, 79, 103, 235–36, 337, 397
Easton, Elliot, 140–41, 308–12, 317, 320, 439–40
Edmonds, Bill, 176–77
Ehart, Phil, 22–23, 23, 73, 74, 172, 175, 253, 453
Einstein, Sandy, 282–83
Elefante, John, 15, 23, 253, 254, 256, 281, 283–86, 292, 318
Elliott, Dennis, 64, 77, 206, 207–8
Elliott, Joe, 12, 59, 195–99, 257–63, 260, 429–34, 442, 455
Elliott, Paul: Bon Jovi, 403; Boston, 59, 60, 291–92, 414; Bryan Adams, 347;

Def Leppard, 257–58; Foreigner, 353; Jim Peterik, 249; Journey, 217; Pat Benatar, 162, 165; REO Speedwagon, 343; Steve Perry, 315; Toto, 232, 237
Ellis, Don, 108–9
Ellis, Stephan, 153
Elson, Kevin, 215, 284–85, 400
Emerick, Geoff, 237
Emerson, Lake & Palmer, 66, 107, 110, 241
Emotions in Motion, 252
"Endlessly," 376
Ennis, Sue, 295
Entwistle, John, 410
Equinox, 25, 95
Ertegun, Ahmet, 325–26, 354, 398, 435
"Eruption," 379
Escape, 1–2, 213–19, 272–75, 277
Estevez, Emilio, 372
Europe, 396–402
Everly Brothers, 13
Everybody's Crazy, 376
"Every Time I Think of You," 91, 325
Evolution, 152–53, 275
Eye of the Tiger, 248–49, 328–29
"Eye of the Tiger," 249, 329
"Eyes of the World," 438
Ezrin, Bob, 70–71

Fahrenheit, 409–10, 414, 415
Fairbairn, Bruce, 59, 152, 181–82, 186, 417, 420
"Faithfully," 275
Fandango, 202
Fawcett, Farrah, 362–63
"Feeling All Right," 63
"Feels Like the First Time," 64–66, 77–78
Feldman, Sam, 181
Feusi, Suzanne, 122, 159–61
Fight to Survive, 400
Filipetti, Frank, 350

"Final Countdown, The," 399–402, 407
Fire of Unknown Origin, 198
Fisher, Mike, 29–37, 60, 82–85, 124–27, 171, 361
Fisher, Roger, 29–37, 60, 81, 83, 84, 124–27
Fitzgerald, Ella, 87
5150, 381–83, 416
Flashdance (movie), 391–92
Fleetwood Mac, 60, 79, 103, 114, 177
Fleischman, Robert, 106–9
Flicker, Mike, 33–34, 35, 37, 123, 250
Flock of Seagulls, 222
Fogelberg, Dan, 20
Foghat, 61
"Fooling Yourself," 94–95
"Foolish Heart," 314
"Fool on the Hill," 11
Footloose (movie), 333, 392
Foreigner, 4, 75–80, 113–17, 139–43, 147–48, 284, 437, 448; *Agent Provocateur*, 350–55, 436; *Double Vision*, 113–17, 139–40, 143–44; formation of, 66–67; *4* (album), 2–3, 5, 206–12, 351–52, 398, 453; *Head Games*, 140–43; induction into Rock and Roll Hall of Fame, 454; *Inside Information*, 436–37; and Toto, 128, 130
Foreigner, 75–80
Fossen, Steve, 29–37, 80, 81–85, 123–27, 171, 250–52, 361–62
Foster, David, 5, 116, 307–12, 375, 376; Chicago, 240–45, 307–12; John Parr, 371–72; Kansas, 282; Rick Springfield, 201, 203–4
4, 2–3, 5, 207–12, 351–52, 398, 453
461 Ocean Boulevard, 147
Frampton Comes Alive!, 53, 58
Frampton, Peter, 20, 139, 148
Frankie and the Knockouts, 305
Franklin, Aretha, 10, 75, 352
Fraser, Mike, 186

Frederiksen, Fergie, 330–31, 332, 409–10, 411
Free (band), 63
Freud, Sigmund, 218
"Friday on My Mind," 432
Frontiers, 273, 275, 276, 277
Frumious Bandersnatch, 21

Gabriel, Peter, 298, 318, 368
Gagliardi, Ed, 64, 139–40
Game, The, 196
Gang, James, 40
Garland, Judy, 12
Garland, Les, 51–53, 190–91, 363, 391, 442; Billy Squier, 318–21; Foreigner, 78; Jefferson Starship, 366–70; "'Mr. Roboto," 280; MTV, 220–25, 318–21; Toto, 132
Gatica, Humberto, 244, 308
Geffen, David, 229, 230, 253, 292, 422, 423, 426, 427
Genesis, 296–97, 298
Gennaro, Sandy, 146
"Georgy Porgy," 150
Get Nervous, 252
Giant, 446–47
Gilmour, David, 139
Giraldi, Bob, 290
Giraldo, Neil, 164–65, 175, 201, 253, 289, 377
Girl (band), 259
"Girl Is Mine, The," 237
Girls with Guns, 340
Glaub, Bobby, 313
Glee (TV show), 451
Glitter, Gary, 12
Glixman, Jeff, 23, 73–74, 88–89, 175
Glover, Roger, 134–38, 202, 285
Goldberg, Julian, 222
Goodrum, Randy, 313–15
Good Trouble, 252
Gottfried, Joe, 200
Goudreau, Barry, 292, 415; *Barry Goudreau*, 172–73; Boston, 55, 57, 60–62; departure from Boston, 172–75, 324; *Don't Look Back*, 113, 115, 116; formation of Boston, 38–42; *Orion the Hunter*, 324, 327; touring, 60–61, 86–87
Graham, Bill, 22, 80, 225
Grammatico, Benie, 65
Gramm, Lou, 104, 148, 163, 376, 426, 435–37, 454; *Agent Provocateur*, 350–55; Black Sheep, 64–65; *Double Vision*, 114–16; early music influences, 13; *Foreigner*, 76–80; formation of Foreigner, 65–67; *4* (album), 206–12; *Head Games*, 140–43; *Inside Information*, 436–37; *Ready or Not*, 435–36
Grand Illusion, The, 93–96, 118–19
Grateful Dead, the, 15, 39–40, 275
Gratzer, Alan, 19, 20, 23–24
Grease (movie), 111
Greenberg, Jerry, 66–67
Green, Nigel, 430
"Green Onions," 39–40
Greenwood, Al, 64, 206–7, 376
Grierson, Don, 359, 360, 361, 438
Grombacher, Myron, 164–65
Guns N' Roses, 179, 443

Hagar, Sammy, 68–70, 172–73, 253, 254, 381–83, 426, 455
Hall, Bruce, 15, 119, 188–89, 265, 343
Hamilton, Susan, 394–95
Hammer, Jan, 219
Hanks, Tom, 400–401
Hansen, Rick, 372
"Harden My Heart," 228–29, 230
"Hard Habit to Break," 310
"Hard to Say I'm Sorry," 244
Harrison, George, 155–56
Hashian, Sibby, 38, 54–56
Haslip, Jimmy, 144–49
Hawkes, Greg, 440
Head First, 120–21
Head Games, 140–43

Heart, 60, 81–85, 436–38, 454; affairs of, 123–27; *Bad Animals*, 436; *Bébé le Strange*, 171; *Dog and Butterfly*, 123–25; *Dreamboat Annie*, 33, 35, 361; formation of, 30–37; induction into Rock and Roll Hall of Fame, 454; *Little Queen*, 82–85, 361; *Magazine*, 82, 84; *Private Audition*, 250–52, 294; reinvention and resurrection, 359–65; woes of, 291–94
Heartbeat City, 308, 310–12, 439–40
"Heartbreaker," 165
"Heart's Done Time," 419
"Heat of the Moment," 244, 262
"Heaven," 348–49
"Heaven's on Fire," 323–24
Hefner, Hugh, 45
Helm, Levon, 149
Hendrix, Jimi, 13, 15, 49, 72, 110, 167, 240
Henley, Don, 5, 235–36, 238, 334–38, 414
Herbert, Herbie: Journey, 21–22, 106–12, 152, 166–70, 215, 217–19, 273, 275, 276, 385–87, 390; Kansas, 282–87; Steve Perry, 315–16
"Here I Go Again," 425, 427
"Higher Power," 294
High 'n' Dry, 195–96, 257–58, 430
Hi Infidelity, 2–3, 187–89, 192, 252
"Hold the Line," 129–30, 132, 153
Holland, Dave, 400
Holly, Buddy, 10
Horn, Trevor, 75, 298, 299–300, 350, 351, 439
"Hot Blooded," 80, 114–15
Hotel California, 60, 79, 292, 434
"Hot Fun in the Summertime," 129–30
Houston, Whitney, 304
Howard, James Newton, 233
Howe, Steve, 241, 243, 296
Huff, Dan, 447
"Human Nature," 236–38

Hungate, David, 45, 46, 103, 105, 130, 234, 235
Hunger, The, 420
Hunter, Ian, 75
Hydra, 153–54
Hyman, Rob, 335, 336, 338
Hysteria, 5, 429, 433, 455

I Can't Stand Still, 235
Ides of March, 15, 150–51
"I Didn't Mean to Stay All Night," 446
"If Looks Could Kill," 360
Ignition, 253
"I'll Be There," 15
"I'm Cryin'," 166
I'm Only Fooling Myself, 438
Independence Day (movie), 294
"India Was the Town That I Was Born In," 14
Indiscreet, 400
Inside Information, 436–37
In the Heat of the Night, 165
Into the Fire, 443–45
Iovine, Jimmy, 250–51
Iron Eagle (movie), 438
"Isn't It Time?," 91
Isolation, 330–31
"It's Only Love," 347–48
"I Want to Hold Your Hand," 11
"I Want to Know What Love Is," 3, 352–55, 452–53
"I Want You to Want Me," 91–92
"I Was Made for Loving You," 155–58
"I Won't Hold You Back," 233

Jackson Five, 15
Jackson, Michael, 5, 236–38, 289, 290, 315, 321
Jackson, Randy, 388
Jagger, Mick, 320, 436
Jamison, Jimi, 248, 329, 331, 437
"Jane," 367
Jay-Z, 149
Jefferson Airplane, 370

Jefferson Starship, 366–70, 440–41, 446
"Jessie's Girl," 203, 205, 253
J. Geils Band, 9–10, 368
Joel, Billy, 76, 350
John, Elton, 12–13, 72, 132, 229, 233, 253, 305
Johnson, Dennis, 151
Jones, Grace, 351
Jones, Kenney, 45–46
Jones, Mick, 139–43, 446–47; *Agent Provocateur*, 350–55, 436, 452–53; *Double Vision*, 113–17, 139–40, 143–44; early music influences, 10; *Foreigner*, 75–80; formation of Foreigner, 65–67, 66–67; *4* (album), 2–3, 5, 206–12, 351–52, 398, 453; *Head Games*, 140–43; induction of Foreigner, 454; *Inside Information*, 436–37; Spooky Tooth, 63–65, 78; Van Halen, 381–83
Jones, Mike, 435–37
Jones, Quincy, 236–38
Jones Road, 227–28
Joplin, Janis, 14, 15, 30–31
Journey, 1–3, 4, 284, 446–47; comes back together and breaks apart, 384–90; *Departure*, 166, 275, 384; *Escape*, 1–2, 213–19, 272–75, 277; *Evolution*, 152–53, 275; finding missing link, 166–70; formation of, 21–23; *Frontiers*, 273, 275–77; induction into Rock and Roll Hall of Fame, 454; *Raised on Radio*, 385–90; resurrection of, 449–52; Steve Perry joins, 106–12
Judas Priest, 107, 400
"Juke Box Hero," 208
"Jump Street," 45–46
"Just One Night," 378

Kalodner, John, 16, 192, 264, 267, 452, 453; Aerosmith, 417–20; Asia, 241, 242, 244–45, 300; Bon Jovi, 305, 407; Boston, 58–59, 293–94; Cher, 441; Foreigner, 66–67, 75–77, 139–43, 140–43; Journey, 170, 213–14, 272–73, 275; Quarterflash, 230; Sammy Hagar, 70, 253, 381–82; Steve Perry, 315–16, 448; Survivor, 151–52; *Top Gun* (movie), 392–93; Whitesnake, 422–28
Kansas, 22–24, 53, 74, 88, 172, 175, 253, 254, 281–87
Kant, Hal, 216–17
Kantner, Paul, 366–67
Kath, Terry, 240
Kaye, Tony, 297–300, 439
Keagy, Kelly, 284, 285, 377
Keenlyside, Tom, 181–82
"Keep On Loving You," 189–90, 192
Keltner, Jim, 130
Kicks, 176
Kid Courage, 282–83
Kilroy Was Here, 278–80, 339–40
Kimball, Bobby, 412; Kansas, 282; Prism, 269–70; Toto, 104–5, 130–31, 154, 265–67, 328–29
Kinnear, Ken, 126–27
Kipner, Steve, 310
Kirke, Simon, 398
Kirshner, Don, 23, 74
Kiss, 145, 155–58, 306, 323–24, 374–75, 403–4, 421
Kleber, Mick, 364
Knee Deep in the Hoopla, 366–69
Knight, Gladys, 10
Knight, Holly, 288–89
Kortchmar, Danny, 218, 292, 307, 377, 380, 453; Bon Jovi, 403–4, 407; Don Henley, 235–36, 334–38; Styx, 279; Toto, 44–46, 101, 235–36
Kulick, Bruce, 376, 443; Aerosmith, 420–21; Billy Squier, 177–79; Blackjack, 144–49; Kiss, 323–24, 374–75
"Kyrie," 376

"Lady," 19, 24–26, 160
"Lady Marmalade," 289
Lambert, Dennis, 368
Lamm, Robert, 243–44, 308–9, 310
Landau, David, 156
Landau, Jon, 156
Landau, Michael, 313
Lane, Brian, 241, 399
Lange, Robert John "Mutt," 5, 6, 446; the Cars, 307–12; Def Leppard, 195–96, 197, 199, 257–63, 429–30, 432–34; Foreigner, 114, 207–11, 350
Lap of Luxury, 444
Larson, Laurie, 51, 53, 191–92
Last of the Runaways, 446
Lauper, Cyndi, 5, 334–38
Lawrence, Martin, 304
Led Zeppelin, 15–16, 31, 32, 66, 72, 79, 92, 95, 146, 396
Leese, Howard, 33–34, 362
Leftoverture, 73, 74
Lennon, John, 12–13, 169, 229, 243, 253, 289
Le Roux, 330
"Let Me Take You Dancing," 186
"Let Me Take You Home Tonight," 55
Lewis, Phil, 259
Linn, Roger, 234
Lippman, Michael, 360
LiPuma, Tommy, 414
"Little Miss Intent," 177
Little Queen, 82–85, 361
Little Richard, 212
"Live and Let Die," 233
Live from Earth, 288
Livgren, Kerry, 23, 72–74, 88, 253, 254, 284, 285
"Livin' on a Prayer," 3, 404–7, 453
Loggins, Kenny, 103, 392
Loizzo, Gary, 160
Londin, Larrie, 313, 386–87, 388
"Long, Long Way from Home," 65
Loughnane, Lee, 242
Love Among the Cannibals, 446

"Love Bites," 433
Love Bomb, 375
"Love Is a Battlefield," 288–90
Loverboy, 183, 186, 203, 225, 230, 377, 404
"Lovin', Touchin', Squeezin'," 167–68
Lowe, Rob, 373
"Lucille," 212
Lukather, Steve, 1, 292, 293, 308, 312, 377, 447, 449, 451, 452; Chicago, 242; early music influences, 10–11, 13; Foreigner, 116; MTV, 226, 320–22; Toto, 43–47, 101–5, 128–33, 150–54, 191, 197–99, 231–39, 264–67, 328–33, 379, 391–94, 409–15, 455–56; the Tubes, 201, 203–4, 282, 286
Lynch, David, 332–33
Lynch, Stan, 377
Lynn, Cheryl, 129
Lynne, Jeff, 196
Lynott, Phil, 305

Mabel, 396–97
McCartney, Linda, 237
McCartney, Paul, 12–13, 46, 233, 237, 243
McDonald, Ian, 64, 76, 140, 206
McDonald, Michael, 103–4
McGhee, Doc, 306
McGillis, Kelly, 392
McKenzie, Charlie, 54
McLuhan, Marshall, 224
McNeice, Andrew, 195, 212, 255, 293, 337–38, 386, 416, 433
Machine Head, 14
Mack, Reinhold, 196, 255
Mad Dogs and Englishmen, 44
Made in Europe, 397
Madness, 222
Madonna, 327
Magazine, 82, 84
Magical Mystery Tour, 11–12
"Magic Man," 35

Mailer, Norman, 269
Mallaber, Gary, 89
"Man in Motion," 372–73
Mann, Michael, 391
Mariah (band), 151
Marley, Bob, 351
Marotta, Ricky, 377
Martin, Eric, 315, 380, 413, 438–39; early music influences, 13–14; Eric Martin Band, 282–87, 377, 378; Foreigner, 78–79, 354; Journey, 21, 22, 108, 385
Martin, Frederick, 14–15
Martin, George, 237
Martunes, 438–39
Masdea, Jim, 39, 40, 41, 54–57, 411
Mason, Dave, 149
May, Brian, 196
Mayfield, Curtis, 110
Meat Loaf, 145, 325–27, 399–400
Mensch, Peter, 262, 431
Mercury, Freddie, 2, 23
Miami Vice (TV show), 391
"Midnight Blue," 350–51
Millar, Adrian, 69, 70
Miller, Steve, 89
"Miss America," 94
"Missing You," 324–25, 327
Mr. Mister, 330, 375–76
"Mr. Roboto," 279–80
"Mistral Wind," 124
"Mistreated," 135
Mitchell, Joni, 227
Mitchell, Lindsay, 204
Mitchell, Mitch, 167
Modern Times, 367
"Money," 122
Money, Eddie, 89–91, 133, 173–74, 225, 412, 444
Money Pit (movie), 400–401
Monroe, Ally, 182–83
Montrose, Ronnie, 68–70, 111–12
Moody, Mickey, 135
Moore, Demi, 372–73

"More More More," 144
"More Than a Feeling," 3, 41, 56–59
Moroder, Giorgio, 196, 392–94
Morris, Doug, 221, 325
Morrison, George Ivan "Van," 209
Moss, Jerry, 65
"Mother, Father," 214
Mother's Milk, 40–41
Mott the Hoople, 23
"Move Over," 30–31
Mraz, Barry, 151–52
MTV, 222–26, 255–56, 276, 283, 317–22, 362, 364
"Mull of Kintyre," 78
Muni, Scott, 77–78
Murray, Neil, 422–28
My Aim Is True, 201
"My Sharona," 141

"Naughty Naughty," 326–27, 371–72
Nazareth, 35
Neil, Vince, 418–19
"Never," 363
Nevison, Ron, 5, 91, 121, 152, 174, 247, 330, 359–61, 421
New Jersey, 443, 445
Newton-John, Olivia, 310, 321
New York Dolls, 176
Next, 106
Nicks, Stevie, 114, 315, 321, 377
Nielsen, Rick, 13, 91–92, 131–33, 173–75, 444
"Night Moves," 347
Night Ranger, 282, 286–87, 377, 438
90125, 297, 299, 300, 350, 439
1987, 424–25, 428
Nine on a Ten Scale, 70
Nolan, Jerry, 176
Nolan, Kenny, 289
"Nothing's Gonna Stop Us Now," 440–41
Nugent, Ted, 70, 114
Nunn, Terri, 393–94
Nyro, Laura, 15, 31

Ocasek, Ric, 308–9, 439–40
Offord, Eddie, 149, 178
Offspring, 253–54
"Oh Sherrie," 314–15, 316
Oliver, Derek, 48, 54, 57, 78, 217, 446
Olsen, Keith, 5, 114, 116, 200, 294, 426
"Once You Love Somebody," 385
"Only the Young," 273
On the Edge, 169
On Through the Night, 195
"Open Arms," 2, 215, 275
Orion the Hunter, 324, 327
Ostin, Mo, 382–83
"out of the box add," 132
Outside Inside, 282
Overland, Steve, 52, 189–90, 397–401, 404, 405, 407
Overnight Angels, 75
"Owner of a Lonely Heart," 297, 299, 300

Padgham, Hugh, 50, 296–300
Page, Jimmy, 5, 13, 163, 212
Page, Martin, 367–68
Page, Richard, 330, 375–76
Paich, David, 289; Foreigner, 116; Toto, 43–47, 101–5, 128–33, 150–54, 199, 231–38, 328, 329–33, 392, 393, 410, 413–15, 452; Van Halen, 379–80
Paich, Marty, 43–44, 116
Palmer, Carl, 241, 243, 298
Panozzo, Chuck, 17–18
Panozzo, John, 17–19
Paradise Theatre, 196
Parker, Graham, 114
Parker, Ray, Jr., 46–47
Parr, John, 50, 224, 238–39, 325–27, 332, 371–73, 453
Pasqua, Alan, 89–90, 254, 255, 308, 382
Passionworks, 294–95, 359
Pat Travers Band, 146
Payne, Bruce, 136, 286

"Peace of Mind," 41
Pearlman, Sandy, 198
Permanent Vacation, 417–20
Perry, Joe, 416–21, 417–18
Perry, Richard, 128–29, 289
Perry, Steve, 1–3, 5, 152, 258, 315, 448; early music influences, 9–10, 13; *Escape*, 1–2, 213–19, 272–77; finding missing link, 166–70; goes solo, 313–16; joins Journey, 108–12; *Raised on Radio*, 384–90; resurrection, 450–51; *Street Talk*, 313–16, 386
Perry, Tom, 46
Peterik, Jim, 10, 15–16, 61, 150–54, 246–49, 264, 328–33, 444
Petersson, Tom, 131, 173, 175
Phillips, Ricky, 121–22, 330
"Photograph," 261–62
"Physical," 310, 321
Pieces of Eight, 118, 119–20, 159–61
Pierce, John, 201
Pierce, Tim, 101–5, 108–9, 133, 253, 255, 304–6, 330, 390, 442
Pinnick, Chris, 243
Piper, 62, 177–78
Pittman, Bob, 50, 51, 220–26, 280, 317–20, 363, 391–92
Plant, Robert, 32, 163, 212
Playing for Keeps, 174
"Please Hold On," 309–10
Point of Know Return, 88
Police, the, 201, 222
Popovic, Steve, 59–60
Porcaro, Jeff, 43–47, 44–47, 236, 309, 332, 413
Porcaro, Joe, 43
Porcaro, Mike, 235
Porcaro, Steve, 101–5, 232, 237
"Pour Some Sugar on Me," 432, 433
Powell, Cozy, 134
Powell, Terry, 330
Prager, Bud, 63–64, 66, 77, 78, 142, 446

Presley, Elvis, 10
Prince, 174, 233, 311, 410
Prism, 182–83, 203, 268–71
Private Audition, 250–52, 294
Private Dancer, 347
Pumpkin, 159–60
Purple Haze, 15
Pyromania, 258, 262–63, 429, 430

Quarterflash, 229–30, 286
Queen, 23, 75, 196, 255, 261, 449
Quinn, Martha, 222–25, 317–19, 380

Rabin, Trevor, 297–300, 439
Rainbow, 134–38, 202, 204–5, 254, 283, 286
Raised on Radio, 385–90
Raitt, Bonnie, 13
Ramones, the, 153
Rascals, 223
Ready or Not, 435–36
Reagan, Ronald, 4, 272, 319
Reckless, 345–49, 443–44
Redding, Otis, 108
"Renegade," 119–20
Reno, Mike, 183–86, 196–97, 225, 445
REO Speedwagon, 2, 4, 20–21, 87, 107, 187–92, 222, 342–44, 438
Rescue You, 376
Richie, Lionel, 309–10, 347
Richrath, Gary, 13, 20–21, 24, 71–72, 87–88, 188–89, 343, 445
Roberts, Elliot, 292
Robinson, Jim, 221
Rock and Roll Hall of Fame, 454
Rock, Bob, 186
"Rock & Roll Band," 41
"Rock Me Tonite," 318–19, 321–22
"Rock of Ages," 258, 260
Rock, The, 410
"Rock the Night," 399
Rocky III (movie), 247–49
Rocky IV (movie), 332
"Rocky Mountain Way," 40

Roeser, Donald, 61, 72–73, 197, 198, 217, 274, 321
Rolie, Gregg, 21, 22, 107–8, 110–11, 166, 168–69, 214
Rolling Stones, the, 49, 79, 117, 251, 319–20
"Roll with the Changes," 119
Ronstadt, Linda, 163, 229
"Rosanna," 2, 231–33, 238, 332
Rose, Axl, 179, 226
Ross, Marv, 227–29
Ross, Rindy, 227–29
Ross, Steve, 221
Roth, David Lee, 306, 379–80, 397–98
Rouge, 155, 157–58
Roxy Music, 139
Rumours, 60, 79, 114, 177, 434
"Runaway," 304–5
Rundgren, Todd, 376, 430
Run-DMC, 432–33
Running Man, The (movie), 373
"Run to You," 346, 348
Rural Still Life, 43–44
Rutherford, Mike, 298
Ryder, Mitch, 305

Sadkin, Alex, 351
St. Elmo's Fire (movie), 371–73
Saints and Sinners, 425
Sambora, Richie, 303–6, 403–8, 445
Santana, 21, 22
Sartori, Maxanne, 177
Saturday Night Fever (movie), 111
Saturday Night Live (TV show), 220
Sayer, Leo, 103
Scaggs, Boz, 45–47, 103
Schermie, Joe, 104
Schlosser, Herb, 220
Schmidt, Timmy, 269–70
Schmitt, Al, 233
Schnee, Bill, 244
Schneider, Jack, 221
Scholz, Tom, 6, 174, 454; early music influences, 10; *Escape*, 1–2, 272–77;

follow-ups, 113–17; formation of Boston, 4–5, 38–42; Sammy Hagar, 172; signing of Boston, 54–62; *Third Stage*, 409–15; woes of Boston, 291–94

Schon, Neal, 1, 166, 167, 378, 420, 455; the Babys, 168; *Escape*, 214–15, 216, 218–19; formation of Journey, 21–22; *Raised on Radio*, 385, 386–90; resurrection, 450, 451; Steve Perry joins Journey, 106–12

Schumacher, Joel, 372–73
Schwarzenegger, Arnold, 371, 373
Scotti Brothers, 151, 246
Scott, Tom, 131
Scrubbaloe Caine, 183, 184
Seafood Mama, 228–29
Seals & Crofts, 44–45
"Search Is Over, The," 331
Sebastian, John, 51, 52
Seger, Bob, 347
Sellers, Peter, 430
"Separate Ways (Worlds Apart)," 1, 273, 276
Seraphine, Danny, 240, 309
Setzer, Brian, 340
Seven the Hard Way, 374–75
17, 307–8
7800° Fahrenheit, 375
Sex Pistols, 59
Shaffer, Paul, 377
Shaw, Tommy, 14, 25–26, 93–97, 118–20, 122, 278–80, 339–41
Sheehan, Fran, 38–42, 86–87
Sheeran, Ed, 189
"She's a Beauty," 282, 286
She's So Unusual, 335
Shipley, Mike, 211, 258
Shock, 181
"Shooting Shark," 321
"Shot Through the Heart," 404
Sidewinders, the, 176
Siegel, Shelly, 35, 37
"Signed, Sealed, Delivered," 237

Silk Degrees, 45–47
Simmons, Gene, 156–58, 323–24, 374–75, 421
Simon, Carly, 350
Simpson, Don, 392–93
Sinatra, Frank, 43–44, 169, 324, 435, 451–52
"Since You Been Gone," 136–37
Sinclair, John, 75
"Sister Christian," 284, 285, 287, 377
"Sittin' on the Dock of the Bay," 420
"Sixteen Tons," 10
Slick, Grace, 366–70, 440–41
Slippery When Wet, 5, 404, 407–8, 416, 443
"Slow Down," 45
Sly and the Family Stone, 129–30
Small Change, 205, 269–70
Small, Henry, 183, 203–5, 269–71, 330, 393–94, 395, 410
Smith, Gary, 151
Smith, Steve, 1, 316; *Escape*, 1–2, 213–19, 272–75, 277; *Evolution*, 152–53; finding missing link, 166–70; Foreigner, 78; *Frontiers*, 276, 277; induction of Foreigner, 454; *Raised on Radio*, 384–90; resurrection, 451–52; Ronnie Montrose, 111–12
Smyth, Patty, 325, 326, 381
"So Long Now," 14
Song Remains the Same, The, 92
Sonny & Cher, 44–45
"Sonny Think Twice," 240
Sopranos, The (TV show), 6, 450, 451
Soul, David, 78
"Space Oddity," 12, 399
Spector, Ronnie, 412
Spero, David, 50, 59–60, 190, 320
Spooky Tooth, 63–65, 78
Springfield, Rick, 14, 200–205, 252–53, 254, 304, 317

Springsteen, Bruce, 156, 305, 327
Squier, Billy, 176–79, 191, 235, 274–75, 293, 445–46; Boston, 59, 62; Def Leppard, 262, 432–33; *Don't Say No*, 196; early music influences, 9–10, 12, 49; *Emotions in Motion*, 252; Foreigner, 79; MTV, 225–26, 317–22; Piper, 62, 177–78; Queen, 255; "Rock Me Tonite," 318–19, 321–22; "The Stroke," 198–99, 432
Squire, Chris, 297, 298
SS Fools, 104
"Stagefright," 259
"Stairway to Heaven," 32, 72, 95
Stallone, Sylvester, 246–49, 332
Stanley, Michael, 59–60
Stanley, Paul, 155–58, 323–24, 374–75, 421
Starr, Ringo, 410
Steely Dan, 44–45, 46, 103, 129, 233, 331
Steinhardt, Robby, 23, 281
Steinman, Jim, 145, 430–31
Stern, Laura, 15
Stewart, Rod, 35, 45, 325
"Still of the Night," 424–25, 427
Stills, Stephen, 13, 26, 72, 326
Stone, Mike, 215, 244, 245, 273–76, 426
Straight Between the Eyes, 254
"Straight from the Heart," 186
Stranger Things (TV show), 452
Stray Cats, 340
Streetheart, 183
"Street of Dreams," 284
Streets, 256
Street Talk, 313–16, 386
"Stroke, The," 198–99, 432
Stronach, John, 71
Styx, 61, 93–97; *Crystal Ball*, 71–72, 93–96; formation of, 17–20, 24–26; *The Grand Illusion*, 93–96, 118–19; *Kilroy Was Here*, 278–80, 339–41; *Paradise Theatre*, 196; *Pieces of Eight*, 118, 119–20, 159–61; surge of, 118–20

Styx (album), 61
Such, Alec John, 305
Sucker for a Pretty Face, 284–85
Sugarman, Joe, 425
Sullivan, Ed, 10, 11
Sullivan, Frankie, 151, 246–49
Summer, Donna, 111, 253
"Summer of '69," 3, 346–47, 452
Supernatural (TV show), 453
"Superstars," 94–95
Supertramp, 148
"Surrender," 91–92, 132
Survival, 351
Survivor, 443–45
Survivor (album), 151–52
Sutton, Derek, 95, 279–80
Sweeney Todd, 183
Swift, Taylor, 6, 262, 434, 455
Sykes, John, 423–28

"Take It on the Run," 189
"Take My Breath Away," 393–94, 395
Tale of the Tape, The, 178–79
"Talk to Ya Later," 203–4, 205, 282
Taupin, Bernie, 360, 368, 370
Tempest, Joey, 12, 59, 396–402, 407, 443, 447
Thatcher, Margaret, 4
"These Dreams," 360, 362, 437
Thin Lizzy, 305
Third Stage, 409–15
Thomas, Dylan, 336–37
Thomas, Mickey, 103, 366–70, 440–41, 446
Thompson, Bill, 368–69
Three Dog Night, 104
Three Men and a Baby (movie), 373
Thriller, 5, 236
Tickner, George, 22
"Time After Time," 5, 336–38
"Time for Me to Fly," 119
"To Be a Man," 411–12
Too Hot to Sleep, 444
"Too Late," 153

Top Gun (movie), 392–93, 395, 438
Torres, Tico, 305
Toto, 2–3, 101–5, 128–29, 150–54, 231–39, 328–33, 391–94, 413, 455–56; excess and drug use, 264–67; Fergie Frederiksen joins, 330–31, 332; formation of, 43–47, 101–2; "Human Nature," 236–38; *Hydra*, 153–54; "Rosanna," 2, 231–33, 238, 332; *Turn Back*, 197–99
Toto (album), 103–5, 128–29, 150
Toto IV, 2, 231–33, 238–39, 331, 453
Toto V, 331–32
Touch of Evil (movie), 117
Townshend, Pete, 13, 20
Tradewinds, 17–18
Tramp, Mike, 396–402, 420, 443
Trigger, 64, 67
Tropico, 324
True, Andrea, 144
Tubes, the, 22, 201–2, 205, 282, 286, 376
Turgon, Bruce, 350–51
Turn Back, 197–99
Turner, Joe Lynn, 254, 255, 266, 304, 376, 377–78, 388, 394–95; Fandango, 202; Rainbow, 204–5, 283, 286
Turner, Joe Lynn, Sr., 304
Turner, Lonnie, 89
Turner, Tina, 347–48, 360, 403
Tusken, Ray, 198
Twain, Shania, 6, 260
Twister (movie), 251
"Two Tickets to Paradise," 89–90
Tyler, Bonnie, 403
Tyler, Steven, 416–21, 454

U2, 315
UFO, 259
Untold Passion, 219
"Up from the Skies," 167
"Urgent," 209–10
"Used to Be Bad News," 115

Vallance, Jim, 11, 59, 180–86, 268–71, 345–49, 443–45
Valory, Diane, 107
Valory, Ross, 21, 22, 106, 107, 109, 166, 275, 385, 386
Vance, Tommy, 4
Van Halen, 80, 111, 233, 282, 306, 379–83, 397–98, 400
Van Halen, Alex, 381–82
Van Halen, Eddie, 238, 289, 379–83
Vega, Carlos, 309
"Vehicle," 15–16
Vidal, Maria, 156, 157, 404–5
Villanueva, John, 21
Vinyl Confessions, 254
Vital Signs, 330

Wachtel, Waddy, 377
Waite, John, 68–71, 91, 168, 253, 304, 324–27; the Babys, 120–22, 168–69, 360; "Missing You," 324–25, 327; Montrose, 68–70; MTV, 255–56
"Waiting for a Girl Like You," 209
"Walk on Water," 444
"Walks Like a Lady," 167
"Walk This Way," 432–33
Walsh, Joe, 236
Walsh, Steve, 23, 53, 172, 175, 253, 256
"Wanted (Dead or Alive)," 406
Warren, Diane, 440–41
"Warrior, The," 326
"Wastin' Time," 186
Waybill, Fee, 201, 203–4, 282, 375, 376
"We Built This City," 367–70
Weiss, Steve, 145–46, 149
Welcome to the Real World, 376
Welles, Orson, 117
Wenner, Jann, 415
West, Kanye, 149
West, Leslie, 63–64
West Side Story (movie), 27
Wetton, John, 241, 243–45, 296–98, 300

"What About Love," 360–62
"What You're Missing," 309
"Wheel in the Sky," 107, 112
White, Alan, 297
White Lion, 420
Whiteside, Bobby, 160
Whitesnake, 135, 416, 422–28
Whitlock, Tommy, 395
"Who's Crying Now," 2, 214–15
Who, the, 69, 410
"Why Can't This Be Love," 382–83
Wildfire, 398, 399
Wildlife, 398
Williams, Joseph, 413–14
Williams, Richard, 73, 74, 88, 89
Willis, Pete, 196, 259
Wills, Rick, 139, 206, 209, 351
Wilshires, the, 81–85
Wilson, Ann, 81–85, 436–37, 444, 447, 454; affairs of, 123–27; *Bébé le Strange*, 171; *Dog and Butterfly*, 123–25; *Dreamboat Annie*, 33, 35, 361; early music influences, 10, 11–13, 27–29; formation of Heart, 29–37; *Little Queen*, 82–85; *Passionworks*, 295; *Private Audition*, 250–52; reinvention and resurrection of Heart, 359–65
Wilson, Brian, 27–28, 29, 81
Wilson, Lois Dustin, 27–28, 29, 36–37
Wilson, Nancy, 81–85; affairs of, 123–27; *Bébé le Strange*, 171; *Dog and Butterfly*, 123–25; *Dreamboat Annie*, 33, 35, 361; early music influences, 10, 11–13, 27–29; formation of Heart, 29–37; *Little Queen*, 82–85; *Passionworks*, 294–95; *Private Audition*, 250–52; reinvention and resurrection of Heart, 359–65
Wings, 78, 233
Winter, Johnny, 145–46
Wolf, Peter (producer), 368–69
Wolf, Peter (singer), 9–10
Working Class Dog, 201
Worlds Apart, 149
Wyman, Bill, 410

Yardbirds, the, 20, 49
Yetnikoff, Walter, 291
"You Are the Flower," 104
"You Better Run," 223–24
"You Give Love a Bad Name," 403–4, 453
Young, James "JY": *Crystal Ball*, 71–72, 93–96; formation of Styx, 18–19, 24–26; *The Grand Illusion*, 94–97; *Kilroy Was Here*, 278–80, 339–41; *Pieces of Eight*, 119–20, 160–61
Young, Neil, 13, 233
"You're the Inspiration," 309

Zander, Robin, 91–92, 131
Zito, Richie, 393, 410
ZZ Top, 37, 199, 279, 286–87

RAISING READERS
Books Build Bright Futures

Thank you for reading this book and for being a reader of books in general. We are so grateful to share being part of a community of readers with you, and we hope you will join us in passing our love of books on to the next generation of readers.

Did you know that reading for enjoyment is the single biggest predictor of a child's future happiness and success?

More than family circumstances, parents' educational background, or income, reading impacts a child's future academic performance, emotional well-being, communication skills, economic security, ambition, and happiness.

Studies show that kids reading for enjoyment in the US is in rapid decline:

- In 2012, 53% of 9-year-olds read almost every day. Just 10 years later, in 2022, the number had fallen to 39%.
- In 2012, 27% of 13-year-olds read for fun daily. By 2023, that number was just 14%.

Together, we can commit to **Raising Readers** and change this trend. How?

- Read to children in your life daily.
- Model reading as a fun activity.
- Reduce screen time.
- Start a family, school, or community book club.
- Visit bookstores and libraries regularly.
- Listen to audiobooks.
- Read the book before you see the movie.
- Encourage your child to read aloud to a pet or stuffed animal.
- Give books as gifts.
- Donate books to families and communities in need.

Books build bright futures, and **Raising Readers** is our shared responsibility.

For more information, visit **JoinRaisingReaders.com**

Sources: National Endowment for the Arts, National Assessment of Educational Progress, WorldBookDay.com, Nielsen BookData's 2023 "Understanding the Children's Book Consumer"